INSIDERS' GUIDE® TO

THE GREAT SMOKY MOUNTAINS

DATE DUE

HELP US KEEP THIS GUIDE UP TO DATE

We would love to hear from you concerning your experiences with this guide and how you feel it could be improved and kept up to date. Please send your comments and suggestions to:

editorial@GlobePequot.com

Thanks for your input, and happy travels!

INSIDERS' GUIDE® SERIES

INSIDERS' GUIDE® TO

THE GREAT SMOKY MOUNTAINS

SIXTH EDITION

KATY KOONTZ

INSIDERS' GUIDE

GUILFORD, CONNECTICUT
AN IMPRINT OF GLOBE PEQUOT PRESS

All the information in this guidebook is subject to change. We recommend that you call ahead to obtain current information before traveling.

INSIDERS' GUIDE®

Copyright © 2001, 2003, 2005, 2007, 2009 Morris Book Publishing, LLC
A previous edition of this book was published by Falcon Publishing, Inc. in 2000.

Interior design: Sheryl Kober
Maps: XNR Productions, Inc. © Morris Book Publishing, LLC
Layout artist: Maggie Peterson

ISSN 1542-5193
ISBN 978-0-7627-5038-2

Printed in the United States of America
10 9 8 7 6 5 4 3 2 1

CONTENTS

Directory of Maps

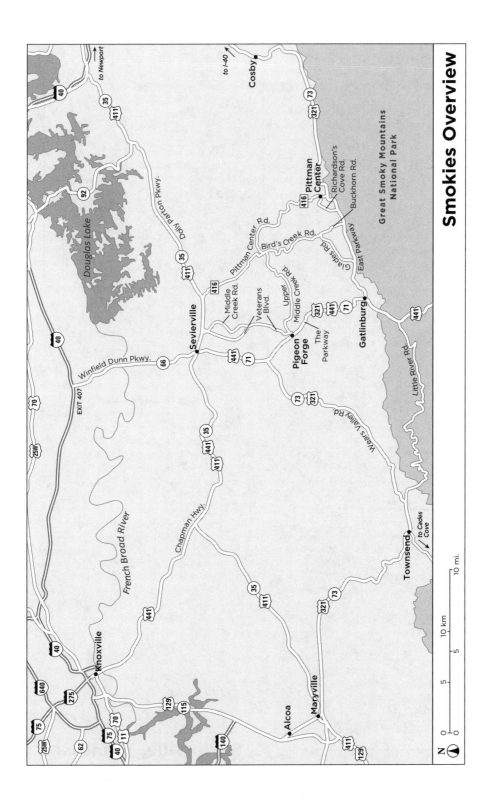

Smokies Overview

N

to Newport

Douglas Lake

French Broad River

Knoxville

Alcoa

Maryville

Townsend

to Cades Cove

Little River Rd.

Gatlinburg

Pigeon Forge

The Parkway

Sevierville

Winfield Dunn Pkwy.

EXIT 407

Chapman Hwy.

Dolly Parton Pkwy.

Pittman Center Rd.

Middle Creek Rd.

Veterans Blvd.

Upper Rd.

Middle Creek Rd.

Bird's Creek Rd.

Glades Rd.

East Parkway

Wears Valley Rd.

Pittman Center

Richardson's Cove Rd.

Buckhorn Rd.

Great Smoky Mountains National Park

Cosby

to I-40

0   5   10 km
0   5   10 mi.

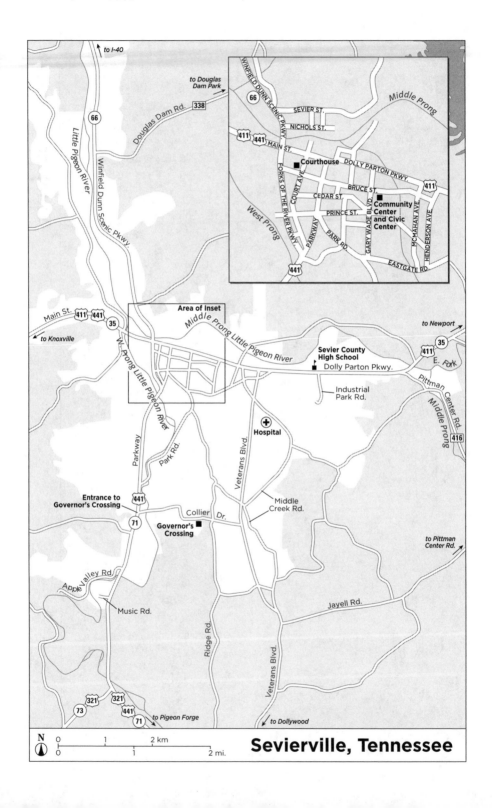

to I-40

to Douglas
Dam Park

Little Pigeon River

Douglas Dam Rd.

66

338

Winfield Dunn Scenic Pkwy.

Area of Inset

WINFIELD DUNN SCENIC PKWY.

66

SEVIER ST.

NICHOLS ST.

411   441   MAIN ST.

Middle Prong

Courthouse

DOLLY PARTON PKWY.

411

FORKS OF THE RIVER PKWY.

West Prong

CEDAR ST.

BRUCE ST.

COURT AVE.

PRINCE ST.

PARKWAY

PARK RD.

Community
Center
and Civic
Center

GARY WADE BLVD.

MCMAHAN AVE.

HENDERSON AVE.

EASTGATE RD.

441

Main St.

411   441

35

to Knoxville

Middle Prong Little Pigeon River

W. Prong Little Pigeon River

Sevier County
High School

Dolly Parton Pkwy.

to Newport

411   35

E. Fork

Pittman Center Rd.

Middle Prong

416

Industrial
Park Rd.

Hospital

Veterans Blvd.

Park Rd.

Parkway

Entrance to
Governor's Crossing

441

71

Collier   Dr.

Governor's
Crossing

Middle
Creek Rd.

to Pittman
Center Rd.

Apple Valley Rd

Music Rd.

Ridge Rd.

Jayell Rd.

Veterans Blvd.

321

321

73

441

71

to Pigeon Forge

to Dollywood

N

0   1   2 km

0   1   2 mi.

Sevierville, Tennessee

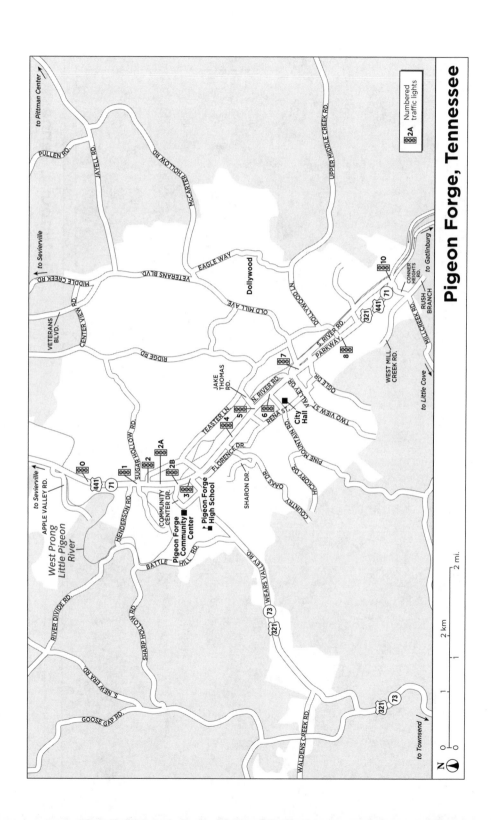

Pigeon Forge, Tennessee

2A 　Numbered traffic lights

N

0   1   2 km
0   1   2 mi.

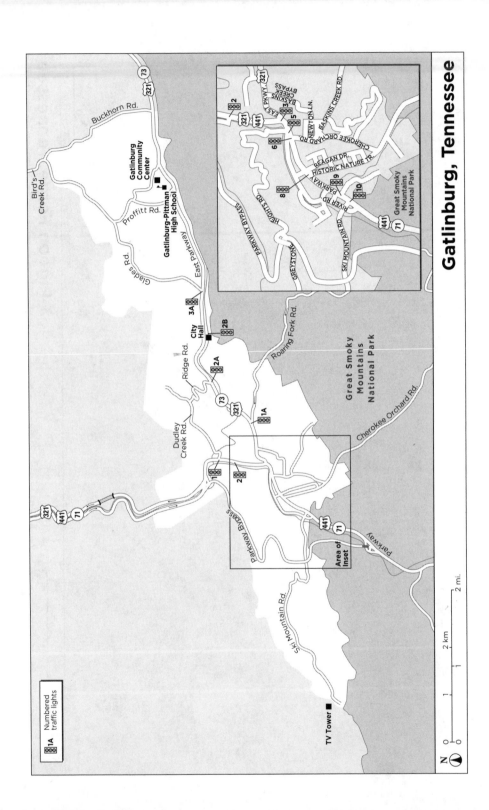

Gatlinburg, Tennessee

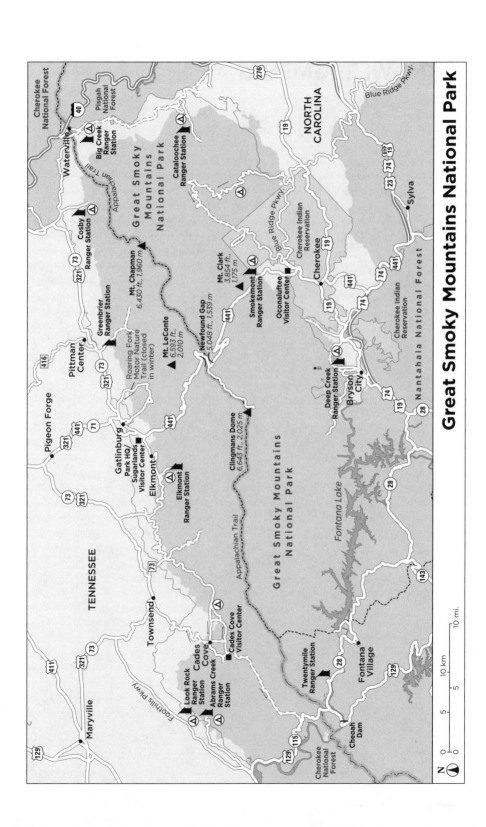

Great Smoky Mountains National Park

ACKNOWLEDGMENTS

Updating this book was a huge undertaking, and I am grateful to many people who were generous with their time and knowledge in helping me pull everything together. First, kudos go to Dick McHugh and Mitch Moore, who did such an encyclopedic job writing the original version of this book. Thanks also go to the unfailingly pleasant and helpful Walter Yeldell at the Gatlinburg Department of Tourism; to Tom Adkinson (a real public relations pro who epitomizes the phrase "southern gentleman") at Bohan as well as Lila Wilson and Sherri Kirby (gracious ladies both) at the Pigeon Forge Department of Tourism; to the always cheerful and ever-obliging Amanda Maples Marr at the Sevierville Chamber of Commerce; to Dollywood's Trish McGee, who works at lightning speed; and to Nancy Gray (an indefatigable source of park information, no matter how obscure) in the public relations office of Great Smoky Mountains National Park. I am also indebted to my fabulous editor Amy Lyons at the Globe Pequot Press for her considerable wit and wisdom. Finally, I'd like to thank my significant other, Colby McLemore, not only for his stunning cover photography but also for his unfailing love and support while I worked on this book, and my daughter, Sam Friedlander, for her cheerful cooperation in the face of yet another pressing deadline.

PREFACE

If you've decided to visit the Smokies, you're in pretty good company. Some nine million visitors each year come to see Great Smoky Mountains National Park (which turns 75 in 2009), making it the most visited national park in the country. And for good reason: A profusion of wildflowers bursts forth here every spring. Hiking trails and cold mountain streams beckon in the summer. The Smokies' fall foliage never fails to paint the mountainsides with fiery colors come autumn. And ice and snow glisten on the trees each winter, adding plenty of sparkle to the scenery. No matter when you visit, chances are you'll get an up-close view of Mother Nature at her best.

But walking in the woods (or toasting marshmallows over a campfire) is just part of the fun here. The gateway communities where park visitors sleep and eat are absolutely overflowing with fabulous accommodations (from log cabins to ritzy condos), a stunning array of family-fun attractions, and lots of great restaurants—most costing a fraction of what you'd pay in other vacation hot spots around the country.

Visitors find plenty of creative ways to fill their time. Adrenaline junkies can roll down a hill inside a giant plastic sphere, float in midair above an airplane's jet engine, or hurtle themselves through the trees on the country's longest zipline. Those wanting tamer adventures can hop on a moving sidewalk through one of the world's longest underwater aquarium tunnels, snap up bargains in one of the country's largest concentrations of outlet malls, or watch Appalachian artisans at work in their studios. Go-karts and miniature golf? Check. Haunted-house attractions and Chinese acrobats? Check. Idyllic wedding chapels and romantic honeymoon cabins with Jacuzzis and fireplaces? Checkmate. You win.

And no matter how much you manage to pack into a trip to these environs, you can't possibly do it all. So whether you come here to steep yourself in the pristine beauty of the national park or to experience the zaniness of the surrounding commercial attractions (or perhaps to enjoy a little of both), you'll undoubtedly find the Smokies worth coming back to again and again. Let this book be your guide for each ensuing exploration.

HOW TO USE THIS BOOK

A destination that has as much going for it as the Smokies takes a lot of explaining. That's why this book is divided into a number of helpful chapters, each reflecting a different subject you're likely to need information about during your stay here. Feel free to carry it with you in your travels to help bring the kaleidoscope of things to do in the Smokies into focus. If you need help finding anything, look in the table of contents under the subject heading that fits your question, then go directly to that chapter. You'll find the subject arranged geographically from north to south, always starting with Sevierville and going south through Pigeon Forge and Gatlinburg. If you're looking for a specific place or business, flip to the comprehensive index to see where it's mentioned in the book. You'll also find detailed maps in the front of the book that will help you get the lay of the land.

Although this book focuses mainly on the park's busiest and most popular gateway (the Sevierville, Pigeon Forge, and Gatlinburg corridor), you'll also find a chapter with information on both Cherokee and the area in North Carolina immediately south of the national park, as well as Townsend, the Blount County community between Pigeon Forge and the national park's Cades Cove. (For much more information on beautiful western North Carolina, pick up a copy of the *Insiders' Guide to North Carolina's Mountains*.) Great Smoky Mountains National Park itself is pretty well covered in its own chapter, but campgrounds, annual events, and other things that are as common to the park as they are to the surrounding communities are also mentioned in the appropriate chapters.

Finally, at the end of the book, you'll find a chapter for people who are relocating to the Smokies. Here, you'll find lots of basic information on real estate, schools, health care and wellness, and various places of worship in the area.

Throughout the book, you'll also find Insiders' Tips (marked with an **i**) and Close-ups that will take you a little deeper into area lore, history, and customs. Be sure to pay special attention to these if you want to feel more like a local than a tourist.

AREA OVERVIEW

As the host area for the most-used entrance to America's most-visited national park, Sevier (say "severe") County, Tennessee, has become a magnet for tourism, with all the advantages and disadvantages that attend such status. As a mostly rural county in some of east Tennessee's most beautiful and fertile countryside, it's a place where the family values generated by an agricultural lifestyle are still practiced and considered socially important. And as an area leader in light industry, Sevier County is undergoing significant change to attract new industrial business and new people to run it.

At 660 square miles, Sevier County is among the largest in Tennessee, but the settled area this book deals with takes up less than 10 percent of that space. There is also the little matter of about 240 square miles of wilderness at the southern end of the county that's not available for any kind of development and hopefully never will be—it comprises about 30 percent of Great Smoky Mountains National Park. It's as much a matter of topography as any other consideration that the corridor itself—defined by Winfield Dunn Parkway (Tennessee Highway 66) south from exit 407 on Interstate 40 to its merge with U.S. Highway 441 in Sevierville, and then south through Pigeon Forge and Gatlinburg to the national park entrance—bisects the county from top to bottom. The Smokies Corridor does, however, encompass all four of the incorporated cities in Sevier County and includes about two-thirds of its 83,000-plus permanent population.

OVERVIEW

Sevier County is politically divided into four cities and a whole lot of unincorporated communities. The unincorporated areas depend on the county for educational services, police protection by the county sheriff, fire control by volunteer departments, ambulance service, and electric service. An elected commission of representatives from 15 civil districts oversees the operation of those facilities and departments necessary to govern any county; day-to-day operations are supervised by an elected county mayor. Although the influx of new population is bringing profound change to the political and economic face of the Smokies Corridor, it's still not a very good idea for anybody but a Republican to seek elected office in Sevier County.

The cities take care of their own police and fire/emergency services within their city limits, and each city also provides public works services at various levels. The cities deliver their refuse to a county-owned facility for disposal, and unincorporated areas have convenience stations where residents and businesses take their trash. The lone airport is jointly owned and operated by the cities of Gatlinburg and Pigeon Forge and is located within the city limits of Sevierville.

The three principal cities that make up the corridor (the fourth is a very special case explained shortly) are still controlled primarily by the descendants of the original settlers of the area. Each is uniquely different from the others because of what it took to tame the land in the late 18th and early 19th centuries. The chapter on the county's history will cover in greater detail their individual development, but the differences in the roles the cities of Sevierville, Pigeon Forge, and Gatlinburg played in the evolution of the county are central to an understanding of how

Sevier County operates. As usual, the chapter starts with Sevierville and proceeds south, with one significant exception from the norm—the inclusion of the town of Pittman Center, an incorporated area east of Gatlinburg on U.S. Highway 321. Pittman Center is one of Tennessee's newest cities, incorporated in 1974, and it is so dedicated to the preservation of its mountain heritage that it officially discourages commercial development.

SEVIERVILLE

Compared to its neighboring cities, the most unusual thing about Sevierville is its normality. Although Pigeon Forge and Gatlinburg are hopelessly synonymous with the tourism industry, Sevierville has managed to retain much of the virginal character of Small Town U.S.A. In fact, the local chamber of commerce at one time billed itself as "Your Hometown in the Smokies," and there's still a lot of truth to that. If it were plucked out of the county and placed in another part of the state, Sevierville would likely sustain itself as it has for more than two centuries—with farming and industry as well as small businesses that are locally owned and cater to the townsfolk.

To be sure, Sevierville has begun to reap the economic benefits of tourism, as Pigeon Forge did in the 1980s and Gatlinburg before that. Accommodations, restaurants, shopping centers, and even music theaters have gradually become familiar fixtures on the Sevierville landscape. But even today, the town has its own distinct personality that, rather than being defined by tourism, has merely been complemented by it. Economically, the town is viable, not so much because of the influx of dollars from the Johnny-come-latelies, but because it has always been so (see the History chapter).

Much of Sevierville's flavor has as much to do with politics as it does economics. When the city was chosen to be the county seat in 1795, the stage was set for it to become a hub of governmental and commercial activity. Today, the network of offices and agencies that has grown and spread from Sevier County's first rudimentary government not only employs hundreds of residents but also naturally draws to it the rest of the county's citizens that receive its services. From court appearances to license plate renewals, Sevierville is the place you have to go.

Geographically, the town is laid out like many of its size and background. The historic downtown area is wedged between the east and west forks of the Little Pigeon River. Just a few blocks from downtown, you'll find most of the city's schools, the police station, the city's community center, and a former movie theater turned civic center. From its central core, the town has expanded in all four directions with balanced concentrations of residential, commercial, and municipal growth. Although the Smoky Mountains dominate Sevierville's southern horizon, much of the city is actually characterized by relatively flat terrain, with the occasional undulation or foothill dropped in for character.

Radiating from downtown, Forks of the River Parkway, then the Parkway (US 441; it's just named "Parkway") lead south to Pigeon Forge and feature much of the city's commercial and tourist-oriented development. Traveling north from downtown on Winfield Dunn Parkway (TN 66), you'll also find rapid growth in residential areas as well as accommodations, shops, restaurants, and attractions geared toward the vacationer.

Chapman Highway (US 411 and 441 concurrently) leads west toward Seymour and Knoxville; its surrounding areas primarily remain a mixture of residential neighborhoods and undeveloped farmland. As Dolly Parton Parkway (aka US 411) takes you east, away from downtown, you'll notice that much of the old and new growth alike have a more local flavor to them. Fast-food restaurants, retail stores, and service-oriented businesses have seemingly sprung up overnight in an effort to serve the growing numbers of Seviervillians who have moved eastward to escape entanglements with heavy tourist traffic.

One only has to take a drive through the county's three main towns to see how Sevierville is "mundanely unique" to Sevier County. It's the

Vital Statistics

Mayors: Sevierville—Bryan Atchley; Pigeon Forge—Keith Whaley; Gatlinburg—Mike Werner; Pittman Center—Glen Cardwell

Governor: Phil Bredesen

Capital: Nashville

Major cities (in East Tennessee): Knoxville, Chattanooga

Outlying counties (surrounding Sevier): Knox, Blount, Cocke, Jefferson; Haywood (North Carolina)

Permanent population: Sevierville—16,051; Pigeon Forge—6,119; Gatlinburg—5,433; Pittman Center—643; Sevier County—83,527; Tennessee—6,214,888 (data from U.S. Census, 2007 population estimates)

Area (Sevier County): 592 square miles (one-third of that lies in Great Smoky Mountains National Park)

Nickname: The Volunteer State

Average temperatures:

> July (High/Low): 89/67

> January (High/Low): 42/25

State/cities founded: Tennessee—1796; Sevierville—1795; Pigeon Forge—1841; Gatlinburg—1807

Major universities: University of Tennessee, Carson Newman College

Major area employers: Dollywood, TRW, Ober Gatlinburg, Ft. Sanders Sevier Medical Center

Famous native: Dolly Parton

Major airport: McGhee Tyson Airport, Alcoa

Major interstates: Interstates 40, 75, and 81

only city in the county that has a movie theater, new car dealerships, a hospital, factories, an airport, and a good ol' small-town main street. Churches, schools, and banks are in abundance, and although Wal-Mart has taken a healthy bite out of the retail pie, mom-and-pop businesses generally hold their own.

As mentioned earlier, tourism has been both directly and indirectly responsible for much of Sevierville's recent growth—a growth that is unmistakable. In fact, 30 percent of the city's lodging opened in 2008 alone. The total number of available hotel and motel rooms—a number that was not even quite 3,500 two years ago—is now 4,652. Local manufacturing accounts for

another substantial chunk—about 15 percent— of the city's economy.

As Sevierville continues to feel its oats, it regularly faces issues that naturally accompany growth. One issue is the city's liquor laws. Sevierville has no liquor stores. Beer is the only form of alcohol that you can buy over the counter here, and you can find it in most local supermarkets and convenience stores. Although it hasn't always been so, you can now buy beer and wine by the drink in restaurants that have a seating capacity of at least 150 and where at least 50 percent of sales are from food. You can also buy beer and wine at city golf courses, special events, and the minor league baseball stadium.

Public transportation: Municipal trolley systems in Sevierville, Pigeon Forge, and Gatlinburg

Military bases: None

Driving laws: Seat belts, juvenile car seats, speed limits, wipers/headlights, HOV lanes, etc.

Alcohol laws: Age (21), DUI limit (0.08), buy on Sundays, buy in supermarkets

Daily newspapers: The Mountain Press, Knoxville News Sentinel

State sales tax: 7%

Municipal sales taxes: Gatlinburg, Pigeon Forge, and Sevierville—2¾%

Hotel/motel surtax: Gatlinburg—3%; Pigeon Forge—2 1/4%; Sevierville—2%

Restaurant surtax: Gatlinburg—1 1/2%; Pigeon Forge and Sevierville—0%

Amusement tax: Gatlinburg and Pigeon Forge—2%; Sevierville—0%

Chamber of commerce/visitor center addresses and phone numbers:

Sevierville Chamber of Commerce 3099 Winfield Dunn Parkway (800) 255-6411 (865) 932-4458 www.seviervillechamber.com	Gatlinburg Chamber of Commerce 811 East Parkway (800) 568-4748 (865) 436-4178
Pigeon Forge Department of Tourism 1950 Parkway (800) 251-9100 (865) 453-8574 www.mypigeonforge.com	Gatlinburg Convention Center 234 Historic Nature Trail (800) 343-1475 (865) 436-2392

Time/temperature phone number: (865) 453-6171

By the way, there really is a reason behind the odd numbering of traffic lights in Sevierville, from the first light (number 23.5, at the Smokies baseball stadium right off I-40) to the last (number 12.6, at Apple Valley Road near the Pigeon Forge border). Unlike the sequentially numbered lights in Pigeon Forge and Gatlinburg, the lights in Sevierville are given numbers based on how many miles the light is from the border of Great Smoky Mountains National Park. Originally, the hope was that all the lights on the Parkway in all three cities would use the same numbering system. But locals in Pigeon Forge and Gatlinburg were so averse to changing the numbers they had been using for so many years that only Sevierville ended up using the new numbering system.

ℹ️ As you travel along the Parkway, you'll see many establishments claiming to be the "official" tourist information centers. They're usually operated by vacation rental developers whose jobs are to give you some sort of sales pitch. Visitors are certainly under no obligation to participate, but you might want to stick with the city-operated and -sanctioned information centers instead.

PIGEON FORGE

For more than a hundred years, Pigeon Forge was a sleeping giant, a rural farm community nuzzled peacefully against the Smoky Mountains' majesty. Unlike its northern neighbor, Sevierville, which had developed sturdy economic legs of its own from day one, and its southern neighbor, Gatlinburg, which began to prosper in the '40s and '50s because of the national park and mountain crafts, Pigeon Forge suffered from an identity crisis until about 1979. Until then, Pigeon Forge was nothing more than rolling farmland dotted by the occasional restaurant or hotel that lined the Parkway in the hopes of sporadically snagging vacationers on their way to and from the mountains (see the History chapter).

During the '80s, Pigeon Forge reaped benefits from the Knoxville World's Fair and the opening of Dollywood Entertainment Park. And by now, Pigeon Forge has more than made up for lost time, generating gross sales tax revenues surpassing those of Gatlinburg and even surpassing that town in permanent residents. In fact, today Pigeon Forge is a bit Las Vegas–like in appearance, with a "main drag" that's packed full of hotels and motels, restaurants, attractions, music theaters, and shopping outlets. Sign after neon sign pulses brightly in the night, each promising more fun, more entertainment, and more value than the guy next door. And it's still growing!

Unless you are a local, familiar with the residential areas and side roads, the axiom "what you see is what you get" stands as a fair assessment of the city's geography. Pigeon Forge is laid out pretty much along the steady course of the Parkway (US 441), running for approximately 4 miles from the abrupt cutoff of Sevierville's city limits near Apple Valley Drive to The Spur, which leads to Gatlinburg. Small side streets with finite lengths or roads leading into the more rural sections of the county frequently intersect the Parkway. Along these paths is where you'll find most of the city's residences as well as many of its churches, small businesses, and government offices.

There's no denying that Dollywood has been an unqualified boon to the city of Pigeon Forge. Much of Pigeon Forge's early success in tourism came from absorbing some of Gatlinburg's spillover with its hotels and restaurants. Soon, entrepreneurs realized that there was a market for developing attractions in Pigeon Forge that would draw people there for its own sake. Enter Dollywood, which was built on a site that had previously been a Silver Dollar City theme park. Since 1986, thanks to the name recognition of and promotion by Dolly Parton, Dollywood has consistently expanded. It is now the state's most popular ticketed attraction, with 2.5 million visitors each year, and its parent company, the Dollywood Company, is Sevier County's largest single seasonal employer. (See the Dollywood chapter for a more in-depth look at the park.)

The Dollywood Company is also responsible, in large part, for the explosion in the Smokies' music theater business. Several theaters had existed in Pigeon Forge, going back as far as 1984, and the Dollywood Company itself had started Dixie Stampede in 1988. But with the company's opening of Music Mansion in 1994 and the city's creation of an infrastructure for a multitheater development known as Music Road, the era of an outright "theater community" in Pigeon Forge was ushered in. Suddenly, visions of the town nipping at the heels of Branson, Missouri, were dancing through the heads of local developers and promoters.

Although growth in Pigeon Forge sometimes appears to be unbridled, city planners will tell you that they don't want their city to become another Branson, with too much stuff packed into too little space. So far, the city appears to have stuck to its guns. The Parkway's six wide lanes generally allow for smooth travel through town (except during the town's custom auto shows), and Sevierville's widening of the Parkway up to Pigeon Forge city limits has undoubtedly helped with traffic flow. Considering that the average traffic flow on Pigeon Forge's section of the Parkway ranges between 59,800 and 92,900 cars per day, cautious city planning is probably a wise option.

Like Sevierville, Pigeon Forge has no liquor stores, but you can purchase beer in supermarkets and convenience stores and both beer and wine are available in some restaurants. And at Mountain Valley Vineyards, thanks to state agricultural laws, you can purchase wine by the bottle (see the Attractions chapter).

i If you're a shopaholic or a music fan, Pigeon Forge is definitely the place for you. With 6 outlet malls and 13 music and entertainment theaters in the space of just a few miles, you'll have no shortage of places to go for fun in the Smokies.

GATLINBURG

Downtown Gatlinburg has always had a certain charm about it, probably because of the intimacy of the city itself. Despite the fact that any day or night can find upwards of 35,000 people browsing the shops and attractions crammed into a half mile on a couple of streets, Gatlinburg's relaxed atmosphere makes it a pleasant place to spend time. The Parkway strip from the area of traffic light #3 (the traffic lights in both Pigeon Forge and Gatlinburg are numbered—see the Getting Here, Getting Around chapter) to the park entrance is full of enough variety shops and amusements to use up whatever part of a day you want to give it, and you'll find enough variety sprinkled in to keep the kids amused as well.

Gatlinburg today is a city of about 5,000 souls that takes care of a visitor population averaging more than 11 million per year. The only way to accomplish this feat is to pretend you're a city of more than 11 million that has a single main street less than a mile long. All services provided by any city are provided in Gatlinburg on that basis. That's why the downtown is always sparkling clean and heavily planted with seasonal flowers,

and it's also why this so-called small town seems to be crowded with police officers on walking beats, riding bicycles or motorcycles, and in patrol cars.

Gatlinburg is, in fact, one of the safest places you'll ever visit. With the proper warnings and precautions, young children can be left to their own devices in the downtown area in the same manner you'd let them go their own way in a theme park. In the history of the town, there's no record of a child ever being harmed in downtown Gatlinburg. Ever.

It's also probably one of a very few cities its size that has three fully operational fire halls, a 278,000-square-foot convention center, and a 50,000-plus-square-foot community recreation center (when you read about it in the Parks and Recreation chapter, you probably won't believe it). A mass transit system consisting of several trolleys on seven different routes serves locals going to and from work and visitors using it for its convenience.

The downtown business district, however, is a very small part of the corporate package— the city limits of Gatlinburg extend about a mile north of downtown and stretch about 4 1/2 miles out the East Parkway. The Great Smoky Arts & Crafts Community, a few miles east of downtown in an area locally known as the Glades, is almost entirely within the city limits and is more than 10 times larger in area. There are also four residential areas ringing the downtown area that dwarf it in size. Gatlinburg has a lot of vacant land; it just isn't really adaptable to construction. The only property with true development potential is along the East Parkway to the city limits, and it's going fast. (Redevelopment, however, is another issue altogether. Witness the area you drive through when you first come off The Spur into town. Recently dubbed Gateway Gatlinburg, this $150 million complex will include, when it's finished in 2011, five restaurants, three hotels, numerous shops, and a parking garage.)

The city government consists of five city commissioners elected entirely at large. Commissioners serve four-year terms, which are staggered so that elections take place every two years. The commissioners elect a mayor from their body every year. The day-to-day operation of the city is directed by a city manager, who is hired by and responsible to the commissioners. Gatlinburg has 355 permanent employees on the rolls today. Citizen participation in local government is unusually high. There are more than a dozen advisory boards serving the city's community development and recreation departments, involving volunteer participation of close to 100 citizens.

i Gatlinburg has been dubbed "The Wedding Capital of the South," thanks to its 20 wedding chapels and the 600,000 people who come here each year to either get married or watch someone else get married. (Even celebrities such as Patty Loveless and Billy Ray Cyrus have wed here.)

Because it's the only city in Sevier County that allows liquor stores, and because state law mandates that all taxes collected on the sale of liquor be used for education, Gatlinburg has its own board of education, which disburses these funds to the city's two schools. Additional teaching positions and equipment purchases provided for by liquor tax monies were prime considerations in a 1998 poll conducted by the *Wall Street Journal*, which recognized Gatlinburg-Pittman High School as the best high school in the South. The 180 graduates of the class of 2002 at GPHS reaped more than a million dollars in scholarship money, including 10 National Merit Award scholarships.

Gatlinburg has come a long way in a short time as a center for tourism and as a host city to people looking for temporary gratification. It's also done an admirable job of standing still long enough to attract a growing population of people from all walks of life who become willing participants in the city's ongoing drive to continually reinvent itself without losing touch with its pioneer heritage. Content at this point to concede that its only industry is making people happy, and willing to do what's necessary to reach that goal without compromising its singular brand of integrity, Gatlinburg moves forward still believing that all stories that start with "Once upon a time" must inevitably end with "and they all lived happily ever after."

i Late September to mid-October means bear season in these parts. A strange quirk in state law makes it legal to hunt within city limits, regardless of whether city laws forbid the open display of weapons (as Gatlinburg does). You probably won't actually see hunters on the Parkway, but many cruise the roads in the Ski Mountain area.

PITTMAN CENTER

This is an unusual case, and to keep it in perspective, history and overview have been compressed here into a single statement. Pittman Center is an incorporated city east of Gatlinburg that has no business district, no post office (it's served by Sevierville), practically no commerce, and no desire to ever have any of the above. It probably wouldn't even be a city if one of its citizens hadn't gotten crosswise with the Gatlinburg building inspector back in 1974, but that's getting ahead of the story.

The community of Pittman Center was established when the Elmira District of the Central New York Conference of the Methodist Episcopal Church founded a missionary school in the mountains east of Gatlinburg and named it for their own superintendent, Dr. Eli Pittman. The school was operated by the United Methodist Church until 1955, when the Sevier County Board of Education bought the three-story building for $20,000 and assumed responsibility for the education of the fewer than 100 students. The

Methodist Church then donated the 650 acres it had originally purchased to the community. A new school was built next to the original building in the early '60s, and the high school grades were transferred to the new Gatlinburg-Pittman High School when it was built in 1964.

The little mountain community, never wanting anything more than to be left alone, then languished into the 1970s while Gatlinburg continued to grow to the east, slowly annexing land and extending its influence into unincorporated land by enforcing a nebulous "development district" statute that gave it legal control of development within 5 miles of its own expanding city limits. Things came to a head in 1974, when a zealous Gatlinburg building inspector trying to protect Gatlinburg's "development status" by enforcing Gatlinburg's building codes stopped an unnamed Pittman Center man from building a house on his own land.

Into the fray jumped the venerable Conley Huskey (1907–1994), a Pittman Center native and longtime political giant in the area. Knowing that the only way to stop Gatlinburg from exercising its influence in Pittman Center, and eventually annexing it, was to incorporate the area into a city of its own, Conley Huskey drew up and circulated a petition practically overnight to incorporate a new city. He waited two weeks to file the petition so the two pregnant women in the area could deliver their babies and bring the population to the 365 heads the state laws of the time required. The vote to incorporate was 128 for, 24 against, and Pittman Center became a city in 1974. And Conley Huskey's unnamed friend built his house.

Conley Huskey, a longtime Sevier County commissioner, paid most of the costs of incorporation out of his own pocket (he recalled once that he'd have been $10,000 better off if

he'd kept his mouth shut) and was rewarded by being elected Pittman Center's first mayor, an office he held until 1990. The old school building had fallen into disrepair by this time, but it was renovated and is now Pittman Center's city hall. At three stories, it's also the most imposing structure in the city. Pittman Center has gone on record as being dedicated to the preservation of its mountain heritage and, as such, has resisted any sort of commercial growth.

The city's biggest asset at the time of incorporation was Cobbly Nob golf course (now Sunterra Resort), a privately operated facility on municipal land. Pittman Center sold the golf course to a private developer in 1978 and used the proceeds from the sale to pave every road in the city. Pittman Center today is just about what it wants to be: a protected mountain community of less than 10 square miles and a population of about 600. The city is governed by a mayor and board of three aldermen, elected at large every two years. An administrator/recorder oversees the day-to-day affairs of the city as well as directs the activities of the city's other four full-time employees: the police chief, an administrative assistant, and two maintenance men. Fire service is provided by a well-equipped volunteer department.

i From May through September, Gatlinburg's bicycle-riding policemen have become an attraction all by themselves. Tourists are constantly stopping the cycle cops to ask for information. The most frequently asked question is "Why are you riding that bike?" The answer is that the bicycles let the police move rapidly through traffic, increasing their effectiveness at responding to emergency situations.

GETTING HERE, GETTING AROUND

The area known as "the Smokies" is a large chunk of east Tennessee and a smaller portion of western North Carolina with an irregular and totally arbitrary border. The area covered in this book mainly covers the corridor that is described by Tennessee Highway 66 and U.S. Highway 441 along a path of about 30 miles from exit 407 off Interstate 40 to Great Smoky Mountains National Park entrance at the southern city limit of Gatlinburg. Keep going, and you'll eventually wind through the park and into North Carolina.

This chapter will begin with a small section on getting here and will then concentrate on telling you how to get around once you're here. It can be a challenge, and sometimes you'll run into a little traffic, but read on and you'll get where you want to go.

GETTING HERE

By Air

GATLINBURG–PIGEON FORGE AIRPORT
1255 Airport Road, Sevierville
(865) 453-8393

Let's start off with one vital piece of information. When you land at this airport, you won't be in either Gatlinburg or Pigeon Forge—you'll be in Sevierville. Don't ask why. It's probably the same logic responsible for locating the Gatlinburg Municipal Golf Course in Pigeon Forge.

The airport itself is a full-service, fixed-base operator. Its 5,500-foot runway can accommodate aircraft ranging from small, single-engine planes to corporate jets. Although no commercial airlines fly in here, it does frequently receive aircraft chartered by individuals or companies. There are no landing fees, but there is an aircraft parking fee starting at $5 per night.

Amenities available on-site include a maintenance crew, jet fuel, and gas for piston-driven planes. The airport does not operate a shuttle service, but there is an Enterprise rental car office on the premises that you can reach at (865) 908-8512. Of course, you can also leave by taxi, if you wish. See the "Getting Around" section for information on rental cars and local cab companies.

> **i** Piloting your own plane to the Smokies? You'll need to know that the FAA designation for Gatlinburg–Pigeon Forge Airport is GKT, and the runway headings are 10 and 28 for eastbound and westbound approaches, respectively.

MCGHEE TYSON AIRPORT
Alcoa Highway, Alcoa
(865) 342-3000
www.flyknoxville.com

This airport is in the community of Alcoa, approximately 15 miles south of Knoxville on U.S. Highway 129 (Alcoa Highway). The airport accommodates nine airlines providing nonstop flights to 20 major cities including Atlanta, Dallas–Fort Worth, Philadelphia, New York City, Orlando, Chicago, and Washington, D.C. Among the carriers that fly in and out of Knoxville are Northwest Airlink, United Express, U.S. Airways Express, American Eagle, Continental Express, and Delta. Allegiant Air (which has been here since December 2006) and most recently Air Tran (which just returned to Knoxville in 2009 after its brief history here from 1998 to 2000) are the low-fare kids on the aviation block.

Both short- and long-term parking sites are available. In both cases, the first 30 minutes are free, and then you're charged in hourly increments. Maximum per-day rates are $10 for long-term parking and $18 for short-term. Two economy lots behind the Hilton charge only $8 a day.

Entering the main terminal, you'll find the baggage claim areas and a number of rental car agencies on the lower street level. The upper level includes the gates and ticketing areas as well as some typical airport facilities and amenities— a full-service restaurant, two gift shops, and a brand-new food court (that includes Starbucks).

i The McGhee Tyson Airport now has a phone-and-wait lot. If friends are meeting you at the airport, they can park for free in a special lot near the car rental return area. When you land, you can call their cell phone from one of the courtesy phones in the airport, and by the time you've picked up your bags, they can be waiting for you at the curb outside.

Transportation from Mcghee Tyson Airport

For transportation from McGhee Tyson Airport to the Smokies, a number of options are available. The following national car rental agencies maintain fleets at the airport. In addition to the various agencies' toll-free numbers, the list below also includes local numbers providing direct access to each company's airport rental office:

ALAMO
(800) 462-5266 or
(865) 342-3210

AVIS
(800) 331-1212 or
(865) 342-3220

BUDGET
(800) 527-0700 or
(865) 342-3225

ENTERPRISE
(800) 736-8222 or
(865) 342-1650

HERTZ
(800) 654-3131 or
(865) 342-3232

NATIONAL
(800) 227-7368 or
(865) 342-3240

THRIFTY
(800) 367-2277 or
(865) 342-3250

If you're driving to the Smokies from the airport, there are two basic ways you can go. Traveling north on US 129 (Alcoa Highway) will take you directly to I-40 near downtown Knoxville. Head east on I-40 to exit 407, and you'll be at the north end of the Smokies Corridor. An alternate, not to mention more scenic, path would be to take US 129 south from the airport for about 2 miles and bear left, following the signs to Maryville and Alcoa. Tennessee Highway 35 will take you east through those two communities. Once you're in Maryville, follow the signs for US 411 North. That highway will take you north to Seymour and then east, directly into Sevierville. Depending on traffic, both routes to Sevierville are about a 45-minute to one-hour drive.

By Ground
GREYHOUND BUS TERMINAL
100 Magnolia Avenue NE, Knoxville
(865) 522-5144
Unfortunately, if you plan to get to the Smokies by bus, Knoxville is about as close as you're going to get, because there are no major bus routes that run into Sevier County. Knoxville's Greyhound terminal receives approximately 35 to 40 arrivals daily. However, be aware that there are no rental car agencies located at the bus station.

GETTING AROUND

You won't find a more beautiful or peaceful place on the planet than the Smokies. The serenity you'll find here simply is not available anywhere else, and it originates from a combination of several agreeable factors that come together quite nicely.

You might want to repeat this mantra to yourself a few thousand times if you're sitting in the parking lot that the Smokies Corridor is wont to become without notice on any given summer day. Traffic is a problem in any place where upwards of 75,000 people are all trying to go anywhere at the same time. And when 50,000 of them are on the same street at the same time, it doesn't matter how long the street is—you've gotten yourself into a traffic jam that only time will resolve, and you're on your time, and it probably didn't come cheap. So here are some hints that may save you a little time and a lot of frazzled nerves.

Handy Hint #1: The roads in this book are all paved and wide enough for trailers or RVs to pass. Locals may well count on some other routes, and they'll be glad to share them with you, but this book is going to stick with the routes that don't require special handling.

Handy Hint #2: If you're bumper-to-bumper in Great Smoky Mountains National Park, you're stuck. Take whatever comfort you can from the beauty of your surroundings and pray that your gas and your composure hold out until you break free.

First, here's how to negotiate the Smokies Corridor: It begins at exit 407 on I-40, which dumps you onto TN 66, also known and labeled as the Winfield Dunn Scenic Parkway. (The area right around here, now referred to at Sevierville 407, is a mini hot spot of development, thanks to several hotels and restaurants that have popped up after the opening of Bass Pro Shop.) Unless you're coming into the area from the southeast via U.S. Highway 321 into Gatlinburg, or have chosen to forgo the interstate system at a point west of exit 407, chances are you'll enter the area at exit 407. It's the way most travel services recommend for travelers coming from the north, south, or west. People coming from the east (the Carolinas and those folks from Georgia and Florida who don't use Interstate 75) usually get off I-40 at the Foothills Parkway (exit 445) and come in to Gatlinburg on US 321—a route that's discussed later.

A word of caution: There are very few places in the area where roads have only one name or only one state or federal route number. Every road name you will read in this book is the one that observation has proven correct. In cases where one road is identified by maps and highway signs as having several route numbers, the maps here will show only the numbers that are used by the local gentry. For example, the Parkway, the area's main stem and primary reference point, can have up to seven different identifications from Sevierville to the Park entrance. Here, it will be called only "Parkway" and "US 441," with the maps marked accordingly. The section on bypasses and back roads will address the name changes more specifically.

ℹ When you make your hotel reservations, ask the clerk if the hotel provides a shuttle service that can pick you up at either the Gatlinburg–Pigeon Forge Airport or the McGhee Tyson Airport, south of Knoxville.

Eight miles south of exit 407, TN 66 intersects Dolly Parton Parkway (US 411N/441S—see why it's easier to use simpler terms?) in Sevierville. You'll probably see the golden dome of the courthouse as you approach Dolly Parton Parkway. More than a century old, the Sevier (pronounced "severe") County courthouse is one of Tennessee's oldest and one of the prettiest in America (see the Attractions chapter for more). After crossing Dolly Parton Parkway, another mile brings you to the end of TN 66 at US 441 south. Turning right toward Pigeon Forge, you're now on what is locally known as the Parkway, and if you've managed to avoid bumper-to-bumper traffic so far, the honeymoon is about to end.

Remember the intersection where you turned onto the Parkway—it will come up later for visits to a few places. For now, though, you're closing in on your first destination: your home away from home for the duration of your visit (if you're staying in or near Pigeon Forge or Gatlinburg. If you're staying in Sevierville, you've probably already checked in by now).

Proceeding south along the Parkway, you'll notice that the first few miles are crowded with motels, convenience stores, and local services, with a few gift/craft shops and restaurants thrown in. You're still in Sevierville, the county seat, where tourism is now growing rapidly (more on this in the Area Overview chapter).

Keep your eyes peeled for Wal-Mart on the right and Governor's Crossing resort complex on the left. When you pass these places, you're approaching Pigeon Forge, and the landscape will change dramatically. The first building that's actually in Pigeon Forge is the City of Pigeon Forge Welcome Center, and if you still thirst for literature and/or more information, it's a good place to stop and get your bearings. Then, welcome to action-packed Pigeon Forge! You actually left Sevierville and entered Pigeon Forge when you crossed the river, but the sign's hard to see.

The next 3 miles are a steady stream of motels, restaurants, amusements, and shops strung out shoulder-to-shoulder along both sides of the Parkway. If you're staying in Pigeon Forge, start looking for your lodging place as soon as you cross Apple Valley Road. In average conditions, you'll have sufficient time to look because you're probably going to be in really slow-moving traffic. If you know which side of the road you're staying on, get in the lane you'll be turning out of, and resist every temptation to get out of it. If you're going on to Gatlinburg, stay in one of the two center lanes all the way through Pigeon Forge.

Looking at the Parkway today, it seems hard to believe that just a few generations back, Pigeon Forge used to have only one traffic light. The numbering of the dozen lights isn't exactly straightforward (there's no light #9, for example,

and three are designated as some variation of light #2), but it's not too difficult to follow. Here's how they lay out, running north to south:

0. The entrance to the parking lots for Wonder Works, the Miracle Theater, and Tony Roma's, this intersection has become increasingly popular as the road has been developed to wrap around the west side of the Parkway and become Music Road.
1. Henderson Chapel Road boasts several motels and the Convention Center.
2. Teaster Lane goes off to the left, leading to a large concentration of outlet malls. Teaster Lane is also the southern bypass around the Parkway, leading to Veterans Boulevard and Dollywood Lane.
2A. This new light is at Christmas Tree Lane, where you'll find both the Inn at Christmas Place (see the chapter on hotels) as well as a matching Starbucks.
2B. Community Center Drive leads into Pigeon Forge's educational campus, city park complex, and the Pigeon Forge community center described in the Parks and Recreation chapter.
3. Wears Valley Road (US 321S/Tennessee Highway 73W) is no longer the northern terminus of the Forge, but it's where you turn left (east) to go to one of the largest selections of outlet malls—if that's where you're heading and you missed Teaster Lane at light #2. In the other direction, Wears Valley Road is being developed so fast it's hard to stay abreast, but the Pigeon Forge educational complex of three schools is about a half mile down on the right. Several campgrounds are on Wears Valley Road and are described in the Campgrounds and RV Parks chapter.

    Wears Valley Road is also an excellent alternative route to Cades Cove at the extreme western edge of the national park and to the community of Townsend in Blount County.
4. Approaching the center of the downtown area, traffic light #4 gets you into and out

of the busy Pigeon Forge Factory Outlet (see the Shopping chapter).

5. Jake Thomas Road goes off to the left (north), leading to Teaster Lane.

6. Pine Mountain Road goes south (right), leading to the Pigeon Forge city offices and U.S. post office.

7. The intersection at Old Mill Avenue (once the center of town) provides access to the Old Mill Square shopping area and Patriot Park. This is the original traffic signal in the city, and Old Mill Avenue leads to Veterans Boulevard, which is handy to know about as a convenient bypass.

8. The "Dollywood" light is so named because it's where most traffic turns to go to the area's biggest single attraction. Note: This is Dollywood Lane, which leads to Veterans Boulevard (where the new entrance to Dollywood is) as well as to Upper Middle Creek Road, which leads out of town and runs alongside the Gatlinburg Golf Club. Upper Middle Creek is a major "back road" and will be described in depth later on.

9. There is currently no traffic light #9.

10. You'll know when you're out of Pigeon Forge by the sudden disappearance of businesses and the equally sudden appearance of wilderness when you pass through the southernmost traffic light.

The next 4 miles pass through federal property, on what's referred to locally as The Spur. With mountains rising from the right shoulder and the lovely Little Pigeon River on the left, this short respite from the hodgepodge of commercialism behind and before you is a preview of Great Smoky Mountains National Park. This is a flat, twisty road. When you leave Pigeon Forge and when you enter Gatlinburg 4 miles later, you're traveling almost due south. In between, you'll go west, north, and east before heading south again.

Handy hint: This illustrates one of the local phenomena that make visiting here such a hoot sometimes. When you get a general direction from a local, like, "Go east for 3 miles," do what you're told. In the 3 miles you travel, you might think you're going every direction but east, but you'll get where you wanted to go.

As you approach Gatlinburg, you'll notice on the right the Gatlinburg/Great Smoky Mountains National Park welcome center. This is another handy place to pick up literature and information, including a lot of park literature that's difficult to get through the mail. Continuing past the welcome center, a broad sweep in the road takes you past the park bypass and into downtown Gatlinburg. It may also bring you to a screeching crawl as the traffic begins reacting to traffic lights you can't quite see yet. Hello, Gatlinburg!

i Tennessee has a very tough drunk driving (DUI) law. If you are stopped and fail a field sobriety test, you will then be asked to submit to a breath analysis. If that test indicates a blood alcohol level of 0.08 percent or higher, you may be arrested and jailed. You could also lose your driver's license for a year.

Gatlinburg usually doesn't have as much traffic as Pigeon Forge, but it seems like more sometimes, because Gatlinburg doesn't have as much Parkway as Pigeon Forge, either. Two miles long and never more than four lanes wide, the Parkway in Gatlinburg provides exactly zero opportunities to pull over to the side and take stock. There's no "to the side"—the buildings come right to the sidewalk, which comes right to the curb. It's helpful to know where you're going at all times in Gatlinburg. If you plan to park, plan ahead. It's so essential that there's a section devoted to parking lots later in this chapter. For now, let's finish the Parkway portion of the Smokies Corridor.

From the end of The Spur at the north (upper) end of town to the entrance to Great Smoky Mountains National Park 2 miles later, Gatlinburg, like Pigeon Forge, is punctuated by nine numbered traffic lights. They are, in order:

1. The Dudley Creek bypass to US 321N. Details will be explained later.
2. A blinker 200 yards south of #1.
3. (A Biggie)—US 321 comes in from the left and the Parkway swings right. US 321 is the only road out of Gatlinburg to the east, and it leads immediately to a string of motels. Farther east are a scattering of businesses, the U.S. post office, Gatlinburg's city hall complex, the Great Smoky Arts & Crafts Community, and Gatlinburg's two primary grocery stores. Note: This piece of road has gone through several name changes in the last decade. At various times it has been TN 73, East Main, US 321 (its current federal designation), and its current local handle, East Parkway. The locals (except for postal workers and firemen) have given up trying to keep current and will refer to it as either "73" or "321." This guide will use the latter, along with East Parkway.
4. There is no traffic light #4—nobody knows why.
5. River Road goes off diagonally to the right. It travels roughly parallel to the Parkway for less than a mile, past several motels, restaurants, and attractions, and rejoins the Parkway outside of town, near the entrance sign for Great Smoky Mountains National Park.
6. Just a block from #5, Cherokee Orchard Road goes off to the left, leading to another large group of motels and condos in the Bask-ins Creek area. Cherokee Orchard rises as it continues east and south to its intersection with Historic Nature Trail (formerly Airport Road). If you meant to turn onto River Road and missed it, you can recover here by turning right.
7. There is no traffic light #7. (The city recently removed the flashing yellow light at Reagan Drive.)
8. Historic Nature Trail (formerly Airport Road) goes off and up to the left. The Gatlinburg Convention Center, a few attractions, several motels, and most of the downtown churches are on Historic Nature Trail. From the intersection at Cherokee Orchard Road, Historic Nature Trail passes Mynatt Park and a residential area on the right and enters Great Smoky Mountains National Park. More about this later in the chapter.
9. A blinking light at the aerial tramway terminal that's forgettable unless you're staying in a motel on the other side of the river.
10. The last light is at Ski Mountain Road. A right turn will take you through the River Road intersection and up Ski Mountain. Mostly chalets and condos, Ski Mountain Road is the only way a visitor would want to go into the Chalet Village area.

Some hardy souls also think it's the only route to Ober Gatlinburg ski resort. Wrong. The only sensible way to get to Ober Gatlinburg is to park in town and ride the aerial tramway. Think about this: Ski Mountain Road goes straight up from town and straight down from the ski lodge, except for that nifty little double hairpin in the middle, and when it's covered with snow and ice, it still goes straight up and straight down. It's a narrow two-lane road with no shoulder for most of its length. Ride the tram to the top. There's more detail on this in the Attractions chapter.

If you go through traffic light #10 heading out of town, you're in the woods as quickly as you were when you left Pigeon Forge. The big difference this time is that you're now in 50 miles of woods, interrupted only by the Pigeon Forge/Sevierville bypass a mile or so ahead, and the Sugarlands Visitor Center another mile up the road.

That's the Smokies Corridor for everybody that used exit 407 to get here. For those rugged individualists who came a little more overland, here's where you are:

If you came out of Knoxville on US 441, or onto 441 from US 411 in Seymour (a popular route for knowledgeable Georgians), continue east about 12 miles to the traffic light at TN 66 (it's well posted) and hang a right. You're now in the Smokies Corridor, and you'll be on the Parkway in a mile.

If you came through the park from Townsend on Little River Road (TN 73E), turn left at the Sugarlands Visitor Center. You're now on US 441 going north, and if you don't take the bypass to Pigeon Forge, you'll be at traffic light #10 in Gatlinburg in about as much time as it takes you to read this paragraph.

If you came into Gatlinburg from the east on US 321S (a favorite route for people coming out of the Carolinas), you will enter downtown Gatlinburg at traffic light #3.

Finally, if you came into Sevierville from the east on US 411S from Cocke or Jefferson County, turn left at the traffic light at US 441S (if you turn right, you'll be in a supermarket parking lot). If you miss the intersection, you've got two more chances in the next 2 blocks. Take either one and stay on it. Both roads end at the Parkway.

If you got truly crazy and came out of Townsend on Wears Valley Road (US 321/TN 73E), turn right at traffic light #3 after you pass the giant Kroger store. You'll be on the Parkway in Pigeon Forge.

Now that everybody's in the corridor and settled, the rest is remarkably easy. Every direction in the rest of this book will use one of the landmarks previously mentioned (e.g., "from traffic light #7 in Pigeon Forge" or "from the Sugarlands Visitor Center") to get you started. Using this chapter as your guide, go from wherever you are to that starting place, and then enjoy your time in the Smokies. The important thing to note here is that the alphabet soup that makes up the road system in the Smokies Corridor consists of only one north-south road (US 441 in all its descriptions) and four major east-west roads (I-40, US 411/441 [Dolly Parton Parkway] in Sevierville, Wears Valley Road in Pigeon Forge, and US 321 [East Parkway] in Gatlinburg). You'll get used to the various descriptions sooner than you think, but remember these simple pointers to make moving around as simple as possible:

Regardless of what city you're in, the terms "Parkway" and "Main Street" will always refer to US 441. In Sevierville, a short portion of US 441 west of the downtown area is actually named Main Street.

US 411 (note the difference) is Dolly Parton Parkway in Sevierville—it's also Main Street and Chapman Highway on the western end (toward Knoxville), and Newport Highway east of Sevierville.

What you may hear called "73" in Gatlinburg is actually US 321N, and it goes east out of town at traffic light #3.

i Pedestrians in Gatlinburg have the right-of-way in crosswalks. This means that if they step off the curb, you have to stop for them. In the heart of downtown, some visitors think the entire Parkway is a crosswalk. Be very wary; hitting a pedestrian in Gatlinburg would be a capital crime if the locals had their way.

Shortcuts and Back Roads

Now that you're scared to death with all this talk of traffic, you should know that there are ways to get around in the area without using the Parkway. They are known and used by the locals, and the folks who live here are not averse to sharing this knowledge with visitors. The problem is that most visitors don't ask about these byways until they've been burned by the traffic, and then they tend to get specific about where they want to avoid. Herewith, a list of handy little back routes on paved, generally level roads.

For openers, let's go back to your introduction to the area coming off exit 407 from I-40. If you've spent the last 10 minutes or so enjoying the view of the courthouse dome from the Winfield Dunn Scenic Parkway (TN 66) and you haven't seen a traffic light yet, take heart. A light is just around the bend you're creeping up on, but you're probably in a traffic situation that's not going to ease off until you get to Gatlinburg, some 20 miles down the road.

At a daytime average speed of 10 to 20 mph, you're talking an hour or so to Pigeon Forge, and God knows what it'll take to get to Gatlinburg. Here comes a small slice of salvation that can get you to those two towns much quicker. What you want to do is turn left at the traffic signal, so get over as soon as you can.

The traffic light you're approaching is at Dolly Parton Parkway (US 411/441), the main east-west thoroughfare in Sevierville. You're now going to take a detour by turning left on Dolly Parton and putting all that traffic in the rearview mirror. Warning: This gambit is for people staying in Pigeon Forge or Gatlinburg. If you're staying in Sevierville, this shortcut isn't much help—you've got to get back into the traffic jam. Do it by turning right at the second traffic light you come to on Dolly Parton Parkway. That puts you back on the Parkway (US 441). This intersection is where US 411 and 441 part company; US 411 continues east toward the first bypass road, and US 441 drops southward toward Pigeon Forge and Gatlinburg.

Back to the escapees: If your goal is Pigeon Forge, your target is Veterans Boulevard, about a mile from where you fled TN 66. It's clearly labeled, and there's a traffic light at the intersection. Also note that Veterans Boulevard goes off only to the right—it's not a cross street yet (long-range planning projects a new road that will run east off TN 66 south of the French Broad River and will drop south to meet Veterans Boulevard). Hang a right onto Veterans Boulevard.

For the first mile, you'll be in an area of local businesses and professional buildings. You'll pass through 4 or 5 miles of farmland. When you see the entrance to Dollywood's parking lot on your left, you're approaching Pigeon Forge. If you stay on Veterans Boulevard, you'll merge with Dollywood Lane near the center of Pigeon Forge and renew your acquaintance with the Parkway at traffic light #8. This side trip has cost you about 3 miles and probably saved an hour.

If you're headed for Gatlinburg, stay on Dolly Parton Parkway and go through the light at Veterans Boulevard. Less than a mile up the road, you'll pass an industrial park on the right and Sevier County High School on the left. A mile or so later, you'll reach a traffic signal where your only option is to turn right; take it, and you'll be on Pittman Center Road (Tennessee Highway 416).

Settle back and enjoy the scenery for a while. You've begun a journey of some 8 to 12 miles, depending on precisely where you're going, and you're on a road through some real pretty farmland. The road itself will change its name two or three times; pay no attention.

Five miles in from your turning point, Pittman Center Road turns left. Keep going straight, and you're now on Bird's Creek Road. The road coming in from the right is Upper Middle Creek, which comes out of Pigeon Forge as Dollywood Lane. More on that shortly.

Continuing on Bird's Creek, you'll enjoy more rural scenery for the next 4 miles until you come to a stop sign. You're now in the Great Smoky Arts & Crafts Community, which means you're closing in on Gatlinburg. You're also within a mile of the end of Bird's Creek Road.

As you approach the intersection at Glades Road (again, right turn only), notice that Bird's Creek seems to flow onto Glades. If you're headed for downtown Gatlinburg, go with the flow. Glades Road ends at US 321, 2 miles (turn right) from traffic light #3 in downtown Gatlinburg. If your destination is a lodging place more than 5 miles east of Gatlinburg on US 321, skip the turn at Glades Road, and bear just slightly left. Now you're on Buckhorn Road.

(These name changes occur a lot around here, and most of them came about when old roads were rerouted in years past to intersect other roads. When the roads came together, nobody could see a good reason to change the name of one of them just because the intersection formed a straight line instead of a corner.)

Buckhorn Road continues south about 2 more miles to US 321, a little more than 5 miles

i **If you find yourself on a winding mountain or country road with no idea where you are, remember this: Every back road in the county is paved and leads eventually to a highway. When you come to the highway, turn onto it and stay on it until you get to something that looks familiar. It shouldn't take long.**

east of downtown Gatlinburg. A left turn here will take you toward Pittman Center and the condo communities of Cobbly Nob, Brandywine, and Bent Creek.

The two bypass routes described above are the longest alternate routes in the area, but they will cut out long waits in Parkway traffic. Used in reverse, they're handy for getting back to I-40 when you leave the Smokies.

Let's go back to Upper Middle Creek Road for a minute. Remember, this is the one that leaves Pigeon Forge as Dollywood Lane at traffic light #8 and runs past the Gatlinburg Golf Club. Upper Middle Creek intersects Bird's Creek Road (near Pittman Center Road) about midway between Pigeon Forge and the Great Smoky Arts & Crafts Community. If you're out that way and want to get to Pigeon Forge without going back through Gatlinburg, it's the best route. Upper Middle Creek goes left off Bird's Creek just past Caton's Chapel School.

That takes care of the really big shortcuts. Now for the little ones that make in-town travel a little more palatable, starting in Pigeon Forge. There really aren't any shortcuts in Sevierville to speak of because the city's laid out in a very compact fashion. To keep things in perspective, these descriptions assume the Parkway runs north and south through town:

Skirting Pigeon Forge to the East

Teaster Lane is a bypass around the Parkway on the east side of Pigeon Forge that runs from traffic light #2 just north of Wears Valley Road to Veterans Boulevard. Coming south on the Parkway (from Sevierville), turn left at traffic light #2 and follow the road as far as you want to go. The traffic

i From the time you enter the Parkway in Sevierville, think of it as a giant funnel. It starts out as a six-lane road in Sevierville, continues that way through Pigeon Forge, and narrows down to four lanes on The Spur and through Gatlinburg. Once you continue into the national park, the four lanes become two.

light near the southern end is Veterans Boulevard; a left turn will take you to the back entrance to Dollywood and, eventually, back to Sevierville.

You can get to Teaster Lane from the Parkway at Jake Thomas Road (traffic light #5) about halfway between Veterans Boulevard and Wears Valley Road. Teaster Lane includes most of Pigeon Forge's outlet malls.

The Western Side of Pigeon Forge

These directions take you from north to south; if you're traveling north, use Teaster Lane. Florence Street runs off Wears Valley Road a block west of the Parkway (Mel's Diner is on the corner). Running parallel to the Parkway for about half its length, the street goes through a very nice middle-class neighborhood and a kaleidoscope of name changes. You can get back to the Parkway just about anywhere along the way.

When it passes the Pigeon Forge city hall and its name becomes Rena, take the next left. If you don't, you'll wind up out in the countryside, and the only way to get back is to backtrack. Pigeon Forge is planning a western bypass called the West End Connector that will run roughly parallel to Florence/Rena, starting at Conner Heights Road at the southern end of the city and extending to Sharon Drive, about midway to Wears Valley. The second phase of the project will extend the bypass all the way to Wears Valley Road so that when it's complete (although no real firm date exists for either stage of the project), you'll be able to go around Pigeon Forge from Wears Valley Road to the Parkway Spur.

Let's go on to Gatlinburg. As mentioned earlier, the only safe "back way" from Pigeon Forge to Gatlinburg is the Dollywood Lane/Upper Middle Creek–Bird's Creek–Glades route. However, you can take the Parkway Spur south and bypass Gatlinburg on either side before getting into downtown gridlock.

The park bypass runs off The Spur just past the Gatlinburg Welcome Center and that's what you should take if you want to go directly to Great Smoky Mountains National Park. Two roadside turnoffs provide spectacular views of Gatlinburg along the way. You'll come off the bypass inside the park boundary, and the Sugarlands Visitor Center (a must-stop for first-time visitors) is about a mile ahead. The bypass is clearly marked on your return.

In Gatlinburg, the Dudley Creek bypass (turn left at traffic light #1 and follow the signs) will put you on US 321 about a mile and a half east of downtown. If you're heading toward Gatlinburg (west) on US 321, turn right at the traffic light and you'll be headed back to The Spur.

Caution: This route is steep and narrow in some places. Large vehicles and towed loads should think twice.

Finally, Gatlinburg's in-town bypasses are the Baskins Creek/Newton Lane Bypass and Cherokee Orchard Road. These are convenient anytime you're on the east end of town and want to get around the Parkway in the heart of the business district.

First, the Baskins Creek/Newton Lane Bypass: This one requires alertness at both ends. It's clearly marked, but if you miss it on the east end (US 321), there's no turning back, and a whiff on the Cherokee Orchard end could drop you into the busiest intersection in town.

Coming west toward downtown on US 321, the street sign says "Baskins Creek Bypass." It's on the left, about halfway around a sweeping curve, and there's a large earthen breastwork at the corner. If you miss it, the only way to get back is to make an illegal U-turn on a hill in heavy traffic. Just go on down to the Parkway at traffic light #3, turn left to traffic light #6, and turn left again. Now you're on Cherokee Orchard Road, 2 blocks from where you would have come out if you hadn't missed the turn.

Cherokee Orchard climbs rapidly as it goes away from downtown and curves around to intersect Historic Nature Trail (formerly Airport Road) at the equivalent of about 8 city blocks from the Parkway. A right turn on Historic Nature Trail will take you back toward downtown; a left leads out of town.

If you're hurtling down Cherokee Orchard toward town, you'll see two side streets very close together right at the bottom of the hill. The second one is marked as "Newton Lane Bypass." Take it to the right, and you'll go around town to US 321.

Finally, River Road in Gatlinburg is a viable bypass to get to Ski Mountain Road and Great Smoky Mountains National Park. Bear right at traffic light #5. Because River Road is populated primarily by motels and restaurants, pedestrian congestion is lighter.

The alternate routes described in this chapter can be invaluable in terms of saving time and tempers. Remember that even more alternate roads are available, but they're not really intended for heavy traffic or unfamiliar drivers. For the most part, the real "back roads" are not really safe to drive on unless you know what to expect in the way of sudden turns, rapid elevation changes, livestock and wild animals in the road, and other obstacles too numerous to mention. Bring this guide with you and use it frequently; it should help you realize the joy you came here seeking.

Parking in Gatlinburg

If you must drive into town, some parking is available. Several private lots on Historic Nature Trail (formerly Airport Road), adjacent to and across the street from the convention center, operate on a sliding rate scale depending on what's going on in town at the time. They usually work on an hourly basis and sometimes offer an all-day or maximum rate. A few private lots are scattered along the Parkway behind the storefronts, but they fill up early. During the summer when school is not in session, the Pi Beta Phi elementary school PTA operates the school's parking lot as a fund-raiser. The school is on Cherokee Orchard Road, 1 block from the Parkway at traffic light #6.

The City of Gatlinburg operates five parking lots and two multistory decks in and around town. Rates are variable, depending on location, and long-term permits are available at city hall on East Parkway. Two of the seven lots offer free parking.

1. The Welcome Center Park and Ride lot on the Parkway Spur coming from Pigeon Forge (96 spaces). Parking is free, and the purple route trolley will take you into the

center of town for 50 cents a head. The lot is unattended.

2. The North Parkway lot, next to Hillbilly Golf before traffic light #3 (34 spaces). Parking is metered (honor system), and the lot has public restrooms. Convenient to businesses and attractions north of the main business district, it's a hike into town and back if you've got kids to consider. A monthly permit is available at city hall for $30. The lot is unattended.

3. The Fred McMahan Downtown Parking Garage (382 spaces) at the intersection of the Parkway and East Parkway (US 321N), south of traffic light #3. Hourly rates are $1.75 (minimum) for the first hour and $1.00 per additional hour, with a maximum charge of $6.00 per day. A long-term parking permit is available for $30.00 a month. The deck is operated by an attendant.

4. Aquarium Parking Garage (382 spaces). Directly behind the Ripley's Aquarium, this structure has the same short-term rate schedules as the Fred McMahan Downtown Garage; the monthly permit here is $60. It is also attended.

5. City Parking Lot at Traffic Light #5 (84 spaces). (This was formerly known as the Anna Porter Library lot, although the library has recently moved.) Turn left at Cherokee Orchard Road (traffic light #6), go 2 blocks to Newton Lane, and turn left again. The entrance is just past the library. Coming in from US 321, turn left at the Bask-ins Creek Bypass. The lot entrance is on the right just after the road levels out. It's a short walk to downtown, and the lot has a flat rate of $5. An attendant operates the lot.

6. Reagan Drive (148 spaces). Reagan Drive intersects the Parkway at Ripley's Believe It or Not! Museum. The lot is 2 blocks up on the left, next to the fire hall. It's a moderate downhill walk into town and a strenuous uphill walk back. Payment is $3 on weekdays and $5 on Fridays, Saturdays, and holidays. No attendant is present but the lot is gated.

7. City hall park-and-ride (79 spaces). Located on US 321, 2 miles east of downtown, between city hall and the post office. Parking is free; ride the blue route trolley into town. The lot is unattended.

Drivers with handicaps can park for free in city-owned parking facilities if they have proper identification.

Car Rentals

In addition to the Knoxville-based companies mentioned in the "Getting Here" section of this chapter, several car rental agencies operate in Sevier County. Local companies are good for those traveling in larger recreational vehicles who may want a more manageable form of getting around town. They may also be an attractive option for those who experience car trouble and have to put their personal vehicle in the shop for a day or so.

In Sevierville you can contact Enterprise Rent-A-Car at (865) 908-3044. In Gatlinburg, call Southland Car & Jeep Rentals at (865) 436-9811.

These rental agencies maintain fleets with as few as 7 cars or as many as 50. Fleet sizes will vary from season to season, but you might find it harder to find cars during the peak tourist months. Except for the one Ford dealership, most of the companies keep a variety of makes and models on-site, including vans. Most will also deliver their cars to you.

Prices range from as low as $39 per day for subcompact models to $89 per day for luxury and sport models. Although credit cards are the standard form of payment, most of the companies will accept cash. In these cases, a more substantial up-front deposit is required. If you live outside Tennessee and wish to pay with cash, you may want to call ahead to verify if a particular company will accept your cash deposit.

Trolleys

Short of having the use of a car while visiting the Smokies, your next best bet is to use the area's trolley systems. The trolleys are a dependable, inexpensive way to get around that will take you most anywhere you might want to go. Their combined service routes run from the events center in Sevierville all the way into the national park as well as the Great Smoky Arts & Crafts Community. And if you've been on your feet all day, nothing beats just plunking down your 50 cents (or more, in some cases), sitting back, and taking in the sights while someone else does the driving.

PIGEON FORGE FUN TIME TROLLEY
(865) 453-6444
www.pigeonforgetrolley.org
Seven trolley routes cover more than 130 stopping points throughout the cities of Pigeon Forge and Sevierville. The main hub of operations is on Old Mill Avenue at Patriot Park, behind the Old Mill. Most of the 40 trolleys in the system run on ultra-low-sulfur diesel fuel, while a few run on propane and about eight are electric hybrid buses. These trolley routes are operational only from March through December, with reduced service in November and December. The fare is 50 cents for all routes except the trolley going to the Gatlinburg Welcome Center, which is 75 cents.

The Wears Valley Trolley travels to the Pigeon Forge Community Center via Teaster Lane before heading out to the city limits on Wears Valley Road.

Two more trolley routes service Dollywood's main entrance and Dolly's Splash Country, respectively, and another route takes riders to the Gatlinburg Welcome Center on The Spur, near the north entrance to that town.

The courthouse route goes from the events center in Sevierville to Patriot Park in Pigeon Forge, while the North and South Parkway routes go the length of the Parkway in Pigeon Forge.

Although the regular trolley system is basically shut down from early January through February, you can still view the city's holiday decorations on its Winterfest Trolley Tours of Light, which run November through January (see the Festivals and Annual Events chapter). Heated buses and informed hosts will guide you through the history of all the light displays. From mid-November through December, tours depart on Monday through Friday evenings, while in January, the tours run Monday and Friday only. All tours depart from the trolley office beginning at 6:30 p.m. and cost $5 per person.

GATLINBURG TROLLEY
(865) 436-3897
www.ci.gatlinburg.tn.us/transit/trolley.htm
This system services more than a hundred locations and covers 50 miles in and around Gatlinburg. Its base of operations is the Mass Transit Center located downtown, between Ripley's Aquarium of the Smokies and the parking garage located behind the attraction. The schedules change with the season (and sometimes the day of the week), so for the hours of operation and the frequency of trolleys during your stay, call or check online. Exact change is required, unless you purchase a trolley pass ($2 for unlimited rides all day on all but the Pink and Tan routes). You can purchase a pass at any of the three welcome centers, city hall, and the Mass Transit Center.

The system's 20 environmentally friendly trolleys, which run on biodiesel fuel, are green and orange, but don't confuse these colors with the different color-coded routes that traverse the city. Each trolley has a sign posted on its front and sides indicating which route it follows.

Red Route—This trolley originates from the Mass Transit Center, travels up River Road, up the south end of the Parkway, up Historic Nature Trail (formerly Airport Road), and through the Baskins Creek neighborhood before circling back to base. This route operates year round (but with reduced service from November through March). The fare is 50 cents.

Purple Route—The trolley runs from the Mass Transit Center downtown, along the Parkway to the Welcome Center and Park-n-Ride lot located on The Spur (US 441) at the north end of the city. Like the Red Route, this route operates year-round with reduced service from November through March. The fare is 50 cents.

Blue Route—This route runs from the Mass Transit Center, up US 321, all the way out to the Gatlinburg Community Center. It also serves the free Park-n-Ride lot located next to city hall. The schedule is identical to that of the two routes previously outlined. The fare is 50 cents.

Yellow Route—These minitrolleys run along US 321, from downtown Gatlinburg out to the Great Smoky Arts & Crafts Community, making a loop around Glades Road and Buckhorn Road through the community itself. These trolleys run from March through December. The fare is $1.

Tan Route—This circuit runs from the Mass Transit Center, down River Road and the Parkway to Sugarlands Visitor Center in Great Smoky Mountains National Park. From there, it continues farther into the park, to the Laurel Falls parking area and Elkmont campground, eventually returning to downtown. The round-trip travel time is one and a half hours. This route operates from June through October only, and the fare is $2.

Pink Route—This trolley departs from the Mass Transit Center and takes passengers to the Pigeon Forge trolley office at Patriot Park and, of course, Dollywood. In season, daily trolleys depart approximately every hour. The fare is $1.

Green Route—This new trolley route starts at the Mass Transit Center and more or less follows the Red Route only backwards. It travels up Cherokee Orchard Road to the Park Vista Hotel and then continues down historic Nature Trail to the Parkway. From there, it goes south along the Parkway towards the national park entrance and then makes a little loop using M&O Street, River Road, and Ski Mountain Road before returning back on the Parkway going north to its start at the Mass Transit Center. This route operates from May through December. The fare is 50 cents.

Beginning in November, you can enjoy the city's Winterfest Trolley Rides of Light (see the Festivals and Annual Events chapter). Not to be confused with any of the trolleys' winter schedules, these special trolleys offer spectacular views of Gatlinburg's Winterfest lighting displays. Tours depart from the main office by Ripley's Aquarium at 6:30, 7:30, and 8:30 p.m. and cost $5 per person for ages three and older (or for any child who takes a seat). In November and December, they run every night. In January, they run on Saturdays only. Because tours don't run on Thanksgiving, Christmas, and a few other selected days, it's best to call (865) 436-0535 to verify specific times and dates and to make reservations.

HISTORY

The Great Smoky Mountains all started with a geologic cataclysm around 200 million years ago, when continental land masses collided in an event that geologists refer to as the Appalachian orogeny. As layer upon layer of rock strata and ocean sediment were slowly folded and forced skyward, the face of the earth permanently changed, and set the stage for a chain of events that continues to unfold today. After all, history is always being made.

Along with its towering fortresses of stone, nature was busy at work in other areas long ago, carving valleys, leveling pastures, and causing rivers and streams to spring forth with water. As was the case with the native inhabitants and early settlers of other uncharted lands, geography played a crucial role in primeval mountain life. Mountain settlements were valued as much for their protection as they were for their beauty. And locating near a river was imperative. Running waters were the source of life for drinking, washing, fishing, and, in later centuries, grinding corn and generating electricity.

It's a given that the many places and things that make up the Smokies communities are named after the people who influenced their time. But the legacies of mountain and river are readily apparent in today's Smoky Mountain communities. An old settlement and an existing highway share the name Boyd's Creek. Sevierville was originally known as Forks of Little Pigeon, and today's city of Pigeon Forge takes its name from that same water source. Upper and Lower Middle Creek Roads are important thoroughfares through the county, and the names of countless businesses and streets contain the *M* word, the word that never finds its way far from the local vocabulary—*mountain*.

THE FIRST INHABITANTS

Despite their strong association with Cherokee Indians, the Smoky Mountains were first home to various prehistoric Indians who preceded the Cherokee by as many as 20,000 years, according to some scientists. The earliest documented Native American existence in the area points to the Archaic Period Indians, who lived here as far back as 10,000 years ago and as recently as 900 B.C. They lived in small nomadic groups of 25 to 30 people and survived primarily off the hunting of animals.

The Eastern Woodland Indians made their homes in the mountains between 900 B.C. and A.D. 900. Artifacts like arrowheads, pieces of pottery, and crude tools have been recovered from different sites around the county and suggest that the Woodland Period Indians enjoyed a more agrarian, less nomadic lifestyle. This time also marked the advent of the burial mound, a rich source for modern discoveries of Indian relics.

i To learn about the area's Native Americans and early European pioneers, visit the exhibits and interactive displays of the Great Smoky Mountain Heritage Center in nearby Townsend (accessible from Pigeon Forge via Wears Valley Road). See the chapter on Getting Out of Town for more information.

The Native Americans of the Mississippian Period (A.D. 900 to 1600) followed the Woodland Indians. This period saw increases in both tribal populations and the complexity of political organization and is generally regarded as the peak of prehistoric Indian culture. Several notable local digs have revealed much about these people, including excavations on McCroskey Island in the French Broad River, at a site in Pigeon Forge, and at the McMahon Indian Mound located along the east bank of West Fork of the Little Pigeon River in the heart of Sevierville. Today, a hotel and a historical marker stand on the McMahon site (see the Hotels and Motels chapter for more).

The Cherokee were descendants of these early Native American civilizations. They primarily made their homes in present-day North Carolina and used east Tennessee lands as hunting grounds. As white visitors and settlers made their way into Cherokee territory, years of alternating peace and conflict were the backdrop for Indian existence. The tribe maintained a strong presence in the Smokies until they were marched en masse to the Oklahoma territory in the 1840s on the infamous Trail of Tears. Yet not all the Cherokees left. The descendants of those who resisted the feds and hid out in the mountains today make up the Eastern Band of the Cherokees, headquartered in the town of Cherokee in western North Carolina (see the Cherokee, NC, chapter).

EARLY VISITORS

One of the Cherokee's earliest recorded experiences with outsiders was friendly enough, according to historical accounts. Hernando de Soto journeyed into the area in 1540, likely during a gold expedition, and received a warm greeting from the Indians. However, as the years passed, more and more traders, usually white men, infiltrated the region and didn't always receive such warm receptions. In fact, many were killed by the Cherokee, including two Virginia traders named Boyd and Daggett. In 1775, these two men were slaughtered, their bodies thrown into a creek. Incidentally, this was the origin of the name Boyd's Creek, a site that would later play an important role in the development of Sevier County.

In 1776 large numbers of white men were introduced to the area as colonial armies clashed with the British and their allies, the Cherokee. That year, Colonel William Christian from Virginia led 1,800 infantry in a punitive expedition against a number of Cherokee Overhill towns located along the Indian War Path, the area's only travel route of the time, which extended from Pennsylvania to Georgia. Many of the soldiers who passed through this area remembered its beauty and resources and returned here to settle in the years following the Revolutionary War.

Two particular battles from that war relate to local history. Colonel John Sevier led a group of men from Washington County, North Carolina (as Tennessee was known at the time), against the British at the Battle of King's Mountain on October 7, 1780. Although the British were defeated in that clash, what was of more local significance was the subsequent Battle of Boyd's Creek two months later. As Sevier and his men returned from King's Mountain, they discovered that their settlements had been attacked by Cherokee Indians during their absence. At Boyd's Creek on December 16, Sevier led 100 men to victory against the Cherokee in what was to be the first of 35 Indian battles in which the colonel would engage over the years.

i Be sure to check out the bronze statue of Dolly Parton outside the Sevierville courthouse. Sculpted by local artist Jim Gray, the statue depicts a young, barefoot Dolly with guitar in hand, jeans rolled up, and hair pulled back in a ponytail. The country singer and entertainer grew up in the mountains here and is well loved in these parts.

SETTLEMENT AND EARLY GOVERNMENT

At war's end, a number of those who fought for the Continental Armies received land grants in recognition of their service. Many made homes along Dumplin' Creek, just north of the French Broad River, and later along Boyd's Creek and the Little Pigeon River. One of the earliest known of these settlers was Isaac Thomas, a former Indian trader who had been a guide for William Christian in 1776 and was a scout and a guide for John Sevier at Boyd's Creek. He was given

1,000 acres west of West Fork of the Little Pigeon River around 1781 or 1782, making him one of Sevierville's first permanent white residents. He even gave Sevierville its first name, Forks of Little Pigeon.

Over the next couple of years, other notable local fathers made their way toward the Smokies. In 1782 Major Hugh Henry built a homestead at Dumplin' Creek near the present-day community of Kodak. Henry's Station, or Henry's Crossroads as it was known, was typical of the small blockhouses used by settlers in those days; these "forts" were used not only as dwellings but also as protection against Indian attack.

In 1783 Captain Samuel Newell settled near what is now the unincorporated town of Seymour in west Sevier County. Newell was a veteran of battles with both the British and the Cherokee; he was to be prominent in the political structure of the area, from its formative years all the way through Tennessee statehood. His home, Newell's Station, would later be the first "county seat" of an infant Sevier County.

Also in 1783, another prominent figure of early Sevierville, James McMahon, settled on 400 acres between the east and west forks of Little Pigeon River, present-day site of Sevierville's downtown district. It was on this land that the McMahon Indian Mound was first excavated in 1881.

During the early 1780s, pioneers were faced not only with the hardships presented by a rugged wilderness existence but also with the political goings-on of the day. Although North Carolina had passed an act in 1783 reserving much of what we now know as east Tennessee for the Cherokee, it was also issuing land grants and selling land to white settlers in that same territory. Needless to say, this only exacerbated tensions between the whites and the Indians, leading to frequent conflict.

By 1784 the North Carolina treasury was severely drained by the war. It no longer had the resources or the inclination to support and protect its outposts to the west. The settlers of Washington County and the recently formed Greene County had become frustrated with

North Carolina's neglect and inability to protect their settlements from Indian attack. In November of that year, the settlers met in Greeneville and organized their own government for a territory they named the State of Franklin, a moniker that they hoped would ingratiate them with the national government in their efforts to achieve statehood. Despite a noble attempt, however, Franklin fell short of its goal, coming within six votes of becoming the 14th state.

Although it failed in those efforts, Franklin did manage to come to more peaceful terms with the Cherokee. In 1785 a delegation from Franklin, led by its governor, John Sevier, met with Cherokee leaders and warriors at Henry's Station near Dumplin' Creek. With the signing of the Treaty of Dumplin' Creek, much of today's east Tennessee was officially opened up for homesteading. Although the Cherokee were well compensated in exchange, not everyone in that nation was in agreement with the peace accord, and numerous massacres were still led against the white settlers.

Legend has it that Timothy Reagan, the man employed to build Sevier County's first prisoners' stocks in 1795, persuaded the county sheriff to allow himself to be locked in them in order to test them out. Reportedly, the sheriff was left locked in the stocks for a considerable amount of time, much to the amusement of local residents.

THE BIRTH, REBIRTH, AND REBIRTH OF A COUNTY

Sevier County was first formed on March 31, 1785, when the Franklin legislature divided existing Greene County into three smaller counties, one of which was named for Franklin governor John Sevier. The first county court was held at Newell's Station. In 1788, however, the State of Franklin collapsed due to dissension among its citizens as well as North Carolina's failure to recognize it as a sovereign entity. The following year, a brief attempt at reorganization was made with the formation of the State of Lesser Franklin, but when John Sevier and other leaders swore allegiance to North Carolina, Franklin ceased to exist once and for all.

Sevier County went through a second incarnation when the former State of Franklin was ceded to the federal government and became part of the Territory of the United States South of the River Ohio. William Blount was appointed its governor, and by 1794 Sevier County was re-formed, with its first court being held at the home of Isaac Thomas on November 8. Samuel Newell remained active in this new government, becoming one of the Sevier County court officials, as did Samuel Wear and Mordecai Lewis, both of whom will be discussed in the section on the history of Pigeon Forge.

Finally, in 1796 Sevier County as we know it today came into existence when Tennessee achieved statehood. The new state name was derived from Tenasi, the name for Cherokee villages along the Little Tennessee River. Its first court was held on July Fourth in the county's first courthouse, which was located in the heart of Sevierville. Several county notables had represented their home district at Tennessee's constitutional convention, including Samuel Wear, Samuel Newell, and Sevierville resident Spencer Clack. Clack had moved to Sevierville around 1788 and settled on 400 acres on the north side of East Prong of Little Pigeon River. He was an active force in local government, education, and religion.

SEVIERVILLE

Although the legislative act that had reestablished Sevier County in 1794 also called for a commission to locate a county seat, it wasn't until 1795 that the commission finally chose a site at Forks of Little Pigeon; Isaac Thomas suggested the name Sevierville in honor of John Sevier. The commission acquired a 25-acre tract of land from James McMahon, whose centrally located homestead made the property a good prospect. They built a primitive courthouse, a prison, and stocks

on the land. They also parceled off the rectangular piece of land into 50 half-acre lots that they sold to the highest bidders for home construction. The establishment of Sevierville made it the seventh-oldest town in Tennessee, and following the planting of those early roots, the fledgling community blossomed into the center of the county's economic and governmental activity.

Sevier County's first three courthouses, all of which were believed to have been destroyed by fire, were located in a section of downtown where Sevierville's two main thoroughfares, Cross Street (now Court Avenue) and Main Street, intersected. When a fourth brick courthouse was erected on the site in 1856, this one-acre tract came to be known as Public Square; in addition to having a courthouse and a jail, the site also evolved into the commercial and social hub of Sevier County.

Such was the situation until 1896, when the current courthouse opened on a new site just a block away. Shortly after World War I, a major fire devastated several key Public Square businesses, and in 1948, the government widened U.S. Highways 441 and 411 (running concurrently). These events helped usher in a period of general decline during which existing Public Square businesses were either replaced by new ones or eliminated altogether. Today, this section of downtown is unremarkable from a commercial standpoint. Nevertheless, the area is liberally festooned with historical markers and other placards, which remind today's citizens of Public Square's once-strong pulse.

Sevierville was typical of most 19th-century Sevier County communities in that education was a priority among its residents. By 1923, as many as 99 different schools operated throughout the county, most of them small, one-teacher schools. In 1806, Nancy Academy was founded in Sevierville, one of the city's first wobbly steps in the pursuit of public education. Offering a curriculum based on "the three Rs," Nancy Academy thrived for almost a century until internal conflict, a fire, and a theft contributed to the school's demise in 1892.

In 1890, Nancy Academy was succeeded by another secondary school, Murphy College.

Although officially under the auspices of the Methodist Episcopal Church, its curriculum was "free from sectarian teachings," according to its catalog. The school folded in 1935 due to the hardships of the Great Depression as well as the county's expanding public school system. The original Murphy College building was renovated and today houses the administrative offices of the county's school system. The larger, multibuilding facility that was later used by the college is now home to the Church of God Home for Children, a local orphanage.

Sevierville experienced another period of heavy population growth in the early 1800s. Following the War of 1812, veterans were given land grants in the area, just as they had been following the Revolutionary War. Many of Sevierville's early fathers who had fought for our nation's independence also saw action in the War of 1812, including Spencer Clack and Isaac Thomas. By the way, it was the massive enlistment of area residents in that war that helped earn Tennessee the nickname "The Volunteer State."

Although the Civil War touched the town and the county as a whole, neither was as directly affected as some other regions of the South. One reason was that landholders here had few slaves—because of the hilly terrain, farms tended to be smaller and didn't generate the income necessary for the landowners to purchase large numbers of slaves. Nonetheless, the county did have a few plantations, including Wheatlands, near Boyd's Creek, and Rose Glen, located on today's Pittman Center Road.

Officially, Tennessee was a Confederate state, but most of east Tennessee sympathized with the Union. As such, many who wanted to fight for the Union Army had to make their way across the state line to neighboring Kentucky to enlist. Some even dressed up as women to be able to cross the tightly regulated borders. The only major Civil War battle to take place in the county was the Battle of Fairgarden, about 7 miles east of Sevierville. In 1864, a division of Union soldiers attacked a stronghold of Confederate troops and forced them back several miles. Reportedly, 65 Confederate soldiers were killed, and more than 100 were taken captive. Outside of this engagement, the county saw only a few minor skirmishes, and both armies used it as a source of food and supplies.

The turn of the 20th century was an eventful period in Sevierville. One of the darker but still more colorful chapters of local history (literally and figuratively speaking) was the White Cap era of the 1890s. Not to be confused with the racially motivated Ku Klux Klan, the White Caps were a group that practiced what could best be described as vigilante justice, often stepping in to weed out "lewd" and "immoral" people from the county. The group first gave those targeted written notice to leave the county. If they failed to do so, the White Caps severely whipped them. At their peak of influence, around 1894, such whippings of men and women had become almost nightly occurrences.

After several years, however, the White Caps were gradually infiltrated by a more serious criminal element who knew that their crimes would go unpunished as long as they operated within the White Cap ranks. As the vigilantes lost favor with the public, another group, the Blue Bills, were formed to confront them and try to head off their attacks. The Blue Bills were composed largely of local professionals and businessmen who clashed frequently with the White Caps, often with serious consequences.

Tensions finally came to a head when two White Cap members murdered Sevierville residents William and Laura Whaley. The two culprits were convicted and hanged in Sevierville's Public Square in the late 1890s, making them the last to be publicly executed in the city. In the years that followed, legislation and a tough stance by local law enforcement soon turned Sevier County into one of the most peaceful, law-abiding counties in the state. Fortunately, that trend has continued to this day.

The turn of the century also brought a couple of politically relevant changes to Sevierville. The county's fifth courthouse, which is still in operation, was completed in 1896 (see the Attractions chapter), and on April 11, 1901, Sevierville finally became an incorporated town. Several previous attempts to do so had been shot down because the town was divided over the issue of alcohol sales (some things never change!). With the incorporation of 1901, Sevierville became a dry town, and until recently, alcohol still was not sold by the drink (see the Area Overview chapter).

Sevierville continued to thrive in the first half of the 20th century. Its population was still fairly small, but for its size, it was a healthy, self-sufficient community. Over the next 50 years, however, a number of significant events slowly but surely connected it to the rest of the globe. Two world wars were responsible for hundreds of local men either enlisting or being drafted to serve their country. As was the case in many other parts of the nation, thousands of young men changed their lives permanently when they left the safety of their farms to engage in battle halfway around the world. Dozens never returned to their hometown in the Smokies.

In 1909, Sevierville expanded its commercial links with outside markets with the completion of the Knoxville, Sevierville, and Eastern Railroad, the first incarnation of what would be generally known as the Smoky Mountain Railroad. Unfortunately, the railroad languished under several owners until its ultimate demise in 1961; the increased popularity of the automobile limited its success. The railroad did enjoy a brief period of profitability in the 1940s during the construction of Douglas Dam, but today, no vestiges of its existence remain in the city (except for a street named Railroad Street).

Douglas Dam itself brought massive amounts of inexpensive public electricity to the Smokies for the first time. Built on the French Broad River between 1942 and 1943 by the Tennessee Valley Authority (TVA), the dam flooded a lot of good, level farmland, but it helped light up an area that, until then, either had gone without electricity or had relied on small, private companies for power. The TVA was to lay its hands on Sevierville again in the 1960s when it literally rerouted the course of the Little Pigeon River near downtown to help prevent more of the major, destructive flooding that had plagued the city for decades.

It wasn't until the post–World War II era,

however, that the rest of the world would finally start to make its impact on Sevierville. After the war, the interstate highway system and America's intensified love affair with the car brought more and more visitors to the Smoky Mountains. For decades, most of these travelers simply saw Sevierville as a place through which to pass on their way to Gatlinburg and the mountains. When Knoxville hosted the 1982 World's Fair, all of the county's communities prospered from the spillover, including Sevierville. Throughout the 1990s and into the new millennium, the city has continued to develop into a tourist destination in its own right (see the Area Overview chapter).

i The most-asked question at the Sevierville Chamber of Commerce has nothing to do with area hotels and attractions. It's how to pronounce the name of the town! For the record, it's pronounced se-VEER-ville (not SEE-ver-ville), and it was named not for a decidedly unjovial nature but instead after John Sevier, the first governor of the state of Tennessee.

PIGEON FORGE

By the late 1700s, Pigeon Forge had followed a similar course to that of Sevierville, serving as a place of settlement for soldiers after the war for America's independence. At least this was so until Sevierville became the county seat; from that point on, the two communities followed different paths. Sevierville expanded in every sense, while Pigeon Forge remained a small, sleepy mountain village until tourism began to really take root and flourish in the 1970s and 1980s.

In 1781 Samuel Wear became the first permanent white settler in what is now Pigeon Forge. Wear was a Revolutionary War colonel who had been a longtime friend of John Sevier and had served as a captain under Sevier at the Battle of King's Mountain. He received a land grant of 500 acres and built his homestead near the mouth of Walden's Creek, a tributary of the Little Pigeon River. Wear was a key figure in the formation of the State of Franklin and served as Sevier County court clerk for 27 years, starting with the first county court at Newell's Station in 1785.

During this same period, other settlers who were to play major roles in the development of Pigeon Forge put down roots, including Floyd Nichols, Barefoot Runyan, and Mordecai Lewis. It is believed that Lewis probably operated a mill back in those days; it is known that his land occupied the present-day site of the Old Mill (see the Attractions chapter) on the banks of the Little Pigeon River. His land also adjoined that of Isaac Runyan, a son of Barefoot, and his wife, Margaret Rambo.

Most of these early Pigeon Forge settlements were located along the river, where two primary types of businesses developed: mills and ironworks, or forges. Isaac Love, another significant figure in early Pigeon Forge's early days, married a daughter of Mordecai Lewis and inherited the Lewis family mill. By 1820, Love was operating an ironworks on the same site, and 10 years later, Isaac's son, William, built the present-day Old Mill there. Still in operation, the Old Mill may be the oldest existing mill in Tennessee. On May 29, 1841, the Pigeon Forge post office was established, with William Love as the postmaster. In those days, this post office was located on the same site as the Love's mill and forge, making it the center of the town's activity.

The name Pigeon Forge was derived from the existing ironworks as well as the Little Pigeon River. The river itself had gotten its name from the huge flocks of migratory passenger pigeons that had frequently stopped there throughout the 1700s and early 1800s to feed on the abundance of beech trees. Unlike the town that bears its name today, the passenger pigeon dwindled into extinction. The last one died in captivity at the Cincinnati Zoo in 1914.

In the 1840s, the ironworks gradually failed due to the lack of transportation in and out of the area. The Sevier County Turnpike Company had built a "road" that extended into Sevierville, but this was nothing more than a glorified trail. Another factor that led to the decline of the forges was the low iron content of the existing ore veins. And when a blast furnace at the Love's

ironworks exploded, the family packed it in and moved to Missouri, selling their business to John Sevier Trotter, a local miller who later revived the ironworks.

When the Civil War broke out, Pigeon Forge became a northern stronghold; 30 townsmen joined the Union forces. Although no battles or skirmishes took place in the town, hard times befell those who stayed behind to mind the home front. Schools were abandoned, roads deteriorated, and the flow of supplies from the outside dried up.

At the turn of the century, progress slowly crept into this rural Sevier County community. It wasn't until 1890 that the town's second store opened for business, and in 1898 Pigeon Forge's first telephone was finally connected. By 1907, the town's population was still only 154, but the following 30 years brought steady growth—stores, churches, and schools would spring up in greater numbers.

In August 1916, the Pigeon Forge Railroad Company extended the Knoxville, Sevierville, and Eastern Railroad line, bridging the Little Pigeon River in Sevierville and then running southeast into Pigeon Forge. Completed in 1920, this extension contributed to KS&E's revenues and aided with the flow of timber and lumber traffic out of the area. However, the growing popularity of large trucks as a means of transportation contributed to the abandonment of the Pigeon Forge rail extension in 1929.

The establishment of Great Smoky Mountains National Park in 1934 was ultimately to affect the lives of Forge residents in an irreversible manner. The birth of the park naturally led to larger numbers of visitors passing through Pigeon Forge on their way to Gatlinburg and the Smoky Mountains. In 1946, however, the Pigeon Forge tourism industry began in its own right with the city's first sale of a parcel of land smaller than a farm. The tobacco barn that stood on that land eventually became Pigeon Forge Pottery, which did a thriving business across the street from the Old Mill until 2000. That's when its longtime owners, the Ferguson family, sold the shop—perhaps fittingly—to owners of the Old Mill.

As more businesses and accommodations grew to serve the growing tourist traffic, Pigeon Forge found itself being transformed from a sleepy, rural town composed primarily of farmland into a viable economic community. In response to this metamorphosis, residents voted (by a narrow margin) to incorporate the town in 1961. From there, the change in both the character and the physical landscape of Pigeon Forge began to snowball. Tourist-oriented businesses multiplied exponentially, particularly during the '70s and '80s. The 1982 World's Fair in Knoxville and the opening of Dollywood in 1986 both contributed to making Pigeon Forge an actual tourist destination, rather than a mere stopover.

Today, the large expanses of cornfields have morphed into restaurants, hotels, attractions, and shopping malls that host more than three million overnight guests per year, or 10 million total visitors if you count both overnight guests and day-trippers (see the Area Overview chapter). Regardless, the legacies of the Pigeon Forge of old live on in the descendants of the founding fathers who still reside there. Pigeon Forge's present-day residents don't have to look too far beyond the gift shops and go-kart tracks to see the green, wooded hillsides that still roll away toward the horizon and remind them of the way things once were.

i **The parkway that runs through Pigeon Forge was built after World War II. Before then, people going from Sevierville to Gatlinburg traveled down Pittman Center Road to Glades Road, and into Gatlinburg on Tennessee Highway 73, a distance of about 20 miles on dirt roads.**

GATLINBURG

Imagine, if you please, that it's a summer day sometime between 1810 and 1910, and you're vacationing in Gatlinburg, Tennessee, soon to become a prominent national resort. And let's say you're standing at what is now the foot of the space needle, the city's tallest street-level landmark, looking back along the Parkway to the Ferris wheel at Fun Mountain. What do you see?

First, you don't see the space needle or Fun Mountain. In fact, you're probably not even standing on or near a road; you're in a field, probably corn, belonging to either a Reagan, a Maples, or an Ogle, depending on the time. Also, depending on the time, you may be at the edge of White Oak Flats. And one more certainty: You can count on your fingers the number of people you see. If you see any people at all.

Like most cities in most everywhere else, Gatlinburg got its start as a farming community when non-nomadic American Indians (the Cherokee in this case) settled here somewhere around 500 years ago and established farms in the fertile bottomland. The biggest mistake these noble citizens made was to invite certain white men to share the bounty of their fields and forests. By the beginning of the 19th century, the land belonged to the white men through various treaties and the granting of Tennessee's statehood in 1796.

Among the white men who had hunted and fished this particular area as a guest of the Cherokee was a South Carolinian named William "Old Billy" Ogle, whose wife was part Indian. He staked a claim on a choice piece of land (very close to the Arrowmont School campus today) and cut and hewed enough logs to build a cabin. He then returned to South Carolina to grow a crop of food large enough to feed his family for the year he figured it would take to move to Tennessee and establish a home. He never made it back.

When Billy Ogle left his Tennessee property and returned to South Carolina, he walked into a malarial flu epidemic that took his life. His widow, Martha Jane, approaching 50 and still tending to seven grown children (and some of their children), left South Carolina and the flu for an "extended" visit with her brother Peter Huskey in Virginia. From there the brood migrated to Tennessee, stopping briefly at Wears Fort on Waldens Creek (west of Pigeon Forge), and then made their way into White Oak Flats, probably through Wears Valley and Elkmont (history is a little vague on this point, but no other roads existed at the time). Martha Jane's oldest son, Isaac, built the cabin his father had left the provisions for (there's also some historical disagreement on this point—some historians insist Isaac bought 50 acres of land, but from whom is a mystery), and a new community named White Oak Flats was born. The year was 1805.

It's significant to understand that Martha Jane Huskey Ogle and her family were by no means entering an untamed wilderness. They knew exactly where they were going and what they were going to find. The immediate area they inhabited was mountainous and previously unsettled by white people, but the region was not. Sevierville was an established city before 1800, and so was Knoxville. And, despite the fact that Big Orange football was almost a century up the road, the University of Tennessee had been in operation for more than a decade when the Ogles came to town.

White Oak Flats naturally expanded, and in the 1850s the community became known as Gatlinburg when a decidedly unpleasant man named Radford Gatlin arrived and opened a general store. In addition to the rumored possession of a slave (not a social asset in east Tennessee), Radford Gatlin brought with him a sulfurous wife, no children, an attitude that didn't sit well with the locals, and enough government contacts to secure a postal commission, which he used to name the community in his own honor in 1856. By 1859, Gatlin had succeeded in alienating enough of the townsfolk that they invited him to seek his fortunes elsewhere. He agreed to go peacefully if the name "Gatlinburg" would be retained, and the locals bought the deal.

Gatlin disappeared into an uncertain history, but it is known that he worked for the Confederacy during the Civil War. The city was occupied briefly by Confederate troops during the Civil War who mined saltpeter in the nearby mountains for gunpowder production. Union forces came in around Christmas in 1863 and took over the town without firing a shot, and thus ended Gatlinburg's involvement in the war. It was significant only in that the Battle of Gatlinburg was the last known "conflict" that involved Native Americans. They were camp followers of the Confederate troops, and their actual status has never been clearly defined.

The town then remained frozen in time for almost a century. The establishment of the post office in 1856, and the accompanying adoption of the name "Gatlinburg," were the only significant changes in the town's basic operation from around 1825 until 1912, when a curious twist of fate occurred that would change the face of Gatlinburg forever.

Pi Beta Phi Women's Fraternity is a national organization dedicated to education and health care. In the latter 19th and early 20th centuries, the good ladies of Pi Beta Phi worked as American missionaries, bringing the blessings of formal education and basic hygiene to isolated communities. In 1912, Pi Beta Phi considered two locations in east Tennessee as sites for a settlement school; neither site was in Sevier County, but their selection committee chose Sevierville as a central location to meet and discuss the alternatives. During their meeting, someone suggested that they add Gatlinburg to their list of possible sites, and because it was handy, they decided to have a look. They must have liked what they saw, because Gatlinburg is where they established their school.

The Pi Phis brought an ambitious agenda with them. Their primary goal was to provide formal education to the mountain children, which in turn provided alternatives to subsistence farming as a lifestyle. Beyond that, they also brought consistent medical care and hygiene training to the community at large. They didn't really plan to set the town up in an industry, but not too long after their arrival, the Pi Phis found that Gatlinburg had something the nation was crying out for. The handicrafts that had virtually disappeared from America during the industrial revolution (an event that Gatlinburg had apparently slept through) were alive and well here and still used in everyday life.

Enter O. J. Mattil and Winogene Redding. Mattil came to Gatlinburg as a vocational instructor in 1922. After indoctrinating the locals in the latest farming techniques, he set up classes for the boys in woodworking, basketry, and carpentry. Until he was able to afford a generating plant and woodworking machinery (Gatlinburg didn't have electricity at the time), Mattil's students worked with hand tools. While all this was going on in Mattil's workshop, the other members of the Pi Phi staff were finding examples of Gatlinburg's native craftsmanship in most of the homes they visited. Knowing the marketability of the items they saw just about everywhere, the Pi Phis started recruiting the local craftspeople both to teach the youngsters their crafts and to produce their goods for sale.

In 1926, Pi Beta Phi opened the Arrowcraft shop as a local outlet and started shipping the crafts of Gatlinburg to other Pi Phi outlets across the country. Winogene Redding organized and managed the whole program. It wasn't long before the crafts of Gatlinburg were in demand all over the United States. In less than five years, Gatlinburg had gone from an isolated farming community to the craft capital of America, and Pi Beta Phi was the driving force that made it happen.

It is possible that Gatlinburg's crafts would have become nationally known without Pi Beta Phi's intervention. Forces were already at work to create Great Smoky Mountains National Park in Gatlinburg's backyard, and the natural influx of tourism could have given the city its craft market a decade or so later. It's also possible that by the time the park and its visitors arrived, handcrafts would have disappeared from Gatlinburg as they had in most of the country.

But what we know for sure is that the Pi Phis brought about a change in the fortunes of Gatlinburg that is still paying generous dividends. For as long as craftspeople are able to make a living in this industry in this place, the names of Pi Beta Phi, O. J. Mattil, and Winogene Redding should be spoken of reverently. Redding stayed on with Pi Phi through the transfer of the school to the county educational system, and she worked as a weaving instructor and author at the Arrowmont School until her retirement in the early 1960s. She died in Nashville in 1981, having made a profound impact on the weaving industry and those she taught to practice and to love it.

In 1928, O. J. Mattil broadened his horizons and those of several thousand craftspeople in nine southeastern states as a prime mover in the formation of the Southern Highlands Handicraft Guild. He remained a dominant figure in that organization until his death 50 years later. In 1945, long after the school they had established in Gatlinburg had become part of the county educational system, Pi Beta Phi and the University of Tennessee established the Arrowmont School of Arts and Crafts on the land it occupies today in downtown Gatlinburg. The Arrowmont School is considered one of the preeminent institutions of its kind in the world. The Arrowcraft Shop stands today in its original location at the intersection of the Parkway and Cherokee Orchard Road in downtown Gatlinburg. Pi Beta Phi sold the shop to the Southern Highlands Handicraft Guild in 1993.

As the older of the sister cities that play host to more than 10 million visitors each year, Gatlinburg finds itself torn between its gentle past and an uncertain future that promises to be anything but gentle. By the mid-1980s, Gatlinburg had pretty much settled into a routine of busy summers and idle winters with an economy fueled mainly by prosperous, middle-aged tourists, when a couple of strange things happened: The face of tourism changed dramatically, and Pigeon Forge reacted quickly and positively to the change. As suddenly as if it had been swallowed by an unseen and unknown force, the conservative Gatlinburg tourist base was engulfed by a tidal wave of younger, livelier people, married and single, who were looking for a good time and had the money to pay for it. And they brought their kids with them. And poor old Gatlinburg, blindsided by a change it never saw coming and hemmed in on three sides by Great Smoky Mountains National Park, began struggling mightily to accommodate a whole new population in an area that really wasn't big enough for the old one.

Because new development space downtown is unavailable, any new idea means the city must first decide if existing structures are compatible. If so, fine; if not, the first tool used in new construction is the wrecking ball. Faced with the reality that the new tourist population is not as laid-back as previous generations, Gatlinburg is reinventing itself annually to meet the demand of its new clientele and is sometimes even willing to destroy its own history to do it. (Witness the highly controversial attempt in 2008 by the Pi Phis to sell their 70 acres of land now smack dab in the middle of town to a developer with ambitious plans to create a complex that would include retail shops, four hotels, and two water parks. The sale never went through, probably thanks more to the tanking of the economy soon after the announcement than to the uproar in public opinion that followed.)

i Gatlinburg's native craftspeople still include several artisans who learned their crafts from O. J. Mattil and Winogene Redding. The current "older" generation of native craftspeople are the children of the Redding/Mattil generation.

Still an international center for handcrafted merchandise and fine art, Gatlinburg strives to maintain those industries as the primary link to its past while it continues to come up with new ways and new places to accommodate the best guesses it can make for the shape its future will take.

HOTELS AND MOTELS

Once upon a time, Gatlinburg had exclusive bragging rights when it came to hotels and motels in Sevier County. For decades, its proximity to Great Smoky Mountains National Park made it the area's dominant visitor destination. Accommodations in Pigeon Forge initially popped up just to catch the tourist overflow from Gatlinburg, and you could practically count the number of lodgings in Sevierville on one hand.

The climate began to change in the 1980s. When Knoxville hosted the World's Fair in 1982, all of the local communities prospered from the spillover, and when Dollywood opened in 1986, Pigeon Forge picked up steam as a tourist destination in its own right. These days, the number of hotels and motels in Sevierville is growing rapidly as well, evidence of the entire region's phenomenal expansion.

Keeping up with the statistics is difficult when it comes to charting the growth of the hotel/motel industry in the Smoky Mountains. Seemingly, as soon as city and county officials get an accurate tabulation of the number of lodging facilities and rooms in the area, someone else pours another foundation at another construction site. To put things in ballpark terms, however, Sevier County boasts more than 200 accommodations representing more than 25,000 rooms. That's a lot of guest soap. But then again, the supply of rooms usually fights to keep up with demand, and in the Smokies the demand is high and the supply is both eclectic and broad-reaching.

Of course, the properties you'll encounter vary widely in price, amenities, and location. What's unique, though, is that a distinct pattern in the makeup of each community develops as you travel south from Interstate 40. With some notable exceptions, the accommodations on the northern outskirts of the county and in Sevierville itself tend to be well-known franchises that are newer and offer a long slate of amenities tailored to the traveler. The trade-off is that they're often farther away from the bulk of the action in the Smokies. Conversely, the big franchises are less prevalent as you travel through Pigeon Forge and draw nearer to Gatlinburg, where you'll encounter more independently owned lodgings, many family-run for generations. Although these accommodations are closer to the heart of area activities, the range of available amenities can sometimes be narrower. Either way, you'll find real gems in either category.

RULES OF THUMB

A number of policies, services, and amenities are common to the vast majority of the hotels and motels in Tennessee's Great Smoky Mountains, which are generally open year-round (exceptions noted). For example, most rooms provide air-conditioning and cable television (with at least one free movie channel). Other safe bets are that the properties provide both smoking and nonsmoking rooms (although an increasing number have gone to 100 percent nonsmoking), accept most major credit cards, have at least one swimming pool, and don't allow pets. The majority have high-speed Internet connections available, although not always in all guest rooms. Definitely call ahead to confirm any amenities you find vital.

Most hotels offer clean, well-maintained, pleasantly decorated interiors, even when any first impressions you may get from the hotel exteriors are deceiving. In many cases, you'll find older motels you might have ordinarily just given a cursory glance when driving by. However, if you were to take a peak inside, you'd often see plush surroundings. Generally, rates vary with a property's location and the number and types of amenities offered, not necessarily the cleanliness of its rooms.

The following descriptions start at I-40's exit 407 and are presented more or less in the order in which you'll encounter them, until you reach the entrance of Great Smoky Mountains National Park. In Gatlinburg, the descriptions also include those lodgings on secondary roads and parallel streets, but otherwise, these listings will remain faithful to a north-south course.

Most of the hotels and motels listed in this chapter have Web sites. Note that some of the Internet addresses included will take you directly to the properties mentioned in the write-ups, while others lead you to the Web sites of the parent companies. In those cases, you might have to poke around until you find a link to the specific Smokies property you're interested in.

ANY RESERVATIONS?

How far ahead you should make reservations depends mainly on the time of year you plan to travel. For visits during unusually busy times, like the Fourth of July holiday, you'll want to hit the phones as much as six months ahead of your intended arrival. But usually, count on making reservations anywhere from two to six weeks prior to a visit during peak season (traditionally the summer vacation months and October, when the autumn leaves put on a spectacular show of color). During the off-season, it's a buyer's market where you can often arrive in town with no reservations and pick your room (although it's best not to count on that).

Most accommodations require a deposit via credit card when you make your reservations. Cancellation policies vary from one hotel to another. A few hotels require as much as 72 hours' advance notice of cancellation, but the typical time is 24 hours. Check with individual lodgings for specific reservation information as well as cancellation procedures and fees.

Price Code

This book's pricing guide is based on two adults staying in a standard room on a weekend night during the peak season. Although many of the places listed here allow children to stay at no additional cost, what "child" means differs from place to place. Generally, upper limits range from 12 to 19 years old. The room rates at many of the hotels and motels are simply flat fees. In these cases, the customer purchases a room at a single price, no matter how many people occupy it. Keep in mind, though, that many establishments place limits on the number of people allowed in each room and will charge extra for additional adult guests.

$	Less than $70
$$	$70–$90
$$$	$91–$110
$$$$	$111–$130
$$$$$	$131 and more

One exception to this price guide is worth noting. Although some of the more expensive hotels and motels might be out of your budget during the summer, those same properties can have substantially lower rates during the off-season. Hotels that charge more than $100 per night in October may charge only $30 or $40 per night for the same room in April or May. Again, the laws of supply and demand keep things in check.

SEVIERVILLE

The first bunch of establishments are all part of a group of hotels, restaurants, shops, and attractions that in 2009 formed a cadre of businesses that dubbed itself Sevierville 407, referring to the I-40 exit they're all grouped around. This includes but is not limited to establishments on Winfield Dunn Parkway (TN 66), the main route that runs from I-40 to downtown Sevierville, and some are officially located in the small, unincorporated community of Kodak. Almost exclusively franchises of national chains, most of these hotels have been constructed within the past 15 years and many are brand new. Although they are somewhat removed from the lion's share of the Smokies' most visited spots (Pigeon Forge is 8 to 15 miles away, and Gatlinburg is 15 to 20 miles down the road), you'll find that the area is developing its own distinct personality and offers certain advantages.

For one, if you've made a long journey to get to the Smokies, the last thing you want to do is sit in bumper-to-bumper traffic trying to reach your hotel. The Sevierville 407 accommodations tend to be heavy on comfort and amenities, and they can make for a welcome end to what might be a long and tiring drive. Also, these hotels and motels are ideally situated for travelers who also want to visit outlying areas in addition to the Smokies. Those who have Knoxville or Asheville, North Carolina, on their itineraries will greatly benefit from the uncongested and centrally located Sevierville 407 lodgings.

The remainder of the Sevierville section includes hotels that are a bit further down the road and therefore within a few minutes' drive of even more shopping, dining, and entertainment options.

HOLIDAY INN EXPRESS HOTEL AND SUITES $$$
3526 Outdoor World Drive, Kodak
(865) 933-0087, (800) 465-4329
www.hiexpress.com

This Holiday Inn Express is brand spanking new—opening in April 2009. It offers a decidedly tony atmosphere decorated in a bold and colorful modern design but it charges unarguably discount prices. Of its 91 rooms (on four floors), 19 are suites (featuring microwaves and refrigerators). The hotel features an indoor pool, a state-of-the-art fitness center, a business center, free high-speed Internet access, and a free hot breakfast buffet.

FAIRFIELD INN & SUITES BY MARRIOTT $$$
3620 Outdoor Sportsmans Place, Kodak
(865) 933-3033, (888) 236-2427
www.marriot.com/tyskd

Here's a brand-new inn that just opened in the fall of 2008. Of its 91 rooms, 15 are suites. The Fairfield Inn has an indoor pool and outdoor hot tub,

a business center in its lobby, a state-of-the-art exercise room (where the machines all have their own televisions), and wireless Internet throughout the property. A complimentary hot breakfast is also included in the rate.

The inn is located at exit 407 off I-40 at the Bass Pro Shop and is also just across the way from the Tennessee Smokies Baseball Stadium.

SMOKIES INN AND SUITES $
3385 Winfield Dunn Parkway, Kodak
(865) 933-7378, (800) 348-4652
www.innofsmokies.com

Conveniently located just off I-40 at exit 407, this hotel is one of the first you'll encounter on the Smokies Corridor, and it offers a pleasant night's stay for the traveler who's eager to get off the road. Known as the Ramada Limited when it opened in 1992, the recently renamed Smokies Inn is a good pick if you're looking for an attractive room at a price that won't break your pocketbook. The inn's 65 standard rooms and 15 suites are accessible from interior corridors on all three floors. All rooms have two queen-size beds. Some feature whirlpool tubs and balconies as well. The inn also offers an indoor swimming pool. Children stay free, and discounts are available for AARP and AAA members.

BAYMONT INN AND SUITES
2863 Winfield Dunn Parkway, Kodak
(865) 933-9448, (800) 939-9448
www.4lodging.com

Formerly a Holiday Inn Express, this property was voted 1998's "Newcomer of the Year" when it made its debut. Now refurbished and flying the Baymont flag, the inn offers 73 standard rooms with inside access that all feature private balconies and porches as well as high-speed Internet. Fifteen suites offer a broader amenities package, including sleeper sofas, refrigerators, microwaves, fireplaces, coffeemakers, and whirlpool tubs.

The property boasts a breakfast bar, guest laundry room, indoor and outdoor pools, a whirlpool, a new fitness room and a business center. Children younger than 19 stay at no cost; AARP and AAA discounts are extended as well.

Although the hotel is still several miles out of Sevierville, it's convenient to shops, restaurants, and two golf courses.

CLARION INN WILLOW RIVER $$$$$
1990 Winfield Dunn Parkway, Sevierville
(865) 429-7600, (800) 610-0565
www.innofthesouth.com
Old Southern charm abounds at this Clarion Inn, which opened its doors in 1997, from the fastidiously manicured landscaping to the large, stately columns and exterior facade awash in white. Inside, the antebellum decor remains consistent. The lobby blends elegance and 19th-century simplicity, featuring accents of ornate lighting fixtures and intricately carved stair railings. Rocking chairs are prominent, and several pieces of Gone with the Wind memorabilia adorn the walls and tables.

This Clarion's 89 rooms on three floors have either two queen beds or one king bed and a sleeper sofa. Refrigerators, coffeemakers, microwaves, and private balconies with porches are standard for these units. Those who desire fireplaces and whirlpools in their rooms can opt for one of 16 deluxe suites.

Clarion Inn Willow River sets out a generous morning feast in its continental breakfast area and has both laundry facilities and meeting rooms at the disposal of its guests. An indoor pool and hot tub are accessible 24 hours a day. The outside pool area is adorned with a white gazebo and elevated deck overlooking the water. The entire scene is surrounded by the "lazy river," a man-made channel, similar to those in water parks. All you have to do is grab one of the small inner tubes provided and shove off with the current.

The hotel is only a few miles from downtown Sevierville and the Eagles Landing Golf Course. The rates at Clarion Inn Willow River are on a per-room basis and allow occupancy of up to six people, depending on the size and number of beds in the room. The inn honors AAA and AARP discounts and has both group and corporate rates.

SUPER 8 MOTEL $$$
1410 Winfield Dunn Parkway, Sevierville
(865) 429-0887, (800) 800-8000
www.super8.com
In keeping with the tradition of Super 8 Motels, this one is an overall good value. Children younger than 12 stay free, and discounts are available to seniors. This property has 60 rooms, each with a unique split-bedroom layout. The sleeping areas contain either queen- or king-size beds and are separated by a common bathroom. All rooms are tastefully decorated and furnished and open onto a private porch or balcony overlooking a scenic, tree-lined stretch of the Little Pigeon River. Each of this Super 8's three floors has a common area—there's a whirlpool spa on the first floor and a porch with rocking chairs on the second floor. The motel's location provides handy access to nearby Douglas Lake and Eagles Landing Golf Course. Open since 1995, it is family-owned and has received superior quality assurance ratings from its parent company.

WILDERNESS AT THE SMOKIES WATERPARK RESORT $$$$$
190 Gists Creek Road, Sevierville
(865) 428-5770, (877) 325-9453 (Stone Hill Lodge)
1424 Old Knoxville Highway, Sevierville
(865) 429-0625, (877) 325-9453 (River Lodge)
www.wildernessatthesmokies.com
Some hotels offer pools, and some even offer pools with lazy rivers and fancy waterslides. And then there's the Wilderness at the Smokies resort. It offers just a tad more than that—three water parks, to be exact, reserved exclusively for resort guests. It's safe to say that since its opening in 2008, Wilderness at the Smokies has seriously raised the bar to dizzyingly new heights. In fact, the 8-mile stretch of parkway that surrounds it has been nicknamed "Billion-Dollar Highway" by locals because the area is slated for more than $1 billion in development.

In keeping with this why-stop-at-one philosophy, the resort also offers two separate lodges. The Stone Hill Lodge (connected to the Salamander Springs outdoor water park as well as the equally brand-new 240,000-square-foot Sevierville Events Center) opened in summer 2008 and offers 234 upscale rooms (including six suites) all featuring flat-screen TVs, refrigerators, microwaves, and coffeemakers. River Lodge (connected to the Wild Waterdome indoor water park and the three-acre Lake Wilderness outdoor water park) opened six months later, offering more than 400 one- and two-bedroom condominiums with a variety of floor plans and featuring fully furnished kitchens and fireplaces.

The Waterdome, which opened in December 2008, is a 60,000-square-foot, state-of-the-art indoor water park with a wave pool, a surf rider, a waterslide, two tube slides, and the Storm Chaser Water Thrill Ride—the only ride of its kind in the region. Up to four people share a tube that drops right into a huge funnel and buffets you about before shooting you into a pool. The swim-in/swim-out hot tub here seats 70 people, and the see-through roof lets you tan year-round. The Salamander Springs outdoor water park offers more than 40,000 square feet of waterslides, an activity pool, a huge hot tub (seating 25), and a toddler area. The Lake Wilderness, a 3.5-acre outdoor water park, has a huge wave pool and lazy river. Guests can rent cabanas here that come with misting machines, flat-screen televisions, and refrigerators stocked with water. (By the way, there's no separate admission for any of the water parks—entrance is included in the room rate.)

Each of the two lodgings here also offers a restaurant, snack shops, retail shops, a video arcade, and a fitness center. Guests can use any of the resort's facilities, no matter which lodge they're staying in, and a free shuttle bus ferries folks from one to the other. Should you prefer slicing to sliding, the Eagles Landing Golf Course is right next door.

QUALITY INN AND SUITES $$$
860 Winfield Dunn Parkway, Sevierville
(865) 428-5519, (800) 441-0311
www.cisevierville.com
If the comfort and privacy of a suite is what you're looking for, this Quality Inn is a good selection. Originally a Comfort Inn when it opened in 1988,

this three-story facility provides exterior entry to most of its 95 two-room suites. Several are accessible from the inside and face the indoor pool and spa area. From others, you'll enjoy pleasant views of the Great Smoky Mountains from your private balcony. The suites can sleep up to six people and offer various combinations of amenities, including in-room whirlpool spas, wood-burning fireplaces, microwaves, coffeemakers, and refrigerators. Each suite is well furnished and has two televisions, one in the bedroom and one in the sitting room.

The inn offers free continental breakfast, meeting rooms, and both indoor and outdoor pools (the latter complete with waterfalls and whirlpool spa). AAA and senior discounts are honored, and children younger than 18 stay at no additional cost. This establishment has won several beautification awards from the city for its neatly landscaped and often festively decorated grounds.

HAMPTON INN $$$$
681 Winfield Dunn Parkway, Sevierville
(865) 429-2005, (877) 807-6132
www.hampton-inn.com/hi/sevierville
This Hampton Inn's three interior, security-controlled floors and 68 rooms and suites are housed in a compact, stucco-look structure located just on the outskirts of Sevierville proper. The 62 standard rooms each contain two queen beds or one king bed. The six suites are spacious and open, featuring king beds and either a recliner or a sofa. Fireplaces, refrigerators, microwaves, coffeemakers, and whirlpool tubs complete the king suite package. For the hearing impaired, some rooms allow for outside communication via keyboard.

The complimentary breakfast buffet includes a healthy selection of fresh fruit. Constructed in 1994, the hotel provides an exercise room, game room, guest laundry facilities, and fax services. The Hampton Inn offers a variety of discounts for those seeking extra value. Children younger than 18 stay free.

LANDMARK INN $

401 Forks of the River Parkway, Sevierville
(865) 453-0318, (800) 548-9038
www.landmarkinnthesmokies.com

This long-established, independently owned motel extends comfort, convenience, and value in the heart of Sevierville. Its 80 standard rooms have balconies and porches with direct views of the Great Smoky Mountains and the Little Pigeon River. Landmark Inn's 20 specialty rooms contain amenity combinations that may include refrigerators, kitchenettes, coffeemakers, fireplaces, and in-room whirlpool tubs. Thanks to the motel's proximity to the river, kids can enjoy feeding the ducks, and anglers can drop their lines. For peaceful and scenic strolls, check out the city's Memorial River Trail Greenway, a paved walking/jogging trail that flanks the Little Pigeon River and passes directly in front of Landmark Inn.

SLEEP INN $$$

1020 Parkway, Sevierville
(865) 429-0484, (888) 429-0484
www.choicehotels.com

This three-story hotel, built in 1996, contains 70 interior-access rooms (some pet-friendly), each imbued with what could almost be described as an art deco motif. The units are filled with plenty of curves and stylish furnishings; the glass doors in the showers add to the character. Rooms also include coffeemakers, refrigerators, microwaves, and high-speed Internet and are laid out with either two double beds or one king-size bed. Free continental breakfast, an outdoor pool, and meeting/banquet facilities round out Sleep Inn's offerings. This hotel's location puts guests within a mile of the Governor's Crossing development, a multifaceted collective of shops, restaurants, and attractions.

OAK TREE LODGE $$$

1620 Parkway, Sevierville
(865) 428-7500, (800) 637-7002
www.greatsmokiesgreatlodging.com

Although it's in a rapidly developing area between Sevierville and Pigeon Forge, Oak Tree Lodge benefits from its placement among open, green fields bordered by white fences. This pastoral setting, combined with charming, antebellum architecture, makes for a vacation or business stay replete with Southern atmosphere. The three-story structure accommodates 64 standard rooms and 36 suites in a combination of both interior and exterior access. All rooms feature either a double queen bed or single king bed setup, refrigerator, and coffeemaker, as well as private balconies and porches. In suites, you'll discover fireplaces and whirlpool tubs.

Built in 1990, Oak Tree Lodge boasts both indoor and outdoor pools, an exercise room, continental breakfast, and private catering. The hotel lies within a short distance (walking distance, in some cases) of outlet shopping malls and restaurants. Other sites of interest that are either on or near the property include tennis courts, a horseback-riding stable, and an on-site meeting facility that can seat up to 200. Oak Tree Lodge recommends making reservations six months in advance.

i Although the number of visitors to the Smoky Mountains drops off dramatically at the end of summer, a heavy influx always follows to see the stunning fall foliage, which peaks around the second and third weeks of October. If you want to see this colorful show, which is highly recommended, you'll need to make reservations many months in advance.

COMFORT INN APPLE VALLEY $$$$

1850 Parkway, Sevierville
(865) 428-1069, (800) 233-3443
www.comfortinnapplevalley.com

This Comfort Inn is rather well decorated, having been named International Comfort Inn of the Year in 1995, 2001, and 2006. It's also won awards from the City of Sevierville for its Winterfest and Harvest Festival decorations. Inside, the quality continues throughout the hotel's 100 extra-large standard rooms and 10 suites. All rooms are located within three interior-access floors and have either two queen beds or one king-size bed. Standard rooms feature private balconies, refrigerators, and coffeemakers. Suites offer whirlpool tubs and in-room fireplaces.

Comfort Inn Apple Valley has both indoor and outdoor pools as well as an indoor whirlpool spa, and continental breakfast is served each morning. The Apple Valley farms complex is a short walk away. Seniors receive a 10 percent discount.

i Cultivate the friendship of your desk clerk—he or she is a fountain of information and can save you many hours of frustration.

PIGEON FORGE

During the last two decades, the section of northern Pigeon Forge and southern Sevierville have fused into one continuous band of businesses geared to the vacationer. As a result, most people driving south on the Parkway aren't aware when they've crossed from one city to the next. But one particular characteristic of Pigeon Forge's identity is noticeable, if you're aware of it—a heavier concentration of independently owned accommodations. From smaller, mom-and-pop motels to multistoried luxury hotels, fewer of the easily recognized franchise names are represented in this mix. As such, this section will help acquaint you with a healthy dose of unfamiliar names and place less emphasis on the franchises. Because Pigeon Forge has so many properties from which to choose, those presented here are only a sampling (albeit a large one) of the better picks.

Keep in mind another premise when perusing these listings. In Pigeon Forge, especially south of traffic light #3, almost every hotel or motel is within easy walking distance of restaurants, entertainment, attractions, and shopping. The listing will note if a particular lodging is extremely convenient to a local point of interest, but otherwise, assume that most anything you want is just outside your door. Also keep in mind that Pigeon Forge has a trolley system with numerous stops that can take you inexpensively up and down the Parkway. See the Getting Here, Getting Around chapter for more specifics.

MOUNTAIN MELODIES INN $$
1949 Parkway, Pigeon Forge
(865) 453-2250, (800) 838-9777
www.mountainmelodiesinnpf.com
This facility is well placed for those with music and variety shows on their agenda. Directly across the Parkway from the Miracle Theater, it's within a short walk of several other Pigeon Forge music theaters as well. Open since 1995, Mountain Melodies Inn has 60 standard rooms and 25 suites offering queen and king beds. All rooms include private balconies and refrigerators. Fireplaces and whirlpool tubs are available in suites. The hotel is a five-story building that provides interior access to all rooms, and there's plenty of room for the family car in the two-level parking area.

MICROTEL SUITES AT MUSIC ROAD $$$
2045 Parkway, Pigeon Forge
(865) 453-1116, (866) 765-1940
www.pigeonforgemicrotel.com
All of this Microtel's 71 units are suites with a queen bed and queen sleeper sofa. Amenities in all standard suites include telephone with data port and in-room safe as well as kitchenettes with coffeemaker, refrigerator, and microwave. Each of the hotel's four floors has one deluxe-size suite offering more living space. The wheelchair-accessible suites include accessible showers.

Guests have access to a number of common amenities, such as a self-service laundry room, meeting room, outdoor pool, and a breakfast room that serves free continental breakfast each morning. Pets are welcome for a fee (starting at $25, more for larger pets). The Pigeon Forge trolley makes a stop at the hotel's Parkway entrance. Showplaces like the Miracle Theater, Magic Beyond Belief Theater, and Memories Theatre are within easy walking distance.

RAMADA $$$$
2193 Parkway, Pigeon Forge
(865) 428-0668, (800) 269-1222
www.pigeonforgeramada.com
This Ramada successfully puts forth a pleasant country decor without slipping into tackiness. The many wooden fixtures and the stacked-

stone fireplace in the lobby are just some of the elements that help create a cozy, rustic ambience. Guests can take advantage of a spacious indoor pool and whirlpool partially surrounded by numerous large windows. An exercise room, game room, and breakfast room (where deluxe continental breakfast is served each morning) are also part of the offerings here.

All of the 126 standard rooms in this three-story, interior-access hotel feature two queen beds, a refrigerator, a coffeemaker, and a microwave. There are also nine suites that include fireplaces and in-room whirlpool tubs. Overall, the furnishings and trappings combine both elegance and simple country charm. This Ramada is in a location central to the Pigeon Forge music theater community (many are within walking distance) as well as an abundance of restaurants and outlet shopping opportunities. The hotel honors both AAA and senior discounts.

MUSIC ROAD HOTEL $$$$$
303 Henderson Chapel Road, Pigeon Forge
(865) 429-7700, (800) 429-7700
www.musicroadhotel.com
Just 1 block off the Parkway, this seven-story structure towers above lush, colorful landscaping and the peaceful waters of the Little Pigeon River. Guests can relax in rocking chairs along the lobby-level observation deck that runs the entire riverside length of the building. The hotel also has an indoor pool with whirlpool and an outside pool area that's like a mini water park, complete with pool, waterfall, fountain, spiral slide, and lazy river ride. An arcade and snack bar round out the amenities.

The 90 standard rooms and 73 suites (renovated in 2008) all have interior access. The standard rooms are substantially larger than the average hotel room. Each comes with two queen beds and a roster of amenities including a refrigerator, a microwave, a coffeemaker, a private balcony, and free high-speed Internet. The bathrooms are conveniently equipped with two sinks, a linen closet, and a hair dryer. The suites are similarly outfitted but also offer fireplaces, in-room whirlpools, and king-size beds.

The large, open lobby has elegant furnishings, wood floors, and a huge stacked-stone fireplace. Just off the lobby is a large, bright breakfast room serving biscuits and gravy, muffins, pastries, cereals, bagels, and, of course, coffee every morning. Also on the first floor are a number of meeting rooms for groups and businesses as well as another arcade. Music Road Hotel offers senior discounts and group rates.

NATIONAL PARKS RESORT LODGE $$
2385 Parkway, Pigeon Forge
(865) 453-4106, (800) 843-6686
www.nprlodge.com
Formerly known as the Heartlander Country Star Resort, this hotel is near to both outlet shopping malls and music theaters, making it a good choice for many vacationers. Its multisize conference and meeting facilities make it a logical option for the business traveler as well.

Twenty-four standard rooms and 136 suites each contain either two double beds or a king bed as well as private balconies for enjoying Smoky Mountain views. All rooms have refrigerators, microwaves, and coffeemakers. This five-story hotel also has a large game room with a pool table, an outdoor pool, an indoor pool, a whirlpool spa, and a gift and sundries shop. Pets are allowed, but owners are required to pay a one-time, nonrefundable fee of $20. Children younger than 12 stay free.

COMFORT SUITES $$$
2423 Teaster Lane, Pigeon Forge
(865) 429-3700, (800) 531-9308
www.comfortsuitespigeonforge.net
At this property, comfort, convenience, and inspiring views make for a winning Smokies vacation combination. The seven-story, coral-hued building is located a short distance off the Parkway on a quiet hilltop, peacefully removed from the bustle of traffic. This site provides a direct "back road" route to Belz Outlets and Tanger Outlet Mall, both just down the street.

Inside, you'll find a number of services and amenities, including a game room, an expanded continental breakfast, laundry facility, and exercise room. The hotel offers two swimming pools, both indoor and outdoor; the interior site has a whirlpool. Each of the 70 interior units provides a refrigerator, a microwave oven, a coffeemaker, and a private balcony that opens your room to memorable mountain views. Rooms come with either a double queen bed setup or a single king-size bed and sleeper sofa. Five spacious suites provide guests with the added luxuries of hair dryers, irons and ironing boards, fireplaces, and whirlpool tubs. Built in 1995, this hotel offers discounts for AAA members and seniors. Children younger than 18 stay for free.

ECONO LODGE RIVERSIDE $$

2440 Parkway, Pigeon Forge
(865) 428-1231, (800) 632-6104
www.econolodge-pigeonforge.com
In 2000, this motel underwent a complete face-lift; in fact, the new owners did everything but completely tear it down and rebuild it. With about 201 units on the premises, Econo Lodge Riverside provides clean and spacious rooms in a pleasant setting near the Little Pigeon River. If your intent is to dive into the music theaters and shopping opportunities in Pigeon Forge, you'll find this motel to be handily situated. Belz Outlets and Tanger Outlet Mall are a short distance away. When you're not out on the town, you'll find relaxation at the picnic spot down by the river, where you're welcome to feed the resident duck population.

Guests can select a standard room with either double queen beds or one king bed. You may also choose from rooms with Jacuzzi tubs and two-family suites with bunk beds and fold-out sofas. All rooms come with microwaves, refrigerators, and coffeemakers.

Econo Lodge's lobby is warm and welcoming with its thick wood rafters and stone fireplace. They've also added an indoor heated pool with accompanying hot tub and kiddie pool. Guests also receive a complimentary continental breakfast.

INN AT CHRISTMAS PLACE $$$$$

119 Christmas Tree Lane, Pigeon Forge
(865) 868-0525; (888) 465-9644
www.innatchristmasplace.com
If you can't get enough stockings and sugar-plums in December, then this hotel is definitely the place for you. It's constantly Christmas at this 145-room inn, which opened in 2007, right across the street from a holiday-themed store called The Incredible Christmas Place (a huge shop selling everything Christmas all year long, which has been a staple on the Parkway since 1986). The two establishments have the same owners.

The inn has regular guest rooms as well as one-, two-, and three-room suites. Every room has a microwave, refrigerator, and DVD player (you can borrow Christmas movies at the front desk), and some have balconies, fireplaces, and double whirlpool tubs. Each has at least a little Christmas decor (such as holiday throw pillows on the bed, wreaths, holiday artwork, and various Christmas knickknacks), but five of the suites are the most decked out—they each have two seven-foot Christmas trees. The walls throughout the inn are graced with winter-themed art prints by the area's most celebrated artists (including Jim Gray, Robert Tino, G. Webb, Vern Hippensteal, Robert McDonald, Lee Roberson, and Terri Waters).

The rate includes a hot continental breakfast with made-to-order omelets. Santa comes to breakfast every Thursday through Monday from mid-May through December 23 (he's under-standably busy on the 24th, and requires recu-peration on the 25th), and the jolly guy even makes an appearance once a week in the off-season. On most Friday evenings, one of Santa's elves reads Christmas stories in the lower lobby from 7:30 to 8 p.m. (complete with cookies and milk). During Christmas week, the inn has a live nativity out front. Kids can write and mail letters to Santa year-round (there's a special mailbox just for this purpose).

Don't miss the three-story glockenspiel in the lower lobby. Every hour on the hour (from 10 a.m. to 9 p.m.), it plays Christmas carols and chimes while cute little mechanical figures move about the enormous structure.

The Inn at Christmas Place has an outdoor pool with a 95-foot, figure-eight waterslide, as well as an indoor pool with a large hot tub, a video game arcade, and a business center. One more amenity makes this inn stand out—it's the only property in Pigeon Forge with doormen!

MOUNTAIN TRACE INN $$
130 Wears Valley Road West, Pigeon Forge
(865) 453-6785, (800) 453-6785
www.mountaintraceinn.net
This is, perhaps, one of the best-placed accommodations in Pigeon Forge. Two outlet malls, a supermarket, and a coin-operated laundry are all within easy walking distance. It's just off the Parkway on Wears Valley Road, one of the routes to the scenic and historic communities of Wears Valley and Townsend. The building itself consists of four floors and 89 exterior-access rooms. All rooms have two queen beds and refrigerators. The inn offers three family suites with kitchenettes and 10 honeymoon suites with whirlpool tubs and fireplaces. The main part of the motel was constructed in 1992, with 42 units added in 1995. The inn offers an indoor pool and whirlpool facility as well as free continental breakfast. Mountain Trace Inn has AAA and senior discounts. Their rates are flat, per-room fees that allow up to five people per room.

TIMBERS LOG MOTEL $$$$
134 Wears Valley Road East, Pigeon Forge
(865) 428-5216, (800) 445-1803
www.timberslogmotel.com
If you're into outlet shopping, this is the place you want to be! Timbers Log Motel is directly across Teaster Lane from Belz Outlets and Tanger Outlet Mall. While you're shopping, your kids can enjoy the Track, an amusement center across the street featuring go-karts, miniature golf, bungee jumping, and video games (see the Attractions chapter).

The motel itself, however, offers plenty of its own charms. With a hewn-logs-and-mortar exterior, this lodging conveys the feel of a mountain cabin. It offers 22 standard rooms that have either two queen beds or one king bed and include refrigerators, coffeemakers, and microwaves. In addition, 30 woodsy suites offer a variety of configurations, including a two-level layout. Some are tailored to families, with kitchenettes and multi-bed arrangements that can sleep up to six. Some are more suitable for honeymooners, with fireplaces and whirlpool tubs.

Timbers Log Motel was built in 1989 and provides three floors of exterior-access rooms. Pets are allowed with a one-time $10 fee, and discounts are available for the military. The rates are on a flat, per-room basis.

VALLEY FORGE INN $$
2795 Parkway, Pigeon Forge
(865) 453-7770, (800) 544-8740
www.valleyforgeinn.net
Developed in three phases beginning in 1988, Valley Forge Inn supplies a mixed bag of room layouts and amenities. The inn's 150 standard rooms and 21 suites are divided among three buildings, the tallest of which is four stories; rooms are accessible from the outside as well as interior hallways. In the original structure, the typical room has two queen beds and a well-remodeled package of furnishings and decor. The second and third buildings, which went up in the early and mid-1990s, contain both standard rooms and suites, some with refrigerators, microwave ovens, coffeemakers, fireplaces, whirlpool tubs, and private balconies. Some of the newer suites are big enough to sleep six in a single king and two-queen bed combination. On the top level of the newest building are 10 two-level town houses with two bathrooms in each.

Valley Forge Inn supplies free continental breakfast, a coin-operated laundry, indoor and outdoor pools, and in-room satellite television. Seniors get 5 percent discounts on rates. Oh, and if you're wondering about the name, the inn has no ties to Pennsylvania or to George Washington. Owners Jimmy and Joe Cole explain that their father, Jim Cole, who built the inn, named it for both Wears *Valley* Road (which is a quarter mile away) and Pigeon *Forge*.

PARK TOWER INN $$$
201 Sharon Drive, Pigeon Forge
(865) 453-8605, (800) 453-8605
www.parktowerinn.com
Standing just 1 block west of the Parkway, Park Tower Inn is one of the best overall values in this area. The inn offers 155 spacious and colorfully decorated rooms, all of which guests enter from interior corridors. Refrigerators, two queen-size beds, and large, open balconies are the norm for standard rooms. Suites and rooms with kitchenettes offer an expanded range of amenities such as whirlpool tubs, fireplaces, and coffeemakers.

On-site conveniences abound at this hotel, built in 1994. Three elevators provide easy access to all six floors, and microwave ovens are centrally located at each level. In addition to the outdoor pool and whirlpool tub, the inn has a massive indoor aquatic facility, complete with pool, whirlpool tub, and a lazy river ride with inner tubes. Vacationers and business travelers alike will appreciate Park Tower Inn's free continental breakfast, guest laundry, game room, exercise facilities, excellent security-monitoring system, and meeting rooms. AAA and senior discounts are available, and quoted rates are good for up to four people per room.

MAPLES MOTOR INN $$
2959 Parkway, Pigeon Forge
(865) 453-8883, (888) 453-8883
www.maplesmotorinn.com
Found on the Parkway, a short hop from Pigeon Forge Factory Outlet Mall, this family-owned inn is a nice place to bring your own family. Providing agreeable rooms at an equally agreeable price, Maples Motor Inn has 57 units in its original building, all of which have refrigerators, microwaves, coffeemakers and free wireless Internet. Another section was built in 1996, featuring suites with whirlpools and fireplaces in a spacious, well-furnished floor plan. Outside, a large pool is flanked by a smaller kiddie pool, and you'll also find a picnic area and toddler playground on the grassy lawn. Maples Motor Inn is closed during January and February and takes all major credit

cards except American Express. Children younger than seven stay at no additional charge.

MOUNTAIN BREEZE MOTEL $$
2926 Parkway, Pigeon Forge
(865) 453-2659, (888) 453-2659
www.mountainbreezemotel.net
This remodeled, two-story motel in the heart of Pigeon Forge's main drag treats guests to a number of in-room comforts at a hard-to-beat price. Rates for two people vary, depending on the number and size of beds required. The rates are lowest for rooms with one queen bed, higher for one king bed, and higher still for setups with two queen beds. Efficiencies and four new Jacuzzi suites with fireplaces are available as well. Each of the 67 rooms provides guests with a refrigerator, microwave, and coffeemaker. You'll find a heated outdoor pool as well as a kiddie pool and hot tub on the premises. Mountain Breeze Motel gives AARP discounts.

WILLOW BROOK LODGE $$$$
3035 Parkway, Pigeon Forge
(865) 453-5334, (800) 765-1380
www.willowbrooklodge.com
When you first arrive at this motel, your attention is soon drawn to immaculate landscaping, a homey architectural style, and an exterior color scheme that's very easy on the eyes. One hundred fifty rooms and six family suites offer different floor plans, amenities, and sleeping arrangements. Guest rooms have either two queen-size beds or one king-size bed and sleeper sofa. All have refrigerators, and some have balconies. Family suites offer a variety of configurations of queen and king beds, sleeper sofas, whirlpool tubs, fireplaces, microwaves, coffeemakers, and refrigerators. Some have private balconies and separate living and dining areas.

The motel also offers an outdoor pool (with a 75-foot slide) and an indoor pool—each with whirlpool tub. Constructed in 1991, Willow Brook Lodge provides exterior access to all three floors. Guests get free continental breakfast each morning, and AAA and AARP members get discounts. Children younger than 12 stay at no extra cost.

HOLIDAY INN PIGEON FORGE
RESORT HOTEL $$$$$
3230 Parkway, Pigeon Forge
(865) 428-2700, (800) 782-3119
www.4lodging.com

The approximately 200 rooms and six suites at this Holiday Inn have recently undergone an extensive $7 million renovation. Typically, units in the inn's five interior-accessible floors have two extra-long double beds, while a few have king-size beds. All rooms provide coffeemaker, microwave, and refrigerator and all have free high-speed Internet.

The open lobby features a sitting area next to a large stone fireplace. Beyond the video arcade lies a large atrium section featuring an indoor pool and whirlpool tub. The pool is flanked by lush greenery and a waterfall that cascades from a high stone wall. The hotel also offers laundry facilities, an exercise room, and various meeting and conference rooms. This is one of the few lodgings in the area that boasts a restaurant in the hotel itself. Louie's Restaurant and Grill delivers a well-rounded menu and serves breakfast, lunch, and dinner. The restaurant also provides room service during its business hours and caters banquets in the meeting facilities. In addition, the hotel offers a marketplace deli with pizza, yogurt, sandwiches, and other casual fare. The hotel offers AAA and senior discounts. Although room prices are charged as a flat, per-room rate, roll-away beds can be provided for an additional fee.

VACATION LODGE $
3450 Parkway, Pigeon Forge
(865) 453-2640, (800) 468-1998
www.vacationlodge.net

When Pigeon Forge's business district consisted of a couple of gift shops, a general store, and a motel all clustered around the city's only traffic light, the Vacation Lodge was the motel. Like the city, the Vacation Lodge grew in all directions during the 1980s to its present size of 93 rooms in a variety of configurations. Ample parking and a central location make the Vacation Lodge a favorite for people planning to park their cars where they're staying and enjoy Pigeon Forge on foot or by using the Fun Time Trolley. The Old Mill area, one of the city's oldest shopping centers and still the place where most of the handcrafts and truly unique gifts are available, is across the Parkway and a block back on Old Mill Street.

RIVERSIDE TOWER $$$$$
3455 Parkway, Pigeon Forge
(865) 453-5500, (800) 453-5540
www.riversidehotels.com

This is the first of the three Riverside properties listed in this book, all owned and operated by the same old-line area "motel family." Riverside Tower, an imposing six-story structure, provides panoramic views on all four sides. All the rooms have queen beds, fireplaces with gas logs, and balconies with gas grills. Riverside Tower has an indoor pool and meeting facilities to accommodate up to 100 people. Pigeon Forge's historic Old Mill shopping area and Patriot Park are a short walk up River Road, which forms the back boundary of the hotel.

RIVERSIDE MOTOR LODGE $$
3575 Parkway, Pigeon Forge
(865) 453-5555, (800) 242-8366
www.riversidehotels.com

Situated between the Little Pigeon River and the Parkway in central Pigeon Forge, the Riverside Motor Lodge offers a choice of two-bedroom family suites or intimate honeymoon suites that provide all the comforts of home. Every room has its own kitchenette and Jacuzzi, and gas fireplaces add a cozy touch. The solarium setting gives the indoor swimming pool an outdoor feel without the noise and wind of the traffic. Suites on all five floors are easily accessible by elevators at both ends and in the middle of the property.

BRIARSTONE INN $$
3626 Parkway, Pigeon Forge
(865) 453-4225, (866) 883-4225
www.briarstoneinn.net

Convenient to most of Pigeon Forge's amusements and restaurants, the Briarstone Inn offers 55 comfortable rooms on three floors with queen beds, microwaves, refrigerators, coffeemakers, and free wireless Internet. The Jacuzzi fireplace suites are great for honeymooners. The inn also features an outdoor pool (plus a separate pool for smaller children). The Briarstone offers AARP and senior citizen discounts.

ℹ️ **Booking a reservation for a weekend during the peak season? Here are a couple of caveats: (1) Rates may be even higher than indicated here if the city is hosting a major special event, and (2) many hotels require two- and sometimes even three-night minimums during high-traffic weekends.**

NORMA DAN MOTEL $$
3864 Parkway, Pigeon Forge
(865) 453-2403, (800) 219-6809
www.normadanmotel.com

From its small beginnings as a 12-room motel in 1958, the family-owned Norma Dan has expanded to the beautiful 85-room multistory structure it is today, with one of Pigeon Forge's biggest swimming pools. The rooms here all have private balconies, as well as refrigerators, microwaves, and coffeemakers. Some rooms have whirlpool tubs, too. Free continental breakfast is included in the rate. Note that this inn is closed in January and February.

Because of its popularity with tour groups, the Norma Dan also has one of the biggest and best-protected off-street parking lots in the city. Some of the Norma Dan's earliest couples, who spent their honeymoons in the mountains, are still coming back, and now they take advantage of the AARP discount program and bring their grandchildren.

CONNER HILL MOTOR LODGE $
3921 Parkway, Pigeon Forge
(865) 428-0287, (800) 447-9534
www.connerhill.com

Conner Hill is another one of the city's older motels, but it's kept so sparkling clean that it looks new to the first-time visitor. They still get a few first-timers every year, but most of Conner Hill's business is repeaters who found the place in the '70s and early '80s when motels were few and far between in Pigeon Forge. The 65-unit structure is reminiscent of the older buildings, with a lot of wrought iron and wood in its spacious design, but the rooms have a new feel. You can choose between queen-size or king-size beds (or a two-bedroom apartment sleeping six). Shopping and amusements are within easy walking distance to Conner Hill, and Dollywood and the Gatlinburg Golf Course are a five-minute drive away.

GREEN VALLEY MOTEL $$
4109 Parkway, Pigeon Forge
(865) 453-9091, (800) 892-1627
www.greenvalleypigeonforge.com

The Green Valley Motel was built mainly to lodge families, and its 70 percent rate of repeat visitors indicates it was done right. Ground-floor access to some of the 51 rooms and convenient restaurants and gift shops within easy walking distance have made the Green Valley a popular lodging place for generations of visitors to the Smokies. All rooms have coffeemakers, and some also have Jacuzzis, refrigerators, and microwaves. The same family that owns the hotel operates the outlet store adjacent to the Green Valley, and most of the veteran guests do a lot of their shopping without ever leaving the property. The motel also features a heated outdoor swimming pool plus a kiddie pool, and kids under 12 stay free.

CREEKSTONE INN $$
4034 South River Road, Pigeon Forge
(865) 453-3557, (800) 523-3919
www.smokymountainresorts.com

A new standard in gracious living, the Creekstone is a 112-room high-rise hotel on the Little Pigeon River, with a full slate of amenities to please the families and honeymooners alike. Spacious rooms and suites include fireplaces, refrigerators, in-room coffeemakers, microwaves, and Jacuzzis. The inn features a covered parking garage, an outdoor pool, wireless Internet, and private balconies (where you can watch for and even feed the resident flock of ducks). The river running along the back edge of the property is also inviting.

ℹ️ Even if you're visiting the Smokies during the dead of winter, don't rule out packing a bathing suit or pair of trunks. Many area hotels have heated indoor pools for year-round swimming.

GATLINBURG

As the progenitor of the tourism industry in the Smokies, Gatlinburg is still a favorite lodging place for veteran visitors. In fact, Gatlinburg's more than 75 hotels and motels, boasting a total of nearly 8,000 rooms, depend heavily on repeat business. The lodging scene in Gatlinburg runs through the full spectrum of accommodations, from old-fashioned tourist cabins in settled neighborhoods to luxury high-rise hotels in the heart of downtown.

The list that follows is a representative sample of the broad variety of hotels and motels in Gatlinburg, most of which are within walking distance of the downtown business district. Those that require more than a 10-minute walk to the Parkway are all within 100 yards of a trolley stop. All of Gatlinburg's hotels and motels provide wheelchair accessibility with ground-floor entrances to rooms that are specifically designated for smoking or nonsmoking use. Most of the multistory facilities have elevators, and all have ramps between levels. Most offer AARP and senior citizen discounts; call ahead to be sure.

The facilities listed will be in order as follows, and please remember this is a sampling, not a complete list. The listings begin with those on the Parkway, from the entrance to town all the way to the entrance to Great Smoky Mountains National Park. Next, the listings go from traffic light #6 on the Parkway up Cherokee Orchard Road to the idyllic Baskins Creek section. Then, they go from traffic light #5 south and west along River Road and into the Ski Mountain neighborhood west of the Parkway. The next grouping is on Historic Nature Trail (formerly Airport Road) (traffic light #8—the Space Needle corner) and includes a mixture of large convention-oriented and small family-owned motels. The final group of descrip-

tions stretches east out U.S. Highway 321N from traffic light #3, where you will find most of the smaller independent facilities and Gatlinburg's biggest independently owned motel.

On the Parkway

FAIRFIELD INN & SUITES–
NORTH GATLINBURG $$$$$
168 Parkway, Gatlinburg
(865) 430-3659, (866) 430-3659
www.marriott.com

The first lodging establishment on the left as you enter Gatlinburg, the Fairfield Inn has 101 rooms that run the full gamut of accommodations, with most of them containing two queen beds and all providing a coffeemaker and high-speed Internet. The three-story back portion features wooded views. The continental breakfast is on the house. The Fairfield has two heated pools, one with a spiral waterslide, and a fitness center. The purple route trolley stops at the front door if you need it; with a restaurant, a liquor store, and a wedding chapel on the property and a miniature golf course next door, you can meet most of your needs without leaving the property.

COMFORT INN ON THE RIVER $$$$$
293 Parkway, Gatlinburg
(865) 436-5047, (866) 885-5047
www.comfortinngatlinburg.com

Three floors of private balconies directly over the Little Pigeon River (you can fish from your balcony!) make you forget there's bumper-to-bumper traffic right outside the door. From standard two-bedrooms to luxury suites with fireplaces and Jacuzzis, the Comfort Inn's spectacular view of the river and the mountains in the background make you forget you're in a city at all. Built before the tourist boom of the 1970s, this establishment is a classic reminder of what the Smokies is really all about. The inn offers an outdoor pool, refrigerators, microwaves, coffeemakers, and free continental breakfast.

ROCKY WATERS MOTOR INN $$$
333 Parkway, Gatlinburg
(865) 436-7861, (800) 824-1111
www.rockywaters.com

When Ralph Lawson first built the Rocky Waters in the late 1930s, the road ran down the other side of the Little Pigeon River. When the new road was built, the Rocky Waters' owners built a bridge and a new building on the new Parkway, and now it's the only motel in town with units on both sides of the river. A hundred rooms and one cabin provide a broad variety of accommodations, all with private balconies as well as refrigerators, microwaves, and coffeemakers. Some rooms also have wood-burning fireplaces and Jacuzzis. The hotel also offers a guest laundry, two pools, and continental breakfast.

BEST WESTERN ZODER'S INN $$$
402 Parkway, Gatlinburg
(865) 436-5681, (800) 528-1234
www.zoders.com

Wallace Zoder came to the Smokies in 1934 to work as an engineer in the developing national park. Seeing the early potential of the area, Wallace built his motel beside the Parkway (it was called Main Street then) to house the summer guests who were beginning to trickle in. The old building is gone now, replaced over the years by the ultramodern 90-room structure that pampers today's travelers, but Wallace and Dot Zoder's children and grandchildren carry on their traditions of service and comfortable, courteous accommodation.

World-class luxury at surprisingly reasonable rates are the norm at Zoder's. Not content with the continental breakfast you can get most anywhere, the Zoders have added a sumptuous wine-and-cheese reception from 5 to 7 p.m. every evening and a great cookies-and-milk bedtime snack from 8 to 10 p.m., all served in the refreshment bar next to the guest lobby. Zoder's features an exercise and weight room, an outdoor pool, and an indoor pool with its own waterfall. And as if that's not enough to satisfy anybody, a walk along the creek to the back of the six-acre woodland will wash a whole day's cares away.

BEST WESTERN TWIN ISLANDS $$$$
539 Parkway, Gatlinburg
(865) 436-5121, (800) 223-9299
www.oglesproperties.com

How about an island right in the middle of downtown Gatlinburg? Well, the city has two, and the Luther Ogle family built a superb motel that uses up both of them. One hundred nine rooms, all with river views and some with private balconies, surround a central courtyard that makes you feel like you're in a private resort. All of downtown Gatlinburg is just outside the front driveway. Like the rest of the old-line family properties, some rooms have fireplaces and Jacuzzis. The Honeymoon Island suites provide isolation without taking you away from the bright lights. This hotel also offers an outdoor pool.

GREYSTONE LODGE AT THE AQUARIUM $$$$
559 Parkway, Gatlinburg
(865) 436-5621, (800) 451-9202
www.greystonelodgetn.com

If you're in the part of the Greystone that's near the Parkway, you're looking at Ripley's Aquarium of the Smokies (described in detail in the Attractions chapter). If you're at the other end of the Greystone, you're looking at the west prong of the Little Pigeon River. This is a big complex—257 rooms in three buildings (one of which is five stories) plus six cottages, all stretched out along the river for more than a quarter of a mile. (Most of the rooms, in fact, overlook the river.) Room configurations vary from two double beds to queen and king rooms, some with hot tubs and fireplaces. An expanded continental breakfast is served every morning in the refreshment bar beside the lobby.

RIVERSIDE MOTOR LODGE $$
715 Parkway, Gatlinburg
(865) 436-4194, (800) 887-2323
www.riversidehotels.com

The original Riverside Motor Lodge was built in 1925 by local entrepreneur Steve Whaley, who insisted to his amused friends that "Some day a half million people a year will visit Gatlinburg!" A com-

 # Close-up

Gatlinburg Inn

You may be familiar with the feeling: You're walking along the busy main drag of a tourist mecca, trying to take in all of the sights and sounds around you, and suddenly something is very much out of sync. It's not something wrong, it's just suddenly . . . different. It's like a rock group has started playing Brahms.

What's happened here? Well, if you're on the Parkway in Gatlinburg, you've probably come to one of the truly rare sights in town: a section of street that doesn't have a building hovering over the sidewalk. And then you see it, set back from the low stone wall that separates its parking area from the sidewalk. Announced by an unpretentious wood sign, the Gatlinburg Inn appears to have been built at the wrong end of the property.

It seems so serene among the bright lights and carnival sounds. Inside, you're in a time warp. The lobby is like an old movie set with hand-blocked wallpaper and matching curtains covering what little of the walls is not taken up with the huge wood-framed windows, and wrought-iron plant stands loaded with various flora in pots of every description circle the room. Fringed area rugs cover the slate floor, and overstuffed couches and chairs surround tables holding various magazines. If you happen not to see the grandfather clock, its Westminster chimes will announce its presence every 15 minutes.

A row of rocking chairs invites you to sit and regard the scene outside. If you're very lucky, you learn that the gracious lady sitting in one of the rocking chairs is Mrs. Wilma Maples, the manager. And if you sit quietly and pay attention (this part's easy—for all her old-world charm, she's a commanding presence), Wilma Maples will tell you about the inn from its beginnings and about the remarkable, Bunyanesque man who built it.

Rellie L. (Rel) Maples (1905–1985) was a Gatlinburg native who worked as a cook in the Civilian Conservation Corps camp while Great Smoky Mountains National Park was being built. He then built his own cafe on the Parkway in town on land owned by his grandfather Ephraim Ogle. When the log restaurant burned, Rel started making blocks the next day to rebuild it with more fireproof material. The Village shopping mall stands on the site today.

Rel's parents had a patch of farmland a little way up the Parkway from the Log Cabin cafe. In 1937, he started clearing the land with a mule-drawn scoop to build a hotel that would house the growing number of tourists coming to visit the mountains. The Gatlinburg Inn opened its doors in 1937, in very much the fashion it appears today.

The 67 rooms and seven suites were designed and furnished for comfort without compromise, and most of the original furniture is still in use. The chairs and sofas have been reupholstered several times (old will do—shabby won't), but the quality built into the inn endures, and so does its absolute refusal to surrender to any cookie-cutter trends in the lodging industry today. Also in keeping with the fashion of the time, separate quarters in the lower level originally housed the chauffeurs and domestic staffs of the inn's visitors.

Baskins Creek Neighborhood

JACK HUFF'S MOTOR LODGE $$
04 Cherokee Orchard Road, Gatlinburg
65) 436-5171, (800) 322-1817
ww.jackhuffs.com

body alive in Gatlinburg can remember when the Huff family didn't operate several lodging facilities, and Jack Huff's is one of the oldest. Located a block off the Parkway and directly across the street from Pi Beta Phi elementary school, Jack Huff's Motor Lodge is another of the many independent motels in the city that reminds guests of a different time. The hotel memorative plaque on the front wall identifies the Riverside as Gatlinburg's oldest continuously operated lodging establishment. Steve Whaley lived to see his prediction realized and much more. The Riverside has undergone a lot of changes in the ensuing 80-plus years, including the establishment of Gatlinburg's first shopping mall as an attachment to the front of the building.

Today's Riverside is a combination of old and new, with enough repeat business to make reservations hard to come by in the summer, especially on weekends, when the place is taken over by square-dance groups from all over the country. Now in the center of the downtown business district that grew up around it, the Riverside hearkens back to a gentler time with its paneled and carpeted hallways leading to comfortable rooms. Amenities here include private balconies as well as an outdoor pool and free coffee in the lobby. Originally built on ground that led to the banks of the Little Pigeon River, the Riverside now has River Road at its back door, where a separate lobby welcomes the traveler.

FOUR SEASONS MOTOR LODGE $$$
756 Parkway, Gatlinburg
(865) 436-7881, (800) 933-8678
www.reaganresorts.com
The Four Seasons (formerly a Ramada Inn) is as close to the middle of everything as you're likely to find, but its unique layout shelters its guests from street noise. With 148 luxurious units, plus two cabins, this inn offers a variety of accommodations that's hard to match (including Jacuzzi rooms, fireplace rooms, various suites, and a penthouse). The heated indoor and outdoor pool is elegant, and the on-site convention facility has three good-size meeting rooms, a full stage, and its own kitchen. The Gatlinburg Convention Center is just a block away, and you'll also find several restaurants and many attractions nearby.

REAGAN RESORTS INN $$
938 Parkway, Gatlinburg
(865) 436-5607, (800) 933-8674
www.reaganresorts.com
The unique topography of this motel provides a

spectacular view of the mountains out the back and arm's-length availability of more than two dozen attractions and restaurants out the front. The convention center is right next door. Most of the 63 rooms are unusually large and well appointed, with comfortable furniture in addition to home-style amenities. All rooms have refrigerators and coffeemakers, most have microwaves, and three have Jacuzzi tubs. The inn also offers an outdoor heated pool, garage parking, a business center, and a meeting room that seats up to 100 people with its own full kitchen.

QUALITY INN CREEKSIDE $$
125 LeConte Creek Road, Gatlinburg
(865) 436-4857, (800) 473-8319
www.qualityinncreekside.com
This inn features 104 oversize rooms with a choice of bed configurations, some with fireplaces and Jacuzzis. The view of the mountains from the balconies on the back building is spectacular. All rooms have microwaves, refrigerators, and coffeemakers, and the inn serves continental breakfast. The inn has an outdoor pool, and the entrance to Great Smoky Mountains National Park is just a few blocks up the Parkway.

CLARION INN & SUITES $$$
1100 Parkway, Gatlinburg
(865) 436-5656, (800) 933-0777
www.clariongatlinburg.com
Luxury is the minimum standard at the Clario every one of the 130 rooms, from king and q bed double units to the penthouse suites, is appointed. Private balconies in every roo vide great views, and the only rooftop m and banquet facilities in Gatlinburg give ; flavor to large gatherings. And speaking the Clarion's full hot breakfast is rend one of the best in a town famous fo of thing. The aerial tramway to Ober is just across the street, and the entr Great Smoky Mountains National P 100 yards. In addition, several of finest restaurants are steps away, a interesting Calhoun's Village, on many shopping malls.

The dining room of the Gatlinburg Inn was a masterpiece of propriety. The supplier of the hand-painted china, sterling silver finger bowls, and crystal used in the dining room joked that the dining room furnishings cost as much as the rest of the hotel, and he probably was close to right. Wilma Maples remembers the dining room fondly, particularly the Tuesday night dinners when the guests would gather for dinner and then retire to the tennis courts for square dancing. As the nature of tourism changed with the times following the war, the "new" tourists objected to the idea of dressing for dinner, so Rel and Wilma regretfully closed the dining room in 1972 rather than lower their own standards.

Wilma Miller Maples is not a Gatlinburg native. Born to a large family in Union County, she came to Gatlinburg in 1943 as secretary to the chief ranger in the park. She worked summers at the Gatlinburg Inn from 1946 to 1950, when she moved to Oak Ridge to work for a research engineer.

That job lasted until 1953, when she received a letter from Rel proposing marriage and a return to Gatlinburg. "It came out of the clear blue sky," she recalls, "and I really didn't know what to make of it at first." Wilma returned to Gatlinburg and became Mrs. Rel Maples in 1954 for what she calls "the best 31 years of my life."

The Gatlinburg Inn is as important to Gatlinburg's growth as the man who built it. In 1950, Rel helped establish the First National Bank of Gatlinburg, and his inn hosted the first city offices prior to the construction of the original city hall. The city's first large-press newspaper was printed in the basement.

Wilma recalls almost wistfully the days when the inn hosted the cream of American society, from captains of industry to an A-list of entertainment people. Igor Sikorsky, the inventor of the helicopter, was a guest there, and so was Melville Bell Grosvenor, son of the founder of the National Geographic Society. J. C. Penney once stayed at the inn, as did the parents of Stanley Marcus, of Neiman Marcus fame.

Tennessee Ernie Ford brought his parents. Liberace, Ladybird Johnson, and Frank Fontaine were satisfied guests, as was "Pistol Pete" Maravich, the late basketball superstar. Wilma remembers with particular fondness the frequent visits of Boudleaux and Felice Bryant, the hall-of-fame songwriting team, who stayed in room 388 almost every winter for more than 20 years. During their stay in 1967, the Bryants wrote "Rocky Top," Tennessee's unofficial state song. The inn was even the setting for the Ingrid Bergman movie A Walk in the Spring Rain.

If the Gatlinburg Inn seems a little out of step today, it's only because it has refused to change its pace with the rest of the world. The inn remains open from April through October, and 95 percent of its customers are repeat guests who first came as children and are now bringing their own children and grandchildren. They're greeted by employees who've been there for as long as the guests can remember.

The inn is open from April through October and is closed in the late fall and winter. For more information on the Gatlinburg Inn ($$), call (865) 436-5133 or visit www.gatlinburginn.com.

offers 60 clean, comfortable, and recently refurbished rooms with refrigerators (and most also with microwaves) as well as a heated outdoor pool with a waterslide and two indoor Jacuzzis. More than 75 percent of Huff's business is made up of people who've stayed there before, so they must be doing something right! The morning coffeepot in the lobby is a gathering spot for what seems to be an ongoing reunion. Downtown Gatlinburg is just outside the door at the rear entrance to the Village, one of Gatlinburg's most popular shopping malls.

BALES TOWN & COUNTRY MOTEL $
221 Bishop Lane, Gatlinburg
(865) 436-4773, (800) 458-8249
www.balesmotel.com

In addition to standard guest rooms where comfort is the keynote, the 30-room Bales Motel also has a couple of town houses (with Jacuzzis and fireplaces) and a cottage on the grounds for larger parties. Long-term rentals are available, and guests paying for six nights will get their seventh night free. The motel offers an outdoor pool, as well. Two blocks from downtown Gatlinburg in the secluded Baskins Creek neighborhood, Bales Town & Country offers a glimpse of how the local families live. The motel is open from April through early December, although the town houses are available year-round.

BRADLEY'S COURT $
111 Woliss Lane, Gatlinburg
(865) 436-4884
www.bradleyscourt.com

Another time-warp property, Bradley's Court was built in the '50s and '60s by current operator Chuck Bradley's parents. Twenty units, accommodating anywhere from two to eight people each, are built into a mountainside at the end of the street, giving the guest a feeling of total privacy within walking distance of downtown. Some rooms have kitchens, and most rooms have a sleeper sofa. Roll-away beds are available at a nominal charge. The swimming pool has an attached baby pool, and a large grassy area is just right for lying around. Pets are welcome. The hotel is open from April through October.

SCOTTISH INNS & SUITES $
208 Woliss Lane, Gatlinburg
(865) 436-5198, (866) 537-7953

Opened in the 1960s, this is another of Gatlinburg's old-line, family-owned and -operated accommodations. The inn has 32 rooms, including 17 suites, with as good a view of the mountains as you're likely to find anywhere. Stroll a couple of blocks through a quiet neighborhood in the other direction, and you're in the heart of the downtown business district. The hotel also has its own video arcade right next to the outdoor swimming pool (complete with slide).

JOHNSON'S INN $$$
242 Bishop Lane, Gatlinburg
(865) 436-4881, (800) 842-1930
www.johnsonsinn.com

Originally built in 1946 and constantly improved in the years since, Johnson's Inn sits within sight of downtown but not within hearing distance of the hubbub. The inn features a four-story tower with seven rental condos and 16 rooms. The inn has both an elevator and gently sloped ramps for total wheelchair accessibility. The main building offers 32 rooms, some with Jacuzzis and fireplaces but all with refrigerators and coffeemakers. The inn also has an outdoor pool. Johnson's customers are so loyal that the owners publish their own newsletter to keep everyone up-to-date with what's going on in their home away from home.

River Road and Ski Mountain

RIVER TERRACE RESORT & CONVENTION CENTER $$$$
240 River Road, Gatlinburg
(865) 436-5161, (800) 521-3523,
(800) 251-2040
www.riverterrace.com

River Terrace Resort offers guests 205 rooms, all with refrigerator and microwave. One of the city's favorite restaurants is right in the center, and the resort also features two heated outdoor pools, a spa, and a lounge for the nightlife lover. The River Terrace's 20,000-square-foot convention center is large enough to attract good-size convention groups or huge family reunions.

RIVERHOUSE MOTORLODGE $$$$
610 River Road, Gatlinburg
(865) 436-7821
www.riverhousemotels.com

The Riverhouse believes in pampering its guests. The 44 spacious rooms with a choice of beds and native stone fireplaces (choose wood or gas logs—from the end of September to the end of

April) have private balconies overlooking the Little Pigeon River. It's hard to stand on the balcony and believe you're only a block from downtown Gatlinburg. The rooms also include high-speed Internet, refrigerators, and microwaves, and even better, the staff at the Riverhouse will deliver a continental breakfast to your room every morning! Long, easy-grade ramps make the second-floor rooms easily accessible to wheelchairs.

HILTON GARDEN INN GATLINBURG $$$$$
635 River Road, Gatlinburg
(865) 436-0048, (877) 742-8444
www.hiltongardeninn.com
This environmentally conscious hotel, opening in July 2009 where River Oaks Mall once stood, is the first of its kind in the Smokies. In fact, it's the first hotel in the state of Tennessee (and among the first ten in the nation) to be Leadership in Energy and Environmental Design (LEED) certified. The certification attests to the fact that major energy-saving and waste-reduction strategies went into the design and construction process. For example, 20 percent of the construction made use of recycled materials, much of it from the River Oaks shopping mall buildings that used to stand here.

This $15 million property features 118 guest rooms, including 20 luxurious suites, all with coffeemakers, refrigerators, microwaves, and large flat-screen televisions. The hotel also offers a full-service restaurant, a convenience store, a workout facility, a business center, meeting space, a guest laundry, an indoor pool with whirlpool, and an outdoor fire pit. It's next to the tram for Ober Gatlinburg (see the Attractions chapter), and it's just yards from the entrance to the national park.

FAIRFIELD INN $$$$
680 River Road, Gatlinburg
(865) 430-7200, (888) 430-7200
www.greatsmokiesgreatlodging.com
Laid out in a parklike setting along the Little Pigeon River, the Fairfield's 54 rooms all have gas fireplaces and private balconies overlooking the water. The hot-tub suites and extra-large king suites heighten the relaxed atmosphere. The

quiet setting on River Road is just far enough away from downtown to shield the bright lights and noise but close enough to walk in less than five minutes. Ober Gatlinburg's aerial tramway mall is less than a block away and so are several excellent family restaurants.

FABULOUS CHALET INN $$$
310 Cottage Drive, Gatlinburg
(865) 436-5151, (800) 933-8675
www.reaganresorts.com
Just across the river from River Road (turn at the traffic light by the Ober Gatlinburg tramway mall), the Fabulous Chalet has a combination of river views and mountain views. Regardless of whether your room has a single king bed or a suite with a hot tub and fireplace, the view is breathtaking. Each of the 78 rooms has a refrigerator and coffeemaker, and the inn also offers heated swimming pools and complimentary continental breakfast. Set back in one of Gatlinburg's nicer residential areas, the Fab Chalet (local parlance) is a short stroll from a couple of truly outstanding restaurants and the Ober Gatlinburg tramway mall, and it's about 2 blocks from the entrance to Great Smoky Mountains National Park. Downtown Gatlinburg is about 3 blocks in the other direction.

BEARSKIN LODGE ON THE RIVER $$$$$
840 River Road, Gatlinburg
(865) 430-4330, (877) 795-7546
www.thebearskinlodge.com
This entry in the lodging business was opened in 2000 by Gatlinburg's oldest family. An imposing log-and-stone structure, Bearskin Lodge stands partially on the property where the late Hattie Ogle McGiffin, Gatlinburg's matriarch for more than half of the 20th century, was born. The lodge has 96 rooms in its five stories. Eight distinctive room configurations are spread throughout the building, ranging from a single queen bed to luxury suites with everything your heart desires. Most rooms have private balconies over the river. Many have gas fireplaces and whirlpool baths. The hotel provides continental breakfast as well as a heated outdoor pool and a lazy river with inner tubes.

Close-up

Keen on Green

It's not easy being green, but fortunately, Gatlinburg thinks it's worth it. The city's chamber of commerce launched its new Gatlinburg Goes Green sustainability campaign in February 2008 in an effort to help its 500 members reduce their impact on the environment. In the first year alone, more than 100 businesses (about 90 of them in some arm of the tourism industry) signed up—among them giants like Ober Gatlinburg and Ripley's Aquarium of the Smokies as well as more modest players, like the Salt & Pepper Shaker Museum (see the Attractions chapter).

"Our businesses wanted to be more environmentally sensitive, but they needed to do it affordably," says Gatlinburg Goes Green executive director Vicki Simms. "This program helps them find ways to work toward that." Currently, members can join on a bronze, silver, or gold level, depending on their level of commitment. Businesses that enter at one level can advance to higher levels as they get more involved.

Finding out who's a member (so you can support the "go green" effort by deciding where you want to spend your own "green energy") is easy. Participating businesses display Gatlinburg Goes Green stickers on their windows and logos in their advertisements and have listings on the program's Web site, www.GatlinburgGoesGreen.com (go to the "Travel Planning" tab). The Web site also contains several "green" travel tips and ideas, as well as information about the state's first LEED-certified hotel (the new Hilton Garden Inn, profiled elsewhere in this chapter).

The city itself has instituted many "green" measures, including replacing all of the lights in its Winterfest light displays (see the Festivals and Annual Events chapter) with energy-saving LED bulbs. Next up will be converting traffic signals to LED lights. City vehicles with diesel engines (including the garbage trucks, ambulances, and fire trucks) now all run on biodiesel fuel—a cleaner-burning diesel fuel made from natural, renewable sources such as vegetable oils instead of petroleum. In addition, several police cruisers now run on compressed natural gas (CNG).

Such efforts in the Smoky Mountain Corridor aren't restricted to Gatlinburg. Sevier County is also making great "green" strides, most notably by drastically reducing its garbage with one of the most advanced composting facilities in the world. The facility focuses on composting and recycling organic matter, which makes up 60 percent of what sanitation workers collect every week. Since 1992, when the county built the solid waste disposal plant (one of only ten so far in the world), sanitation experts from Europe, Asia, and Australia have come to town specifically to tour the plant to see how they might build a similar one.

Not content to merely reduce landfill by 65 percent (saving 40,000 tons a year), the county is also considering another state-of-the-art program that would boost that figure to a whopping 95 percent or higher. The program would use bioenergy conversion technology that would, to put it simply, turn garbage into electricity. Solid waste would be "cooked," and in the process, gases that the heated waste gives off would be stored and used by generators to produce power.

With efforts like these, before you know it, Gatlinburg will be as green as the mountains that surround it.

RIVERHOUSE AT THE PARK $$$
205 Ski Mountain Road, Gatlinburg
(865) 436-2070
www.riverhousemotels.com

At the southwest intersection of River Road and Ski Mountain Road, Riverhouse at the Park is conveniently situated for a short walk into downtown Gatlinburg or a short hike into Great Smoky Mountains National Park. There's a trail just across the river that's a great favorite with local exercise walkers at all hours of the day and night. Fifty rooms at three levels of accommodation offer private balconies with spectacular views of the Little Pigeon River and the mountains. Creature comforts from whirlpool baths to wet bars and native-stone gas fireplaces abound, and the inn also offers a heated pool with hot tub. The Riverhouse staff brings your continental breakfast to your room every morning.

GRAND PRIX MOTEL $$
235 Ski Mountain Road, Gatlinburg
(865) 436-4561, (800) 732-2802
www.grandprixmotel.com

With the park for its backyard, the English Tudor–style Grand Prix offers special low-cost lodging for hikers among its 34 rooms. Accommodations include four kitchen units that accommodate up to eight people each, as well as honeymoon suites. The inn has a large, clover-shaped heated outdoor pool, a kiddie pool, and an on-site Laundromat. The Grand Prix serves donuts and coffee each morning. Both AAA and AARP discounts apply, and pets under 10 pounds are welcome.

Historic Nature Trail

Historic Nature Trail (formerly called Airport Road) runs uphill from the Parkway at traffic light #8, which is the corner where the Space Needle rises from the street. An eclectic combination of lodging places runs from small (20 rooms and fewer) family-owned motels to two of the city's largest franchise establishments. The Gatlinburg Convention Center and churches representing most Christian denominations are all convenient to the Historic Nature Trail motels.

GILLETTE MOTEL $$$
235 Historic Nature Trail, Gatlinburg
(865) 436-5601, (865) 436-5376,
(800) 437-0815
www.gillettemotel.com

A block up Historic Nature Trail from the Parkway, the Gillette Motel is directly across the street from the Gatlinburg Convention Center. The 80 rooms in this imposing three-story structure are usually filled during the summer by repeat visitors and convention-goers, but the location makes the Gillette worth a look. During the Christmas season, the Gillette is a consistent prizewinner for its spectacular lighting efforts. All rooms here have refrigerators and coffeemakers, as well as free wireless Internet. One unit has a kitchenette and some have Jacuzzis. The motel also has an outdoor heated pool.

ROCKY TOP VILLAGE INN $$
311 Historic Nature Trail, Gatlinburg
(865) 436-7826, (800) 553-7738
www.rockytopvillageinn.com

Named for Tennessee's state song, the Rocky Top is owned by the family of the tune's cowriter, Felice Bryant. Eighty-nine luxurious rooms in several configurations and a guest loyalty rate of more than 75 percent attests to the Rocky Top's hospitable treatment. Guest rooms include microwaves, refrigerators, coffeemakers, and balconies overlooking either the mountains or downtown. The inn also has an outdoor heated pool and offers free coffee and doughnuts each morning. Pets are welcome, although the hotel appreciates advance notice.

If you're staying in a Gatlinburg motel and you want to go downtown, take the trolley. It's easy, dependable transportation, and everybody on the trolley seems to be having fun. It's cheaper by a long shot than parking downtown and a lot easier to find than a parking spot.

SUPER 8 GATLINBURG DOWNTOWN   **$$**
417 Historic Nature Trail, Gatlinburg
(865) 436-2222, (866) 436-2228
www.super8gatlinburgdowntown.com
A lovely front lawn surrounded by flowers greets you at the Super 8 (formerly called the Gazebo Inn), establishing an air of serenity that carries right through the comfortable 60-room structure. Rooms all have refrigerators and coffeemakers, as well as either a balcony or a patio. Eight special rooms offer king beds, fireplaces, and Jacuzzis. You'll also find an outdoor pool and free Internet, and the inn provides continental breakfast every morning. AAA and AARP discounts apply.

GLENSTONE LODGE   **$$$**
504 Historic Nature Trail, Gatlinburg
(865) 436-9361, (800) 362-9522
www.glenstonelodge.com
If this place leaves a light on for you in every room, they'll illuminate a fair stretch of Historic Nature Trail, and that only covers about a quarter of what's available. More than 200 comfortable rooms with king, queen, or double beds and eight deluxe and executive-type suites surround a central atrium that's totally isolated from the street. The lodge has a huge indoor pool with a waterfall in a pleasant atrium, an Olympic-size outdoor pool, and a putting green. Full banquet and catering facilities complement the award-winning restaurant and on-premise meeting rooms. The Gatlinburg Convention Center is a five-minute walk away.

GARDEN PLAZA HOTEL   **$$$$**
520 Historic Nature Trail, Gatlinburg
(865) 436-9201, (800) 435-9201
www.4lodging.com
If the Garden Plaza could float, it'd be a luxury cruise ship. The complex includes a full-service restaurant, a lounge with planned family and adult activities, a market/deli, a pizza counter, a guest laundry, two indoor pools and an outdoor pool, two whirlpools, a health/fitness center, and an activities desk where you can plan your whole vacation, including picking up tickets to most of the local attractions.

Most of the 400 rooms and suites are in the terrace area at the back of the property, where three multistory buildings feature views of the mountains in the (near) distance and LeConte Creek practically at your feet. A full hot breakfast is included with most rates.

Mynatt Park, one of Gatlinburg's real jewels (see the Parks and Recreation chapter), is right next to the terrace section. The Gatlinburg Convention Center and downtown are a couple of blocks in the other direction.

SIDNEY JAMES MOUNTAIN LODGE   **$$$**
610 Historic Nature Trail, Gatlinburg
(865) 436-7851, (800) 578-7878
www.sidneyjames.com
Right at the top of Historic Nature Trail, the Sidney James offers cushy accommodations in what appears to be the middle of the woods. Gatlinburg's beautiful Mynatt Park is right next door, and one of the most popular sections of Great Smoky Mountains National Park is just up the road.

The lodge's more than 180 attractively decorated rooms all have coffeemakers and refrigerators, and they all look out on LeConte Creek and the mountains. The hotel offers both an outdoor pool as well as an idyllic indoor pool with a kiddie pool, sauna, and poolside cafe. The Sidney James prints its own travel guide with discount coupons for lots of local attractions and restaurants.

East Parkway

Following East Parkway (US 321N) east of town from traffic light #3, a succession of smaller, family-owned and -operated lodging places is within a few blocks. These places were built mostly on farmland in the 1950s and '60s and vary in size from intimate to huge. With a few exceptions, these are comfortably furnished, moderately priced accommodations that boast extremely high return percentages and where you'll be treated more like a visiting family member than a guest tenant. The orange trolley route services this strip of road, and the trolley will stop at, or within 50 feet of, the door to every motel listed.

EAST SIDE MOTEL $
315 East Parkway, Gatlinburg
(865) 436-7569
Tom and Marlene Trentham built the East Side in 1971 on land that was part of her grandfather's farm. Four-fifths of the East Side's guests come back, most of them annually, and Marlene says running the motel is a lot like having a great big house and a great big family to fill it. Each of the 30 big rooms has microwaves and refrigerators, and the motel also has an outdoor pool.

The East Side is convenient to both ends of downtown at the same time—traffic light #3 is a short walk or trolley ride from the front door, and the Bishop Lane bypass is just across the street.

BROOKSIDE RESORT $$
463 East Parkway, Gatlinburg
(865) 436-5611, (800) 251-9597
www.brooksideresort.com
The only word to describe the Brookside is *huge*—it has six multistory buildings containing 170 rooms and includes cabins in every imaginable configuration (one sleeping up to 20), all stretching along 3 blocks of the East Parkway, with Roaring Fork Creek at the back. The Brookside's front lawn, featuring the black bear statue that's a favorite landmark, is bigger than most of the lodging properties in town.

Each of the rooms has a small refrigerator. The hotel offers basketball, volleyball, and wallyball courts; a new exercise facility; an event center that can seat up to 200 people; a riverside pavilion with its own kitchen facility; and an outdoor heated pool with a whirlpool, a slide, and a waterfall. The breakfast room is open during the season, and the continental breakfast is complimentary. The blue trolley stops at the inn's front door.

BED-AND-BREAKFASTS AND COUNTRY INNS

The bed-and-breakfast industry in the Great Smoky Mountains is driven by a growing number of great, new, old-looking structures that were mostly built in the 1990s. Regardless of their location (and some of them are going to give you a whole new appreciation of the term *remote*), the bed-and-breakfast inns of the Smokies are in the vanguard of a vibrant, growing addition to the established lodging industry. Designed and built with the specific market in mind, the Smokies' bed-and-breakfast inns are intended to satisfy the demands of a clientele that consists almost exclusively of couples. Children are not actively discouraged, but most of the inns limit the number of occupants in a single room, and the limit is usually three. Several have "couples only" policies, as noted in the individual descriptions.

Being of recent construction, the inns have many of the amenities you'd find at any upscale lodging place: Expect private bathrooms, cable or satellite television with one or more premium channels, air-conditioning and central heating, and some form of hot tub or whirlpool. Telephones and stereo systems are commonplace. With only a few exceptions, the views of the mountains from private or semiprivate balconies and full-width porches are absolutely spectacular—every inn can state with some justification that their view is "the tallest," "the widest," "the highest," ad infinitum.

The "breakfast" part of the equation is usually what you'd expect to find in a place like Tennessee, where bacon and sausage are considered vegetables. The three basic Southern food groups (meat, flour, and grease) are served in copious amounts, with some surprising gourmet touches added. Enough fruit, cereal, and whole-grain baked goods are usually available to satisfy the health-conscious. Most of these inns offer afternoon and pre-bedtime snacks. Some will serve lunch and dinner to large groups with sufficient advance notice. Pets are a universal no-no, and please don't ask for any exceptions—the guests that killed off the pet question brought a pot-bellied pig with them.

The unique nature of this segment of the lodging industry makes it almost imperative that reservations be made well in advance. It's more like you're visiting in a very solicitous house than staying in a motel, and the hosts need as much planning time as they can get. Each of these places welcomes walk-in traffic on the rare occasion when they have vacancies, but *rare* is the operative word here. Conversely, cancellations usually require about 10 days' advance notice for full refunds—specific differences will be individually noted. Check-in times are all mid-afternoon (around 3 p.m.), and the earliest checkout is 11 a.m. Smoking is without exception restricted to outdoor areas.

Be forewarned that except for a few places convenient to downtown Pigeon Forge and Gatlinburg, the inns described here (and this is not a complete list) are in areas of the county where the average tourist probably wouldn't go for any other reason. Therefore, you'll also find clear directions to every one, and they're all accessible on paved roads. As usual, the list begins in Sevierville and moves south—please note that all accommodations are south of Dolly Parton Parkway (U.S. Highway 411/441).

Price Code

The pricing key indicates the average cost of a room for two adults, exclusive of taxes, during the tourist season (April through October). Where two codes are present, the higher code usually applies to guest cottages. Most places accept credit cards—those that don't are so noted.

$.................. Less than $100
$$ ....$100–$130
$$$ ....$131–$160
$$$$ ....$161–$200
$$$$$................Over $200

SEVIERVILLE—EAST

BLUE MOUNTAIN MIST COUNTRY INN & COTTAGES $$$
1811 Pullen Road, Sevierville
(865) 428-2335, (800) 497-2335
www.bluemountainmist.com

Set peacefully among several prosperous farms, Blue Mountain Mist is a haven of country charm and style. The inn is on a 60-acre farm owned by the Ball family, surrounded by mountains on three sides. The 17 rooms include a mix of queen beds, queen plus twin, king beds, king plus twins, and deluxe Jacuzzi rooms, as well as five honeymoon cottages (soon to be more). The innkeepers serve their hearty country breakfast family-style in the sun-drenched dining room, as well as offer coffee and desserts each evening.

The immaculate grounds include beautiful gardens made for strolling, and the hammock on the corner of the full-width front porch is almost irresistible on a warm summer afternoon. Nestled in the woods behind the inn, five quaint honeymoon cottages offer a little more privacy. Each cottage has a bedside Jacuzzi, fireplace, kitchenette and grill (although breakfast is included), and a private yard with a picnic table. It's easy to see why this inn ranked in the top 10 Southern inns at BedandBreakfast.com.

To get there, travel east out of Sevierville on Dolly Parton Parkway (US 411N) for 2 miles and then turn right at the light onto Veterans Boulevard. Then go about 3.9 miles until you see Jay Ell Road on the left. Turn onto Jay Ell and go about 1 1/2 miles to Pullen Road. Blue Mountain Mist is the huge, turreted farmhouse-style structure on the corner.

SEVIERVILLE—PARKWAY

CALICO INN $$
757 Ranch Way, Sevierville
(865) 428-3833, (800) 235-1054
www.calico-inn.com

The Calico Inn is a cozy authentic log cabin with three country-style guest rooms, complete with beautiful patchwork quilts on the beds. School-age children are welcome in one of the guest rooms that's large enough for three people. The attitude and the surroundings are laid-back, with a panoramic view of the mountains forming a backdrop for the nearby woods and fields. The inn has both a wide, welcoming front porch complete with a porch swing and a relaxing back deck graced with lounge chairs. In the great room, you'll find a lovely stacked-stone fireplace. If the country breakfast doesn't fill you to the brim, help yourself to the home-baked goodies on the hospitality cart any time of day. The Calico Inn is 2 miles off the Parkway on New Era Road, just south of Wal-Mart.

WEARS VALLEY

The three inns on and adjacent to Wears Valley Road have addresses in both Pigeon Forge and Sevierville. Political boundaries aside, they're described here in the order you would come upon them if you turned westbound on Wears Valley Road (U.S. Highway 321) from the Parkway in Pigeon Forge.

HILTON'S BLUFF BED & BREAKFAST INN $–$$
2654 Valley Heights Drive, Pigeon Forge
(865) 428-9765, (800) 441-4188
www.hiltonsbluff.com

Close enough to the Parkway that you could hear traffic if the woods didn't get in the way, Hilton's Bluff is a 10-room inn with a variety of bed

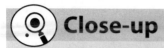 **Close-up**

A True Work of Art

Vern Hippensteal is not your usual artist (if there would ever really be such a thing). Here is an artist who sees things with such clarity that he's able to record them on canvas as accurately as if he'd used a camera, but no camera can breathe life into a scene like Vern can. Maybe that's because he is a scientist by education (he's got a degree in physics), a printer by heritage (it's one of the family businesses), and, in his own terms, an artist by the grace of God. The difference between Vern Hippensteal and most other truly gifted artists is that Vern lives in a disciplined world, with both feet firmly planted in his native soil. And when Vern and his wife, Lisa, decided to build and operate their own inn, the first thing they did was design it themselves, to reflect the peace and beauty of their birthplace.

Vern's artistic and mathematical talents came in handy for the concept and the structural details. Lisa's experience growing up in the famed Mountain View hotel in Gatlinburg, managed for several years by her father, provided the nuts-and-bolts details that separate a classic lodging place from a merely outstanding one. Their impeccably good taste didn't hurt either. The result is Hippensteal's Mountain View Inn, which the couple built and decorated themselves, opening in 1990.

The inn's magic begins on the wide front porch, complete with requisite rocking chairs, where the view of the Smokies range exceeds 200 degrees in width, stretching from Greenbrier pinnacle to the east across Mount LeConte to Mount Harrison. In the impossibly bright lobby, the dominant white of the wicker furniture and imposing limestone fireplace complements the alternating black and white marble floor tile and walls covered with artwork (naturally—and most of it is for sale, too).

By the way, if you look closely, you'll see a secret in many of Vern's prints. He hides faces, animals, and even little gnomes in his pictures—especially in waterfalls and rock-work. It's fun to see how many you can find. If you don't see anything at first, ask someone for a hint. Once you see the first one, you'll see them everywhere!

The breakfast room, where delectable meals are served each morning, is furnished with white wicker chairs and glass-topped pedestal tables. Dessert is served in the evenings. The nine elegantly furnished guest rooms, each named for the painting that the room is planned around, are upstairs. So is the library, while the room at the back is Vern's studio. In an adjacent building, you'll find two guest rooms.

To get to Hippensteal's from traffic light #3 in Gatlinburg, drive 2.6 miles east on East Parkway (US 321) to Glades Road, and then drive through the Arts and Crafts Community about 3.1 miles to its terminus at Bird's Creek Road. Turn left again, and less than half a mile later you'll come to the first of two forks; take the right one up and over the hill to the second fork, which you also take to the right for about another half mile to the inn's driveway (Taten Marr Way) on the left.

For reservations at the inn ($$$$), call (865) 436-5761 or (800) 527-8110, or visit the inn's Web site at www.hippensteal.com.

configurations and plenty of space for corporate meetings, church retreats, weddings, and other groups. All the rooms are bright and airy, and three are honeymoon-style suites with heart-shaped two-person Jacuzzis.

The day begins here with a full country breakfast and ends with delicious surprise snacks and refreshments. The selection of parlor games is outstanding, and the library is excellent. The Pigeon Forge trolley stops at the corner just below the inn. Valley Heights Drive is just half a mile from the Parkway—it's the second street off the Parkway to the left.

i It would be nice to say that the level of service you get at the bed-and-breakfast establishments is typical of the rest of the area, but it isn't—it's much better. Don't be afraid to ask for anything that seems reasonable to you.

GATLINBURG

EIGHT GABLES INN $$$$
219 North Mountain Trail, Gatlinburg
(865) 430-3344, (800) 279-5716
www.eightgables.com
The Eight Gables Inn offers 19 spacious and elegant rooms and suites furnished with a decidedly feminine touch, each with feather-topped beds, private baths, and large windows with great views. Suites also have fireplaces and whirlpool tubs. The inn offers a lovely sitting area, a covered porch, and the ever-popular Magnolia Tea Room—the setting for the inn's gourmet country breakfast (you'll love the potato pie au gratin). The inn also serves scrumptious afternoon tea and offers a decadent evening dessert bar.

Eight Gables is located right between Gatlinburg and Pigeon Forge, and the trolley stop at the Gatlinburg Welcome Center provides service to both cities. Before you even get into Gatlinburg on the Parkway Spur, Eight Gables Inn is across the road from the Gatlinburg Welcome Center.

OLDE ENGLISH TUDOR INN $-$$
135 West Holly Ridge Road, Gatlinburg
(865) 436-7760, (800) 541-3798
www.oldeenglishtudorinn.com
Right in the center of downtown Gatlinburg, the Olde English Tudor Inn is an oasis of comfort and serenity. The innkeepers live in the building, so they are ever at your service. The inn's eight comfortable guest rooms all offer views of the mountains or of downtown. The rear patio and flower garden provide a quiet respite, while the community room is a great place to mingle with other guests.

To get to the inn, turn left at Reagan Drive, left again at Reagan Lane (the first street), and left

one more time at Holly Ridge. The inn is then the first place on the right.

GATLINBURG—EAST

The establishments east of Gatlinburg are spread out in an area accessible by roads running north off US 321, from 2 to 15 miles from traffic light #3 in Gatlinburg.

i The bed-and-breakfast industry in the Smokies probably offers the most intimate experience you'll have with the local population. Don't be surprised if you get emotionally involved with your hosts.

TIMBER ROSE ENGLISH LODGE $-$$$$
1106 Tanrac Trail, Gatlinburg
(865) 436-5852, (877) 235-4993
www.timberrose.com
Timber Rose is more than a lavish couples-only bed-and-breakfast inn housed in a true English-style lodge. When current owners George and Debra Moye acquired the inn in 2000, they turned Timber Rose into an eco-lodge. They did more than just add insulation, recycle, and switch to low-flow showerheads and compact fluorescent bulbs, though. The ambitious list of eco-friendly policies they instituted is easily a mile long, including initiating a towel and linen reuse program; buying only natural, biodegradable, phosphate-free cleaning products; and purchasing fair-trade products whenever possible. (The coffee served at the Timber Rose, for example, is Rainforest Alliance Certified.) Even the bathroom soap is all natural and comes in a recycled (and recyclable) box!

The inn itself is easily as impressive. Each of the five large suites has its own private entrance and nearly every amenity you could wish for: a spacious living room, dining room, full kitchen, romantic bedroom, fireplace (with candelabras), and a hot tub on the private porch. Opulent furnishings appear throughout, as do Corinthian statuary and stained-glass windows. The panoramic view of the Smokies is almost 100 miles wide from the inn, and it's hard to believe civilization is only a mile or so away.

Timber Rose is on the northern edge of Gatlinburg's world-famous Great Smoky Arts & Crafts Community, described at length in the Shopping chapter. To get there, go east 2 miles out East Parkway (US 321) from traffic light #3 to the traffic light at Glades Road. Turn left on Glades and go about 2 more miles to the blinking light at Powdermill Road, where another left turn will lead about 2 blocks to a fork in the road. Take the next left (John's Branch Road) about 1 1/4 miles to Tanrac Trail, and turn right. Follow the road up about 1/3 mile.

BUCKHORN INN   **$$–$$$$$**
2140 Tudor Mountain Road, Gatlinburg
(865) 436-4668, (866) 941-0460
www.buckhorninn.com
The only establishment in the Smokies Corridor that is considered a true country inn, the Buckhorn Inn has been in business since 1938. Set on 25 acres of woodland in a secluded area 6 miles east of Gatlinburg, the inn has its own walking trails and lake, as well as one of the largest meditation labyrinths in the United States. The main building has a lovely sitting area complete with grand piano and a flagstone terrace out back with fabulous views, including Mount LeConte, the third highest peak in the national park.

The inn has 10 guest rooms with private baths (in fact, the newest room has two baths—his and hers!), as well as seven guest cottages with fireplaces and three swank guesthouses. The amenities are luxurious, right down to the robes.

Breakfast is included in the lodging fee, and lunch and dinner are available to guests by reservation only. Special maps prepared by the inn's staff describe nearby hiking trails in Great Smoky Mountains National Park and throw in a few secret locations known even to very few locals.

The inn is located within the boundaries of the Great Smoky Arts & Crafts Community. From traffic light #3 in Gatlinburg, take East Parkway (US 321) about 4 1/2 miles east to Buckhorn Road

and turn left. Tudor Mountain Road is about a mile in on the right.

FINALLY, SOMETHING REALLY SPECIAL

Although this next inn isn't technically in the Smokies Corridor (it's in Newport, about 25 miles east of Sevierville and Gatlinburg in Cocke County), it's notable for an unusual reason. It was the setting for Country Music Television's not-really reality show, *Outsiders Inn* (featuring Maureen McCormick as the innkeeper, Carnie Wilson as the head chef, and Bobby Brown as the entertainment director), which aired all eight of its episodes in 2008.

However, please don't be misled. The show's Pigeon Manor is totally different from Christopher Place. For the record, the inn was closed during filming, the furnishings were switched out, and the producers handpicked the inn's guests, so what you may have seen on the show bears little resemblance to what you'll experience if you stay here. While few locals appreciated the hillbilly stereotype the show presented, folks around here do still very much appreciate the grandeur of this quiet country inn that was lauded long before and will live way beyond CMT's now-shelved show.

CHRISTOPHER PLACE   **$$$$–$$$$$**
1500 Pinnacles Way, Newport
(423) 623-6555, (800) 595-9441
www.christopherplace.com
This regal inn is housed in a Federal-style mansion with a grand three-story vestibule that leads you into several common rooms. To the right are the library and a bar, and to the left are two dining rooms. The library has books, puzzles, periodicals, and comfortable chairs. But the best place to sit a spell is in one of the rocking chairs on the full-width front porch—the view of the mountains is simply stunning.

The inn's seven suites each have private bath, coffeemaker, stereo system, hair dryer, and snuggly terry robes. Mountain Sunrise is a cheery corner room with a brass queen bed and a garden outside. Camelot is a regal suite with a hand-carved mahogany king bed. The Roman Holiday suite features a double whirlpool. Breakfast is hearty country fare, and if you're celebrating a birthday or anniversary, expect a little surprise.

The grounds include a swimming pool, tennis court, gym, sauna, and kitchenette with soft drinks available anytime. A hiking trail takes off from the back of the property and goes up the side of English Mountain, where you might catch a glimpse of wild turkey, red fox, gray squirrels, or raccoons.

Gatlinburg is about 45 minutes away, and Interstate 40 will take you back to Sevierville and Pigeon Forge in about the same time. The Cosby entrance to Great Smoky Mountains National Park is 15 miles south on Tennessee Highway 32, the same road that leads to Gatlinburg.

Christopher Place has won nearly every award available to a bed-and-breakfast and carries the highest designations offered by every rating service that has seen it. The elegance of the accommodations and the effortless grace of the staff are bound to impress.

The inn can be tough to find. The key is to get to English Mountain Road on TN 32, and there are three approaches to that point:

From I-40 East (like from Knoxville or Interstate 81S): Take exit 435 in Newport and turn south (right) 3 miles; English Mountain Road is on the right.

From I-40 West (from North Carolina): Take exit 440 (US 321—Wilton Springs Road) 2 miles west to TN 32; turn right and go 3 1/2 miles to English Mountain Road on the left.

From Gatlinburg: Take US 321 (East Parkway) to its terminus at TN 32 (about 17 miles from traffic light #3 in Gatlinburg). Turn left (north) on TN 32 and go about 10.3 miles to English Mountain Road on the left.

Christopher Place tries to keep a directional sign at the intersection of TN 32 and English Mountain Road, although it sometimes gets "borrowed." However, once you're on English Mountain Road, follow it 2 miles (it'll seem longer) through the rolling countryside of rural Cocke County. The next right turn is Pinnacles Way, and it winds less than a mile up the face of English Mountain to Christopher Place.

VACATION RENTALS

Renting a cabin, chalet, or condo unit is a great way to enjoy all the Smokies have to offer while making your base a literal home away from home. And one of the truly wonderful things about vacationing in the Smokies is that it's possible to rent a place for about the same amount of money (and sometimes even less) as you'd spend on a hotel, depending on your circumstances. Two families traveling together, for example, could easily spend less money sharing one multi-bedroom cabin than they would staying in your average hotel. The larger your group, the more you're likely to save.

The number of rental choices here totals in the thousands and grows larger all the time. In fact, the prospect of narrowing down your vacation lodging may indeed be a little overwhelming. To help you out a bit, this chapter presents you with a basic overview of what kinds of properties and amenities exist, where they're located, what they cost in general, and what to expect when making a reservation. It also includes a listing of a number of rental companies and resorts in the area. Collectively, they'll give you access to just about any type of rental property in whichever area of the Smokies you want to stay in.

WHAT TO CHOOSE

Although infinite variations exist, the styles of Smoky Mountain vacation rental properties can loosely be classified under three basic types, which are primarily distinguishable by their architectural differences: chalet, cabin, and condominium.

The term *chalet* generally refers to the style of home reminiscent of those in mountainous European villages. The classic chalet's most distinguishing characteristic is its A-frame construction. Typically, you'll also find lots of big windows for fabulous mountain vistas as well as ample outdoor deck space. In Sevier County, the largest concentration of chalets is found nestled in the hilly slopes surrounding Gatlinburg.

The word *cabin* on the other hand, inspires images of a sturdy, rustic, log dwelling. Although there is surely an abundance of log structures for rent throughout the Smokies, you might be surprised to find that many of them are anything but rustic. Today's log rentals offer plenty of modern conveniences, often in quite cushy surroundings.

Cabins probably offer the widest berth in terms of architectural range. You'll find smaller one-bedroom cabins, sprawling ranch-style structures, and multistory log homes with heavy-duty square footage. Many incorporate some of the popular exterior features common to chalets, such as large picture windows and porches. While you can find rental cabins throughout the Sevier County area, you're more likely to find them in the middle to northern sections where the terrain is generally less steep and more conducive to construction.

Condominiums most often resemble apartment complexes and normally house a large number of units in a centralized building or set of buildings. They range from multiple groupings of ground-level flats and townhomes to interior-access, high-rise structures. Condominiums are most prevalent in and around Pigeon Forge and Gatlinburg, but you'll also find them in Sevierville and outlying areas as well.

You'll notice in the listings of rental companies later in the chapter that some companies market themselves as "resorts." This means that the company's rental properties are centralized and offer common on-site amenities such as swimming pools, tennis courts, or golf courses. Most resorts are made up of either condominiums or cabins.

ℹ **The state of Tennessee requires that any company in the overnight rental business operate with a vacation lodging license obtained through the Tennessee Real Estate Commission. To be on the safe side, make sure that any overnight rental company you deal with is properly licensed.**

SELECTING A LOCATION

Your first decision in selecting a vacation rental is choosing its general location. If scenic mountain views are high on your list, you might want to be closer to Gatlinburg. If you want quick access to shopping and music theaters, Pigeon Forge is your place. Basing yourself out of Sevierville will help you avoid a lot of the heavier traffic and also allow handier access to surrounding cities like Knoxville or Asheville, North Carolina.

A few specific sections of the Smokies are noted for their abundance of rental choices: Walden's Creek, a few miles off Wears Valley Road, outside Pigeon Forge; Wears Valley, about 10 miles southwest of Pigeon Forge; Ski Mountain, the generic name given to the concentration of chalet homes located a couple of miles from downtown Gatlinburg on Mount Harrison; and Cobbly Nob, a resort area about 12 minutes from Gatlinburg on U.S. Highway 321.

AMENITIES

To the good fortune of the overnight renter, Smoky Mountain properties are usually rife with the luxuries and the "little things" that can make an overnight accommodation seem like home.

But just because a particular property is laden with amenities doesn't mean it's necessarily attractive or offers good views. It may just be a dump that happens to have a lot of bells and whistles. The only way to be sure is to look at

pictures of the property on the rental company's Web site or ask your rental agent to e-mail (or snail mail) images to you along with the property's other marketing materials.

Although you will always find some exceptions to this list, most vacation rentals will include furnished linens and towels; kitchens equipped with dishes, silverware, cooking utensils, and major appliances like refrigerators, stoves, and microwave ovens (although you're responsible for the food!); hot tubs/whirlpool baths; fireplaces; washers and dryers (either in the unit itself or in the complex's laundry room); cable or satellite television; and Internet connections. Some places, especially the resorts, have access to other exterior amenities such as swimming pools, tennis courts, and golf courses.

MONEY MATTERS

How much can you expect to pay for an overnight rental? Size matters. A small, one-bedroom condo will obviously not be as expensive as a seven-bedroom cabin. That said, you'll be hard-pressed to find a price lower than $65 to $85 per night for two people, and prices can go as high as several hundred dollars per night for a multiple bedroom unit.

In most cases, prices are based on the unit's capacity. A one-bedroom condo, for example, might be considered to have a capacity of four (two people in one bedroom and two more on a sleeper sofa in the living room). Similarly, a three-bedroom cabin may have a capacity of eight (three beds plus a sleeper sofa). You will also likely be charged extra for additional occupants beyond the unit's limit. An average figure is $10 per night per person for anyone over 12 years of age.

Although individual policies vary from one rental company or resort to another, the following general guidelines and procedures apply with just about all of them. Even so, be sure to confirm any particular company's specific policies when shopping around.

It's advisable to make reservations months in advance, especially for holiday or peak season periods (during the summer months; October; and holidays like the Fourth of July, Memorial Day, Labor Day, and, of course, Thanksgiving and Christmas). Six months out, you'll probably be safe, but many repeat vacation renters will book their regular unit for the following year on departure. It's typical for most companies to have reservations on their books for one and sometimes even two years in advance.

Most places require that you reserve a minimum number of nights. Two nights is an average minimum, especially when you're dealing with weekends. If you're booking for holidays or peak season periods, you're looking more at a three- or four-night minimum.

You will usually have to post a deposit within a certain time period after making your reservation in order to hold it. The amount can range anywhere from the amount of the first night's rental to 50 percent of the total cost of the stay, depending on your rental agency. Although most places will accept credit cards, double-check with the booking agent to confirm which specific cards are accepted. Some companies also accept cash and even personal checks (if they receive your check well enough in advance). The balance of the total is expected on arrival.

As for cancellation policies, two weeks seems to be a standard cutoff point for safely canceling your reservation (some companies allow as few as 72 hours, while some require a month's notice). If you cancel before that cutoff time, you'll probably have a choice of either rescheduling your reservation or receiving a refund. Some places give a full refund, while some keep a nominal administrative fee.

i **If you are from out of town and interested in booking a vacation rental property in the Smokies, the Internet is an excellent research tool. Most rental company's Web sites contain photos of all the individual properties along with detailed descriptions of amenities and, sometimes, virtual tours. You can usually even handle your reservation requests and bookings online.**

Cancellation within the cutoff period usually results in full forfeiture of the deposit. The same goes for early departure after you've checked in. Exceptions can sometimes be made, however, if the customer can document a family emergency like death or serious illness.

OVERNIGHT RENTAL COMPANIES

A few helpful distinctions are in order that may deflect confusion when sifting through this section. Some rental companies call themselves "resorts," which are noted for their centralized accommodations and amenities. For the purposes of distinction, resort companies are somewhat unique when compared to the rental company whose inventory comprises separate properties located all over the county. In both cases, however, the individual units are commonly owned by absentee investors.

Condominiums present their own peculiarities. Some condo units are marketed through rental companies. It's very common to see individual unit listings within a single condominium complex handled by different overnight rental businesses. On the other hand, the management of that same condominium development may also personally handle the marketing and property management for other units in the development. The choice of who manages a particular unit is usually up to the discretion of that unit's owner.

Some of the companies included below deal exclusively in rentals, but many are also full-service real estate businesses through which you can invest in rental property as well.

The addresses below are for each company's business office—where you go to check in, pay the balance of your rental, and get your keys. You might also receive specific instructions on how to get to your rental, if it's located at a separate site. Be sure to visit the companies' Web sites to see photos of specific properties as well as pricing information and rental policies. In most cases, you can even make your reservations from a company's Web page.

SEVIERVILLE

OAK HAVEN RESORT
1947 Old Knoxville Highway, Sevierville
(865) 428-2009, (800) 652-2611
www.oakhavenresort.com

Oak Haven is easily accessible from Interstate 40 and Tennessee Highway 66 (less than 6 miles from the interstate), but it still offers its guests a fair amount of seclusion with decent mountain views. The property includes 100 one- to seven-bedroom log cabins, each equipped with a hot tub, whirlpool bath, full kitchen, gas grill, DVD player, and TV/VCR/stereo combination. Most also have game rooms. An outdoor pool is available to all guests, along with a community game room with arcade. Housekeeping service is included in the rate. A day spa recently opened here, as well, and you'll find more than 2 miles of walking trails on site.

Douglas Lake is only 5 miles away, and Eagles Landing Golf Course is next door (see the chapters on Parks and Recreation and Golf for more details about both). Several golfing packages are available.

ECHOTA RESORT
110 Echota Way, Sevierville
(865) 428-5151, (800) 766-5437
www.echotaresort.com

More than 60 fairly new but rustic log cabins and a central amenities area make up this resort just a few miles from downtown Sevierville. The one- to four-bedroom cabins feature vaulted ceilings, private hot tubs, kitchens with dishwashers and microwaves, washers and dryers, satellite TV, and gas grills. On-site amenities include a multipurpose clubhouse, swimming pool, and lighted tennis courts. Eagles Landing Golf Course and Douglas Lake are both a short drive away.

If you're in a matrimonial mind-set, Echota is also a wedding provider (see the Weddings chapter). Wedding packages are available to guests, and services can be performed in the clubhouse or even in guest cabins.

THE RESORT AT GOVERNOR'S CROSSING
225 Collier Drive Sevierville
(865) 429-0500; 1-800-497-5749
www.governorscrossing.net

This resort is definitely a trendsetter—it added a 10,000-square-foot indoor water park (open only for guests) at the end of 2007 that offers an "endless" pool with a jet so you can swim in place against the current for fun or for fitness, two "cyclone" tunnel slides that loop outside the building and then deposit you back in the pool inside, and a kids area (among other amenities). The outdoor pool features a 250-foot lazy river, a hot tub, and a kiddie pool.

More than 150 of the resort's 165 condos are available for rental, including studios as well as one-, two- and three-bedroom units. All of the units have full kitchens, and the studio queens have washers and dryers. Most of the units have balconies, and the penthouse units also have fireplaces. The resort also has a fitness center and a game room.

HIDDEN MOUNTAIN RESORT
475 Apple Valley Road, Sevierville
(865) 453-9850, (800) 541-6837
www.hiddenmountain.com

More than 300 cabins, cottages, and villas make up this sprawling resort community, which gives quick access to Sevierville and Pigeon Forge. Hidden Mountain is divided into two main areas. The west section is made up exclusively of cabins, while Hidden Mountain East comprises cabins, Music Mountain Villas, and Old Home Place Cottages (as well as a brand-new Class-A motor coach resort called The Dell). In-unit amenities vary from property to property. Both the east and west sections have swimming pools, and Hidden Mountain East also has a clubhouse and exercise room. Summer Smith, the daughter of the resort's owners, runs the Tin Roof Café just down the street (see the Restaurants chapter).

PIGEON FORGE AND WEARS VALLEY

RIVERSTONE RESORT
212 Dollywood Lane, Pigeon Forge
(865) 908-0660, (866) 908-0660
www.riverstoneresort.com

This resort, which opened in spring of 2007, is quite simply a treat. This luxury condominium unit was designed by the folks who created the Atlantis resort in the Bahamas and Disney's Old Key West Resort. The resort offers one- to four-bedroom condos complete with flat-screen TVs, stone fireplaces, covered patios, kitchens with granite countertops and stainless steel appliances, and walk-in closets. Some have whirlpool tubs.

RiverStone also has a full-service spa, an indoor/outdoor pool complex (with hot tub and a 300-foot lazy river), a playground, a 2,000-square-foot fitness center, and a game room that includes billiards and air hockey. Outside, a walking trail follows the Pigeon River. The Gatlinburg Golf Course is right next door. (Ask about spa and golf packages.) To get there, take a left at light #8. Go 2 blocks, drive over a small bridge, and you'll see the resort on the right.

MIDDLECREEK VALLEY CHALET VILLAGE
Kimble Overnight Rentals
3346 Parkway, Pigeon Forge
(865) 429-0090, (866) 710-1323
www.mvchalets.com

This 44-acre property offers 13 wooded units, both cabins and chalets, for rent. The units vary widely, and they range from having just a single bedroom to having almost more than you can count (two have 14 bedrooms and one has 17). All have full kitchens, and some have hot tubs. The complex features a heated pool, gas grills, a playground, a sand volleyball court, horseshoes, gazebos, walking trails, and a pavilion with picnic tables. The village also has a large conference center and is perfect for groups of up to 400.

ALPINE MOUNTAIN VILLAGE RESORT
Cabin Fever Vacations
2529 Sand Pike Boulevard, Pigeon Forge
908-1919; 866-342-2246)
www.alpinemountainvillage.com

Alpine Mountain Village offers 60 cabins, more than 40 of which are on the rental program. They range from one- to six-bedroom units, sleeping up to 24. All of the units have hot tubs and grills, and many have fireplaces. Some also have home theaters with surround sound. Pool tables and air hockey are common here, and some cabins also offer ping-pong tables and arcade games. The complex features a wedding chapel (seating 35), a playground, an outdoor pool, and a picnic area with a pavilion.

Alpine Mountain Village sits just five minutes off the parkway, but the wooded resort has a secluded feel and is away from all the hustle and bustle of town. The turnoff to the village itself is from traffic light #1, while you'd turn off at traffic light #3 to get to Cabin Fever to pick up the keys.

GREAT OUTDOOR RENTALS
1198 Wears Valley Road, Pigeon Forge
(865) 429-7878, (800) 720-6978
www.greatoutdoorrentals.com

Great Outdoor Rentals offers 80 units throughout the Smokies Corridor—including units in Wears Valley, Pigeon Forge (including some close to Dollywood), and Gatlinburg's Arts and Crafts Community. Rentals range from fairly simple to simply elegant and have anywhere from one to four bedrooms, sleeping from two to 16 people. Some have great views, quite a few have game rooms and pool tables, and almost all have hot tubs. Some have swimming pool access, as well, and some have fishing ponds. Many of the cabins are also pet friendly.

Be sure to ask about discounts and seasonal packages. Year-round savings include a free night when you pay for either five nights or six nights, and repeat customers always get 10 percent off their next stay (excluding holidays). Active military members also receive a 10 percent discount with valid military ID. Among the more fun packages is the romance package, which includes candy, flowers, dinner, and a show for $99. All guests can purchase discounted attraction tickets (including a two-day Dollywood ticket for the price of one day).

COVE MOUNTAIN RESORTS
3202 Wears Valley Road, Sevierville
(865) 429-5577, (800) 245-2683
www.covemountain.com
Cove Mountain offers 220 rental cabins in and around the beautiful Wears Valley community (which is about 10 miles southwest of Pigeon Forge, even though the company has a Sevierville address) in your choice of mountain, forest, or river settings. The cabins have anywhere from one to 11 bedrooms, most featuring a hot tub, gas grill, washer and dryer, cable or satellite TV, and VCR. The properties are just a few miles away from the hustle and bustle of Pigeon Forge, while also offering easy access to Townsend, Cades Cove, and a back entrance to the national park.

EAGLES RIDGE RESORT AND CABIN RENTALS
2740 Florence Drive, Pigeon Forge
(865) 453-2220, (800) 807-4343
www.eaglesridge.com
Eagles Ridge is a centralized village consisting of approximately 150 log cabins and chalets just 1 mile off the Parkway in Pigeon Forge. The accommodations range from one- to nine-bedroom units featuring kitchens, fireplaces, hot tubs, whirlpool baths, and outdoor grills. Common amenities include a swimming pool and clubhouse. Eagles Ridge offers golf and honeymoon packages and can coordinate catering services with area restaurants.

LAUREL CREST RESORT
2628 Laurel Crest Lane, Pigeon Forge
(865) 428-8570
www.bluegreenonline.com
Nearly 300 villas and townhomes with flexible layouts and lots of amenities make up this Pigeon Forge resort, located just a couple of miles from

the Parkway off Wears Valley Road. The villas are one-bedroom units featuring well-equipped kitchens and entertainment centers. The deluxe units have whirlpool tubs and fireplaces, as well. All units have sleeper sofas that increase the sleeping capacity to four people. You can also combine one-bedroom and one-bedroom deluxe layouts to create a two-bedroom configuration that can sleep eight.

The one-bedroom townhomes sleep up to four and have basically the same amenities as the villas, plus washers and dryers. The two-bedroom town-homes feature an upstairs master bedroom suite and can accommodate up to six guests. Both can be combined into a three-bedroom unit that sleeps up to 10 people.

Clubhouse amenities at Laurel Crest include heated indoor and outdoor pools, whirlpool hot tubs, an exercise facility, sauna, game room, and reading lounge. Staff coordinators also plan activity programs for children and teens.

i Buying rental property? In Sevierville, Pigeon Forge, and Gatlinburg, you can vote on local issues if your primary residence is in Tennessee. If you're from out of state, the laws vary from town to town. In Pittman Center, however, vacation home owners may vote no matter where they're from. Outside city limits, owners of second homes generally can't vote here.

GATLINBURG

GATLINBURG CHALET RENTALS
201 Parkway, Gatlinburg
(865) 436-5104, (800) 359-1661
www.gatlinburgchalets.com
The company's rental office has the advantage of being one of the first you encounter as you enter the heart of Gatlinburg from the north on U.S. Highway 441. Their inventory of rental property includes more than 80 chalets and cabins located within 5 miles of downtown. Amenities vary, but include saunas, game rooms, hot tubs, whirlpool baths, fireplaces, and fully equipped kitchens. Units have from one to seven bedrooms.

MOUNTAIN VISTA LUXURY RENTALS (BASKENS CREEK CONDOMINIUMS)

215 Woliss Lane, Gatlinburg
(865) 430-7550, (866) 430-7550
www.mvlr.com

Mountain Vista offers 58 two-bedroom suites and two three-bedroom suites in Baskens Creek. Each has covered balconies, gas fireplaces, vaulted ceilings, free high-speed Internet, and great mountain views. Master suites have double whirlpool tubs. Resort amenities include an outdoor pool, fitness center, business center, and covered parking. The Gatlinburg trolley stops at the front entrance, although the units are also within walking distance of downtown.

Mountain Vista also offers a separate three-story rental property called Mountain Lookout (above Ripley's Aquarium) that has five king bedrooms, five bathrooms, two double whirlpool tubs, three balconies, an outdoor Jacuzzi, game room, and three fireplaces.

THE HIGHLANDS CONDOMINIUM RENTALS

855 Campbell Lead Road, Gatlinburg
(865) 436-3547, (800) 233-3947
www.highlandscondos.com

The Highlands' location gives it the illusion of being cut off from everything (it's bordered on three sides by the national park), but it's actually just off the Gatlinburg Bypass, making it convenient to both downtown and the park. Guests can choose from 77 one-, two-, and three-bedroom condominium units (all with great views facing the national park), all managed by the Highlands on their five-acre site. Each unit comes with a native-stone fireplace, whirlpool bath, kitchen, and private balcony. On-site amenities include two swimming pools, sundeck, sauna, indoor and outdoor hot tubs, and an exercise room. Look for Ober Gatlinburg's aerial tramway, which passes by regularly.

SKI MOUNTAIN CHALETS AND CONDOS

416 Ski Mountain Road, Gatlinburg
(865) 436-7846, (800) 824-4077
www.skimtnchalets.com

You'll find this rental company as you start driving up Mount Harrison (which the locals call Ski Mountain) on Ski Mountain Road. About 100 one-to six-bedroom properties are included on its rental program, all of which are within 4 miles of downtown. The units come with fully furnished kitchens, TVs and VCRs, and barbecue grills. Some have hot tubs, whirlpools, washers and dryers, game areas, and stereos.

MOUNTAIN LAUREL CHALETS

440 Ski Mountain Road, Gatlinburg
(865) 436-5277, (800) 315-4965
www.mtnlaurelchalets.com

This real estate and rental company offers nearly 150 chalets and cabins (ranging from one- to 12-bedroom) that are all located on Ski Mountain and are anywhere from 1/2 mile to 4 miles from the main office. Because Ski Mountain Road meets downtown Gatlinburg at the south end of the city, many of Mountain Laurel's properties provide fairly quick access to the national park. They're also convenient to Ober Gatlinburg.

CHALET VILLAGE PROPERTIES

1441 Wiley Oakley Drive, Gatlinburg
(865) 436-6800, (800) 262-7684
www.chaletvillage.com

Perched along the east face of Ski Mountain (about halfway to the top), the Chalet Village section of Gatlinburg boasts some of the most memorable views in town. The village itself is a collection of chalets and condominiums built mostly on steep, wooded sites. They're connected by Ski Mountain Road, the main thoroughfare to the top of Ski Mountain, and a mind-boggling network of hilly, curvy side roads. All but the most adroit of navigators will need a map to find their way among the maze, but the views make the trip well worth the effort.

More than 100 units in the Chalet Village area are on Chalet Village Properties' rental program. Well-equipped kitchens, whirlpool tubs, cable TV, charcoal grills, fireplaces, balconies, decks, and porches are standard among the properties' features. Units have anywhere from one to 12 bedrooms. Be aware that guests planning to stay from December through March are advised to use a four-wheel-drive vehicle or have snow chains available for travel up the mountain. In recent years, however, snowfall has been less than average, and driving up Ski Mountain Road has not been a hazardous venture.

MOUNTAINLOFT RESORT
110 Mountain Loft Drive, Gatlinburg
(865) 436-4367, (800) 456-0009
www.bluegreenonline.com
This resort lies just off US 321, only a couple of miles from downtown Gatlinburg. The same corporation that runs Laurel Crest Resort in Pigeon Forge owns MountainLoft, and you'll find similar configurations of one- and two-bedroom villas and one-, two-, and three-bedroom townhomes here. Refer to the Laurel Crest write-up in the Pigeon Forge section of this chapter for detailed descriptions of the various layouts and amenities available. MountainLoft, however, also has two-bedroom chalets with lofts that sleep up to eight. The chalets have amenities similar to those in the villas and townhomes.

At the clubhouse, you'll find indoor and outdoor pools, hot tubs, an exercise room, sauna, and game room. Hiking trails are located nearby, and the resort provides nightly security service. With MountainLoft's Courtesy Vacation Planning, staff members help plan activities like golfing, fishing, and rafting trips, horseback riding, and ski trips. The resort also plans activities specifically for children and teens as well as adults.

STONY BROOK CHALETS
1663 East Parkway, Gatlinburg
(865) 436-7428, (800) 633-5652
www.stonybrooklodging.com
Stony Brook manages about 40 cabins and chalets located throughout Gatlinburg—ranging from the Ski Mountain area to US 321 between Gatlinburg and Cosby. Accommodations are as small as one-bedroom units that sleep only two and go as large as six-bedroom homes that can handle up to 26. Amenities vary, but all have hot tubs. Many have grand views and quite a few are pet-friendly.

GREENBRIER VALLEY RESORTS
3629 East Parkway, Gatlinburg
(865) 436-2015, (800) 546-1144
www.cobblynob.com
You'll have to travel a little out of your way to get to Greenbrier Valley Resorts in Cobbly Nob, but the properties you'll find there offer quality accommodations in a peaceful, secluded notch of the county, well removed from all the hurly-burly of Gatlinburg and Pigeon Forge. This company is approximately 11 miles from downtown Gatlinburg on US 321 and has about 75 properties, including log cabins and chalets.

Units have from one to 11 bedrooms and amenities that include fireplaces, hot tubs, TVs, stereos, washers and dryers, barbecue grills, and well-outfitted kitchens. Pets are welcome. Guests have full use of the tennis courts and three swimming pools at the Village of Cobbly Nob, the residential community in which Greenbrier's properties are located. Most of Greenbrier's properties offer views of the Smokies or of Bent Creek Golf Course, adjacent to Cobbly Nob (see the Golf chapter).

i Most rental companies require that you book a minimum of two nights, but if you've got your sights set on a one-night stay, check to see if your rental office has an odd night that they need to fill between other reservations. They won't pass up the chance to book it if you're otherwise dead-set against a longer stay.

DEER RIDGE MOUNTAIN RESORT
3710 Weber Road, Gatlinburg
(865) 436-2325, (877) 333-7743
www.deerridge.com
If views are your thing, this scenic vacation resort won't disappoint. Located 12 miles from downtown Gatlinburg, just off US 321, Deer Ridge sits high atop a foothill peak with views of mountains that are so close they take your attention hostage. A little more than 80 one-, two-, and three-bedroom condominium units are available on-site, all having sleeper sofas and some having lofts. Each unit comes with a wood-burning fire-

place, TV, VCR, two phones with data ports, and a fully equipped kitchen.

Clubhouse amenities include indoor and outdoor pools, sundeck, hot tub, sauna, steam room, lighted tennis court, game room, and video rentals. The resort's playground area features a children's playhouse, swings, half-size basketball court, volleyball area, picnic tables, grills, and a covered pavilion. Bent Creek Golf Course is less than 2 miles from Deer Ridge at the bottom of the hill. The resort offers its guests golf packages as well as discount tickets for Dollywood.

CAMPGROUNDS AND RV PARKS

Maybe it's the pioneer spirit of our forefathers, but for many Americans, camping is simply in the blood. Sitting around a campfire, sleeping under the stars, and maybe even listening to a babbling brook nearby can make for a memorable family vacation. And there's no better place for any of that than the Great Smoky Mountains.

Most of the campgrounds and RV parks described here are listed in order as they appear along the Smokies Corridor in a north-to-south progression, starting at exit 407 on Interstate 40. Diversions will run away from the Parkway in whatever direction they occur.

From this point forward, the term *campground* will denote any commercial or government-operated facility that rents space for a temporary shelter that you bring with you. Several of the campgrounds will actually rent you a trailer, and they'll be handled individually.

Naturally, Great Smoky Mountains National Park itself is a camper's paradise, and four of its campgrounds that are contiguous to the Smokies Corridor are outlined here in detail in the last section of this chapter.

RULES OF THUMB

The commercial campgrounds tend to provide creature comforts that hook up to your portable home. Unless otherwise stated, you can expect 30- to 50-amp electrical service at all permanent sites, and most also have cable TV. Water and sewer hookups are common, and those that are more than 5 miles from a downtown area usually have well-stocked stores and well-maintained on-site recreational facilities. Swimming pools are as commonplace at campgrounds as they are at hotels, and laundry facilities are also usually available. Public bathrooms with showers are pretty standard, particularly in those facilities that feature separate tenting areas.

One of the true advantages of RV-type travel is the ability to bring your pets along. Unless specified otherwise, all of the campgrounds in the area (including those in the national park) permit pets on leashes.

Because facilities and prices vary based on several factors (convenience to the bright lights is foremost), prices are included for each campground, based on a single camping space for two people in a single camping unit. (A separate fee averaging less than $5 is charged for vehicles in tow.) Unless

stated, all prices quoted are plus tax. Additional-person charges run between $3 and $4 for everyone over five years old. Most campgrounds also will give you a seventh night free when you reserve and pay for a six-night stay in advance. It's also safe to assume that major credit cards are accepted unless specifically stated otherwise.

Most of the campgrounds are affiliated with national associations or publications. The competition is fierce, and you are the beneficiary. Expect immaculate surroundings, except in places that cater to the more seasoned "primitive" camper, and don't be afraid to mention problems or shortcomings to the management.

RESERVATIONS

Like any other lodging facilities in the Smokies, campgrounds are at their peak from early April through October, and reservations couldn't hurt. If you plan to be in the area at peak times like July, August, or October, reservations are highly recommended. If you're a seasoned trailer traveler, you know when your fellow RVers are on the road. Cancellations are normally accepted with seven days' notice required for a full refund of deposits.

SEVIERVILLE

Sevierville campgrounds fall into two categories—along the main corridor or in the vicinity of Douglas Dam Park, a TVA facility about five miles east of Tennessee Highway 66. (See the Parks and Recreation chapter for more on Douglas Dam Park.) Those along the corridor are described first, followed by the Douglas Dam facilities.

RIPPLIN' WATERS CAMPGROUND AND RENTAL CABINS

1930 Winfield Dunn Parkway, Sevierville
(865) 453-4169, (888) 747-7546
www.ripplinwatersrv.com
Right on the highway about midway between I-40 and downtown Sevierville, Ripplin' Waters is convenient to just about everything and a short walk from a couple of antiques malls and amusements. This campground is on a level plain with the Little Pigeon River at its back. Its 155 RV sites have full hookups, and you can fish directly from the riverside sites. A full hookup site is $26 to $29 per night ($28 to $31 for riverside sites), and four furnished cabins are available at $75 per night for two, plus $5 per person for anyone older than three. Ripplin' Waters is open year-round and offers monthly rental rates.

> **i** Off-season rates for park model trailers and cabins can sometimes be negotiated to a figure low enough to make it worthwhile for you to leave your trailer home and still come to the Smokies and live in the style you're accustomed to enjoying.

RIVER PLANTATION RV PARK

1004 Parkway, Sevierville
(865) 429-5267, (800) 758-5267
www.riverplantationrv.com
Just south of downtown Sevierville, River Plantation has more than 250 total sites, with 200 full hookups. Eight cabins are also available. A quiet walking trail along the Little Pigeon River provides a nice view of the mountains in the distance. All sites have full hookups and range from $30.50 to $49.50 in season. Cabins with kitchen

and bathroom are $74 per night in season. Special consideration is given for groups to provide adjacent sites around the pavilion.

DOUGLAS DAM

When the Tennessee Valley Authority dammed up east Tennessee's rivers to provide electric power, they also created a bunch of pretty cool lakes that became vacation spots in their own right. One such place is Douglas Dam in northeast Sevier County, where the TVA improved the situation by building a park around the dam. Several campgrounds also sprang up in the area.

First, a word of warning: There are two roads named Douglas Dam Road. Both go east off TN 66 (about 4 miles apart), and they merge in Douglas Dam Park. The northern version is Tennessee Highway 139, and it enters the park below Douglas Dam. The southern road, Tennessee Highway 338, is about 2 miles outside of Sevierville, and it's the one you should take to get to the campgrounds in this section. TN 338 stays above the dam until it crosses the French Broad River right in front of the dam and merges with TN 139.

MOUNTAIN COVE MARINA & RV PARK

1590 Dyke Road, Sevierville
(865) 453-3506
www.mountaincovemarina.com
The only commercial campground actually on Douglas Lake, this campground is adjacent to a full-service marina and has about 71 full hookup sites (including sewer) at $35 a night (for two adults and two kids) and one water/electric site for $30. The campground is within easy walking distance of a public park and has its own boat launch. Well-placed signage guides you into the campground from Douglas Dam Road, a little more than 5 miles from TN 66.

DOUGLAS LAKE CAMPGROUNDS

Douglas Dam Park, Sevierville
(800) 882-5263
www.tva.com/river/recreation/camping.htm
This listing is actually for two separate camp-

grounds in the park that operate under identical rules. The headwater campground is on the lakeshore right at the dam and has 65 sites (plus a swimming beach, and walking trails), while the tailwater camp on the French Broad River directly under the dam has 62 sites (plus a bait and tackle shop). Public restrooms are adjacent to both campgrounds, and both have boat ramps and wildlife viewing areas.

Both are self-service campgrounds, so to establish a campsite at either spot, find a campsite, fill out the form provided at the entrance, and drop the completed form with payment in the deposit vault at the entrance within 30 minutes of arrival. Campsites are $20 a night with hookups, and $16 a night without hookups. Holders of Golden Age or Golden Access passports receive a 50 percent discount on rates. Credit cards are not accepted, but personal checks are. The campsites are patrolled by TVA rangers, who also monitor the deposit vaults.

PIGEON FORGE

The campgrounds in Pigeon Forge are set in clustered groups at both ends of the city, with a couple of exceptions. The first group is spread along 2 miles of Wears Valley Road (Tennessee Highway 321)—turn right at traffic light #3. The Wears Valley Road campgrounds are all on the south (left) side going away from the Parkway, and all have camping sites and picnic facilities on Walden's Creek, which forms the back boundary of all of them. The rest are at the southern end of town, and all are within sight of or a short walk from the Parkway.

CLABOUGH'S CAMPGROUND
405 Wears Valley Road, Pigeon Forge
(865) 428-1951, (800) 965-8524
www.claboughcampground.com
A half a mile from the Parkway, Clabough's is actually two campgrounds bisected by a city street. The 320 full-hookup sites here include 15 along Walden's Creek, and the fees range from $33 to $37 in high season. The campground is large enough for two swimming pools, and it also

includes a game room arcade, three laundries, and a playground.

The campground is situated far enough off the road to provide seclusion from the traffic, and for convenience, the campground also offers an on-site grocery store/gas station/deli. The Pigeon Forge Fun Time trolley stops at the entrance to Clabough's as well as inside the campground.

KING'S HOLLY HAVEN RV PARK
647 Wears Valley Road, Pigeon Forge
(865) 453-5352, (888) 204-0247
www.hollyhavenrvpark.com
More like a city of temporary shelters than anything else, King's has been a family-owned operation since the 11-acre park was part of a farm purchased by the family in 1928. King's is open year-round, with special activities during the summer season. The Friday night gospel sing in the pavilion is a local tradition. Full-hookup rates vary from $22 to $32, depending on the time of year. Monthly rates are available on request.

EAGLE'S NEST CAMPGROUND
1111 Wears Valley Road, Pigeon Forge
(865) 428-5841, (800) 892-2714
www.eaglesnestcampground.com
Eagle's Nest is open year-round and its 200-plus sites feature extra-wide spaces for units with slide-out rooms or awnings. Seasonal rates are $30.00 to $32.50 (slightly higher in October) for full hookup, $29.00 for water and electric service, and $26.00 for tent spaces. Off-season rates are lower. The campground also offers nine air-conditioned cabins from April to mid-October that include a small refrigerator. Cabin rates are available on request.

PIGEON FORGE KOA CAMPGROUND
3122 Veterans Boulevard, Pigeon Forge
(865) 453-7903, (800) 562-7703
www.pigeonforgekoa.com
Opened in what was really an out-of-the-way location in the 1960s, KOA is now the campground nearest to downtown Pigeon Forge. Nearly 200 trailer/tent sites and 15 "Kamping Kabins" are arranged near and along the west

prong of the Little Pigeon River, with the business district on the other side. KOA is open April through November, with rates varying from $32 for a primitive site to $80 for a full hookup. The cabins rent for $55 to $60 for a single room unit and $65 to $70 for a two-roomer. The central location and KOA's long history make advance reservations highly recommended. In addition to the heated pool, hot tub, game room, and playground, this campground also offers a fitness center.

The following two campgrounds are west (turn right) of the Parkway at traffic light #10. Following these descriptions, the listings will return to the Parkway and pick up a sizable group on the east side.

SHADY OAKS CAMPGROUND
210 Conner Heights Road, Pigeon Forge
(865) 453-3276
www.shadyoakscampgroundpigeon forge.com
About a half-mile up Conner Heights Road, Shady Oaks is one of Pigeon Forge's older camping facilities. Built by the Graham family in 1969, the campground is filled with shade trees that have grown up around the 107 sites. Although campers feel as though they're way out in the woods, the Pigeon Forge trolley makes an appearance every 20 minutes or so, providing an easy connection to downtown. The year-round campground offers 87 full-hookup sites and 23 large tent sites for $30 a night. Shady Oaks also has two-bedroom cabins that sleep six to eight, with air conditioning, TV, and full bathroom ($25 a night for two, plus $5 for each additional person), as well as smaller, more rustic camping cabins that sleep four, with air-conditioning and refrigerators but not bathrooms ($40 per night).

MILL CREEK RESORT & CAMPGROUND
449 West Mill Creek Road, Pigeon Forge
(865) 428-3498
www.mcresort.com
The sprawling layout of the Mill Creek Resort makes for easy access to its 85 sites, available

year-round for $32.50 per night, with tax. Eighteen park model trailers and five log cabins, each designed for a maximum of six people, rent for $85 a night for up to four people ($5 for each additional person) when you can get them—there's usually a waiting list in midsummer and October. The mountain view is splendid, and the back road access to Pigeon Forge is a real asset in the peak season. The campground offers worship services on Sundays and free Bible School for children in the summer.

To get there from Sevierville, after stop light #8 in Pigeon Forge, make a right onto West Mill Creek Road. The campground is 3/4 mile on the left.

The last leg of Pigeon Forge campgrounds is so jammed together at the southern extremity of the city that the unsuspecting traveler might assume they're all one really huge campground. Despite the different addresses, it is actually possible to drive from the Twin Mountain RV Park through the middle of Riveredge RV Park and into Foothills RV Park without going on another street. Alpine Hideaway Campground is at the southern end of the line and is set back off the Parkway.

TWIN MOUNTAIN RV PARK & CAMPGROUND
304 Day Springs Road, Pigeon Forge
(865) 453-8181, (800) 848-9097
www.twinmountainrvpark.com
Twin Mountain has an interesting choice of 120 sites, equally divided among the riverside, the woods, and the center of the park. Twin Mountain is open year-round, with rates ranging from $34 for center sites to $38 for riverside sites during the peak season. Sites are $24 to $32 a night December through March and range from $26 to $32, depending on location, in April, May, and November. In addition to a swimming pool, this campground also offers tennis and basketball court.

If you're southbound on the Parkway in Pigeon Forge, the best way to get directly into Twin Mountain is off South River Road, a block east of the Parkway, before you get to traffic light #10. If you're northbound, go through the traffic light and take Golf Drive, the third street to the right. This will keep you from driving through another campground to find your spot.

RIVEREDGE RV PARK & LOG CABIN RENTALS
4220 Huskey Street, Pigeon Road
(865) 453-5813, (800) 477-1205
www.stayriveredge.com

The entrance to Riveredge is right at traffic light #10 on the Parkway, right before the entrance to the national park. The resort itself is separated from the Parkway by the Little Pigeon River and a whole lot of trees.

Landscaped campsites in the woods and along the river—175 of them—belie the convenience to all of Pigeon Forge's attractions, and the on-site arcade is an attraction in its own right. Complete hookups are $38 a night from April through December and $27 a night from January through March. Twenty-one cozy camping cabins with full-size beds and bunk beds run $48 for two people during the season ($4.50 per additional person over four years old) and $35 on the off-season. For the ultimate in roughing it, Riveredge offers seven one- and two-bedroom cabins with all the amenities, including gas fireplaces and Jacuzzis. These cabins rent for $125 per night, with a $12 charge per additional guest over 13 years old. In off-season, these cabins run $75 weekdays and $99 on weekends.

i Most of the campgrounds that have campfire facilities also have or provide firewood. Check with your operator before foraging for something to burn.

FOOTHILLS RV PARK & CABINS
4235 Huskey Street, Pigeon Forge
(865) 428-3818
www.foothillsrvparkandcabins.com

A quiet, comfortable, family atmosphere prevails at Foothills RV Park, tucked in the woods less than 100 yards from the Parkway. Its 38 full-hookup sites on shady level ground are complemented by 21 log cabins with great views of the mountains, as well as smaller A-frame cabins and rustic camping cabins.

Foothills is open from April through October, with sites renting for $29 a night. The one-room cabins have heating and air-conditioning, cable TV, microwaves, refrigerators, outdoor charcoal grills, and picnic tables, and some also have covered porches with rocking chairs. They start at $30 and go up to $75 a night for two people. The camping cabins are $40. Downtown Pigeon Forge is less than a mile up the Parkway, and the trolley stops at the office.

ALPINE HIDEAWAY CAMPGROUND & RV PARK
251 Spring Valley Road, Pigeon Forge
(865) 428-3285
www.alpinehideawaycampgroundandrv.com

Just off the Parkway at the extreme southern end of Pigeon Forge, Alpine has a full spectrum of camping options, including 76 full-hookup RV sites, 13 camping cabins, one park model trailer, a pair of two-bedroom cottages, and three primitive tent sites. Although it's just 400 feet off the parkway, its location at the end of town gives Alpine a secluded feel.

Alpine is open March through September. Full-hookup trailer sites are $29.95 a night, while tent sites with water and electric service are $20. The park model trailer is furnished with one queen and one sofa bed (bring your own linens) at $500 a month, and the fully furnished two-bedroom cottages can sleep up to eight people for $75 (bring your own linens). Additional people in the park model trailer and cottages are free. The 13 camping cabins each have a double bed and two twin beds and will sleep four people comfortably. Air-conditioning and cable TV are included, but linens aren't. Nightly rental is $35 to $55 for two adults.

i Be sure to read the rules posted in your campground (and often printed on the campground map) and honor the quiet hours—your neighbors will appreciate it!

GATLINBURG

Again, the older, more established lodging places in the Gatlinburg area are generally more independent than you'll find in Pigeon Forge and Sevierville. In fact, every campground that's actually within the city limits is independently owned. As you move east out of town on East Parkway/ US 321N (the only direction where you can find commercial campgrounds), some larger camp-grounds with franchise affiliations pop up. The last campground in this section is actually in Cosby, which is in Cocke County. It's included in the Gatlinburg section because it's on the same road as every property east of the city. Great Smoky Mountains National Park also has a camp-ground at Cosby, and it's covered in the next section of this chapter.

TWIN CREEK RV RESORT
1202 East Parkway, Gatlinburg
(865) 436-7081, (800) 252-8077
www.twincreekrvresort.com

The highest-rated RV park in the state of Ten-nessee, upscale Twin Creek is tucked into the foothills just off East Parkway. The park is open from mid-March through November (after the Christmas parade) and allows no tents on its large 85-space property. Every RV site is paved, with its own deck and fire ring. The resort is heavily wooded and beautifully landscaped and features a game arcade and a Sunday morning worship service.

Site rental ranges from $46 to $50 for two, based on location. Twin Creek's two one-bed-room-with-loft cabins run $100 per night. Given the park's secluded setting, it's hard to believe downtown Gatlinburg is merely 2 miles away. It's just a quick trip on the blue trolley, which runs by the campground.

CAMPING IN THE SMOKIES— GATLINBURG RV PARK
1640 East Parkway, Gatlinburg
(865) 430-3594
www.gatlinburg.com/campinginthesmokies

This RV park located within the boundaries of the world-famous Great Smoky Arts & Crafts Com-munity opened in 1966 on a flat space alongside Little Dudley Creek that's not quite as secluded as it used to be. Still, Camping in the Smokies— Gatlinburg RV Park provides a lot of privacy. Its 53 full-service sites are convenient to the highway

and Little Dudley Creek. The blue trolley stops right in front of the campground. Gatlinburg is 3 1/2 miles to the left, and the biggest golf commu-nity in the county is about 10 miles to the right. Open April through October, the park offers sites with full hookups that rent for $31.95 to $47.95 per night. Tent sites with water, electric and cable are $18.95 to $29.95 a night.

GREENBRIER ISLAND CAMPGROUND
2353 East Parkway, Gatlinburg
(865) 436-4243

Greenbrier Island is exactly what it says it is: an island campground in the pristine middle prong of the Little Pigeon River. It isn't being immodest when it claims to be the "best campground in town"—it's the only one in the town of Pittman Center. Greenbrier Island offers 48 full-hookup RV spaces for $30 a night, 36 water/electric spaces for $28, and 38 primitive campsites for $26 each. "Flint Rock," the swimming hole at the north end of the campground, has been a favorite of locals for generations. The entrance to the camp-ground is a short distance off East Parkway on Pittman Center Road (Tennessee Highway 416), 6 miles from traffic light #3 in Gatlinburg. The campground is open April through October.

OUTDOOR RESORTS OF AMERICA
4229 East Parkway, Gatlinburg
(865) 436-5861, (800) 677-5861
www.outdoor-resorts.com

The largest facility in the southern section of Sevier County, Outdoor Resorts is a "condo" campground (for lack of a better description), offering permanent sites for members' trailers and RVs, overnight sites for public rental, and fully furnished rental trailers. Sites with and without trailers are also available for sale to interested campers. The facility's 376 sites include more than 100 along the banks of Webb's Creek and 32 around the lake in the center of the resort. Two swimming pools complement the full spectrum of recreational facilities. A nondenominational church service is held Sunday mornings in season at 11. Trailer space rents for $40 to $45 a night for a family of four during the season, or for $35 in

November through April. Rental trailers run from $75 to $80 per night, with some restrictions and deposit requirements.

ADVENTURE BOUND CAMPING RESORTS AT GATLINBURG
4609 East Parkway, Gatlinburg
(865) 436-5653, (800) 528-9003
www.abgatlinburg.com

Centrally located for both east- and west-flowing traffic, Adventure Bound is 12 miles from downtown Gatlinburg and 15 miles from the Wilton Springs exit (exit 440) on I-40. The Foothills Parkway exit (exit 443) is closer yet, but not recommended for towed loads.

Adventure Bound has 212 camping sites about evenly divided between full hookup and water/electric, and 14 cabins in various configurations. To accommodate a usually high population, Adventure Bound has three laundries, three bathhouses, a private trout pond, and a 500-foot waterslide. The Jack Tales Theater, at the back of the park, is a long-standing local favorite and will give campers and their families a chance to act in a series of plays adapted from fairy tales and local legends. Adventure Bound is open from April through November. Peak season is June through August and October.

Full-hookup sites are $30 to $47 per night, and water/electric sites are $28 to $39. Full hookup 50 amp sites range from $37 to $49. Camping cabins with heat and air-conditioning as well as small refrigerators sleep six for $52 to $69. The one-room Tennessee Cabin sleeps four and is $72 to $99 a night. Seven one-bedroom log cabins with all the amenities sleep up to four occupants for $82 to $109. Two deluxe cabins with two bedrooms each (sleeping a maximum of six) cost $92 to $139 for two adults.

i If you're towing a trailer or driving a large vehicle, avoid the Dudley Creek and Bishop Lane bypasses in Gatlinburg. Both are steep and curvy, with long downhill approaches to a usually busy US 321.

SMOKY BEAR CAMPGROUND
4857 East Parkway, Gatlinburg
(865) 436-8372, (800) 850-8372
www.smokybearcampground.com

Smoky Bear is set on a large knoll 15 miles east of Gatlinburg. Forty-six good-size sites surround a clubhouse that includes a swimming pool, public hot tub, and a playground. The owner-operators pride themselves on running a spotless operation and live on-site to provide 24-hour security. Smoky Bear opens on Easter weekend and stays open through November. RV/camper sites with full hookups run $32 to $44 a night for two adults and two children.

YOGI BEAR'S GREAT SMOKY JELLYSTONE PARK CAMP
4946 Hooper Highway, Cosby
(P.O. Box 282, Gatlinburg 37738)
(423) 487-5534, (800) 210-2119
www.greatsmokyjellystone.com

Don't let the name fool you: This isn't an amusement park. It's a campground for families who are happiest in a place where there's always something going on. Jellystone offers bingo, live entertainment, ice-cream socials, and wagon rides. Saturday night is cartoon night, and you can watch family movies on the other six nights of the week. During the high season, a local resort ministry runs a day camp here that includes games, activities, and crafts. Jellystone's backyard is Great Smoky Mountains National Park, with the popular Maddron Bald hiking trail jumping off right out of the campground. This pleasant 1-mile walk takes you to a lovely picnic grove.

Jellystone is open from mid-March through November, with 70 trailer/RV sites, three fully furnished cabins, two rustic cabins (with heat and air but no plumbing), two rustic suites (with color TVs, coffeemakers, microwaves, and half-baths), and 18 tent sites. Most of the trailer sites are on an island surrounded by the stream. Some premium sites are available that are almost twice as big as standard sites.

Streamside sites with full hookup are $37 to $57 per night, and sites with water/electric hookup are $30 to $50. Off-stream full hookup sites run $37 to $47, and off-stream sites with water/electric hookup are $29 to $33. Tent sites with water and electric service are $30 to $34, and primitive tent sites are $23 to $25. The three full cabins sleep five at $95 to $115 a night, and the rustic cabins will accommodate six for $55 to $70. The rustic suite sleeps five and costs from $70 to $95.

GREAT SMOKY MOUNTAINS NATIONAL PARK

As you might expect, Great Smoky Mountains National Park has a lot of opportunities for camping. The park service maintains 10 developed campgrounds with more than 1,100 total sites, none with hookups. The campgrounds do have restrooms with cold running water and flush toilets, but no showers. Most of the sites are accessible by RV or towed trailer. This section will list four of the 10 campgrounds in the park, including one in North Carolina. The remaining six are all some distance from the Smokies Corridor (four are in North Carolina) and are described in detail in the chapter devoted to the national park.

Only two of the campgrounds (Cades Cove in Tennessee and Smokemont in North Carolina) are open year-round, while the others close in the winter months. (Exact dates of operation vary with the individual campground and also from year to year.) Sites are limited to six people, with either two tents or one RV plus one tent permitted per site. Pets are welcome as long as they are either on a leash or otherwise contained. You can stay for up to a week during the summer and fall, or for a maximum of two weeks in the off-season. Reservations are accepted for peak season only up to six months in advance at Cades Cove, Elkmont, Cosby, and Smokemont campgrounds. To reserve, call (877) 444-6777 between 10 a.m. and 10 p.m. or visit www.recreation.gov. Otherwise, sites are available on a first-come-first-served basis. For more information and a complete list of national park campgrounds, visit the park's Web site at www.nps.gov/grsm and follow the links for camping.

The following descriptions cover the four campgrounds in the national park that are contiguous enough to be considered part of the Smokies Corridor, starting with the easternmost and moving west, then south. Check out the chapter on the park for detailed information on some of the recreational opportunities available (including junior ranger programs for kids and ranger talks and walks).

COSBY CAMPGROUND
Route 321

Set on the northeast edge of the park, Cosby campground is 2 miles off of East Parkway (US 321N), about 20 miles east of Gatlinburg. You'll find a picnic area, a 1-mile self-guided nature trail, an amphitheater for ranger programs in-season, and the trailheads for several hiking trails here, including hikes to Hen Wallow Falls and rare old-growth forest. Cosby campground is open from mid-March through October and has 165 campsites. Site rental is $14, and RV length is restricted to 25 feet. Group sites for eight to 20 people are available by reservation only and cost $26.

ELKMONT
Little River Road

Situated 9 miles southwest of Gatlinburg and 5 miles from the Sugarlands Visitor Center, Elkmont is one of the original campgrounds in the park. This is one of the larger and more popular of the park's campgrounds, and it fills up quickly in the summer. The campground features a self-guiding nature trail that's less than 1 mile long, an amphitheater for ranger programs, and a concession area that sells wood and ice as well as a variety of convenience items (including the makings for s'mores). Elkmont is open mid-March through November and has 220 single sites at $17 to $23, as well as four group sites (maximum 15 to 30 people, depending on the site) from $26 to $33, available by reservation only. The campground has a 32-foot maximum for trailers and a 35-foot maximum for motor homes.

CADES COVE

Laurel Creek Road

One of the most popular day-trip locations in the park, Cades Cove is closer to Townsend, TN, than it is to Gatlinburg or Pigeon Forge. To get there, you'll drive 27 miles from Gatlinburg on Little River Road, which turns into Laurel Creek Road. This is one of the most popular campgrounds in the park, and it offers a snack bar, a camp store, a gift shop, a large picnic area, riding stables and a new half-mile-long self-guiding nature trail.

The 11-mile, one-way Cades Cove loop drive begins just past the entrance to the campground (see the chapter on the national park for more details). You can also rent bikes here, a popular option in the summer when the loop drive is closed to cars on Wednesday and Saturday mornings. Cades Cove is also one of the best places in the park to see wildlife, and sightings of white-tailed deer along the loop road are all but guaranteed. The campground's outdoor amphi-theater and pavilion make this a favorite for large groups, so you'll want to make reservations as early as possible.

The campground is open year-round. One hundred fifty-nine sites for trailer, tent, and family camping each rent for $17 to $20. Group sites for 20 to 30 campers are available for $35 to $65. RVs are limited to 40 feet.

SMOKEMONT CAMPGROUND

U.S. Highway 441, NC

Just about the time Newfound Gap Road (US 441) levels off in its descent from the gap into North Carolina, the Smokemont campground comes into view on the north side of the road (left if you're going south out of Tennessee). The campground has an amphitheater, the base for many ranger programs in season, as well as a 3/4-mile self-guiding nature trail. Near the entrance, you'll also find riding stables (where there's a concession selling firewood and ice) and a dump station. The park's Oconaluftee Visitor Center and Pioneer Farmstead is 3 miles away, and the town of Cherokee is just beyond that.

Smokemont has 142 sites open year-round. Campsites run $17 to $20 a night. Group camp-sites handle 15 to 20 people and are available for $26 to $35, by reservation only. The campground has a 35-foot maximum for trailers and a 40-foot maximum for motor homes.

i Follow the park's strict rules about food storage and disposal, or you may find a bear in your tent. (This bear, should you come nose-to-nose with it, will most definitely not be cuddly nor will it be cute.) And yes, bears can smell food—even in coolers.

RESTAURANTS

Millions of people visit the Great Smokies every year, and every one of them must eventually answer that nagging daily question of where to eat. Fortunately, you never have to go too far to find sustenance in these mountains. It takes little more than a casual stroll down the Parkway in any of the Smokies Corridor cities to come face-to-face with enough dining options (including those serving massive portions of down-home Southern cooking) to cover your mealtime decisions for an entire week and more.

Naturally, you'll find an abundance of both fast-food and sit-down national chain restaurants, although this chapter will take you in a different direction. Some of the places highlighted here are less expensive, hole-in-the-wall cafes, while others offer more pricey, upscale dining. Some are favorite local haunts, while others are tourist "musts." What they all have in common, though, is fairly good food in a pleasant environment. (One note: the list of Gatlinburg eateries shared here stretches the envelope slightly to include some regional chains that merit inclusion because they've gone to extra effort to fit into the local picture.)

By the way, the phrase *dress code* isn't a part of the local vernacular. No matter how elegant the setting or how refined the cuisine, restaurants here don't require you to don any fancy duds. Dressing for dinner in the Smokies usually means putting on jeans instead of shorts. Most restaurants don't take reservations, either (exceptions will be noted). They simply don't need to. So just show up and put your name on a waiting list if necessary.

The subject of parking must necessarily hinge on the city you're planning to visit. If you're dining in Sevierville or Pigeon Forge, parking spots are plentiful and free. In Gatlinburg, though, you'll be more dependent on public transportation or on parking lots and garages that charge a fee. Most restaurants along Gatlinburg's Parkway have limited parking, if any at all.

Bear in mind that most places have a less expensive lunch menu as well as a reasonably priced children's menu (the cutoff age is usually between 10 and 12 years old). Unless the description below says otherwise, you can assume the restaurants here accept most major credit cards. Traveler's checks aren't a problem, but don't even bother trying to pay with a personal check drawn on an out-of-town bank.

Finally, a word about alcohol sales. Restaurants in Gatlinburg and now also in Sevierville may serve liquor by the drink. (That means it's legal, not necessarily that all restaurants in those cities choose to do so.) In Pigeon Forge, you can't order a mixed drink anywhere, although many restaurants can serve you beer or wine.

Price Code

The following code is based on the price of two entrees from the dinner menu, not including appetizers, desserts, beverages (alcoholic or otherwise), taxes, or gratuities—unless they are included with the price of an entree.

$	Less than $20
$$	$20–$35
$$$	$36–$50
$$$$	$51 and more

SEVIERVILLE

ISLAMORADA FISH COMPANY
RESTAURANT $$–$$$
3629 Outdoor Sportsmans Place, Kodak
(865) 932-5500
www.fishcompany.com

Although this restaurant is indeed part of a chain, it's notable because it's located inside of the huge Bass Pro Shop at exit 407 off Interstate 40. The restaurant offers both indoor and patio seating, not to mention a 13,000-gallon saltwater reef aquarium. Popular menu items include venison stuffed mushrooms and the hand-breaded alligator for appetizers, as well as the Islamorada Portofino blackened tilapia topped with grilled shrimp in a creamy lobster sauce.

DOUBLE PLAY CAFE $–$$
3540 Line Drive, Kodak
(865) 286-2300, (888) 978-2288
www.smokiesbaseball.com

Speaking of restaurants in unusual locations, this one is inside the Tennessee Smokies baseball stadium (just off I-40 at exit 407), right behind third base on field level. (You'll find more information about the Smokies and the stadium itself in the Attractions chapter.)

The cafe, open only during baseball games, serves an all-you-can-eat buffet that begins when the gates open and runs through the first pitch (after that, you can order appetizer-type items off the menu). The cost is $10 per person ($7 for kids), plus beverages (which includes beer on tap and by the bottle). There's a fish fry on Fridays and sandwiches on Saturdays.

NEW ORLEANS ON THE RIVER $$
2430 Winfield Dunn Parkway, Kodak
(865) 933-7244
www.neworleansotr.com

What's a five-star chef from Louisiana doing in the Smokies? Creating quite a following with his Creole masterpieces, of course. Chef George Lovell, who has trained at Paul Prudhomme's K-Paul's Louisiana Kitchen in New Orleans, dishes up such Nawlins favorites such as crawfish étouffée, red

beans and rice, and bread pudding with praline sauce. This restaurant, opened in early 2009 by owners Marion and Glenda Sheffield, is located on top of a bluff, overlooking a bend in the French Broad River. It's hard to tell which is better here, the views or the food. What's for sure is that you won't find more authentic New Orleans food anywhere else in the area.

TONY GORE'S SMOKY MOUNTAIN
BBQ AND GRILL $$–$$$
1818 Winfield Dunn Parkway, Sevierville
(865) 429-7771
www.tonygore.com

If you like your grub with gospel, you'll be in heaven at Tony Gore's. Gore is not only an area gospel singer, but he's a great cook, too. All the meats on the menu are fresh here, and Gore even has his own smokehouse. Some of the more popular dishes include ribs, pulled pork, pig wings (shank of pig that tastes like a cross between ham and ribs), burgers, beef brisket, and seasonal specials like all-you-can-eat catfish in the summer. The homemade desserts are definitely angelic. Gospel music plays constantly over the sound system, and Gore himself performs live a few days each month, often sharing the billing with other gospel singers. When he's not singing or cooking, Gore is wandering from table to table, personally greeting his customers. Tony Gore's is open for lunch and dinner daily.

THE DINER $–$$
550 Winfield Dunn Parkway, Sevierville
(865) 908-1904
www.thediner.biz

Here's an eatery right out of the 1950s, complete with shiny metal exterior, juke box, pressed-tin ceilings, black-and-white tile floors, Formica tables, neon accents, and waitresses dressed in '50s attire. The menu covers a lot of ground, including char-grilled Angus burgers, a variety of sandwiches, steaks, and good old-fashioned Southern specialties (like fried green tomatoes, liver and onions, and grits). Another plus: you can order breakfast all day long here. The pies and cakes on the dessert menu are all handmade, and the hand-dipped milk shakes are simply scrumptious to the very last slurp. From May to October, The Diner offers a Casual Cruise-in on Saturday nights. Parties who drive up in classic cars get a 10 percent discount on their bill.

WALTERS STATE COMMUNITY
COLLEGE $–$$
Rel Maples Institute for Culinary Arts
1720 Old Newport Highway, Sevierville
(865) 774-5817
Put yourself at the mercy of the aspiring young chefs at this community-college culinary arts program, and you'll end up with a wonderful meal with great service at a remarkably low price. Located at the Walters State Community College campus in Sevierville, the institute serves a cafe-style lunch to the public Monday through Thursday from 11:30 a.m. to 12:30 p.m. throughout the academic year, as well as reservation-only gourmet lunches and dinners offered about once a week.

A typical meal might feature a lineup of potato skins, Caesar salad, chicken breast Parmesan, pork loin, rice pilaf, and vegetables. Occasional "international weeks" feature cuisine from various ethnic cultures. Space fills up quickly, so the best way to snag a reservation is to get on the institute's mailing list and call as soon as you get the e-mail announcement.

The institute, begun in 1998, now takes up an entire wing of the college's $6.5-million building, which boasts three state-of-the-art kitchens where food is prepared for 75 to 100 guests per meal. The cafe-style lunches are $6 per person (tax included), and any tips left behind help cover the culinary arts program's scholarship fund and operational expenses. The reservation-only events generally cost between $12 and $15 per person.

CLINT'S BBQ AND
COUNTRY COOKIN' $$–$$$
2334 Newport Highway, Sevierville
(865) 453-5150
www.clintsbbq.com
Clint Carnley learned to cook on his back porch

and got to be such a master at barbeque that dozens of friends and family members at a time would flock to his place for supper. So many people told him he should open his own restaurant that Clint eventually did just that. But he does more than cook for this family-owned and family-operated restaurant. On Tuesday nights, the former professional musician has been known to get out his guitar and walk around the place, strumming and singing for his customers.

Clint's menu includes everything from grilled cheese to shrimp and steaks, but the specialty here is barbeque (including pulled pork, chicken, and ribs). Leave room for the homemade desserts, as well.

COBBLERS $
160 Court Avenue, Sevierville
(865) 908-8700
www.cobblersbistro.com
Starbucks must surely be quaking in their croissants. Cobblers offers locals and visitors alike a genuine European-style espresso bar, gourmet sandwich shop, and wireless Internet cafe. Located across the street from the Dolly Parton statue outside the Sevier County Courthouse, Cobblers serves cleverly named sandwiches (like Miss Piggy Gone A Rye), homemade desserts (including killer cobblers), and specialty coffees and teas. You can also get boxed lunches here. Open only for breakfast and lunch.

CHIANG HOUSE $–$$
624 Parkway, Sevierville
(865) 428-5977
This versatile house of Far East cuisine offers traditional Chinese dishes, meals served Japanese hibachi-style, and even a sushi bar. It's a big draw among locals and tourists both. You can select from more than 60 entrees on the Chinese menu or, for a little entertainment with your dinner, you can opt for the Japanese teppanyaki meals, where the food is prepared at your table hibachi-style. The highly trained chefs juggle, twirl, and spin their cutlery like masters, making cooking your order into a real show. Teppanyaki dinners include a shrimp appetizer, Japanese soup, salad,

an entree (shrimp and scallops is one popular option, as is the filet mignon), rice, and vegetables. The sushi bar offers more than 15 types of sushi and sashimi, as well as sushi rolls and larger combination platters. The lunch and dinner buffets feature soups and entrees from the Chinese menu and even sushi rolls. Chiang House also carries a good selection of domestic beers in addition to several imported Japanese labels. The restaurant is open seven days a week for lunch and dinner. Reservations aren't required, but they are accepted.

THE SMOKY MOUNTAIN
CHOP HOUSE $$-$$$$
1649 Parkway, Sevierville
(865) 774-1991
www.thechophouse.com
This Chop House, located in the Tanger Five Oaks Outlet Center is one link in a very small chain of similar restaurants found in the Southeast and Midwest. In addition to both pork and lamb chops, the menu offers a diverse selection of steaks, including prime rib, New York strip, and medallions Anthony (grilled tenderloin served with a rich Bordeaux sauce, Burgundy mushrooms, and a béarnaise sauce—a deceptively small but filling portion). You'll also find a number of chicken dishes as well as seafood entrees like North Atlantic salmon, baked scrod, and seafood pasta. Entrees include a choice of soup or salad and a choice of potato, and you can add a half or full skewer of char-grilled shrimp to any entree. Sandwiches, burgers, and salads are available, too, with popular choices including Oriental chicken salad, lunch chops, and a portobello veggie burger.

The warm atmosphere reflects a simple but tasteful elegance, featuring dark woods, fireplaces, and shelves full of interesting knickknacks. You can also dine in the bar area, located just off the foyer. Choose among foreign and domestic beers or wine coolers, or bring your own alcoholic beverages with you. Reservations are not accepted, but you can call ahead for seating before your arrival.

CONNORS STEAK & SEAFOOD $$-$$$$
1641 Parkway, Sevierville
(865) 428-1991
www.thechophouse.com
Connors is owned and operated by the same folks as the Smoky Mountain Chop House (the previous entry), and like its sister restaurant, it's also a favorite with both locals and the shopping crowd at the Tanger Outlet shops. Desserts, soups, biscuits, sauces, dressings, and other side items are prepared daily from scratch. Connors, open for lunch and dinner daily, is known for dishes like cilantro lime-grilled shrimp, soy mustard-glazed grilled salmon, shrimp and Cajun sausage with cheese grits, and sautéed pork tenderloin. Lunchers can get fat, juicy burgers and one of the few authentically prepared Reubens you'll find in the area. Even the soups and salads excel. Take note: No self-respecting visitor in the South should pass up the opportunity to try Connors fried green tomatoes appetizer. Served with cheese grits, tasso, and white gravy for dipping, these 'maters will make you think you've died and gone to the Whistle Stop Cafe.

For dessert, buckle under the temptation of the caramel fudge cheesecake, the key lime pie, or the bananas Foster served with a cup of home-ground Colombian coffee. If you think a beer would hit the spot, you can order from a wide selection of domestic and imported labels.

If the restaurant you choose does not take reservations, ask if it has call-ahead seating. If so, you can call in and get your name on the waiting list before you get there.

APPLEWOOD FARMHOUSE GRILL $$
220 Apple Valley Road, Sevierville
(865) 429-8644

APPLEWOOD FARMHOUSE
RESTAURANT $$-$$$
240 Apple Valley Road, Sevierville
(865) 428-1222
www.applewoodrestaurant.com
Apple Valley Farms is an operational apple farm

in Sevierville that has grown into an immensely popular tourist stop. Besides sporting two full-service restaurants, it's also home to the Apple Barn General Store and Cider Mill, the Apple Butter Kitchen, the Candy Apple and Chocolate Factory, the Creamery, the Apple Barn Winery, and the Christmas and Candle shop. (See the Close-up in the Shopping chapter for more details).

The two restaurants—Applewood Farmhouse Restaurant and the newer Applewood Farmhouse Grill—have similar menus, so this write-up will focus on the original Farmhouse Restaurant before including a few distinguishing facts about the newer Farmhouse Grill.

The restaurant is located in what was once an actual farmhouse, built in 1921. It was refurbished and opened as a restaurant in 1987. The building has retained much of its original charm. A friendly, whitewashed exterior welcomes you into a world of country simplicity. Inside, you'll find wood floors and big windows offering views of the rest of the Apple Valley complex and the lazy Little Pigeon River just beyond.

As you might well expect, the apple reigns supreme here, and you'll get plenty of apple-licious side dishes whenever you visit, whether for breakfast, lunch, or dinner. Traditional breakfast favorites include omelets, pancakes, eggs, and biscuits. Big appetites appreciate the Farmhouse Special Breakfast, featuring your choice of eight different main items, including bacon, country ham hash, and even rainbow trout. Each main dish comes with an Applewood julep, applesauce muffins, apple fritters, homemade apple butter, biscuits, fried apples, grits and sausage gravy, home-fried potatoes, and two eggs cooked to order.

Lunches and dinners (in generous portions) are also loaded with extras but include a few different side dishes, like homemade vegetable soup, mashed potatoes, and a vegetable. As for the entrees, some of the "Farmhouse Favorites" include Southern fried chicken, old-fashioned chicken and dumplings, chicken potpie, and applewood pork loin (a tender, boneless pork loin smoked over applewood and served with homemade apple relish).

Next door, the Applewood Farmhouse Grill was opened in 1995. Although the construction is newer, it was designed to resemble its older sister. The breakfast and lunch menus are very similar to those of the original restaurant, but side salads and desserts are not included in the price of the dinners as they are at Applewood Farmhouse Restaurant. Overall, however, the prices on the dinner menu are a little less expensive. Both restaurants have a reasonably priced children's menu with kids' favorites like grilled cheese sandwiches, burgers, bologna and cheese sandwiches, and fried chicken.

THE TIN ROOF CAFE $

304 Apple Valley Road, Sevierville
(865) 365-0515
www.underthetinroof.com
Down the street a bit from the Apple Valley Farms is a very different sort of eatery housed in a converted 1900 farmhouse. The Tin Roof Cafe started out in 2008 as a coffeehouse (with free wireless Internet) that soon expanded into a bakery/cafe offering fabulous lunches and dinners with celebrated desserts. The menu has included such dishes as leek and potato soup; curry chicken salad; and turkey, apple, and brie paninis. The delectable desserts here include lemon tarts, sweet potato pie, and Oreo cupcakes, to name just a few. Speaking of sweets, try the frozen hot chocolate. In the summer, it's the most popular drink order. You can dine inside or out (choosing either the front or back porch), in a peaceful setting just across the road from the river.

PIGEON FORGE

BULLFISH GRILL $$-$$$
2441 Parkway, Pigeon Forge
(865) 868-1000
www.bullfishgrill.com
This fairly upscale restaurant has a fancy interior (check out the four-sided fireplace) to match its classy hand-cut steak and seafood menu, although you an also order a good old-fashioned hamburger or a salad entree, as well. Specialties here include Parmesan-crusted grouper, New

Orleans shrimp pasta, and the meat loaf stack with white cheddar mashed potatoes. The restaurant is also known for its Black & Bleu Salad—sirloin steak over greens with Cajun fried onions and bleu cheese crumbles. If you're an onion ring fan, you'll love the signature onion ring appetizer with jalapeno ranch dressing. You can get draft beer here as well as bottled domestic and imported brews, and you'll find the wine list impressive.

FLYING HORSE GRILL $$–$$$
2485 Parkway, Pigeon Forge
(865) 428-7561
www.flyinghorsegrill.net

Right next door to Bullfish is the Flying Horse Grill, Bullfish's sister restaurant. It's named for the custom-made Italian carousel you can see through the window from the parkway (complete with 17 classic horses, a pair of rocking horses, a rocking chariot, and a spinning teacup, all aglitter with 550 lights). Feel free to grab a ride while you're waiting for your table; the attraction is a big hit with kids and kids at heart alike. The contemporary American menu here includes such dishes as barbeque baby back ribs, pecan trout, a variety of specialty salads and pastas as well as a chicken potpie that's easily enough for two.

BLUE MOOSE BURGERS & WINGS $
2430 Teaster Lane
Pigeon Forge, TN 37863
(865) 286-0364

This inexpensive and relatively new family sports grill tucked back from the road in Teaster Crossing has quite the local following already. For starters, the homemade fried pickle chips with ranch dip are surprisingly crunchy, tangy, and totally addictive. You can order cold beer and hot wings (they have 18 different flavors) while you watch sports on the flat-screen TVs. The burgers here are quite good, and you'll also find an unusually extensive menu of hot dogs, of all things. The dessert menu has only a handful of options, but it includes a peanut butter pie that will send you into orbit. The Blue Moose also dishes up live music on the weekends.

LITTLE TOKYO HIBACHI & SUSHI RESTAURANT $–$$$
2430 Teaster Lane, Pigeon Forge
(865) 908-0555

Here's another local's favorite in the Teaster Crossing shopping center. Little Tokyo offers a solid selection of Japanese steak and seafood, as well as hibachi meals and a sushi bar. The restaurant is known for its excellent lunch specials, which start at $6.

MEL'S DINER $–$$
119 Wears Valley Road, Pigeon Forge
(865) 429-2184
www.melsdinerpf.com

Mel's is a classic silver-sided diner sitting just 1 block off the Parkway on Wears Valley Road. Although it was built in 1993, you can easily believe you're revisiting the '50s here, thanks to the restaurant's cozy, sleek interior, retro color scheme, and rows of booth seating.

One of the neat things about Mel's is that it's one of the few dining establishments in the Smokies that's open 24 hours a day, seven days a week. For breakfast, they serve traditional morning fare like eggs and omelets, pancakes and waffles, and biscuits with gravy (you are, after all, still in the South!). The rest of the menu consists primarily of American staples like burger and sandwich baskets and dinner platters. Platter entrees include hefty portions of pork chops, ham, meat loaf, country-fried steak, and other staple diner offerings. The entrees come with bread and a choice of two side vegetables. Be sure to allow room for dessert at Mel's. The cakes, pies, and sundaes are delicious, as are the milk shakes.

BENNETT'S PIT BAR-B-QUE $–$$$
2910 Parkway, Pigeon Forge
(865) 429-2200
714 River Road, Gatlinburg
(865) 436-2400
www.bennetts-bbq.com

Just because you're surrounded by Eastern mountains doesn't mean you can't dig into the hearty, zesty flavors of the Southwest. Both Sevier

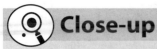 **Close-up**

How 'bout a Fried Bologna Sandwich?

Surrounding the grandeur of the Smokies and the glitter created by the cities that host their visitors, Sevier County still lives in a kind of time warp that's disappearing fast. While it holds on, the rural atmosphere that exists just outside the Smokies Corridor hides a lot of treasures that a lot of people thought gone from the American scene forever: the mom-and-pop general store.

This is a place few will remember, where locals, mostly farmers and other close-to-the-earth laborers, stop by daily for a loaf of bread or a dozen fresh eggs and, as often as not, stick around for a sandwich and a soft drink while they're at it. If you're here for the "whole hog," your meal will probably include:

- a fried bologna sandwich (self-explanatory).

- a MoonPie—a purely Southern concoction made in Nashville for close to a century. A Moon-Pie is a round graham cracker cookie sandwich filled with marshmallow cream and coated in chocolate, vanilla, strawberry, or banana (although some newer flavors like peanut butter also exist).

- a big dope—a carbonated beverage, typically a 12-ounce Coke, Pepsi, or (if you're really Southern) RC Cola.

Most of these establishments are small grocery stores with a grill and a counter, and most serve breakfast and lunch. These places aren't real long on ambience, and sometimes they don't even have a place to sit, but they do have a short menu of honest-to-God food that'll stick to your ribs and drive a nutritionist to the brink of madness. And it won't cost you an arm and a leg to eat.

With a few noted exceptions, these businesses are on roads that ring the Smokies Corridor, and you'll probably find them on your way to some attraction or accommodation mentioned elsewhere in this book.

The places listed here meet three simple criteria: (1) They have to sell some other commodity (usually gas and/or groceries) besides food; (2) everything they serve must be cooked before your eyes; and (3) their menu must offer either a fried bologna sandwich or home-baked biscuits (most have both).

This section won't include a price code, but the price of a fried bologna sandwich (noted as "FBS") is thrown in to give you an indication. In each case, a five-dollar bill will probably return a little change for each person eating.

County Bennett's serve satisfying portions of pork, beef, chicken, and ribs prepared just the way barbecue aficionados like them. The lunch and dinner menus present a broad selection of hickory-smoked and mesquite-grilled entrees; a 40-item, all-you-can-eat soup and salad bar; barbecue sandwiches; and much more.

Separately, or in various combinations, Bennett's offers five basic meats from its hickory smoker: chopped pork, sliced beef brisket, sliced sausage, chicken, and pork spareribs. Other entrees like steaks, shrimp, and chicken breasts are flamed over the mesquite grill. Interestingly, Bennett's serves breakfast as well. That menu contains morning favorites like pancakes, omelets, and biscuits, but it also features a number of breakfast specials like hickory-smoked ham, bacon, pork chops, and even a 10-ounce strip.

Bennett's cooking methods are true to good Texas form and result in foods that are moist, tender, and packed with flavor. The meats start with a generous basting in Bennett's special-recipe

Poppa Kent's
FBS: $2.79
508 Dolly Parton Parkway, Sevierville
(865) 453-9236
Real country cooking for breakfast, lunch, and dinner. The menu includes burgers, pizza, and lasagna, as well.

Frank Allen's Market & Grill
FBS: $2.51
1415 Parkway, Sevierville
(865) 453-3617
Here's a Shell station with just a few booths and a lunch counter. They serve up amazing chipped ham sandwiches in addition to a classic FBS.

Dunn's Market and Grill
FBS: $2.09
2650 Upper Middle Creek Road, Sevierville
(865) 429-5804
Seven tables are scattered through Dunn's Market, with seating for as many as you can fit around them. Get here early in the morning for biscuits, considered by a highly prejudiced clientele to be the best thing on the menu.

McCarter's Market
FBS: $2.50
103 Mills Park Road, Gatlinburg
(865) 436-4951
Don't let the address fool you—this place is on East Parkway, about 4 1/2 miles east of downtown Gatlinburg. (The mailbox is on Mills Park Road.) A local landmark for more years than anyone recalls, McCarter's serves a house special they call "Ron & Giff's Burger," a patty melt on special bread. Their soup beans are locally famous. One of the larger places, McCarter's has seating for about 10 at the counter and several tables.

barbecue sauce. They're then smoldered over hickory wood and smoked for up to 14 hours. Then it's on to the open-pit hickory fire where selections are grilled to order.

Bennett's is a Denver-based chain with about 20 franchises nationwide. The Pigeon Forge Bennett's opened in 1991, and about a year later, the second one appeared on River Road in Gatlinburg. The Gatlinburg location also has a full-service cocktail lounge where you can relax with a game of pool, darts, video games, or televised sports. Both restaurants are open year-round.

ALAMO STEAK HOUSE $$–$$$$
3050 Parkway, Pigeon Forge
(865) 908-9998
705 East Parkway, Gatlinburg
(865) 436-9998
www.alamosteakhouse.com
Owned by the same folks who own Bennett's, the Alamo offers a Texas theme, right down to the cactus. This place is known for its Black Angus steaks, cooked over an open oak fire, although the menu also includes a selection of chops, seafood, and chicken dishes. You can order beer or

wine in either, and the Gatlinburg restaurant also features a full bar.

KINKAKU JAPANESE STEAKHOUSE $$–$$$$
3152 Parkway, Pigeon Forge
(865) 774-7698
www.pigeonforgejapanese.com

If you're not amused by the crazy hibachi chefs here, you're bound to be entertained by owner Tommy Kinkaku, who used to be (believe it or not) a chemical engineer. Dinner entrees at Kinkaku come with soup, salad, fried rice, and vegetables. Two of the most popular entrees include the filet mignon and scallops and the salmon and tuna. Japanese beer and sake are also among the offerings. Kinkaku plans to add a sushi bar in the near future.

RED ROOSTER PANCAKE HOUSE $
3215 Parkway, Pigeon Forge
(865) 428-3322

Here's one of the better locally owned pancake places, featuring two tractors out front and an antique 1925 Farmall in the dining room to highlight the farmhouse theme. Red Rooster serves big, fluffy omelets, country ham, pork chops, French toast, waffles, and pancakes with such flavors as chocolate éclair (three buttermilk pancakes layered with Bavarian crème and drizzled with chocolate), pineapple upside down, berrylicious (with blueberries, blackberries, raspberries, and strawberries), caramel peach, and peanut butter and chocolate chip. The signature Red Rooster omelet includes everything but the farmhouse sink (onions, green peppers, mushrooms, tomatoes, sausage, bacon, ham, and your choice of cheese) and comes with three buttermilk pancakes. The Red Rooster is open for breakfast and lunch.

THE OLD MILL RESTAURANT $$–$$$
2944 Old Mill Avenue, Pigeon Forge
(865) 429-3463
www.old-mill.com

This restaurant stands next door to one of Pigeon Forge's most famous historical sites, the Old Mill. (See the Attractions chapter for more on this working mill.) The Old Mill Restaurant, however, is a veritable newcomer, having opened in 1993. From an architectural standpoint, these two neighbors on the banks of the Little Pigeon River blend together well. The restaurant is a sprawling timber-look building that has gone a long way toward matching the exterior ambience of the mill. Inside the restaurant, wood floors, rafters, and simple country furnishings add consistency to the motif. The main dining room is split between two levels, allowing most diners pleasant views through large picture windows overlooking the Little Pigeon River below.

Down-home Southern fare is the specialty here. The country breakfast is based on pancakes with grits, eggs, muffins, and biscuits. You can then add extras like bacon, ham, or sausage. Both the lunch and dinner menus feature Southern specialties, including country-fried steak, sugar-cured ham, and chicken potpie for lunch; or pork loin, chicken and dumplings, and pot roast and gravy for dinner. The dinner menu also has a large selection of both fried and grilled entrees, including beef liver, catfish, and rib-eye steak. Most dinner entrees come with the Old Mill's trademark corn chowder and homemade fritters plus salad, vegetables, and dessert. For lighter dining, you can choose among the several salad, fruit, and vegetable plates.

In 2003 the Old Mill complex expanded with the opening of a restaurant now called the Old Mill Pottery House Café & Grille (formerly the Old Mill Bakery Café). It's located in a renovated home that used to belong to Douglas Ferguson, a renowned local potter who passed away in the year 2000.

Both the restaurant and the cafe use flour and cornmeal that's ground at the old mill, and they serve meals on pottery from the adjacent Pigeon River Pottery shop.

DUFF'S FAMOUS SMORGASBORD $$
3985 Parkway, Pigeon Forge
(865) 453-6443
www.duffssmorgasbord.com

Many of you may recognize the Duff's name. For years these buffet-style family restaurants were fixtures throughout Middle America. Slowly, the chain dwindled away, and today only one Duff's still stands—this one in Pigeon Forge. It's open from mid-February through December, serving lunch and dinner only in the off-season months and adding a breakfast smorgasbord from May through October.

For one price, you have your choice of at least six hot entrees (always including fried chicken), six vegetables, nine salads, and 10 desserts plus beverages. Carving stations with roast beef and ham are open after 3:30 p.m. on weekdays and all day on Saturday and Sunday. Duff's signature dessert is the Hurricane Cake, a spice cake topped with a gooey, buttery, brown sugar topping. Repeat visitors ask for it by name.

i Cracker Barrel is famous for its old-fashioned Southern cooking, as well as for its tendency to place its restaurants near interstate exits. Yet the company's first "destination location" (where the town was targeted instead of an exit) was in Pigeon Forge, miles from the nearest interstate (I-40). The gamble clearly paid off, because now Pigeon Forge has two Cracker Barrels.

GATLINBURG

Down the Parkway

SMOKY MOUNTAIN TROUT HOUSE $$-$$$
410 Parkway, Gatlinburg
(865) 436-5416
They're a little vague about how long the Trout House has been in business, but Trout Eisenhower, the establishment's signature dinner (served with bacon butter and sautéed mushrooms and onions), was so named during Ike's administration (1953–1961). While the usual restaurant fare is available, the pièce de résistance here is the local king of the game fish, caught fresh daily and offered in a dozen different presentations, some of which you'd never associate with a fish. You've probably heard of trout almondine, but how about cheese-baked trout,

Parmesan trout, or trout with lemon rice stuffing? (Not to mention the trout fritters appetizer.)

The Trout House is one of those "urban myth" places you hear about from time to time, a place that looks as unpretentious as a "greasy spoon" but leaves you knowing you've encountered culinary greatness. It's a Smoky Mountain classic. Just outside of the bustle of downtown, the Trout House recommends reservations for groups larger than six. Municipal parking facilities are within easy walking distance of the restaurant in both directions, and the purple route trolley stops at their door.

ATRIUM PANCAKES $
432 Parkway, Gatlinburg
(865) 430-3684
One of Gatlinburg's favorite local spots, the Atrium serves breakfast and lunch in a restaurant with atrium-style curved windows and its own four-story, man-made waterfall. In addition to the dining room, an outdoor balcony overlooking the waterfall is open upstairs in the summer. The light and airy setting is enhanced by a profusion of plant life in hanging baskets and wall planters. The Atrium offers 25 varieties of pancakes for breakfast (including the baked apple pancake featured in Taste of Home magazine) and a wide selection of soups, sandwiches, and entrees for lunch. You'll find free parking at the front door.

HAVANA DREAMS CAFE $$-$$$
449 Parkway, Gatlinburg
(865) 436-4755
If you're looking for something besides typical Southern (or even classic American) fare, consider some Cuban cuisine at Havana Dreams Cafe. Owner Juan Carlos hails from Cuba, and you can be sure that the dishes here are the real thing. The extensive menu includes such Cuban and Spanish specialties as fried green plantains, roast pork, wild rice and black beans, and the grilled Cuban sandwich (ham, roast pork, Swiss cheese, and pickles with mustard).

Save room for flan—including cheese, chocolate, coconut, guava, and caramel. You can even order a papaya or mango milk shake (or chocolate, vanilla, or strawberry if you aren't feeling particularly daring).

You can't miss this establishment—its vivid red and yellow exterior is festooned with bright, multicolored lights and neon palm trees on the roof. If you eat in the rear dining room, you can sit at a table overlooking the river.

HARD ROCK CAFE $-$$$
515 Parkway, Gatlinburg
(865) 430-7625
www.hardrock.com

As one of the world's biggest full-service restaurant chains (more than 100 worldwide, nearly 40 in the United States), Hard Rock wouldn't normally rate a specific write-up in an Insiders' Guide. The difference here is that when Hard Rock moves into a new city, it does so with the intent to become a member of the community. The Ambassador's Club, an organization of Hard Rock employees, gets deeply involved in community affairs from the day they open their doors. Local beneficiaries of this establishment include Friends of the Great Smoky Mountains and several environmental groups.

The restaurant itself is a comfortable, 221-seat facility offering a menu heavy on barbecue and smoked-meat entrees, with a broad selection of steak and pasta dishes and, of course, the burger selection that triggered the whole Hard Rock concept in London in 1971, when the Tennessee-born originator of the franchise couldn't find a decent hamburger.

This is also the only Hard Rock Cafe in the world that has its own wedding chapel, perhaps reason alone to mention it in these pages. On your way out, you can browse through the distinctive logo merchandise displayed by the cash register.

NO WAY JOSE'S CANTINA $-$$
555 Parkway, Gatlinburg
(865) 430-5673
104 Walden's Main Street, Pigeon Forge
(865) 429-7779
www.nowayjosescantina.com

The appearance of No Way Jose's may take authen-ticity to an extreme—the place looks like an urban renewal program somebody forgot about, say 10 years ago. Don't be fooled: When you get past the cluttered exterior and into the dimly lit dining room that really doesn't look like it seats 160, you're in for a treat. Daily deliveries of fresh meat and vegetables are cooked in authentic Mexican style and served in generous portions, and the cooks make the tamales, salsas, and sauces fresh daily. The menu includes enough "gringo" grub to satisfy any less-adventurous palates in your group, and margaritas and Mexican beers complement the meals. Free parking is available at the front door, and if the lot is full, the downtown aquarium parking deck is just across the street. The Pigeon Forge location opened a few years ago in the Walden's Landing shopping complex.

PANCAKE PANTRY $-$$
628 Parkway, Gatlinburg
(865) 436-4724
www.pancakepantry.com

Arguably the favorite visitors' breakfast spot in the downtown area, the Pancake Pantry doesn't really need parking—it's within 3 blocks of more than a thousand motel rooms. Some mornings, it seems like each and every overnight visitor in Gatlinburg is standing in line to score a table here, so if you get a hankering for their hotcakes in high season, you better get up early (they open at 7 a.m.). The breakfast menu includes more ways to fix a pancake than you'd ever believe possible, and the lunch menu includes burgers, sandwiches, soups, and salads. Established in 1960, the Pancake Pantry was the first pancake house in the state of Tennessee. Its outstanding architecture and quick, friendly service have

You may just flip over the number of pancake restaurants in the Smokies. The Smokies Corridor is home to almost two dozen such places with some version of "pancake" (or "flapjack") in their name, with only a few representing national chains. Countless additional establishments serve them, as well. Bring on the maple syrup!

made it a landmark in downtown Gatlinburg. But be sure to bring cash—they don't accept credit cards (although there is an ATM machine in the lobby).

LINEBERGER'S SEAFOOD CO. $$-$$$$
903 Parkway, Gatlinburg
(865) 436-9284
www.linebergersseafood.com
A refugee from the low country of South Carolina, Lineberger's features one of the most complete lines of fresh Atlantic seafood in the area. The restaurant, a family-owned business established in 1948, is strongly reminiscent of the seafood houses that line Murrell's Inlet, just south of Myrtle Beach, with an extensive variety of seafood dishes and platters cooked to your order. Land-lubber offerings like steaks, chicken, and chops will suit the aquatically challenged, but a visit to Lineberger's shouldn't really be for that type of eating. Another plus: The window views afforded from most seats make Lineberger's a great place for people-watching.

BEST ITALIAN CAFE AND PIZZERIA $$-$$$
968 Parkway, Gatlinburg
(865) 430-4090
www.bestitalian.com
The name may seem a little arrogant at first, but nobody who's ever eaten at "the Best" walks away complaining. Opened in 1975 in half the space it currently occupies at the back of Elk's Plaza, this is as authentic an ethnic restaurant as a native of New York City can make it. Atmosphere? "Fuggedaboudit!" People come here to eat. Again and again. If it's Italian, they make it; if not, see the quote above.

"The Best" made its local reputation in the '70s when it was the only pizza place in town (it's still the overwhelming favorite of locals) and grew from that start to a full-fledged eatery. From antipasto and garlic rolls that defy description as appetizers through absolutely authentic entrees to the sinful desserts, "the Best" justifies its name. Parking is convenient in the small Elk's Plaza lot adjacent to the restaurant and in the commercial parking deck across the Parkway.

HOWARD'S RESTAURANT $-$$$
976 Parkway, Gatlinburg
(865) 436-3600
www.howards-gatlinburg.com
Since its opening in 1946, Howard's has been that memorable place in the middle of downtown where people sat right out in the open along the Parkway. Now closer to the south end, it's still the same people serving the same great food in a bigger setting. As close to an old-fashioned eatery as you'll find anywhere, Howard's features a full line of hearty steaks and gourmet burgers, skillet-cooked trout, and baby back ribs cooked just the way you like 'em, on both the grown-up and children's menus. Long famous for homemade french fries, desserts, and salad dressings, Howard's includes a spacious upstairs lounge where you can relax until it's time to get serious about eating. The lounge has live entertainment Wednesday through Saturday evenings. Howard's is convenient to the Elk's Plaza parking lot.

THE PARK GRILL STEAKHOUSE $$$-$$$$
1110 Parkway, Gatlinburg
(865) 436-2300
www.parkgrillgatlinburg.com
One of the city's architectural wonders, the Park Grill is built almost entirely of huge peeled spruce logs 2 feet in diameter that came from trees killed by beetles and harvested from a national forest in Idaho—no live trees were cut for the construction. The stonework you'll see came from dismantled rock fences from the area around neighboring Cosby. The combined effect makes the restaurant, located just 200 yards from the park's entrance, look exactly like the type of classic national park lodge you'd find out west. The waitstaff is even outfitted in park ranger uniforms to echo the theme. If you want to steep yourself even further in the outdoorsy atmosphere, ask for one of the tables by the huge picture windows that face the woods.

The menu here includes a wide variety of steak, fish, and chicken, although the pork tenderloin is one of the more popular entrees. The restaurant also features an all-you-can-eat salad bar and homemade desserts made fresh daily.

The Park Grill is open for dinner only and offers call-ahead seating, as well as limited free parking.

THE PEDDLER STEAKHOUSE $$$–$$$$
820 River Road, Gatlinburg
(865) 436-5794
www.peddlergatlinburg.com

Just off the Parkway, the Peddler is located in one of Gatlinburg's most historic buildings: The center of the structure is the log cabin that was the home place of the late Hattie Ogle McGiffin, the city's acknowledged matriarch. To build it in 1958, Charles "Earl" Ogle Sr., a fourth-generation Gatlinburg merchant, used the logs of four other area log cabins. (Earl's great grandfather, Noah Ogle, was the town's first grocer.) The Peddler is part of a small regional chain that operates like an independent restaurant, and the local management is deeply involved in civic and national park affairs.

Custom-cut steaks (they bring the loin to your table, and you tell them how big a steak you want) and fresh seafood dishes make the Peddler a special-occasion favorite. The salad bar is considered one of the best in the area. The restaurant is also known for its cantilevered bar (which hangs out over the West Prong of the Little Pigeon River), added in 1993. The Peddler has its own parking lot in front of the building—if the lot's full, and you didn't take advantage of the call-ahead seating, figure you're going to wait the better part of an hour to get seated. Open for dinner only.

i Leave your ties and high heels at home; dress codes are casual in almost every Sevier County restaurant. You can even wear shorts to dinner! As one local puts it, "Only bankers and lawyers wear ties here!"

Out East Parkway from Traffic Light #3

GREENBRIER RESTAURANT $$–$$$$
370 Newman Road, Gatlinburg
(865) 436-6318
www.greenbrierrestaurant.com

Convenient but well removed from any other distractions, the Greenbrier is located on a mountaintop just 1½ miles from traffic light #3. Take East Parkway out to the traffic light at Newman Road, turn right, and drive up into the parking lot where the road ends. Some member of the Hadden family will probably be waiting to show you to your table. If you ask about the history of the log building (which dates from 1939), you'll likely hear about how it was once the Greenbrier Lodge, sporting Gatlinburg's first concrete swimming pool.

Although beef dishes (particularly the prime rib) are the staple here, the Greenbrier also offers an extensive seafood menu and does more with chicken than anyone else in the area. Because of the size of its several dining rooms, the Greenbrier can accommodate groups of up to 30 people. The barroom is a local favorite during televised football games.

MOUNTAIN LODGE RESTAURANT $
913 East Parkway, Gatlinburg
(865) 436-2547

The Mountain Lodge is a huge local favorite for its extremely Southern breakfast menu. The staff (which usually includes several members of the Smith family that owns the place) will treat you as though you're the most special thing that's happened to them all day. The deceptively large building can hold 125 guests, which means you probably won't have to wait long to get seated. Ample parking is available on both sides of the restaurant, which is open for breakfast and lunch only.

MA'S KITCHEN $
680 Glades Road, Gatlinburg
(865) 430-7799

This may be the most appropriately named restaurant in the area; it's a small converted house that has just one room, and that room is a kitchen. Donna and Sue (and frequently their kids) will take your order from a basic Southern menu, and then they'll pitch in to help Jamie cook your order and serve it. There's nothing real fancy on the menu, and the rest of the place is

The Great Smoky Arts & Crafts Community

It wasn't that long ago that a day in the Great Smoky Arts & Crafts Community meant a leisurely drive of a few hours to visit a few dozen shops. Today, with upwards of 100 shops and galleries, a day gets you halfway through if you hurry. It's fortunate that as the number of businesses has increased, three excellent eateries have sprung up throughout the community, all offering plenty of convenient parking. Unlike downtown eateries, the hours of operation in these places can be somewhat abbreviated, so call ahead before you make the drive out.

is so authentic that the fish and chips even comes served in newsprint. The menu includes such English delicacies as bangers and mash, toad in the hole, Cornish pasties, scones, and Eccles cakes (as well as some sandwich combinations you may actually have heard of). Being a pub, the Fox & Parrot also offers 160 different beers (make that ales, lagers, and stouts)—10 of them on draft. If you order hot tea instead, you'll have your pick of 15 varieties. Only one traditional pub element is (thankfully) missing: This is a no-smoking establishment that is perfectly appropriate for families.

The pub serves lunch and dinner every night, although it closes at 6 p.m. on Sundays. If you come on a Thursday night, you might catch the local darts league. Feel free to throw a few yourself—the steel-tipped darts are authentic, too.

THE WILD PLUM TEA ROOM $-$$
555 Buckhorn Road, Gatlinburg
(865) 436-3808
The oldest of the craft community's eating establishments, the Wild Plum Tea Room is a great favorite with several local ladies' social and service clubs. The gourmet menu in this Austrian-style tearoom housed in a Smoky Mountain log cabin begins with a fabulous soup du jour followed by an equally delicious salad-and-sandwich menu. All entrees include a serving of the restaurant's signature wild plum muffins. The beverage list includes a selection of beers and wines, and if you liked the muffins, you'll probably love the wild plum tea. Open for breakfast and lunch only (closed Sundays) from March through mid-December.

every bit as unpretentious—they serve good, honest, salt-of-the-earth food in generous portions. Weather permitting, you can eat in the front yard's parklike setting. Ma's Kitchen is generally open for lunch every day, plus breakfast on Saturdays (closed Sundays).

THE FOX & PARROT TAVERN— A BRITISH PUB $
1065 Glades Road, Gatlinburg
(865) 435-0677
www.fox-and-parrot.com
This place may look like a log cabin from the outside (because it is), but as soon as you step inside the Fox & Parrot, you'll feel as though you've been instantly transported to the other side of the pond. (Owner Brian Papworth hails from Michigan, although his heritage and his heart are as British as they come.) This British pub

i If you're dining as a group, be prepared for a gratuity to be automatically added to the tab. Some places add the tip for parties with as few as 6 people, while others draw the line at 10 or 12 guests.

MUSIC AND ENTERTAINMENT THEATERS AND NIGHTLIFE

As fun as it may be to roast marshmallows around a campfire (s'mores, anyone?), that's hardly the only evening entertainment option in the Smokies. Basically, the nightlife here can be separated into two categories. The most popular choice is attending any of the area's many music and variety theaters, all of which are profiled in the beginning of this chapter. These wholesome, family-friendly shows often include dinner (or breakfast), but no alcoholic beverages (with one exception, noted below). Visitors to the Smokies without kids in tow who prefer more traditional after-dark fun will find that here, too—complete with locally brewed beer, karaoke, and even a little dancing on bar tops. (Let it never be said that the Smokies doesn't have it all!)

MUSIC AND VARIETY THEATERS

Most of the shows you will find in the Smokies are music-oriented, with an emphasis on country tunes. However, if your tastes reside elsewhere, you won't feel left out. Some area shows tip their hats to other musical genres, such as rock 'n' roll, Broadway, gospel, and bluegrass. A few theaters skip the music entirely and focus more on comedy and variety. The result is a diverse menu of entertainment choices.

All of the area's music and variety theaters are wheelchair-accessible, nonsmoking facilities. They also have adequate free parking, except in one case (noted later) where you'll have to pay. Each is equipped with concession stands and, in most cases, souvenir shops filled with coffee mugs, T-shirts, and CDs by the theater's artists. Those that serve meals also generally serve a variety of refillable soft drinks, coffee, and tea.

The theaters tend to be very audience-friendly. You can take your drinks and snacks into the auditorium with you, and although video- and audiotaping are prohibited, most venues allow flash photography during performances. All theaters sell reserved seats, so it pays to buy early if you know which shows you want to see because you'll have a better chance at a good seat (especially in peak season).

Note that the ticket prices quoted in the write-ups below do not generally include tax (exceptions are noted). Although prices were current at press time, be sure to verify any theater's ticket prices when making reservations, and if you're buying for a group, don't forget to ask about discounts.

If you buy your tickets in advance by phone, you'll need to give your credit card number. If you purchase your tickets ahead of time at the theater's box office, both cash and credit cards are accepted; personal checks are not.

Finally, although you'll find a general sketch of each theater's seasonal schedule below, call to verify specific dates and times, since all schedules are subject to change. Many theaters close down in January and February, and those that don't usually cut way back on their performances, ramping up again in the spring before getting in full swing for summer and fall. Most theaters also have special holiday-themed shows from mid-November through December.

Sevierville

SMOKY MOUNTAIN PALACE THEATER

179 Collier Drive, Sevierville
(865) 429-1601, (800) 826-2933
www.smokymountainpalace.com

You simply will not believe that a person could artfully bend his or her body the way the performers do in the amazing Cirque de Chine show at the Smoky Mountain Palace Theater. Cirque de Chine, Sevierville's only live theater show, has been wowing audiences since 2007 with its incredible displays of what can only be described as human origami. But you'll see much more here than just contortion and acrobatics. Other popular acts include the Thunder Drums (featured in the opening ceremonies of the 2008 Beijing Olympics as well as in the Jet Li movie Fearless) and the Flying Motorcycles (five motorcycles driving around in different directions inside a 26-foot metal sphere-shaped cage—noted in the *Guinness Book of World Records*). Hoop diving, plate spinning, and Chinese yoyos are included, as well, and every single act in the show has won at least one gold medal in international competition. (Several have won more than once.)

Cirque de Chine generally performs nightly from April through December, with additional matinees on Tuesday and Saturday. Tickets are $29.95 for adults, $15.95 for teens ages 13 to 17, and $9.95 for children ages 6 to 12. Children five and under are free, and seniors 55 and up get $2 off. Please note that the Cirque de Chine's prices include tax.

i If anyone in your party is having a birthday or anniversary (or even if you're on your honeymoon), make sure to let the theater know when you make reservations. The emcee will be glad to recognize your special event.

Pigeon Forge

THE MIRACLE THEATER

2046 Parkway, Pigeon Forge
(865) 428-7469, (800) 768-1170
www.miracletheater.com

The Miracle Theater (housed in the old Louise Mandrell Theater) is now the largest-scale production staged in the Smokies. The faith-based musical about the miracles of Jesus appropriately held its grand opening on Good Friday, 2006. The show begins with a depiction of creation and then illustrates various major events in Jesus's life from his birth through the crucifixion and resurrection. No stodgy Sunday-school play, this two-and-a-half-hour show features an enormous cast of actors, singers, dancers, stunt professionals, and even live animals. Specialty technicians work state-of-the-art special effects, including three-dimensional video using front- and rear-screen projection and surround sound. You'll watch angels soaring through the air in some impressive acrobatic battle scenes, Roman centurions on horseback, and the three kings astride camels arriving in Bethlehem.

Tickets for *The Miracle* are $34.95 for adults and $9.95 for children ages 2 to 11. Those age two and under are admitted free.

For a special treat, you can also take a VIP backstage tour beginning about an hour before showtime ($5 per person, including tax; reservations recommended). Escorted by one of the show's actors, you'll be able to watch what happens as everything comes together backstage. You'll see the cast exercising, the fly fighting, the dressing rooms, the wardrobe rooms, the sets, the lighting and sound booths, and the stables where all the camels, donkeys, sheep, and other animals (except for the snakes) are kept. You can even walk on the stage (behind the curtain and before it goes up, that is). In the afternoon before each show, anyone can also ride one of the camels around the oasis in front of the building ($5 per person, including tax).

On Sundays at 8 p.m. and on Wednesdays at 3 p.m., the theater presents *Exalt*. In this brand-new show, cast members from *The Miracle* give a concert filled with contemporary Christian songs, old-time gospel tunes, church hymns, and even a camp song or two. Tickets to *Exalt* are $29.95 for adults and $9.95 for children ages 2 to 11. Those age two and under are admitted free.

The Miracle's parent company, the Fee/Hedrick Family Entertainment Group, is offering an impressive combo price for 2009 that allows you to save big when you buy any two of six different shows in four separate Pigeon Forge theaters. In addition to *The Miracle* and *Exalt*, the shows covered by the deal include *The Black Bear Jamboree*, *Magic Beyond Belief*, *The Comedy Barn*, and The Blackwood Breakfast Variety Show (in the *Black Bear Jamboree*'s theater). These special combo tickets cost $49.95 for adults, and $9.95 for children ages 2 to 11 (the same price normally charged for a single child admission) and tickets are good for one week. This is an especially good deal for shows like *The Black Bear Jamboree* that include a meal.

HOOT N' HOLLER DINNER SHOW
WonderWorks
100 Music Road, Pigeon Forge
(865) 868-1800, (800) 768-4971
www.wonderworkstn.com
The two-hour Vaudeville-style music and dance performance inside the WonderWorks interactive museum follows the adventures of a traveling troop of dancers and singers and their ever-comical would-be chef Scraps, who doubles as the emcee. As with many such entertainment shows in the area, Hoot N' Holler has lots of audience participation.

The three-course Italian dinner is served family style. The menu includes salad, bread with homemade whipped garlic butter, baked ziti, stuffed shells, and chicken Parmesan. Dessert is strawberry shortcake with homemade whipped cream.

Tickets are $32.95 for adults and $14.95 for children ages 4 to 12. Those age three and under are free if they sit on their parent's lap and share the parent's meal.

BLACK BEAR JAMBOREE
119 Music Road, Pigeon Forge
(865) 908-7469, (800) 985-5494
www.blackbearjamboree.com
This $10 million dinner show features a family of larger-than-life animatronic black bears and

several comical humans in a high-energy musical performance that includes oldies rock, country, gospel, and patriotic tunes. The bears include the amiable Momma Bear, Papa Bear, and Baby Bear, as well as three craftier characters named Weezer, Big Ben, and Gobo.

Dinner consists of creamy soup and biscuits followed by Southern-style chicken, hickory pit barbecue ribs, corn on the cob, a vegetable medley, and seasoned potatoes. Chocolate mousse is the dessert. A live bluegrass band plays during mealtime, before the show begins.

The Black Bear Jamboree show runs year-round, generally with two shows a night, plus matinees in high season. Tickets are $39.95 for anyone aged 12 and up, and children 11 and under are free (one per paid adult admission); seniors receive a $2 discount.

The 650-seat theater is also the home of the *The Blackwood Breakfast Variety Show,* starring a Grammy-award-winning family gospel group known as the Blackwoods whose roots go back more than six decades. Today's incarnation of the group includes founding Blackwood Quartet member R. W. Blackwood and his wife, Donna, as well as three additional nonfamily singers. The show's songs cover oldies rock and country in addition to gospel. The husband-and-wife ventriloquist and comedy team of Bob and Marty Hamill also lend their talents to the show. The hearty breakfast includes eggs, bacon, sausage, hash browns, buttermilk biscuits, muffins, and fruit.

The Blackwoods perform Tuesday through Sunday mornings, March through December. Tickets are $29.95 for adults and $9.95 for children 11 and younger.

The Jamboree's parent company, the Fee/Hedrick Family Entertainment Group, is offering an impressive combo price for 2009 that allows you to save big when you buy any two of six different shows in four separate Pigeon Forge theaters. In addition to *The Black Bear Jamboree* and the Blackwoods, the shows covered by the deal include *Magic Beyond Belief, The Comedy Barn*, The Miracle, and Exalt (in The Miracle Theater). These special combo tickets cost $49.95 for adults and

$9.95 for children ages 2 to 11 (the same price normally charged for a single child admission), and tickets are good for one week.

i If you want to get an autograph from a performer or even pose for a photograph with one, they're usually very accessible and willing to oblige after a performance (and sometimes during intermission). If you didn't bring your own memorabilia for your favorite star to sign, the theater gift shops will be happy to sell you something.

MAGIC BEYOND BELIEF THEATER
2135 Parkway, Pigeon Forge
(865) 428-5600
www.pigeonforgemagic.com

Master magician Terry Evanswood, who earned the Merlin Award (the magician's equivalent to an Oscar) from the International Magicians Society, is truly amazing. He brings everything from large-scale illusions to close-up sleight of hand to his show. Consummate skill, top-notch assistants, dramatic lighting and music, and various special effects (not to mention four and a half tons of props and equipment) all contribute to the wow factor. By incorporating comedy, live animals (from doves to tigers), and even audience participation into his show, Evanswood has crafted a well-rounded routine that will absolutely amaze you.

During the two-hour performance, guests witness Evanswood's variations on a number of classic feats of prestidigitation, such as levitation, sawing a person in half, disappearing in a box, and escaping from a trunk, as well as some tricks of his own unique design.

In 2007 Evanswood moved from doing morning shows only at the Country Tonite Theater to nightly shows and three matinees a week in his very own place (in the building that once housed the *Ole Smoky Hoedown*). A Chicago native, he has appeared all over the world, including Las Vegas and the famed Magic Castle in Hollywood. At the age of 21, Evanswood became the youngest person ever to perform at the Magic Castle,

which is also the headquarters for the Academy of the Magical Arts.

Tickets are $29.95 for ages 12 and older. Children 11 and under are admitted free (one per paying adult, with additional children $10 each).

Magic Beyond Belief's parent company, the Fee/Hedrick Family Entertainment Group, is offering an impressive combo price for 2009 that allows you to save big when you buy any two of six different shows in four separate Pigeon Forge theaters. In addition to *Magic Beyond Belief*, the shows covered by the deal include The Black Bear Jamboree, *The Comedy Barn, The Miracle, Exalt* (in The Miracle's theater), and *The Blackwood Breakfast Variety Show* (in the *Black Bear Jamboree*'s theater). These special combo tickets cost $49.95 for adults and $9.95 for children ages 2 to 11 (the same price normally charged for a single child admission), and tickets are good for one week. This is an especially good deal for shows like *The Black Bear Jamboree* that include a meal.

i Lots of the music theaters (including the Dixie Stampede and the Comedy Barn) feature audience participation. Volunteering doubles your fun, so don't hesitate to participate!

MEMORIES THEATRE
2141 Parkway, Pigeon Forge
(865) 428-7852, (800) 325-3078
www.memoriestheatre.com

Memories Theatre is one of the longer-running shows in Pigeon Forge. Since 1990, *Memories* has made its mark with the musical tribute, honoring a host of country, gospel, and rock 'n' roll greats through the songs that made them famous. The first half of the show is devoted to tributes to artists such as Roy Orbison, Kenny Rogers, Buddy Holly, and even Cher by the seven-piece Memories Showband as well as the Three Inspirations, a female vocal trio. The cast has such a large repertoire to its credit that it frequently changes the show's makeup from night to night.

The anchor of each *Memories* show is the Elvis Presley tribute by Lou Vuto, the longest-running Elvis show in Smokies. Vuto has no less than 30 Elvis costume replicas, so every night he chooses something different. As he belts out hit after Presley hit, you have to constantly remind yourself that you're not watching the real thing.

Memories Theatre generally gives one show an evening, up to six nights a week in high season and limited to weekends only in the off-season. Tickets are $29 for adults, $20 for ages 13 through 19, and $5 for ages 6 through 12. Ages 5 and younger are admitted free. Seniors ages 55 and up receive a $2 discount.

Memories has recently added a new matinee show called *Can't Stop the Beat* that showcases '50s and '60s rock 'n' roll three afternoons a week. Tickets are $18 for adults, $16 for seniors and teens, and $5 for ages 6 through 12. You can also save by purchasing combo tickets for both shows.

Some dinner theaters provide vegetarian entrees upon request, so do ask your server if you would prefer this option.

COUNTRY TONITE THEATRE
129 Showplace Boulevard, Pigeon Forge
(865) 453-2003, (800) 792-4308
www.countrytonitepf.com
Since opening in Pigeon Forge in 1997, Country Tonite Theatre has presented a fast-paced, high-energy show brimming with a broad spectrum of country music. With a beautiful, 1,500-seat auditorium as the setting, Country Tonite's cast of musicians, dancers, and featured vocalists give a two-hour-plus salute to country music's legendary performers, both past and present.

The ensemble (including some notable young singers) pays musical tribute to many country artists, including Patsy Cline, George Jones, Charlie Daniels, and Dolly Parton. Country Tonite's funnyman is Bubba, a slow-witted park ranger.

Country Tonite generally gives two shows daily (one in the afternoon and one in the evening) seven days a week from late March through December. Tickets are $27.75 for adults, and $17.75 for children ages 13 through 17 (both

including tax). Children ages 12 and under are admitted free (two per paid adult admission), while seniors 50 and up get a $2 discount.

Once a month from March through December, Eddie Miles does a Friday-night tribute to Elvis. Tickets are $24 for adults, including tax, and children 12 and under are free. Anywhere from one to five mornings a week during the same period, singer/songwriter, musician, and comedienne Patty Waszak does a morning show. Tickets are $20 for adults, including tax, and children under 13 are free. Seniors 50 and up get a $2 discount

In addition, the theater hosts several special-event shows throughout the year. In 2009 they will include performances by the likes of Loretta Lynn, Ronnie Milsap, and George Jones. Prices vary with the event.

SMITH FAMILY DINNER THEATER
2330 Parkway, Pigeon Forge
(865) 429-8100, (966) 399-8100
www.smithfamilytheater.com
The three Smiths (Charlie, his brother Jim, and Charlie's son Charlie Bob) deliver a blend of country, gospel, and oldies rock 'n' roll with plenty of comedy thrown in as well. The brothers also do some fabulous impersonations of various stars as well as a tribute to *The Andy Griffith Show*. If you're good with hula hoops, you may want to raise your hand when they ask for audience volunteers.

The show recently added an all-you-can-eat buffet, starting an hour before showtime. The spread includes fried chicken strips, grilled chicken, meat loaf, pot roast, jumbo cheese stuffed Italian shells, mashed potatoes, corn, macaroni and cheese, coleslaw, green beans, carrot cake, chocolate cake, and banana pudding. You can also opt to get just a dessert and beverage.

The Smith Family generally gives one show a night, six days a week, with two shows a night in the autumn. Tickets run $37.95 for adults and $18.95 for children ages 13 to 17. If you opt for just a dessert and drink with the show, tickets are $29.95 for adults and $14.95 for children ages 13 to 17. For either option, children ages 12 and under are free (one per paying adult), while seniors 55 and up receive $2 off.

The Smith Family Theater also hosts a relatively new '50s show called *Matt Cordell's Blast From the Past* that also includes a tribute to Elvis. This show is not a dinner show, but a beverage and popcorn are included in the price. Performances are generally three days a week, year-round. Tickets are $16.95 for adults and $8.49 for children ages 13 to 17. Children ages 12 and under are free (one per paying adult), while seniors 55 and up receive $2 off.

In 2009, the theater also began hosting a new Sunday night dinner show (Friday nights as well in high season) starring T.G. Sheppard singing a variety of his hits. Tickets are $39.95 for adults and $19.95 for teens ages 13 to 17. Children 12 and under are free (one per paying adult), but there's no senior discount. If you want to see this show and just have a dessert and a beverage, the tickets are $34.95 for adults and $17.49 for children ages 13 to 17.

GRAND MAJESTIC THEATER
125 Music Mountain Drive, Pigeon Forge
(865) 774-7777, (888) 472-6308)
www.thegrandmajestic.com
Big Band music from the '40s is the main element of this show off Teaster Lane (in the theater where *American Jukebox* used to be). The lead actor plays retired Colonel Edwin Parker, who takes the audience on a two-hour trip down Memory Lane to hear the songs of Glenn Miller, Benny Goodman, and the Andrews Sisters. There's lots of singing, dancing, and even a little '50s rock 'n' roll thrown in for good measure.

The Grand Majestic Theater generally gives one show a night year-round, as well as a Wednesdays morning show and two matinees a week during high season. Tickets are $29.95 for adults (although everyone can take advantage of a $10 coupon on the theater's brochure, available at the front counter) and $15 for ages 13 to 17. Entry is free for children ages 12 and under. The matinee shows are $3 less.

TENNESSEE SHINDIG
2391 Parkway, Pigeon Forge
(865) 908-3327, (888) 908-3327
www.tnshindig.com
The Tennessee Shindig (formerly Fiddler's Feast) isn't a dinner theater, but you do get dinner with your ticket—at the Western Sizzlin's Wood Grill Buffet next door. The two-hour show begins with a tribute to Tennessee, with country, gospel, and bluegrass music from Dolly, Elvis, and other stars who made it big on Nashville's Music Row. And what's a tribute to Tennessee without "Rocky Top"? So be prepared to hear the unofficial state song as well. The second half of the show focuses on music from each decade, starting with the '50s and moving through the '90s, with a patriotic grand finale. Cody Slaughter does a great young Elvis tribute in both halves of the show.

The Shindig generally gives two shows a night during high season and one show a night the rest of the year. Tickets are $31.95 for adults, $28.95 for teens and seniors, $9.95 for children ages 11 to 12, and $4.95 for children ages 6 through 10. Admission is free for children age 5 and younger. (If you don't want the all-you-can-eat buffet dinner, you can get a $5 discount per person).

THE COMEDY BARN THEATER
2775 Parkway, Pigeon Forge
(865) 428-5222, (800) 295-2844
www.comedybarn.com
You can't miss this place when you're driving down the Parkway. It is a huge, metal, barnlike structure that towers high above most of the buildings around it. Since it opened in 1994, *The Comedy Barn* has become one of the most popular shows in the area. It's one of the few theaters here that places an emphasis on comedy, although a bit of magic and some good ol' country music is also thrown into the mix.

While the show definitely has a bit of a country flavor, that "twang" is more of an accent than a traditional lampooning of Southern stereotypes. The ensemble cast includes jugglers, fire-eaters, ventriloquists, magicians, and, of course, stand-up comedians who have credits ranging from

Hee Haw to Evening at the Improv. You'll also see the Comedy Barn Canines, a troupe of rescue dogs from various animal shelters who do tricks.

Everyone in the cast (even the owners) gets directly involved in running other operations of the theater—everything from selling concessions to parking cars!

The show's lineup is staggered with segments of country and bluegrass music courtesy of the Comedy Barn All-Star Band and its gifted pickers. The host for each performance is Grandpa Duffy, an animatronic hillbilly character perched in the window of his old country cabin. On closer inspection, however, you realize that Duffy is actually playing a real banjo! His mechanical head and body are combined with the real hands and voice of one of the Comedy Barn's cast members, providing the Smokies' only "manimatronic" experience.

The Comedy Barn generally presents two shows a night in high season, although performances peter off to weekends only in the off-season. They even do shows on Thanksgiving and Christmas Day. Tickets are $24.95 for adults and free for children 11 and younger (one per paid adult admission).

The Comedy Barn's parent company, the Fee/Hedrick Family Entertainment Group, is offering an impressive combo price for 2009 that allows you to save big when you buy any two of six different shows in four separate Pigeon Forge theaters. In addition to The Comedy Barn, the shows covered by the deal include The Black Bear Jamboree, Magic Beyond Belief, The Miracle, Exalt (in The Miracle Theater), and the Blackwood Breakfast Variety Show (in the Black Bear Jamboree's theater). These special combo tickets cost $49.95 for adults and $9.95 for children ages 2 to 11 (the same price normally charged for a single

i Be sure to check area hotels and restaurants as well as the Internet for money-saving coupons to area shows. You'll typically receive a $1 or $2 discount. Also, don't forget to pick up those free tourist-oriented magazines that are usually rife with coupons.

child admission), and tickets are good for one week. This is an especially good deal for shows like The Black Bear Jamboree that include a meal.

GREAT SMOKY MOUNTAIN MURDER MYSTERY DINNER SHOW
2682 Teaster Lane, Pigeon Forge
(865) 908-1050, (888) 641-7183
www.murder-mystery-theater.com
This theater in the Riverview Outlet Mall across from Belz Outlets presents something you don't normally see in the Smokies—a show rated PG-13. You can bring your kids if you want, but you're warned that although there's no profanity, there is adult humor. The theater gives two alternating three-act shows: Murder on American Idle (where volunteers from the audience play judges as well as contestants on a karaoke version of American Idol; the winner goes home with a trophy) and WhoDunit Lucy (where the audience tries to solve a murder when Lucy tries to break into Ricky's show at the Tropicana; audience volunteers get to join the cast).

The dinner menu consists of creamy vegetable soup, salad, rolls, your choice of chicken or beef, garlic mashed potatoes, green beans, corn on the cob, and cheesecake for dessert. Alcoholic beverages are available. The murder mystery dinner show generally gives one performance per night, with an additional afternoon matinee in high season. Tickets are $32.95 for everyone.

DP'S CELEBRITY THEATER
1020 Dollywood Lane, Pigeon Forge
(865) 428-9488, (800) 365-5996
www.dollywood.com
Located just inside Dollywood's front turnstiles, this large theater is the site of Dollywood's largest performance venue. Performances vary depending on what festivals are currently running at Dollywood. Times and hours vary, too, so call Dollywood for specific information. Prices to these shows are included with park admission, except for occasional special concerts by Dolly herself. For details about theme park admission prices and general park information, see the Dollywood chapter.

DIXIE STAMPEDE
3849 Parkway, Pigeon Forge
(865) 453-4400, (800) 356-1676
www.dixiestampede.com

For more than two decades, the Dixie Stampede (part of the Dollywood family) has been one of the top theater draws in the Smokies. Each performance in the large, oval-shaped arena is a multifaceted event that includes trick riding, horseback competitions, music, magic, comedy, and a four-course meal.

The premise of the *Dixie Stampede* show is a friendly, Civil War–style rivalry; the audience is divided into "North" and "South" sections that "battle" each other during the evening through a series of horse-riding contests and other competitions (before being united in a rousingly patriotic grand finale). The show features a host of special effects, including pyrotechnics. At one point, a thunderous stampede of longhorn steers even storms the arena.

The meal consists of a whole rotisserie chicken, a slice of barbecued pork loin, creamy vegetable soup, biscuits, corn on the cob, potatoes, a hot apple turnover, and a beverage. By the way, if you're finicky about table manners, you can check your etiquette at the door. There's no silverware at Dixie Stampede—it's strictly hands-only!

Dixie Stampede is open four days a week in February, and seven days a week from March through the end of the year. Usually, the arena hosts two shows a night, but in peak season, there are up to five shows a day. Admission is $41.99 for adults and $21.99 for ages 4 through 11. Children ages 3 and younger are admitted free if they sit in a parent's lap and share his or her meal.

Gatlinburg

SWEET FANNY ADAMS THEATRE
461 Parkway, Gatlinburg
(865) 436-4039, (877) 388-5784
www.sweetfannyadams.com

The Smokies' oldest music variety theater has celebrated more than 30 seasons, featuring shows six nights a week from April through October and a holiday show on weekends in November and December. Tickets are $21.75 for anyone 13 or older, and $7.95 for children 12 and younger. Seniors (60 and up) get a $2 discount. Anyone in a wheelchair is free. (See the next Close-up in this chapter for more information on the show itself.) City parking, by the way, is available across the street.

ℹ Although most area theaters offer free admission to younger children, always be sure to ask if any stipulations go along with that discount. For example, some theaters request that small children sit in their parents' laps to be admitted free, while others will admit only one child free per paying adult.

NIGHTLIFE

REEL THEATRES MOVIES ON THE PARKWAY
713 Winfield Dunn Parkway, Sevierville
(865) 453-9055
www.seviermovies.info

If you want to catch a flick while you're in Sevier County, there's only one game in town, and it offers first-run box office attractions seven days a week on six screens. Each auditorium is equipped with Dolby Surround Sound and Digital Theater Sound. A video arcade and, of course, a well-stocked concession stand round out the offerings.

Throughout the year, the theater generally presents two shows each evening, plus two matinees. Admission is $7.75 for anyone age 13 and older and $5.75 for children ages 4 through 12 as well as seniors (age 60 and up). Children younger than 4 are admitted free but may be required to sit in a parent's lap during sellout situations. Movies that begin before 6 p.m. are bargain matinees; tickets are only $6.

BIG MAMA'S KARAOKE CAFE
10605 Chapman Highway, Seymour
(865) 609-0208
www.karaokecafe.com

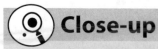

Close-up

Madness in the Heart of Gatlinburg

There's comedy, and then there's Sweet Fanny Adams Theatre, which presents a two-hour musical comedy extravaganza that is definitely like no other in the area. The 200-seat auditorium may be relatively small, but the comedy is dished out in huge portions. The humor is broad, full of slapstick, and downright silly, but it's also undeniably hilarious. And it's appropriate and enjoyable for all ages.

The first half of each evening consists of a short musical comedy. Each season features two new shows that play on alternating nights of the week, including such memorable examples as *Not Quite Snow White, A Knight's Tail and Other Acts of Superficial Foolishness, Once Upon a Pirate,* and *Déjà Vu All Over Again.* Since opening the theater in 1977, owners Don and Pat MacPherson have written, directed, and produced each show, some of which have gone on to play in Las Vegas and Atlantic City. The MacPhersons have extensive backgrounds in theater, having worked at one time or another as singers, dancers, actors, and directors throughout the United States and Europe.

Bringing these comedy gems to the boards nightly is the Great Victorian Amusement Company, the theater's troupe of performers that includes the MacPhersons and about five other thespians, some of whom have been Fanny Adams mainstays for years. (One of the troupe, Chris, is the MacPherson's son, a former clown with Ringling Brothers; the MacPherson's daughter, Jennifer, is the general manager.)

After the intermission, the show forges ahead with an old-fashioned sing-along and a vaudeville-style revue of music and comedy sketches. From beginning to end, the audience is very much a part of the show, making for a night of interactive fun that most area theaters can't duplicate.

Are you one of those people who likes to sing in the shower or in the car on the way to work? Don't keep your vocal talents to your self! Haul yourself over to Big Mama's Karaoke Cafe in Seymour, about 10 miles northwest of Sevierville on Chapman Highway. At Big Mama's, you can lend your voice to your favorite songs and be the singer you always knew you could be—at least in your own mind.

Part of the appeal of doing karaoke at Big Mama's is, no doubt, its simplicity. You select your favorite song from their catalog of more than 8,000 titles, and when your turn comes up, you take the stage, grab the mic, and wail to your heart's content. About 15 people per hour take the stage, and once the action starts for the day, it continues nonstop with no intermission.

While you're watching the singers (or waiting to go onstage yourself), you can order from Big Mama's full menu of appetizers, sandwiches, and entrees. House specialties include the Big

Mama Burger and the "Love Me Tender" chicken tenders. Beer is also available for those who need to steady their nerves before taking the stage.

The hours at Big Mama's Karaoke Cafe vary, although it's generally open Thursday, Friday, and Saturday, with a $5 cover charge on weekend nights. If you can't get enough of being at Big Mama's Karaoke Cafe, you can take the fun home with you. They offer karaoke systems for both sale and rental.

HOGG'S & HONEY'S SALOON & GRILL
745 Parkway, Gatlinburg
(865) 436-8515
www.hoggsandhoneys.net

If you've ever wanted to dance on a bar, this is your chance. Hogg's & Honey's was originally known as Coyote Ugly for its first year or so in business, which tells you a thing or two about what happens here. All the waitresses and even the female manager jump up on the extra-wide bar once an hour to get the crowd going. Anyone who is game is welcome to crawl on up and have at it. (Some brave booty-shaking souls have even been known to dive off the bar!) During high season, you'll find karaoke here on Wednesday nights and live music on Thursdays.

Hogg's & Honey's has a few other claims to fame as well, including its fabulous balcony overlooking the Parkway—possibly the best spot for unobtrusive people watching in town. They have anywhere from 50 to 60 different beers on the menu, not to mention locally award-winning chili, ribs, and wings. Because entrance is limited to those ages 21 and up, this is one of the few smoking bars in Gatlinbug.

CRAWDADDY'S RESTAURANT AND BAR
762 Parkway, Gatlinburg
(865) 430-3755
www.crawdaddys-gatlinburg.net
Crawdaddy's also has a fabulous balcony overlooking the Parkway. Kids are admitted here, though, and those age 10 and under even eat free. Crawdaddy's serves up seafood, steak, ribs, and Cajun specialties (such as alligator bites, po'boys, and gumbo) and offers a full drink menu, including a diverse selection of margaritas, martinis, and signature shooters. Every night is karaoke night, year-round.

BLAINE'S GRILL & BAR
812 Parkway, Gatlinburg
(865) 430-1978
www.blainesgatlinburg.com
Every night the tables are cleared from Blaine's main floor, and the deejay cranks out dance music from 10 p.m. to 1 a.m. (The deejay is live Friday and Saturday nights.) Many of the tunes are contemporary, while some are modernized dance mixes of older rock 'n' roll favorites. The clientele is mostly in the 20-something age range, but those 30- and 40-something folks who get into dancing to a loud, pounding dance beat will love Blaine's, too.

Blaine's is a full-service restaurant and bar, located on the corner of Parkway and Historic Nature Trail (formerly Airport Road). From the

outside, the three-story building is reminiscent of a Bourbon Street facade with its upper-level porches and iron railings. Inside, the main bar, dining areas, and dance floor are on the second level. A smaller bar area with limited seating occupies the third level.

Blaine's stops serving food at 9 p.m. on Friday and Saturday nights, which is when the dancing starts. At that time, there's a $3 cover, and you must be 21 to enter (photo ID required). Blaine's also hosts a big New Year's Eve gala every year with four different packages.

SMOKY MOUNTAIN BREWERY
1004 Parkway, Gatlinburg
(865) 436-4200
www.smoky-mtn-brewery.com
This restaurant and microbrewery is located in a Bavarian-style timber and stone building at Calhoun's Village near the south end of Gatlinburg's Parkway. The village itself is unique in that it offers visitors plenty of free parking.

Smoky Mountain Brewery provides entertainment six nights a week. Typically, you'll find karaoke Monday and Tuesday and live bands Wednesday through Sunday. The bands present varied styles ranging from light rock to bluegrass. The shows run from around 9:30 p.m. to 12:30 a.m., and there's never a cover charge. You don't have to be 21 to enter, but naturally, you must be to consume alcohol.

The main dining room, full-service bar, and entertainment section are upstairs. The heavily raftered room provides a simple and casual tavern-style atmosphere. There is a large-screen television, which is the center of attention during televised sporting events (especially Tennessee Volunteer football games). Those ordering from the menu will find a hearty selection of subs, sandwiches, and calzones as well as the restaurant's specialty—pizza. You can enjoy your meal in the main dining area or on the glassed-in porch.

Downstairs is where you'll find the microbrewery. The menu features as many as 13 different beers. Seven house beers are always on tap, including Cherokee Red Ale, Mountain Light,

Black Bear Ale, Old Thunder Road, Tuckaleechee Porter, and Velas Helles Lager. In addition, several brewmaster's specials and seasonal selections complement the overall selection.

This location is the company's first microbrewery, although another has opened in the Walden's Landing shopping area in Pigeon Forge. The Pigeon Forge location (at 2530 Parkway, call 865-868-1400 for information) offers the same beers and the same menu, but in a more modern setting.

THE FOX & PARROT TAVERN—
A BRITISH PUB
1065 Glades Road, Gatlinburg
(865) 435-0677
www.fox-and-parrot.com
This Smoky Mountain pub may not look exactly the same as its British brethren (it's in a log building), but it really is the real deal, as one quick look at the menu will tell you. (See the chapter on Restaurants for more details.) The tavern offers more than 60 brands of foreign and domestic beers and ales available bottled or on tap. This is a favorite spot for locals, with the dart league playing on Thursday nights. The proprietor, Brian Papworth, is an American Anglophile with British roots.

The Fox & Parrot is open until 8 p.m. from Monday through Thursday, until 10 p.m. on Fridays and Saturdays, and until 6 p.m. on Sunday.

ATTRACTIONS

From the fringes of Sevierville all the way to the national park entrance, the Smokies offer a little bit of everything—museums, historical sites, haunted houses, professional baseball, alien-infested miniature golf courses, go-kart tracks, and even indoor skydiving—although not necessarily in that order. In fact, you'll find almost any form of family-fun attraction you could possibly imagine (except the one that's going in next month). If you don't much care for viewing shrunken heads or gliding through prehistoric swamps, just glance around and you'll easily find a dozen other options vying for your attention in the immediate vicinity. Whether you consider this conglomeration of commercial fun to be awesome or awful, you must admit one thing: The Smokies don't do boring.

This chapter attempts to cover the highlights, moving as always from north to south. Those places that are off the main drag are included at the point on the Parkway where you'd turn off to get there. Hours of operation at all of these attractions vary widely. Basically, if area hotels and motels are full, hours expand and attractions are open late (sometimes even until 1 a.m.). When things calm down, the lights go off earlier. Several establishments cut back to weekends only or some other limited schedule during the off-season, which varies with the weather and demand. Your best bet for exact opening and closing times is to call ahead. Also, be aware that unless otherwise indicated, the prices in this chapter do not include tax.

Do take note that some amusements, including thrill rides and go-kart tracks, have minimum age and height requirements. Needless to say, pregnant women and people with heart and back conditions shouldn't participate in these activities. You'll also notice that several of the go-kart tracks are referred to as "slick tracks." This means that the driving surface is smoother than normal surfaces. Speeds are a little slower, but drivers have fun spinning their wheels on the turns!

Most Smoky Mountain attractions provide adequate free parking, especially those in Sevierville and Pigeon Forge. In Gatlinburg, you will probably have to rely on the city lots or garages, or you can simply leave your car at your hotel and walk or take the trolley.

By the way, if you're looking for coverage of Dollywood theme park or Dollywood's Splash Country water park, you won't find it in this chapter. Dollywood is such an expansive subject that it deserves its very own chapter. Likewise, active outdoor adventures, like rafting, tubing, horseback riding, and a few other unusual options guaranteed to provide an adrenaline rush, are listed in their own chapter, following this one.

SEVIERVILLE

TENNESSEE SMOKIES BASEBALL
3540 Line Drive, Kodak
(865) 637-9494, (888) 978-2288
www.smokiesbaseball.com
This AA minor league affiliate of the Chicago Cubs plays ball at Smokies Park in Sevierville, located just off Interstate 40 at exit 407. The facility features 6,000 fixed seats, grass berm seating for an additional 2,000 spectators on the hillside beyond the outfield, 18 private suites, and two patio areas. Ample restrooms and concession areas open directly onto the concourse that runs above and behind the stadium seating. The Double Play Cafe inside the stadium overlooks

the field and is open during ball games (see the Restaurants chapter). Visitors can also stop by an area welcome center located on the 25-acre site.

The Southern League season runs from April through early September, and the Smokies play more than half of their 140 games at home. The team runs countless special promotional nights during home stands, and they give away lots of prizes during the games themselves. Between innings, they usually run contest events for kids that take place on the field, including things like musical chairs, throwing water balloons, or racing the Smokies mascot around the bases. The stadium includes three separate "no alcohol" seating areas—two bleacher-level sections and one field-level section.

The team's history goes back to 1896, when they were founded as the Knoxville Indians. They've had many names since then, but finally settled on the Smokies in 1993. They still played in Knoxville until they moved to their current dugout digs in 2000.

Ticket prices range from $5 to $10, including tax, and on-site parking costs an additional $3. Season tickets are available in different packages.

SCENIC HELICOPTER TOURS
113 Helicopter Ride Boulevard, Sevierville
(865) 453-6342, (877) 359-7236
www.scenichelicoptertours.com

One of the most memorable ways to experience Smoky Mountain views is from high up in the air. This tour operator with more than 25 years' experience will take you on local helicopter flights that cover different areas between Douglas Lake and Pigeon Forge. These flights range from two-minute introductory flights for $10 per person to 24-mile trips over the Pigeon Forge foothills for $67 per person. Longer flights going as far as Gatlinburg and Wears Valley range from 28 to 80 miles and cost between $85 and $233 per person. (Exact flight times are flexible.) Riders wear headsets and listen to in-flight narration. If you're in town to get married, you might also consider Scenic's aerial weddings and honeymoon flights.

Scenic Helicopter Tours is open year-round, but flights run only when weather permits. Chil-
dren younger than two fly free. Ask about their combination packages with Wahoo Ziplines (see the Active Outdoor Adventures chapter for information on zipline tours) and their "light flights" during Winterfest.

GREAT SMOKY MOUNTAIN HELICOPTERS
1101 Winfield Dunn Parkway, Sevierville
(865) 429-2426

This helicopter tour company flies a number of local routes, starting with an introductory two-minute flight for $10 per person. The longest tour is an hour's ride, covering 120 miles, that costs $350. The company also offers custom flights for $1,200 per hour for up to six people. Great Smoky Mountain Helicopters is open year-round, weather permitting.

FLOYD GARRETT'S MUSCLE CAR MUSEUM
320 Winfield Dunn Parkway, Sevierville
(865) 908-0882
www.musclecarmuseum.com

If you're a "gear head," you'll feel like a kid in a candy store at this showplace of American custom and vintage performance cars. Open since 1996, the museum houses a collection of 90-plus "muscle cars" and occupies a massive 35,750 square feet of floor space. Most of the vehicles on display belong to Floyd Garrett, and each has been reconditioned to virtual perfection. Automotive fans have enjoyed up-close inspections of cars like NASCAR star Richard Petty's 1977 STP Monte Carlo as well as speedsters driven by racers Bobby Allison and Dale Earnhardt. You'll also see specialty cars like a 1940 Ford Coupe that was confiscated for running moonshine. The collection is always evolving, so the lineup of cars may change from visit to visit. Visitors can also view walls lined with racing memorabilia, check out a display of rare racing engines, and browse the gift shop, which is stocked full of souvenirs for the NASCAR junkie.

Admission is $8.95 for adults and $3.00 for children ages 8 through 12; children younger than 8 are admitted free.

SEVIER COUNTY COURTHOUSE
Court Avenue, Sevierville
No general phone

After the Great Smoky Mountains, the towering 75-foot spire of this century-old structure is usually the second thing that grabs your attention when driving into the city of Sevierville. One of the most recognized and photographed courthouses in Tennessee, the building maintains a stately presence in an otherwise rapidly developing tourist market. In 1976, it became the first Tennessee courthouse to be placed on the National Register of Historic Places. The exterior is predominantly red brick with a foundation of large, locally quarried limestone blocks. The architecture is Victorian and features an imposing clock tower surrounded by a number of smaller domed structures on the rooftop. The clock is the same one that was installed in 1896, and to this day it still faithfully chimes the hour and half hour.

The present structure is the fifth to serve as county courthouse and was completed in 1896 at a total cost of just over $21,000. In 1971, plans to do away with the aging building were scrapped in favor of a complete renovation, which included gutting virtually all of the wood used in its interior to minimize the risk of fire (after a fire devastated an earlier Sevier County courthouse). In the years that followed, two architecturally compatible annexes were added to the original building.

Don't miss the statue of a young Dolly Parton on the courthouse's east lawn. Sculpted by noted local artist Jim Gray, the life-size, cast bronze figure rests on a large rock base, dangling her bare feet, holding her guitar in her arms and sporting her trademark wide grin. She looks much as she did when she lived here, dressed in rolled-up jeans and a simple, button-down shirt and with her hair pulled back in a ponytail—a rare view of Sevier County's most famous native. Because most of the courthouse's noteworthy attributes can be seen from the outside, you can visit any time of day, even if all you do is pull your car up to the curb and snap a few pictures.

SEVIER COUNTY HERITAGE MUSEUM
167 East Bruce Street, Sevierville
(865) 453-4058

Take a trip back through time at this museum, just down the street from the courthouse, and see cherished relics and artifacts that tell the story of Sevier County's rich history. Inside, visitors can take a chronological tour that offers glimpses into the lives and times of the people who settled and developed the area. From the tools and arrowheads of early Indian inhabitants to an authentic telephone operator's switchboard from the mid-1900s, the museum's multiple displays and tributes bring treasured legends and memories to life.

The museum explores all aspects of the lives of area pioneers and settlers. Looking over preserved treasures like spinning wheels, butter churns, pantaloons, and corn shellers allows the visitor to conjure up images of a vanished era. See materials used in the construction of 18th- and 19th-century homes and marvel at the handcraftsmanship of muzzle-loading flintlock rifles. Other displays pay homage to Sevier Countians who served their country on the battlefield in the Civil War and World War II. Many of the items on hand, including photographs and newspapers, were donated by residents whose families had helped shape the events of their day. Those who wish to delve deeper into the past can peruse an extensive catalog of newsletters published by the Smoky Mountain Historical Society or purchase one of many different books on various facets of local history.

Located in downtown Sevierville, the building that houses the museum is historically significant itself. Erected in 1940, it served for years as the city's post office. The museum originally opened in the summer of 1995 in conjunction with Tennessee's bicentennial celebration. Although admission is free, the museum also welcomes donations. Volunteers staff the museum, so hours vary, but it's generally open on Monday, Tuesday, Thursday, and Friday from noon to 5 p.m. and on Saturday from noon to 3 p.m. You can park for free anywhere along Bruce Street.

ℹ️ The Sevier County History Center (next door to the Sevier County Public Library) has a wonderful genealogy department that can help you research your family history—even if you aren't from around here. For more information, call the center at (865) 908-7988 or visit www.sevierlibrary.org/NewGen/Homepage.htm.

SEVIER COUNTY PUBLIC LIBRARY
321 Court Avenue, Sevierville
(865) 453-3532
www.sevierlibrary.org

Every Wednesday is story day at the library! Story hour starts at 10:30 a.m. for preschool children and their parents. During the session, volunteers read aloud to the children from age-appropriate books. Participation by preschool and day-care groups is especially high during the school-year months.

In addition to the normal morning story, the children can also listen to guest speakers from the community, such as firefighters, veterinarians, and even clowns! These folks will use their time to tell the children about their occupations. The kids especially enjoy going outside to check out the real squad cars when a local police officer is part of the program.

The library itself has a separate section for children's books and has hundreds of children's videos on its shelves. Sevier County residents (including anyone who owns property in the county, even if it's not your main residence) can easily obtain a library card, of course, but out-of-county residents can also check out materials with a nonresident library card, which costs $25 per year.

To get to the library from the Parkway, turn east on Prince Street and go 1 block. Then turn left on Court Avenue. The library will be on your left.

TENNESSEE MUSEUM OF AVIATION

TENNESSEE AVIATION HALL OF FAME
135 Air Museum Way, Sevierville
(865) 908-0171, (866) 286-8738
www.tnairmuseum.com

Aviation and history fans alike will enjoy this 50,000-square-foot museum and hangar located near the Gatlinburg–Pigeon Forge Airport in Sevierville (yes, Sevierville). The Tennessee Museum of Aviation, which opened in December 2001, is home to a host of authentic memorabilia that tells the story of powered flight. Items such as photos, scale models, military flight suits, and aircraft paraphernalia bring the history of aviation to life through a series of professionally designed displays.

Although several of the sections showcase the role that aircraft played during times of war, one area taps more into the museum's theme, detailing the contributions that Tennesseans have made to aviation. Exhibits include a large jet aircraft engine, a hands-on flight simulator, and a wall-size time line of national and statewide aviation milestones.

The museum's main attraction, however, is the 10,000-square-foot Warbirds Hangar, displaying as many as 20 active, flying vintage aircraft on a rotating basis. If you visit at the right time, you might even be fortunate enough to watch the museum's owner, Neal Melton, as he takes one of the birds up for a flyby.

The facility is also home to the Tennessee Aviation Hall of Fame, which celebrates the men and women from the Volunteer State who have made significant contributions to flying. In 2002 the museum inducted its inaugural slate of honorees, including Evelyn Bryan Johnson, a resident of Morristown, Tennessee, who has racked up more flying time than any woman in the world and until recently was the oldest living flight instructor. "Momma Bird" turns 100 in 2009.

The Tennessee Museum of Aviation and Hall of Fame are open year-round. Admission is $12.75 for those 13 and older; $6.75 for ages 6 through 12; and free for those under 6. Seniors (ages 60 and older) are $9.75. All admission prices include tax. To get to the museum, turn off the Parkway at Connie Houston Drive and then turn right at Park Road.

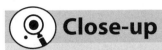

Close-up

All the Deer That's Fit to Feed

You don't have to worry about the llamas spitting at the hands-on Smoky Mountain Deer Farm and Exotic Petting Zoo, located on a 140-acre farm way off the beaten path in Sevierville. That's because the animals there that look like llamas aren't llamas—they're guanacos (the animal the llama was bred from), and guanacos don't spit.

Roam the grounds at your own pace and enjoy the many different animal species—some of which, like the kangaroos and wallabies, are a long way from home. You can go inside two of the pens to pet and feed the animals. Be aware, however, that if you're carrying feed (and do use only the feed provided by the petting zoo), you'll soon become very popular with the "locals." If you have smaller children in tow, watch out for them to be sure they don't get overwhelmed. If you prefer, you can have the little ones feed the goats and deer from outside the fence.

You're also welcome to feed the various breeds of donkeys, zebras, and miniature horses you'll encounter while winding through the complex's pathways. (When feeding any of the "horse-like" animals, make sure you feed them with a flat, open palm.) However, you definitely must not feed the kangaroos and wallabies, because they consume a special diet provided by the owners. As the farm's name implies, you can also visit many varieties of deer, including the fallow deer and the reindeer. Along the way you'll see Rocky Mountain elk, potbellied pigs, prairie dogs, exotic cattle, emu, and even sheep (which definitely aren't deer, and they definitely aren't exotic, but they're still fun to pet and feed).

---

i Many Smoky Mountain amusements give discounts to those with military ID, so if you're a member of the armed services, remember to ask about special prices.

SMOKY MOUNTAIN DEER FARM AND EXOTIC PETTING ZOO
478 Happy Hollow Lane, Sevierville
(865) 428-3337
www.deerfarmzoo.com
About 7 miles from the intersection with the courthouse (turning east on Dolly Parton Parkway; call for exact directions) is Smoky Mountain Deer Farm and Exotic Petting Zoo. For more than a decade, visitors have been coming here to feed and get face-to-face (and often hand-to-mouth) with a live menagerie that includes camels and zebras, kangaroos and llamas, ferrets and reindeer. It's a great alternative to arcades and miniature golf courses. (See the Close-up in this chapter for more details.)

Admission is $10.95 for ages 13 and older; $5.95 for ages 3 to 12; and a nickel for children ages 2 and younger. Feed for the animals (please use only the special feed provided) is $2.50 for a 22 ounce cup. Pony rides for children weighing less than 100 pounds are $6.50.

The facility is open year-round, but it's best to call ahead to verify hours during periods of bad weather. Owners Greg and Lynn Hoisington also operate Deer Farm Riding Stables, which is located on the same property. See the Active Outdoor Adventures chapter for more information on horseback-riding opportunities.

FORBIDDEN CAVERNS
455 Blowing Cave Road, Sevierville
(865) 453-5972
www.forbiddencavern.com
Although you won't exactly journey all the way to the center of the earth here, you'll get a good feel for what it might be like in this large underground cave located approximately 15 miles east of downtown Sevierville (accessible via Dolly Parton Parkway/Highway 411N; call for directions). Stalactites, stalagmites, towering natural

ATTRACTIONS

chimneys, and grottoes are among the many natural formations you'll witness on your adventure, as well as the largest known wall of rare cave onyx. Enhanced by special lighting effects and a stereophonic sound presentation, your guided, 55-minute tour is chock-full of memorable sights and will take you a half-mile into the heart of English Mountain.

The trails are well lighted, with handrails where necessary. In addition to the rock structures, you'll also see a running stream that's believed to flow from a lake deep within the mountain. Your guide will tell you about the people who carved out the cavern's colorful history, from the Eastern Woodland Indians who used the cave as shelter to the moonshiners of the 1920s and 1930s.

Forbidden Caverns is open from April through November. Admission is $13 for adults and $7 for children ages 5 through 12; prices include tax. Souvenirs and refreshments are also available, as is plenty of free parking.

i With more than 8,350 registered caves, Tennessee has more caves than any other state in the Union.

RAINFOREST ADVENTURES
109 NASCAR Drive, Sevierville
(865) 428-4091
www.rfadventures.com
This museum of reptiles and amphibians, located behind the NASCAR Cafe in the Governor's Crossing development, slithered into the Smokies in 2001. Throughout the facility's 15,000 square feet of exhibit space are snakes such as cobras, mambas, pythons, and boa constrictors (sorry, Indiana Jones) as well as other interesting species, including lizards, alligators, frogs, turtles, tarantulas, scorpions, ring-tailed lemurs and serval cats. Habitats replicate each animal's natural surroundings and create the feel of an Amazon rain forest. Try to catch one of the live shows and demonstrations, scheduled every two hours. If they volunteer, your kids might get to hold one of the critters!

Out back (no pun intended) is the Aussie Walkabout, which doubled Rainforest Adven-

ture's size when it opened in 2008. The Walkabout features a 4,600-square-foot aviary with Australian birds, an Aussie Sheep Station where guests may feed and pet sheep, and an enclosure where guests can interact with kangaroos and wallabies.

Admission is $11.99 for adults and $6.99 for children ages 3 to 12. Seniors 55 and up are $9.99.

HILLSIDE WINERY
229 Collier Drive, Sevierville
(865) 908-8482, (877) 908-9460
www.hillsidewine.com
This brand-new winery specializing in sparkling and Italian-style wines made its debut November 2008. Owner Don Collier also owns and operates Mountain Valley Winery (which specializes in French and German wine) and the Apple Barn Winery (specializing in fruit wines)—both of which are described later in this chapter. If you visit all three wineries (following what's now referred to as the Rocky Top Wine Trail), you will get a free gift.

Hillside is a cork-free winery—all their wines feature screw caps. The label for each variety of wine displays a stunning photo of a different species of butterfly, all photographed by Tennessee nature photographer Patricia Ferguson.

Tours and tastings are free. The winery also has a shop that sells natural springwater originating from an area spring and locally made goodies that include cheese, jams, and jellies. You can buy bottles of wine to take with you, or Hilltop will ship wine anywhere in the U.S.—except within the state of Tennessee.

NASCAR SPEEDPARK
1545 Parkway, Sevierville
(865) 908-5500
www.NASCARSpeedPark.com
As a licensed activity of NASCAR, this attraction has a lot in store for fans of one of the fastest-growing spectator sports in the country. All of the park's downsize race cars are custom-designed and custom-built. Four actual NASCAR show vehicles are on display throughout the property

as are more than 100 items of NASCAR memorabilia and hundreds of photos of NASCAR events and stars.

With eight tracks spread out over 26 acres, this $15-million speed park, which opened in 1999, is Sevier county's third-largest attraction by acreage (after Dollywood and Ober Gatlinburg). The tracks are each different and cater to every driving preference and skill level. At one end of the spectrum is the Baby Bristol track for drivers who are at least 40 inches tall. The small, single-loop circuit is just right for youngsters. At the other extreme is the quarter-mile Smoky Mountain Speedway track, which requires drivers to be at least 5 feet tall. Kids who aren't quite tall enough can try the Rookie Experience on the same quarter-mile track. Participants need only be 54 inches tall for this one.

In between are other courses—the Qualifier, Young Champions, Slidewayz, the Intimidator, and the Competitor—that range from basic oval shapes to multiple-turn surfaces. Minimum height requirements for these tracks range from 48 inches for the Qualifier to 62 inches for the Competitor. The Family 500 track has double-seat karts so that adults and children can burn rubber together. Drivers must be at least 48 inches tall (or 60 inches tall for a double car), and passengers must be at least 40 inches tall.

Inside the main building is the 28,000-square-foot Speed Dome arcade, featuring more than 60 racing games and driving simulators. You'll also find the Pit Stop Grill and souvenir shops full of SpeedPark memorabilia and apparel. Rounding out the amusements are bumper boats, a climbing wall, and two miniature golf courses.

NASCAR SpeedPark is open year-round. The number of tickets required ranges from one ticket for the Baby Bristol track to four tickets for the Smoky Mountain Speedway. Individual tickets sell for $3 each, with packages of 9 tickets for $20 or 25 tickets for $50. An all-access wristband pass for all ages costs $32 and includes access to all rides and attractions except the Smoky Mountain Speedway and the NASCAR Silicon Motor Speedway Simulator.

i Prices posted at most attractions don't include tax. For your information, state and local sales taxes combined are a whopping 9.75 percent in Gatlinburg, Pigeon Forge, and Sevierville. Pigeon Forge and Gatlinburg tack on an additional 2 percent amusement tax, for a total tax of 11.75 percent in those cities.

RIPLEY'S OLD MACDONALD'S FARM MINI GOLF
1639 Parkway, Sevierville
(865) 428-1699, (888) 240-1358
www.ripleysgatlinburg.com
This miniature golf course proves that at least in the Smokies, pigs really do fly. Three imaginative 18-hole courses are each bedecked with colorful animated barnyard animals (including—you guessed it—a porker with wings). The complex also has an impressive 4,000-square-foot state-of-the-art arcade.

The cost for players 12 and older is $9.99 for 18 holes, $13.99 for 36 holes, and $15.99 for all 54 holes. For players ages 5 to 11, the costs are $7.99, $9.99, and $10.99, respectively. For children 2 to 4, the cost is $2.99, $4.99, or $5.99. This attraction is part of the Ripley's You-Pick voucher, which gives discounts on Ripley's attraction combos when you visit Ripley's Aquarium of the Smokies. See the detailed description of the voucher in the listing for the aquarium in the Gatlinburg section of this chapter.

PIGEON FORGE

MOUNTAIN VALLEY VINEYARDS
2174 Parkway, Pigeon Forge
(865) 453-6334, (866) 453-6334
www.mountainvalleywinery.com
This Pigeon Forge winemaker provides free guided tours of its operation. The grape-crushing machine, the massive steel fermenting tanks, and the automated bottler all give visitors a firsthand glimpse at a process that has produced national award-winning vintages. Those interested in tasting the finished product can sample, at no

charge, any of Mountain Valley's 14 labels at their tasting bar. Of the three Don Collier wineries, this one specializes in French and German varieties. (To read about the other two Collier wineries, see the description of Hillside Winery in the Sevierville section, as well as of the Apple Barn Winery, later on in this chapter.)

Mountain Valley Vineyards, one of 33 wineries in the state of Tennessee, primarily uses grapes from regional vineyards. Seven of the vineyards are located within a 60-mile radius of the winery itself. Because 85 percent of the grapes used are grown in-state, Tennessee agricultural laws allow Mountain Valley Vineyards to market its product in a city that otherwise is not permitted to sell wine. Forty different types of grapes and a variety of other fruits such as raspberries, blackberries, and strawberries are put through a fermenting process that can take anywhere from one to five years. The result: a respectable menu of dry, semisweet, and dessert wines. Mountain Valley Vineyards does ship wine out of state, but by law they can't ship within the state of Tennessee.

DINOSAUR WALK MUSEUM
106 Showplace Boulevard, Pigeon Forge
(865) 428-4003
www.dinowalk.com

A menacing two-story-high T-Rex is one of the 60 life-size replicas of prehistoric creatures that greet visitors as they tour this fun and educational collection. But they're not all giants. The smallest 'saur represented here is the tiny 12-inch-tall, one-pound Microraptor. Other exhibits include giant sea lizards; flying reptiles; and replicas of bones and skulls of ancient prehistoric creatures.

The fascinating dinosaur sculptures here are called "flesh replications." To create them, the artists use actual fossils, footprints, and other information. First, they build a wooden skeleton, which they then cover in clay and sculpt to the dinosaur's actual size. To do that, they analyze modern-day animals to figure out what muscle mass a creature of that size would have. The artists then make molds from the clay models and cast the beasts in fiberglass. When the pieces are painted and fully assembled, the effect is eerily realistic.

The Dinosaur Walk Museum also shows high-definition educational films and offers a monthly series of dinosaur-related activities, hands-on studies, and demonstrations by paleontologists as part of its innovative Kids Club program.

Admission is $9.95 for adults; $6.95 for children ages 4 to 11; and free for children under 4.

MAGIQUEST
2491 Parkway, Pigeon Forge
(865) 686-5586
www.magiquest.com

The moment you see this fanciful gray-stone castle with a green cartoon dragon peaking out a side window, you know you're in for a fantastic experience—quite literally. Fantasy becomes reality here, where you get to see what it's like to step into a video game. To begin your adventure, select a magic wand (yours to keep) and then receive training in how it works. When you set off on your quest, your interactive wand tracks your progress and remembers all your tasks and all your powers as well as your experience level as you play. The quests have multiple parts, just like a video game, and they all end with you using your wand to battle the dragon. You can progress as fast or as slowly as you want, and you can even stop in the middle and return later that day or another day—or even to another MagiQuest location in another city. Your wand will remember exactly where you left off, and you'll pick up the game from there. (This pause feature is a good thing, because each quest takes between 10 and 15 hours to finish!)

MagiQuest was just added in May of 2009 to this attraction, which originally opened in 2008 as Adventure Quest. The Adventure Quest elements are all downstairs, including pirate-themed black light golf, a laser maze (where you must make it through a maze in a room filled with lasers without touching any of the beams), and a 500-square-foot mirror maze.

Admission for the mirror maze is $11.95 for adults; $6.95 for children ages 4 to 12; and free for those under 4. The laser maze costs $3.95. Black light golf costs $9.95 for adults and $6.95 for children ages 4 to 12. Combo tickets that get you into all the downstairs fun are available at $14.95 for adults and $9.95 for children. Prices for MagiQuest were not available at press time.

WALDEN'S LANDING FIREHOUSE GOLF
2528 Parkway, Pigeon Forge,
(865) 908-1933
www.waldenslanding.com
These two 18-hole firefighter-themed miniature golf courses are smack dab in the center of the Walden's Landing shopping center. It's a cute course, with forest creatures like a big bear and a raccoon dressed up in firefighters' hats and bright red suspenders. The six waterfalls add a nice touch, too. Outside the entrance is a big, bright red 1939 fire truck that kids are welcome to climb on. Tickets cost $8 for adults and $6 for children ages 3 to 11 for one course. If you want to play the second 18 holes, it's half price.

THE TRACK
2575 Parkway, Pigeon Forge
(865) 453-4777
www.pigeonforgetrack.com
Although there's a lot to take on at this sprawling family amusement center, the focus is on go-kart racing, including two twisty, curvy, outdoor tracks. The first, simply called the Track, uses one- and two-seat karts. Solo drivers must be at least 4 feet 6 inches tall, and those driving the two-seaters must be at least 16 years old. Passengers in the two-seaters must be at least 3 feet tall. The cost to drive either a single or double car is two tickets. Passengers 4 feet 6 inches tall and under ride for free, while passengers taller than 4 feet 6 inches pay two tickets.

When the other outdoor track, the Wild Woody, was added in 1999, it helped usher in the advent of wooden go-kart tracks in the Smoky Mountains. The driving surface is actually a hybrid combination of the original, ground-level, concrete track and a newer, add-on section—a multi-tiered wooden track that goes through several humps and corkscrew twists. The driving is a little slower than on the run-of-the-mill go-kart track, but like wooden roller coasters, the wooden tracks give karsters a ride you can really feel.

To drive on the Wild Woody, you must be at least 4 feet 10 inches tall. Drivers with passengers must be at least 16 years old. Two-seater passengers on the Wild Woody must be at least 3 feet tall. The cost to drive either a single or double car is three tickets. Passengers 4 feet 10 inches tall and under ride along for free, while passengers more than 4 feet 10 inches tall pay three tickets.

If you're in search of an even bigger adrenaline rush, bungee-jump from the Track's 75-foot tower ($16, half-price for repeat jumps). Or try the Sky Flyer thrill ride, which goes back and forth horizontally and takes up to three people at once ($16; riders must be 3 feet 6 inches tall).

Gator Golf provides two 18-hole miniature courses adorned with various animal figures. The cost is three tickets per person per 18-hole round for ages 13 and older. Ages 6 to 12 can golf for two tickets, and kids 5 and younger can tag along for free with a paid adult. Bumper cars are available for two tickets to anyone taller than 4 feet 2 inches (although anyone shorter can ride with an adult driver).

The Kid's Country area is for younger children and features a number of carnival-style rides that cost one ticket each. There's even a Kiddie Kart Raceway where the smaller ones can burn rubber on their own track. Drivers of the Kiddie Karts must be at least 4 years old, and drivers of the Rookie Karts must be at least 4 feet 2 inches tall. Both karts cost two tickets. (Note that Kid's Country is closed during most of January and February, even when the rest of the Track is open.)

Pigeon Forge's much-anticipated Belle Island Village—a huge dining, retail, and attraction complex already under construction—was in limbo at press time. Darrell Waltrip's Racing Experience (a variety of racing simulators), Otter Cove river otter habitat, and Debbie Reynold's Hollywood Motion Picture Museum ($50 million worth of Hollywood memorabilia, the world's largest collection) are momentarily on hold. Check www.belleisland.com for updates.

Individual tickets are $2.99, or you can purchase discounted bundles of 6 tickets for $16.50 or 14 tickets for $36.40. The Go-Kart Fun Pack is the biggest package. For $70.84, you get 28 tickets and the chance to buy additional tickets for $1.50 each any day you want until the end of the year.

ELVIS MUSEUM
2638 Parkway, Pigeon Forge
(865) 428-2001, (866) 683-5847
www.elvismuseums.com

Elvis may have left the building, but he sure left a lot of stuff behind! Get an up-close peek at the first Elvis museum outside the walls of Graceland and the world's largest privately owned collection of Elvis Presley memorabilia—everything from clothes to cars, guns to guitars. The museum has been around since 1979, but it got a major overhaul in 2005.

The sounds of Elvis's music fill the air as you approach the front doors. Inside, you'll see plenty of authentic personal effects that belonged to the King, including stage costumes, backstage notes, sports gear, gifts from fans, jewelry, and sunglasses. There are several larger items in the collection as well, like the last limousine owned by Presley as well as the fire-engine red 1967 Cadillac Coupe de Ville that Elvis and Priscilla drove on their honeymoon. You can also take a gander at the living-room furniture from his Hollywood home, as well as his karate uniform, the original TCB ring, and the first dollar he ever earned in 1951 (complete with his autograph). For those interested in adding to their own collection of Elvis trinkets, four separate souvenir shops carry a healthy selection of music, videos, books, and other assorted knickknacks. If you work up an appetite, Houndawg's Snack Shop will oblige.

The museum complex also includes the TCB Theater (located directly above the museum), where you can watch a two-hour live Elvis tribute show anywhere from one to three nights a week, often starring Tennessee native and award-winning professional Elvis impersonator Matt Cordell. True-blue Elvis fans may want to check out the overnight accommodations in the TCB Suite, a luxury suite with pictures of the King on the walls.

Admission to the museum is $17 for adults; $15 for children ages 12 to 18; and $12 for children ages 6 to 11. Seniors (ages 65 and up) are $15, and children younger than 6 are free. A family pass for parents and their children is $45. Tickets to the TCB Theater are $25 for adults, or $22.50 for children ages 12 to 18 and for seniors (children under 12 are free). Combo tickets for the museum and theater are also available.

i Titanic Pigeon Forge opens in spring 2010 near WonderWorks. This $25 million ship-shaped attraction will include exact replicas of the grand staircase, a first-class suite, a third-class cabin, and the Marconi wireless room. Interactive features will allow you to touch an iceberg, sit in an actual lifeboat, "steer" the ship, and send an SOS message. Check www.TitanicPigeon Forge.com for updates.

STAR TRACKS
2757 Parkway, Pigeon Forge
(865) 908-1097
www.lazerportfuncenter.com

In addition to a fairly large indoor arcade and laser tag, this amusement center features the Family Slick Track, a covered track open to drivers 4 feet 8 inches and taller where they can go at speeds up to 40 mph. Admission is $10 per ride (or $12 for a two-seater; drivers must be at least 16 years old), and every ride after that is half off for the rest of the day. Laser tag costs $8.

You can also get a special Park Hopper pass that lets you mix and match rides at any of four amusement centers (Star Tracks, Rockin' Raceway, Lazerport Fun Center, and Speed Zone Fun Park). The pass gives you five rides for $25 or 10 rides for $45 per person.

Close-up

Anything but Ordinary at WonderWorks

You can't miss this interactive science museum on the Parkway. The marble mansion that houses WonderWorks seems to have been mercilessly tossed upside down, with its roof crushed in and its palm-tree landscaping hanging from its uprooted lawn like fringe on a sombrero. The premise, you soon discover, is that the attraction is really a top-secret science institute that was located in the Bermuda Triangle until an experiment went wrong; the resulting explosion propelled the building sky high until it landed here, forever inverted. You even have to walk through hissing and billowing steam from the burst and groaning pipes to get inside.

It's well worth the effort. The two-story museum offers more than 120 displays and activities, including the chance to experience a 5.3-magnitude earthquake as well as 65-mph hurricane winds. At a computer simulator, you can try to land the Discovery space shuttle. The museum even includes a rock-climbing wall and specially designed bicycles that, when pedaled hard enough, make 360-degree loops. A section on optical illusions is particularly intriguing.

Perhaps the most unusual offering is the opportunity to lie on a bed of nails to learn about the principle of weight distribution. (Warning: The nails really are sharp!) The museum also has a video arcade, a laser tag attraction, and the Hoot n' Holler dinner show (see the Music and Entertainment Theaters and Nightlife chapter).

WonderWorks (865-868-1800; www.wonderworkstn.com) is at 2046 Parkway (on the site of the former Music Mansion). Tickets are $19.95 for ages 13 and up, and $12.95 for children ages 4 to 12. Laser tag costs $5.95 for the first game, and $2.95 for each additional game. Combo tickets with various combinations of the museum, laser tag, and/or the dinner show are also available.

If you're looking for a good deal on go-kart racing, try visiting the amusement centers before noon, when the majority of the tracks have some kind of two-for-one deal going. Plus, showing up in the morning is a good way to beat the intense heat of those Tennessee summers.

LAZERPORT FUN CENTER
2782 Parkway, Pigeon Forge
(865) 453-0400
www.lazerportfuncenter.com

Lazerport offers an outdoor, roller-coaster-style go-kart track that's three stories high and includes a 40-foot plunge. Drivers must be at least 4 feet 8 inches tall, and to drive a two-seat kart, you must be at least 16 years old. Passengers on the two-seaters must be three years old.

Inside Lazerport, you'll find high-tech black-light laser tag inside two labyrinth arenas. After a short briefing on how to play the game and use the equipment, players suit up and let loose, blasting their opponents away. Games last for 15 minutes, and players get infinite lives and infinite shots, eliminating the need to reload. Players as young as five or six years old can participate, depending on their size. You'll also find a massive indoor arcade, an 18-hole black-light mini-golf course, and the brand-new Sweet Sensation ice-cream parlor (which sells ice cream, funnel cake, milk shakes, popcorn, and candy).

Tickets are $10 per person including tax for the first activity, and then $5 for any additional activities for the rest of the day. Two-seater go-karts are $12 for the first ride, and $6 for any other double-kart ride. You can also get a special Park Hopper pass that lets you mix and match rides at any of four amusement centers (Lazerport Fun Center, Star Tracks, Rockin' Raceway, and Speed Zone Fun Park). The pass gives you five rides for $25 or 10 rides for $45 per person.

JURASSIC JUNGLE BOAT RIDE
2806 Parkway, Pigeon Forge
(865) 908-7599

This indoor boat ride takes you on a 15-minute journey down a winding river through a creepy dinosaur-infested jungle, complete with waterfalls and a geyser. Some 15 to 20 unruly reptiles move and roar (and one even spits at you) as you glide by. Admission is $13.99 for those ages 12 and older, $9.99 for children ages 5 to 11, and $4.99 for children ages 3 and 4. Kids under 3 are admitted free.

ROCKIN' RACEWAY
2839 Parkway, Pigeon Forge
(865) 428-3392
www.rockinraceway.net

Rockin' Raceway offers a very large, well-equipped video arcade, as well as a figure-eight slick track. You must be three years old to ride, and 56 inches tall to drive. To drive a double kart, you must be at least 16 years old. Admission is $10 per ride, and every ride after that is half off for the rest of the day. Kids who are too short to drive can ride free. You can also get a special Park Hopper pass that lets you mix and match rides at any of four amusement centers (Rockin' Raceway, Star Tracks, Lazerport Fun Center, and Speed Zone Fun Park). The pass gives you five rides for $25 or 10 rides for $45 per person.

FAST TRACKS
2879 Parkway, Pigeon Forge
(865) 428-1988

The centerpieces of this multifaceted entertainment center are the two outdoor go-kart tracks. The pro track is a fast road course for racing enthusiasts, while the elevated track spirals up 45 feet in the air and then races down through tunnels and hills. On either of the tracks, you must be at least 10 years old and 4 feet 6 inches tall to drive alone. To take a passenger, you must be at least 16, and your passenger must be at least 3 years old and 3 feet tall. The go-kart tracks are $8 per person, or $12 for a two-seater. Combo tickets that allow you to ride both the pro and the elevated track are $12. All prices include tax.

For a different sort of thrill, try the Sky Scraper, a large pendulum-like contraption that whirls occupants around in vertical loops. Tickets are $20 (or $30 for two people). Other Fast Tracks offerings include a trampoline jump ($7) and the VR Voyager roller-coaster simulator ride ($6). At the Junior Track, drivers ages four through eight can zip around a small, single-loop track for $6 each. Younger children will probably prefer the many kiddie rides, which cost $2.50 each or six for $10.00.

SPIN CITY USA SKATE CENTER
2891 Parkway, Pigeon Forge
(865) 774-5998
www.spincityusa.com

Spin City is, as you may imagine from the name, a roller-skating rink. This wildly colorful place is open year-round, and a live deejay entertains on the weekends. Admission usually ranges from $6 to $8, but it's $10 on Friday and Saturday nights when there's a live deejay. Skate rental is $2 extra. All prices include tax. Spin City runs specials on different days. On Tuesdays rentals are included in the skating price, and on Sundays a family of four can skate for $20 (including skate rentals) and can also get a large pizza for $7 ($3 less than the usual price). Downstairs, there's a figure-eight go-kart track that usually gives extra-long rides. Single tickets are $8, including tax, and a double car is $12.

ADVENTURE GOLF
2925 Parkway, Pigeon Forge
(865) 453-9233

Adventure Golf is one of the more attractive and interesting miniature golf courses in the area. In fact, its owners claim that it's the oldest commercial miniature golf course in Pigeon Forge. Here, you'll be putt-putting amid mammoth versions of a dinosaur, a shark, an octopus, and more. Large shipwreck and castle scenes add to the landscaping. Adventure Golf has two 18-hole courses that cost $7.50 each, including tax; you can play a second round for only $3 more. Children ages four and younger are admitted free.

ADVENTURE RACEWAY
2945 Parkway, Pigeon Forge
(865) 428-2971

Adventure Raceway features one outdoor track—another of the several wooden go-kart tracks that sprang up on the Parkway in 1999. Since then, a curvy, multilevel wooden section was added to the existing figure-eight, ground-level track. The cost is $7.50 per ride, including tax (or $10.00 for a double car), and drivers must be at least 4 feet 8 inches tall.

Adventure Raceway also has bumper boats that cost $7 per ride. You must be 3 feet 6 inches tall to operate the boats. Children who are more than three years old but who are still under the minimum height requirements may ride free as passengers on both the go-kart track and the bumper boats. The attraction also has a large arcade.

SMOKY MOUNTAIN CAR MUSEUM
2970 Parkway, Pigeon Forge
(865) 453-3433

Since 1956, this showplace of rare and vintage cars has offered self-guided tours through the history of the automobile. The collection of more than 30 cars and trucks features such notable vehicles as the silver Aston-Martin driven by James Bond in the films *Goldfinger* and *Thunderball*, Al Capone's bulletproof Cadillac, Elvis Presley's 1971 Mercedes Benz, and the "Silver Dollar" car owned by Hank Williams Jr. A number of classic antiques are on display as well: a 1930 Duesenberg, a 1909 Hupmobile, and a 1915 Ford Model T, just to mention a few. All of the cars on display have been reconditioned and are in running order.

What makes this museum truly unique is that it's much more than just a "car museum." Most of the wall space and virtually every spare nook and cranny are packed with hoards of interesting antiques and memorabilia. Many of the relics are, of course, automobile-related: newspaper clippings, photographs, model cars, antique gas pumps, and mechanic's tools. You'll also see items that would seem equally at home in any antiques mall: old manual typewriters, nickel-odeons, gum-ball machines, and even a display of different types of barbed wire! The gift shop has a wide assortment of collectible books and magazines.

Admission is $7.50, including tax, for adults and $2.00 for children ages 3 through 10. Children younger than 3 are admitted for free. The museum is open from early spring through late fall.

PROFESSOR HACKER'S LOST TREASURE GOLF
3010 Parkway, Pigeon Forge
(865) 453-0307
www.losttreasuregolf.com

Although this attraction is devoted exclusively to miniature golf, there's not very much that's "miniature" about it. An Aztec pyramid, a volcano, and a twin-prop plane reminiscent of the Indiana Jones films are among the life-size props that tower above street level and scream out for your attention as you drive down the Parkway.

The twin 18-hole courses are built around the theme of exploration and adventure. According to the course "legend," Professor Ephraim A. Hacker discovered an abandoned mining train that had been built by the Germans during World War I for the purpose of helping finance their war effort. Once you've selected your putter and ball, a train takes you and your fellow golfers up an inclined railway to the top of the park. From there, you can choose either the Gold course, which takes you past a 60-foot waterfall and through several caves, or the slightly harder Diamond course, which takes you through the pyramid and also through a pirate ship.

Lost Treasure Golf costs $9 per course for those age 13 and older, $8 for children ages 5 through 12, and $5 for kids four and younger (or free if they use a plastic putter). Prices include tax. For $5, any age can play a second round. If you get a hole in one at the day's mystery hole (which changes every day), you win a free round.

ULTRAZONE
3053 Parkway, Pigeon Forge
(865) 428-2444

At Ultrazone, laser tag gamers can hunt each other down in a 3,800-square-foot play area designed to resemble a destroyed city. The layout also features three sniper areas where shooters can pick off their opponents from aerial vantage points. After a 10-minute period of equipment briefing and suiting up, players enter the game area and compete in a three-team system with up to six players on each team. Each game lasts about 15 minutes. Tickets are $8.75, including tax, for anyone seven and older. Each additional game is $5.75.

FLYAWAY
3106 Parkway, Pigeon Forge
(865) 453-7777
www.flyawayindoorskydiving.com
Flyaway is the first indoor skydiving simulator in the country, providing novices and seasoned skydivers alike the opportunity to experience the sensation of high-speed free fall in a safe, indoor environment. First-timers start off with a half-hour training session that includes safety and body positioning techniques. After you don a special flight suit and protective gear, you're ready to soar in Flyaway's 21-foot-tall vertical wind tunnel. A large jet engine, located under the mesh wire floor, generates wind speeds of up to 115 mph and creates a column of air on which participants can learn the fundamentals and intricacies of free-fall flight. Five "divers" enter the padded tunnel simultaneously and divide 15 minutes of flight time between them, helped by a flight instructor. Participants normally fly no higher than six to 12 feet.

Flights run on the hour and half hour. The cost of the training and first flight is $31.95 plus tax, but you can tack on an additional flight for $20.95 more. Spectators can watch the "dive" sessions for free. Group rates (11 or more), coaching packages, and five-ticket books are available. You can also buy a DVD of your adventure at an additional cost.

Participants at Flyaway are required to be in good physical condition and weigh at least 40 pounds. Maximum weight allowances are 220 pounds for men under 6 feet tall and 230 pounds for men over 6 feet. Maximum weight for women up to 5 feet 6 inches tall is 160 pounds; for women between 5 feet 6 inches and 5 feet 11 inches tall, it is 180 pounds; and for women 6 feet and taller, it is 200 pounds. Children younger than 18 must be accompanied by a parent or guardian. Casual clothing with socks and sneakers is suggested.

FANTASY GOLF
3263 Parkway, Pigeon Forge
(865) 428-7079
Fantasy Golf now has an enormous, 75-foot-high, bright-blue sea serpent guarding its two 18-hole courses, which were already populated with an ogre, a Pegasus, a dragon, a bear, a mermaid, and two dinosaurs before this recent addition. The giant castle and huge waterfall definitely make a splash. Admission is $8 for adults, $7 for children ages 5 to 12, and free for kids 4 and younger with a paying parent. Playing a second 18 holes is half price.

SMOKY MOUNTAIN SPEEDPARK
3275 Parkway, Pigeon Forge
(865) 429-4639
This Parkway amusement operation has an elevated oval go-kart track for drivers age 12 and older (without height restrictions). One-seat karts cost $8 per ride (or $70 for 10 rides); two-seaters cost $12. Speedpark's kiddie track (for ages 4 to 11) costs $7 per ride. All prices include tax.

If you'd rather go up and down rather than round and round, look for the Sky Scraper. Riders are strapped into a cage that swings over and over like a pendulum in 360-degree loops. You must be at least 3 feet 6 inches tall (and slightly insane) to ride. The cost is $30 for either one or two. If you'd like to try a reverse bungee, the new Sling Shot ride will shoot you straight up into the air about 120 feet at anywhere from 80 to 100 mph ($30 for two people). The traditional Bungee Jump costs $20 ($10 for a second jump if the jumper is still in the harness). The Screaming Swing (which swings back and forth, 65 feet off the ground at 60 mph) is $10 per person (minimum height 48 inches). Other Speedpark activities include a multi-axis gyro ride and a trampoline jump, each of which costs $7.

The Speedpark offers a thrill ride special for $55 per person, including tax, that includes one ride each on the Screaming Swing, the Bungee, the Sky Scraper and the Sling Shot.

SPEED ZONE FUN PARK
3315 South River Road, Pigeon Forge
(865) 908-7255

Speed Zone has three outdoor go-kart tracks at the raceway's location just off the Parkway near the Old Mill neighborhood. The single-loop slick track has both single karts ($8 each, or three for $18, including tax) and two-seaters ($12). The Tennessee Twister is a wooden go-kart track with multiple levels and corkscrew turns ($8 for one-seaters and $10 for two-seaters). Sprint and Kiddie Karts will set you back $5 per person. You must be at least 4 feet 8 inches tall to drive, and drivers of all two-seat cars must be 16 years old. Passengers on two-seaters must be at least three years old.

You can also get a special Park Hopper pass that lets you mix and match rides at any of four amusement centers (Speed Zone Fun Park, Star Tracks, Rockin' Raceway, and Lazerport Fun Center). The pass gives you five rides for $25 or 10 rides for $45 per person.

THE OLD MILL
130 Old Mill Avenue, Pigeon Forge
(865) 453-4628
www.oldmill.com

Just a block off the Parkway (turn at traffic light #7 and cross the river) stands the Old Mill, a still-working gristmill built in 1830. It was the center of all activities in the old days and is still in the middle of the shopping area most long-term visitors remember. The mill, on the National Register of Historic Buildings, still grinds corn into flour for sale in the general store. Guided 25-minute tours of the mill are available from April through October, beginning every half hour. The tour costs $3.00 for adults and $1.50 for children ages 6 through 12, including tax. Children age five and younger are admitted free.

MOVIE RIDER
3370 Parkway, Pigeon Forge
(865) 428-8511

At this movie attraction, you won't just be a passive spectator—you'll feel like you're part of the action. Viewers are strapped into chairs mounted on moving platforms that tilt, dip, and shift in synchronicity with the 70-mm film, which is displayed on a giant 40-foot-by-30-foot screen in digital surround sound. The 20-minute movie features four different roller coasters, including one moderate and three extreme. Movie Rider also has an arcade.

Tickets cost $12.99 for adults and $9.99 for children 12 and under. Seniors (50 and up) are $9.99 plus tax. You must be 42 inches tall to ride, and participation by pregnant women, claustrophobic people, or anyone with back, head, or neck problems is discouraged. (Non-motion seats are available free for anyone who wants one.)

GATLINBURG

The scene here isn't as frantic as it is in Pigeon Forge because amusement-type activities have to shoehorn themselves in among the shops that gave Gatlinburg its original reputation as a tourism center. Some of the older attractions hark back to the days when tourism first came to the Smokies, and the newer ones are striving to achieve the state-of-the-art condition found in the two cities to the north.

Everything in Gatlinburg is convenient, and attractions are no exception. All but a small handful sit in a 4-block section of town, and almost all the others are on River Road, a block off the Parkway.

RIPLEY'S DAVY CROCKETT MINI-GOLF
188 North Parkway, Gatlinburg
(865) 430-8851, (888) 240-1358
www.ripleysgatlinburg.com

This course takes miniature golf to a new level of fun. As you put around the two 18-hole courses here, various animals pop up and converse with you, sometimes even offering golf advice. The courses feature several holes with curves, elevation changes, and where the tee is on a different level from the green, making every putt a challenge. The 17th hole on the Fort Crockett course may be the longest in miniature golf history—it's about 40 yards from tee to green down a sluice filled with water. Perhaps the most whimsical hole is the one where a hillbilly outhouse flushes when your putt is right on target (never mind that outhouses don't flush—it's still fun).

Adult greens fees (for age 12 and up) are $9.99 for 18 holes and $13.99 for 36 holes. Children ages 6 to 11 pay $7.99 and $9.99, respectively, while children age 2 to 5 pay $2.99 and $5.99. Wheelchair accessibility is provided for 18 full holes, 9 on each side. You'll find plenty of free parking, although you can also take the trolley.

This attraction is part of the Ripley's You-Pick voucher, which gives discounts on Ripley's attraction combos when you visit Ripley's Aquarium of the Smokies. See the detailed description of the voucher in the listing for the aquarium, later in the Gatlinburg section.

HILLBILLY GOLF
340 Parkway, Gatlinburg
(865) 436-7470

This oldie but goodie actually offers two attractions in one. Hillbilly Golf's two 18-hole courses are on a mountaintop 300 feet above the Parkway, and the only way to get to them is to ride an incline railway. While you're waiting for the railcar, you can visit the arcade or get in a few strokes on the practice green. Once you get to the top, you can play on your choice of courses, set in the wilderness with mountaineer hazards like stills and rock walls to make your shot selections a little more difficult. The cost is $9.50 for adults (ages 12 and up), and $7.50 for children ages 3 to 11. Seniors (ages 60 and up) are $7.50, and children under 3 are free. Prices include tax. Hillbilly Golf is open from early Spring through late fall.

THE SALT AND PEPPER SHAKER MUSEUM
461 Brookside Village Way, Gatlinburg
(865) 430-5515, (888) 778-1802
www.thesaltandpeppershakermuseum.com
Here's a slice of Americana you won't see any-

where else—the world's only salt and pepper shaker museum. Originally opened in nearby Cosby in 2002, it moved two years later to its present location in Winery Square on East Parkway/Route 321 (half a mile east from traffic light #3 downtown). It's taken owner Andrea Ludden (a retired archaeologist from Belgium) more than 25 years to collect the 20,000-plus sets of shakers you can see here, and she is always adding to her collection.

The shakers come in all shapes and sizes, made from ceramic, wood, walnut shells, horn, eggs, rock, glass, metal, plastic, nuts, seashells, and crystal. They're displayed in themed sections that have a few humorous twists. For example, in the vegetable section, you'll find a few snails and bugs interspersed here and there. In the American Southwest section, aliens (representing Roswell) share space with the cowboys and Indians. The transportation section displays not only trains, sports cars, and carriages, but also roller skates and witches on brooms.

Still other themed sections include cooking (with pots and pans, stoves, chefs), food and beverages (with beer bottles, liquor bottles, and even a few monks and nuns—because they made the wine); chickens, dogs and cats, marine life (including Jonah in the belly of a whale), weddings, and both international and domestic souvenirs. You'll even find a section devoted to Lucille Ball. And of course, since the museum is in the Smokies, you'll also find plenty of bears. As if all that wasn't enough, the museum also boasts the largest pepper-mill collection in the world.

Tickets are $3, including tax, and children 12 and under are free. The price of admission goes toward any purchase in the gift shop, which features thousands of both modern and vintage shakers, spices, handcrafted jewelry (made by Andrea's husband, Rolf, and her daughter, who is also named Andrea) and photographic prints created by her son, Alex.

ANNA PORTER PUBLIC LIBRARY
158 Proffitt Road, Gatlinburg
(865) 436-5588
www.annaporterpl.org

It used to be there were two things you could never do in a public library—talk and eat. But Gatlinburg has changed all that. In 2009, the local library moved into a brand-new $1.7 million building near the high school and adjacent to the community center (way out East Parkway/Route 321), replacing the older library building that used to be on Cherokee Orchard Road several miles away.

The new facility includes an Internet cafe with wireless access where you can buy a cup of coffee and check your e-mail, as well as a "phone zones," where patrons can chat on their cell phones (as long as they don't get too loud, of course). This is the first library in the country to be built from the ground up as a bookstore-style library. The shelves are lower than you're used to seeing, and you'll also find lots of signs announcing sections by topics, making it easy to browse. One section will display new books, and the circulation area comes complete with a fireplace.

The summer reading program for school-age children is quite popular (call ahead for times and days, which vary). During the school year, the reading program shifts to preschoolers, with age-appropriate stories and games. You might also want to check out the library's Smoky Mountain Archives, which contain historic writings and photos of the area.

COOTER'S FAMILY FUN CENTER
542 Parkway, Gatlinburg
(865) 430-9909
www.cootersplace.com

This family-fun center (which moved in 2009 to the place where Camp Thunder used to be) is owned by Ben Jones, who played the sidekick mechanic Cooter in The Dukes of Hazzard TV show (which ran from 1979 to 1985). Jones and other cast members, including Catherine Bach (Daisy Duke), Sonny Shroyer (Enos), and Rick Hurst (Cletus), make occasional appearances at the fun center, greeting fans and signing autographs. The General Lee (the Dukes' car from the series) has a place of honor by the front door.

Cooter's Place offers an 18-hole Dukes-themed indoor miniature golf course, as well as

a slick track with single and double go-karts. The gift shop sells various Dukes of Hazzard memorabilia. Prices for either attraction are $8.95 for anyone 12 and up, and $5.95 for children age 4 to 11. If you want to do both, the price is $14.95 or $9.95, respectively. Children ages three and under are free.

THE HISTORIC OGLE CABIN
Parkway at Cherokee Orchard Road
Gatlinburg

Absolutely the oldest building in Gatlinburg, the Ogle cabin on the grounds of the Arrowmont School and the Arrowcraft Shop dates from 1807, when the sons of Billy Ogle took the logs their father had cut and hewed and built the cabin on a site about 300 yards back on Baskins Creek. The cabin was occupied by various members of the family until 1910. The walls and rafters of the original building were moved to the current site, and the present dwelling restoration was completed in 1969 as a cooperative effort of the city of Gatlinburg, Pi Beta Phi Fraternity, the Arrowmont School, and the Daughters of the American Revolution. The cabin is free if you want to take a look around inside to speculate how Martha Jane Huskey Ogle cared for seven grown children and some of their 82 children in that kind of space. Be aware, however, that the hours are somewhat irregular because the cabin is staffed by volunteer docents, and it's closed completely from November to Memorial Day.

RIVERWALK
River Road, Gatlinburg

One of the most pleasant results of a massive ongoing urban beautification program begun in 1997, Riverwalk is an island of serenity on the northern edge of the downtown business district. The renewal project actually begins before traffic light #3, where the utilities have been buried to leave an uncluttered skyline, but the stretch that joins the river itself where River Road runs diagonally off the Parkway at traffic light #5 is the highlight here. From that point to Maples Lane, about half a mile away, Riverwalk is a pleasant stroll along the west prong of the Little Pigeon

River at a reasonable enough remove from the downtown activity to make the noise and lights seem a million miles away.

The variegated sidewalk—sometimes brick and cobblestone, sometimes faux boardwalk, sometimes just plain cement—is flanked by old-fashioned globe streetlights, reminiscent of gaslights at the curb, and a wrought-iron fence along the riverbank. The fence is festooned with thousands of planters filled with homegrown flowers, courtesy of the Parks and Recreation Department's full-time horticultural staff. Early on, a footbridge across the river provides the main access to Ripley's Aquarium. That bridge and the sidewalk leading to Gatlinburg's Mysterious Mansion a few blocks down are the only two points where businesses are accessed directly from the Riverwalk; for the rest of the way, it's just you and the water and those millions of fresh flowers.

If you want to get a closer look at the river or go fishing in it (for fishing regulations, see the Parks and Recreation chapter), several stairways along the way lead to the river's edge, where the local duck population nests. And if strollin' and sittin' are more your style, you have your choice of several benches and gazebos. In a way, the Riverwalk is a reminder of what Gatlinburg used to be: a sleepy, friendly little town where you could just forget about your troubles for a while in nature's beauty.

RIPLEY'S AQUARIUM OF THE SMOKIES
88 River Road, Gatlinburg
(865) 430-8808, (888) 240-1358
www.ripleysaquariumofthesmokies.com

This downtown Gatlinburg attraction has made a big splash since opening in late 2000. In its first full year of operation, Ripley's Aquarium of the Smokies pulled some two million visitors through its turnstiles, making it the most visited aquarium in the nation.

This $70 million, 115,000-square-foot facility offers a multilevel, self-guided tour of its impressive collection of aquatic life-forms that hail from all the world's oceans. The tour is divided into major themed sections, such as Tropical Rainforest, Coral Reef, and Ocean Realm. In its numerous display tanks, you'll find some of the earth's most interesting undersea creatures, including piranha, jawfish, and seahorses. One of the more unusual collections is in the Gallery of the Seas area, home to jellyfish, sea dragons, giant octopi, and the sprawling Japanese spider crab—the world's largest crustacean.

Several of the tanks are quite large. In the Coral Reef and Stingray Bay sections, schools of exotic, colorful reef fish and hordes of stingrays make their respective homes. In both tanks, scuba divers interact with the fish during hourly dive shows. Spectators can watch the critters being fed and learn about them in the process. At one point, near the end of the tour, guests themselves are allowed to pet the stingrays from topside.

The centerpiece of Ripley's Aquarium of the Smokies is Shark Lagoon, which alone holds nearly a million gallons of man-made seawater. Ten-foot sand tiger sharks, sandbar sharks, and nurse sharks as well as sawfish, eels, and a giant green sea turtle glide silently by as visitors travel through the tank in a fabulously fun underwater aquarium tunnel (that was the world's longest when it was built, although a newer aquarium in Asia outdid this one recently). A 340-foot-long moving walkway snakes through the tunnel, which is built with 6-inch-thick acrylic that allows you to see fish all around you and directly overhead. The sharks appear close enough to touch!

The Discovery Center near the end of the tour is brimming with dozens of interactive exhibits that let you touch, twist, turn, and poke. There are places to crawl into as well as a "touch tank" where you can pet live horseshoe crabs. The Discovery Center also has rooms where staff educators deliver hourly multimedia presentations on a variety of sea life–related topics. Although most of what you see at Ripley's Aquarium of the Smokies is part of its permanent collection, you'll also find some special exhibits displayed on a temporary basis.

Overall, allow several hours to do the aquarium justice and another hour if you plan to take in a temporary exhibition. The aquarium is laid out in roughly a one-way path, although it leaves you room to double back and see things twice, if you like. Along the way, you'll find the Feeding Frenzy snack shop; the Veranda, a lunchtime country buffet open in the summer; and the Cargo Hold gift shop.

Admission prices are $19.99 for those age 12 and older, $10.99 for ages 6 through 11, and $4.99 for ages 2 through 5. You can also get an annual pass for $38.99, $23.99, and $12.99, respectively.

Ripley's You-Pick voucher allows you to get discounts on other Ripley's attractions when you visit the aquarium. The vouchers are good for one year, so you can use them on different visits, if you want. The aquarium-plus-two-attractions voucher is $43.47 for adults or $28.96 for children ages 6 to 11; the aquarium-plus-three voucher runs $53.48 and $34.52; the aquarium-plus-four voucher costs $62.39 and $40.09; the aquarium-plus-five voucher is $71.29 and $43.42; and finally, the aquarium-plus-six voucher is $79.09 and $46.75. The You-Pick voucher prices include tax.

MYSTERIOUS MANSION
424 River Road, Gatlinburg
(865) 436-7007

Things go bump in the Mysterious Mansion at all hours of the day and night. It's easy to find the place: Just go over to River Road and look for the only turn-of-the-century building with a big black hearse parked in front. Things get even creepier once you get inside. Secret passageways, dark dungeons, rooms with no exit, and floors that suddenly give way await you. Ghouls and ghosts and all manner of ghastly otherworldy creatures appear out of nowhere, and then disappear as suddenly as they arrived. Even if you've been before, you will want to go back to see what new terrifying twists and turns the mansion has made since your last visit. Admission is $8.97 for ages 13 and older, $6.95 for children 4 to 12, and free for children 3 and younger.

THE GUINNESS WORLD RECORDS MUSEUM
631 Parkway, Gatlinburg
(865) 436-9100, (888) 240-1358

Take just about any adjective you can think of, add "est" to the end, and you'll find it at the Guinness World Records Museum. From the moment you walk through the unusual whale's mouth and belly that forms the museum's opening, the Guinness folks will show you the biggest, smallest, baddest, longest, shortest, and richest of everything they've been able to uncover in nearly half a century of research. Since it's entertaining as well as educational, there's a little bit of the silliest thrown in as well. It's two jam-packed floors of superlatives in the worlds of art, sports, music, movies, television, and human nature. Admission is $9.99 for adults and $5.99 for children 6 through 12. Children younger than 6 are admitted free. (Although this attraction is indeed owned by Ripley's, it's not part of the Ripley's You-Pick combo program.)

TREASURE QUEST GOLF
653 Parkway, Gatlinburg
(865) 436-3972

Treasure Quest is an 18-hole indoor miniature golf course (so you can play even when it rains), set in an ancient jungle temple infested with pirates and other treasure-hunters. Rock 'n' roll music plays in the background as you putt. Admission is $8.99 for ages 12 and up, $6.99 for children 5 to 11, and free for children 4 and younger (with a paying adult).

EARTHQUAKE—THE RIDE
653 Parkway, Gatlinburg
(865) 436-9765

Shake-and-bake on the Parkway. A simulated subway car gets caught smack in the middle of an earthquake, and you're right in the center. Motion and electronic wizardry combine to provide a gut-wrenching eight-minute ride that'll leave you gasping for air and wondering if you want to do it again right now, or maybe wait a little while 'til all the body parts get back where they belong. Admission is $7.99 for those 12 and older, and $5.99 for those 5 to 11.

FANNIE FARKLE'S
656 Parkway, Gatlinburg
(865) 436-4057
www.gatlinburg.com/fanniefarkles

One of Gatlinburg's original arcades, Fannie

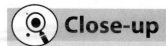

Close-up

New Kid on the Block Gives Back

It's no secret in Gatlinburg that most of the major property owners and business operators are members of the city's founding families. Although the names Ogle, Ownby, Trentham, McCarter, and Reagan are not as visible as they used to be, most of those families have leased their downtown properties to incoming businesses and so still call most of the shots in town. But there's a new name in town these days that is instantly recognized all over the world: Ripley's. And Ripley's Entertainment, Inc. has quietly become a major player in Gatlinburg's business community.

The Ripley name first appeared in Gatlinburg in 1970 with the opening of Ripley's Believe It or Not! Museum, one of the company's first permanent museums, now the third oldest still-existing Ripley's museum in the United States. By the mid-1980s, the Ripley family had shrunk to two brothers who didn't really have much expansionist blood in their veins, and the company lapsed into a comatose state.

In 1985, the company was purchased by Canadian millionaire Jim Pattison, who hired all the right people to quickly build the company into the world's largest chain of museum-type entertainment venues by acquiring existing attractions and developing new ones. Based on the success of their ventures in Gatlinburg, Ripley's Entertainment decided in 1998 to make their biggest ever investment in a state-of-the-art aquarium in the middle of the downtown business district. Ripley's Aquarium of the Smokies opened in late 2000 and became the most-visited aquarium in the Western Hemisphere before its second birthday. Only Dollywood gets more visitors in the entire state of Tennessee.

With eight uniquely different attractions that are open year-round (seven in Gatlinburg and one in Sevierville), Ripley's provides permanent employment for about 400 residents (275 in the aquarium alone), which represents 10 percent of the city population. Not only that, but the aquarium also generated enough revenue to increase the city's overall figure by 20 percent.

In addition to making money, Ripley's has become a good corporate citizen as well. It's a major player in the Gatlinburg Goes Green initiative (see the Close-up about this in the chapter on Hotels and Motels), and it contributes generously to local charities, including the Sevier County Food Ministry and the Friends of the Great Smoky Mountains.

Ripley's has even set up a program that allows employees to help distribute a slice of the company's wealth. A four-member charity committee made up of cashiers and supervisors (read that: not the usual bigwig corporate honchos) decides how to distribute $50,000 a year among largely unsung charitable pursuits. It's a drop in the bucket compared to what the corporation has already earmarked for donations, but it's enough to make a huge difference in the lives of many people in the community. For example, that money has gone to help Gatlinburg residents whose homes have burned down, to those with unusual medical needs, and to kids whose families can't afford to send them on school field trips.

So although it may seem to the casual observer that Ripley's has become a juggernaut, taking over the downtown in a major way, the company has proven to be a kind and gentle giant that understands the principle of giving back and demonstrates the spirit of partnership with those around them.

Farkle's is distinguished by the fact that the premiums offered to the game winners include high-quality collectibles like porcelain figurines and crystal accessories. In business since 1980, Fannie Farkle's is the only stand-alone arcade in this section. The foot-long "Ogle Dog," available at the snack bar, is a local favorite, as are the smoked sausage subs. In addition, Fannie Farkle's also offers Internet access and claims to have the cleanest restrooms in town.

WORLD OF ILLUSIONS
716 Parkway, Gatlinburg
(865) 436-9701

Just about nothing is real at World of Illusions. These people do more with smoke, mirrors, and lighting than anyone around. Consider this: You can stand there and see an Imperial Warrior beam down from his starship, but you can't touch him, and you can turn the tables on Superman by spotting him with X-ray vision. Your friend can disappear while holding your hand, and a laser illusion will convince you that Elvis is alive. You can walk away from your shadow and watch Count Dracula turn into a flying bat, and Merlin, the world's best-known wizard, will appear before you and levitate. Watch carefully—you never know what will happen (or seem to happen) next. Admission is $7.99 for adults, $5.99 for children 5 to 11, and free for children younger than 5.

FORT FUN
716 Parkway, Gatlinburg
(865) 436-2326
www.smokymountainfun.com

Several different amusement venues (including on-site arcades with the latest in high-tech competition) stretch across the back of Reagan Square Mall in the heart of downtown Gatlinburg. The first of these activities are two unusual miniature golf courses laid out on the hillside that integrate old buildings into the play. Gatlinburg's Old Town Square Course delivers a local history lesson at every hole, including how the city got its name. The Smokies Old Mountain Trail Course describes the development of Great Smoky Mountains National Park in a peaceful setting reminiscent of the park itself. One hole plays through a replica of the old Elkmont post office. And for the modern-at-heart, Fort Fun also offers a black-light golf course. The complex also contains gem mining, a laser tag game with spectacular sound and light effects, a 3-D movie theater with special glasses and special effects, a motion-ride movie, a bumper car track, and Boogie Bodies (which uses green-screen technology to put you in your own music video). Prices are $9.99 for one amusement or activity, $13.00 for two activities, and $15.99 for six (the best value), the Do It All pass.

HAUNTINGS
716 Parkway, Gatlinburg
(865) 436-4636

Here's a new slant in haunted houses: At Hauntings, the house comes to you as you sit frozen in fascination in a room filled with things that go bump. And wiggle. And giggle. And scream their heads off. It's truly a terrifying collection of sights and sounds, complete with spooky lighting and otherworldly sounds (in stereo, yet) from the dark side. If it doesn't remind you of your worst-ever nightmare, it'll probably provide you with a new one. Admission is $7.99 for those ages 12 and up, and $5.99 for children under 12.

GATLINBURG SKY LIFT
765 Parkway, Gatlinburg
(865) 436-4307
www.gatlinburgskylift.com

When it opened in 1954, the Sky Lift started from a point almost as sparsely settled at the bottom as it was at the top. Now leaving the Parkway in the center of downtown, it travels across River Road and 700 feet up the south face of Crockett Mountain. At the summit, the panoramic view of Gatlinburg and the surrounding Smokies is breathtaking. Safe, two-person chairlifts stay comfortably close to the ground during the ascent, and if you look down as you go up, you might even see a deer or two under the lift. An automatic camera takes your picture as your chair approaches the top (you can buy a copy if you like the photo), and other souvenirs and snacks are also available at the summit's rustic gift shop. The Sky Lift is most popular in autumn, when the fall colors make the panorama even better. Don't forget your camera—you can take one-of-a-kind shots of downtown Gatlinburg and Mount LeConte together.

Admission is $12.75 for adults, $9.50 for children ages 3 to 11, and free for those under 3. You can also opt for the new all-day pass, which allows you to ride at whim throughout the day for not much more ($16 for adults and $12 for children). Prices include tax.

RIPLEY'S BELIEVE IT OR NOT! MUSEUM
800 Parkway, Gatlinburg
(865) 436-5096, (888) 240-1358
www.ripleysgatlinburg.com

Robert Ripley (1893–1949) was a cartoonist by trade and an adventurer and world traveler by choice. Supported by his syndicated radio show (the first program ever broadcast simultaneously to a worldwide audience) and his world-famous comic strip (begun in 1918 and still running), Ripley traveled to 198 countries. He collected unusual (some may say bizarre) facts, legends, and artifacts from places most people hadn't even heard of before Ripley went there. It's not stretching a point to call Ripley the father of modern trivia.

Your believe-it-or-not experience starts with a leap of faith at the entrance. Don't be concerned that the museum is going to collapse around you—the "interesting" architecture is just a warm-up for what you'll see during your self-guiding tour through three stories of more than 500 exhibits. Those exhibits range from the actual stuffed remains of a two-headed calf born in Gatlinburg to rare film footage shot in the early part of the 20th century. Many are "hands on," allowing the visitor to experience such delights as actually touching a real shrunken head or playing a giant keyboard by dancing on it (remember the Tom Hanks movie Big?). No matter how quickly you think you'll get through, you'll probably spend a lot more time than you expect to here.

You'll also find a 4,000-foot-square state-of-the-art arcade on the ground level, as well as a new wax hands gallery that allows you to create your own souvenir—a wax replica of your own hand (or hands, in the case of a couple). Hot wax artists help you create the replica and even decorate it for you with your choice of colors and extras. Prices for the wax hands start at $6.99.

Admission is $14.99 for ages 12 and older, $7.99 for children ages 3 to 11, and free for children younger than 3 when accompanied by a paying customer. This attraction is part of the Ripley's You-Pick voucher, which gives discounts on Ripley's attraction combos when you visit Ripley's Aquarium of the Smokies. See the detailed description of the voucher in the listing for the aquarium, earlier in the Gatlinburg section.

RIPLEY'S MARVELOUS MIRROR MAZE
623 Parkway, Gatlinburg
(865) 430-1834, (888) 240-1358

The mirror maze, which opened in spring of 2008, is the newest of the Ripley's family of attractions. The 2,000-square-foot maze is made of more than 100 mirrors tilted at 45-degree angles for extra-added disorientation. The corridors are lined with grand archways and pillars, and LED lights on the floor reflect a million times in every direction as the beat of techno tunes resounds around you. You'll think you're headed down a hallway, but it's just a reflection of the way you really want to go. It's a good thing the mirrors are shatterproof, because you'll be bumping into them with regularity. You can't even count on smudges for clues to what's a passageway and what's a solid surface, because everyone has to wear disposable plastic gloves (and because one employee does nothing but keep the mirrors sparkle-clean full-time). You can also buy 3D Holo-Specs glasses for $1 each that turn every light into a starburst, making it even harder to find your way around.

The pathways are changed every so often, so even if you've memorized your way around on your first visit, it's bound to be different the next time you come to town. During Halloween, the attraction becomes a haunted mirror maze for horrific holiday hilarity. At the entrance, Ripley's operates a fabulous candy store that sells more than 100 types of sweet stuff in bulk bins.

Admission is $8.99 for anyone age 3 and up, and children under 3 are admitted free. Your admission is good for the entire day, so you can come back later if you want to take another go at the maze. (Some people time themselves alone or in teams, trying to beat their best time.)

This attraction is part of the Ripley's You-Pick voucher, which gives discounts on Ripley's attraction combos when you visit Ripley's Aquarium of the Smokies. See the detailed description of the voucher in the listing for the aquarium, earlier in the Gatlinburg section.

HOLLYWOOD WAX MUSEUM
903 Parkway, Gatlinburg
(865) 430-1800
www.hollywoodwax.com

Here's your chance to don Playmate bunny ears and lounge on Hugh Hefner's bed, sing karaoke with pop divas like Britney Spears, shoot hoops with Michael Jordon, stand on the bow of the Titanic with Leonardo DiCaprio, and even putt with Bob Hope. Other figures include Donald Trump, Angelina Jolie, Johnny Depp, and Tom Hanks as Forest Gump. Visitors to Gatlinburg have been able to have these thrills and more every since the Hollywood Wax Museum came to town in 2007.

The 90 world-famous celebrities represented in wax here are arranged in 50 movie sets with no ropes or glass, so you can get into the scene yourself and pose however you want. But please don't touch the figures—they're fragile. It can take up to three months and $25,000 to create each figure, thanks to a team of sculptors, makeup artists, hair stylists, costume and set designers, special-effects technicians, and a few other assorted experts. To add some chills to your thrills, check out the horror section, including Linda Blair as Regan from The Exorcist, Michael Myers from Halloween, and the title characters from Freddie vs. Jason.

The gift shop offers plenty of movie memorabilia, and you can also make a replica of your hand in wax (starting at $8.99) and buy a matted photo of yourself with King Kong ($9.99). Admission is $13.99 for adults, $7.99 for children ages 6 to 12, and free for children under 6. Seniors get $2 off.

i A number of area rides and attractions have minimum height, weight, and age requirements. Most of that information is included in this chapter, but it's a good idea to call ahead before visiting these places, especially if you plan on taking children.

RIPLEY'S MOVING THEATER
904 Parkway, Gatlinburg
(865) 436-9763, (888) 240-1358
www.ripleysgatlinburg.com

Once you're strapped into your custom chair, the 70-mm screen comes alive and the reverberations from the six-channel digital sound system enter every pore in your body. For the next 12 minutes, expect to be buffeted in eight different directions (sometimes all at once) as your seat moves with the action on the screen. You'll see two shows—Glacier Run (a runaway alpine bobsled) and Secrets of the Lost Temple (an Indiana Jones-like adventure), and you'll experience wind, snow, and rain at the appropriate times during the films. At the end of the experience, you'll be thankful that white knuckles don't glow in the dark.

Admission is $12.99 for anyone 12 and older, and $7.99 for kids up to 12 years old. Children must be 40 inches tall to ride. This attraction is part of the Ripley's You-Pick voucher, which gives discounts on Ripley's attraction combos when you visit Ripley's Aquarium of the Smokies. See the detailed description of the voucher in the listing for the aquarium, earlier in the Gatlinburg section.

RIPLEY'S HAUNTED ADVENTURE
908 Parkway, Gatlinburg
(865) 430-9991, (888) 240-1358
www.ripleysgatlinburg.com

The headless horseman outside that rears up 12 feet should be warning enough, but those who willingly join this trip through an abandoned casket factory should be prepared for some extremely scary stuff. From the time you enter the funicular railcar that takes you up to the second floor until you scramble out of the elevator that delivers you back to the safety of the Parkway, the Haunted Adventure is an intense journey. Even if you've been here in years past, you'll want to go through again, lest you miss the new maggot room, the Cave of the Slime Beast, and "the big squeeze." Various shady characters (and that's putting it mildly) keep showing up, including a grisly butler and an escaped prisoner who only wants to "play" with you. Remember, though, that as the saying goes, "It ain't over 'til it's over."

Admission is $12.99 for adults and $7.99 for children ages 6 to 11. Because of the intense nature of this attraction, Ripley's asks that children younger than age six not be taken along. The Haunted Adventure is part of the Ripley's You-Pick voucher, which gives discounts on Ripley's attraction combos when you visit Ripley's Aquarium of the Smokies. See the detailed description of the voucher in the listing for the aquarium, earlier in the Gatlinburg section.

STAR CARS
914 Parkway, Gatlinburg
(865) 430-7900
www.starcarstn.com

When it comes to way-out designs for special cars, nobody does it better than George Barris. Starting back in the 1960s with the customized Pontiac GTO used by the Monkees and the first Batmobile, George Barris designed cars that actually became stars (as did the actors portraying the characters who drove them). This self-guiding, two-story tour of specialty cars begins with several George Barris designs and continues with other venerable vehicles, including those owned by Elvis Presley and Frank Sinatra. A special NASCAR exhibit features video highlights of the careers of several drivers.

Each of the 40 cars is in its own setting with scenes from its movie or television show and accompanying soundtrack. Examples include a vehicle from the movie Transformers, the Ecto-1 from Ghostbusters, the Munsters' Drag-u-la, "General Lee" from The Dukes of Hazzard, and the jalopy driven by the Beverly Hillbillies. Recent additions include the Back to the Future time machine, the Mello Yello race car from Days of Thunder, and The Beach Boys' 1955 Thunderbird. Star Cars also houses the country's largest collection of James Bond movie props.

Admission is $11.99 for adults, $6.99 for children ages 6 through 12, and free for children ages 5 and younger with a paying adult.

AMAZING MIRROR MAZE
919 Parkway, Gatlinburg
(865) 436-4415

This mirror maze features a wild show of lights that flash and change color to the beat of the music. Thanks to the disposable plastic gloves they give you to wear as you navigate your way through the maze, the walls remain challengingly smudge-free. The maze is handicapped accessible so just about everyone can have fun. Admission is $8.75 for adults and $6.75 for children ages three to nine. Admission is good all day, so you can go through as many times as you want, and even return later in the day. Combo tickets with Circus Golf (see the following listing) cost $14 for adults and $10 for chidren.

CIRCUS GOLF...IN 3D
919 Parkway, Gatlinburg
(865) 436-4415

This 18-hole, indoor, black-light miniature golf course features a circus theme with computer animation, special effects, and animatronic characters. For an extra charge, you can don 3-D glasses that add to the fun. At the last hole, Dunk-a-Babe, the fat lady sings if you get a hole in one. Admission is $10 for adults, and $7 for children ages three to nine. Combo tickets with the Amazing Mirror Maze (see the previous listing) cost $14 for adults $10 for children.

OBER GATLINBURG
1001 Parkway, Gatlinburg
(865) 436-5423
www.obergatlinburg.com

Sitting 1,400 feet above town (and peering down over it) is Ober Gatlinburg, which began life as a ski resort but which has morphed over the years to a year-round mountain of both indoor and outdoor fun. Southern skiing is, of course, still Ober Gatlinburg's main claim to fame, but for descriptions of that option (as well as the resort's new snow-tubing hill), see the Active Outdoor Adventures chapter, which follows this one.

The listing in this chapter concentrates instead on everything else you can do here—and that's quite a lot. The first thing you must realize is this: A large part of the fun of Ober Gatlinburg is indeed about the journey, and not just the destination. Getting there entails a 2-mile ride from the tram terminal on the Parkway (highly recommended) or 7 miles of driving on a two-lane mountain road (not recommended at all, especially since the road is frequently closed to all but local traffic during the ski season).

The aerial tramway is a wonder all by itself. Two counterbalanced tramcars run continuously, transporting up to 120 people and their equipment on each 10-minute trip (complete with guided narration). The views alone are worth the cost of the ride ticket. Round-trip fare is $10 for adults and $8.50 for children ages 7 to 11. Ober Gatlinburg upgraded the tram in 2007, replacing the cars with entirely new ones that offer 15 percent more glass viewing area.

The tram drops you off at a huge indoor mall at the top, where the Smoky Mountain Wildlife Encounter (formerly the Municipal Black Bear Habitat) is to your immediate left. This recently redesigned area not only offers renovated bear enclosures (housing non-releasable bears), but now it also has an aquatic exhibit with river otters and a nocturnal house with raccoons, skunks, and flying squirrels. Coming soon are exhibits of birds of prey and native mammals (including bobcat, fox, and others). Admission is $6.

The indoor mall also offers souvenir shops, snack bars, an arcade, and a variety of midway-type attractions. They include the usual kiddie rides and games of skill and chance, as well as some slightly-more-way-out-there attractions. Those include the Spider Web, a Velcro-covered cushion that kids in padded Velcro suits can hurl themselves at to see if they stick, and the Bungee Run, where two kids with bungee cords around their middles see who can run the farthest down a 35-foot alley before being snapped back into an air cushion. These attractions cost one or two coupons a piece. You can buy coupons at the kiosk in the mall, near where you get off the tram. Coupons cost $3.50 each or $31.50 for a book of 10.

One floor down on the second floor, a restaurant with large windows overlooks the mountains on one side and the ski slopes on the other. An additional lounge overlooks the ski slopes. On the ground level, you'll find a 10,000-square-foot indoor skating rink that operates year-round. Skating costs $9 for three hours of ice time and includes skate rental.

Outside the mall, on the top level, you'll find a bunch of outdoor activities that generally operate year-round, weather permitting. Among them is the longest scenic chairlift in the South, which goes to the summit of Mount Harrison. It's a 15-minute ride to the top, where a bluegrass band will entertain you while you enjoy the view. If you get off at the halfway point instead, you can ride the alpine slide (a dry-track simulated bobsled run) the rest of the way down in true white-knuckle fashion. The manually controlled sled lets you set your own speed through the woods and curves as you drop 200 feet in a 1,800-foot ride. Speeds range from scary to horrifying. Round-trip fare for the chairlift is two coupons, and two more will buy a ride on the Alpine Slide.

In summer, three water raft rides add to the fun. The Blue Cyclone Rapids features an inflated bobsled with handles that carries up to two people twisting, turning, and usually screaming at the top of their lungs, more than 600 feet through a closed tube on a cushion of water. The Lightnin' Raft Ride and the Shoot-the-Chute are basically identical, each sending a raft down a 240-foot course with a vertical drop of 40 feet. The Lightnin' River Raft is open all the way, and the Shoot-the-Chute is covered for most of its distance. Each of these rides is one coupon. Kiddie Land offers slides, ladders, crawling nets, swinging bridges, and rides on cars, snowmobiles, and the Rio Grande train for kids ages 3 to 11. Admission is two coupons and lasts all day.

Ober Gatlinburg is closed for maintenance from about mid-April to early May.

ACTIVE OUTDOOR ADVENTURES

If you prefer your adventures in the great outdoors (maybe with a bit of a wild and crazy flavor not supplied by Mother Nature), you've thumbed to the right chapter. A number of Smoky Mountain outfitters are only too willing to provide you with tons of al fresco fun. The listings in this chapter start with a handful of one-of-a-kind adventures that defy categorization and then move on to cover tubing, white-water rafting, horseback riding, and skiing (along with snow tubing). There's even a little llama trekking thrown in (see the Close-up).

Within each category, the listings move from north to south, as always, although hardly any of them are actually on the Parkway, so do expect to go a bit further afield for most of them. (Even so, they aren't exactly hard to get to—most of them are just a short drive away from the main fray.)

Do take note that most of these offerings have minimum age and height requirements, and many also have maximum weight restrictions. All adventure outfitters will invariably require you to sign a release form in which you agree not to hold the business responsible if you happen to get hurt. In other words, you play at your own risk.

The Smokies Corridor offers two other fairly active adventures that really should be acknowledged here because if you love this chapter's sort of outdoor fun, you'll love these activities, as well. But because they actually take place indoors, both ice-skating (at Ober Gatlinburg) and the skydiving simulator (at Flyaway in Pigeon Forge) are covered in the Attractions chapter. Fishing, by the way, is covered in the Parks and Recreation chapter, as well as the chapter on Great Smoky Mountains National Park .

WAHOO ZIPLINES
1200 Matthews Hollow Road, Sevierville
(865) 453-7301, (877) 924-6621
www.wahoozip.com

You won't need wings to fly if you go see the folks at Wahoo Ziplines (which offers the longest zipline course in North America). Before you take off, you'll suit up in a snug harness, a helmet, and canvas work gloves. A short bus ride takes you to the start of the course, where you'll climb steps up to a rough-hewn wooden platform at treetop height. Your fully trained professional guide (or in zipline lingo, sky ranger) will then clip your harness to a pulley that's suspended on a stainless-steel cable strung between two pillars, the takeoff side higher than the destination side.

After you push off and lift your feet, gravity takes over as you fly at speeds up to 40 mph, the ground a dizzying blur beneath you, for any-

where from 1,000 to 1,500 feet—zipping above, underneath, and through the forest canopy. Once everyone in your group has had a turn, you'll walk a short distance to the next zipline, where you'll do it all over again. Wahoo's two-hour tour covers five single ziplines and one double course (where you can fly in tandem), for a grand total of more than 10,000 feet (that's almost 2 miles) of wahooing. The ziplines here range from a minimum of 50 feet high to a maximum of 250 feet above the ground. It's fair to say that since Wahoo arrived on the Smoky Mountain scene late in the summer of 2008 (when they were temporarily known as EcoZip), getting "on-line" has never been so exhilarating!

Wahoo is also dedicated to ecologically sound "green" practices. The ziplines themselves use no electricity or gas, and the course was designed so as few trees as possible would have to be cut down. The roads that had to be cut through the woods to get the construction equipment in were turned into walking paths connecting the lines, and the trees that were felled were recycled—ground up for mulch spread along the paths. Also, the wood used to build the decks isn't pressure treated, because such wood contains toxins like arsenic that can be harmful to the surrounding plants.

Ziplining (which began in Costa Rica in the late 1990s and commercially debuted in the U.S. in 2002) is one of the fastest growing eco-tourist attractions in the world—although so far, less than 1 percent of Americans have done it. As an eco-tourism attraction, Wahoo wants to give you a greater appreciation for the environment you're zipping past. Guides have been specially trained by botanists and geologists, and they share fun facts about the mountains, trees, plants, and birds in the Smokies to make your trip more interesting. Various information stations along the trail give even more details.

Wahoo Zipline Tours cost $89 per person. Anyone staying at one of the 30 to 40 rental cabins at Sterling Springs Resort (where the zipline course is located; see www.sterlingspringsresort .com) receives a 50 percent discount for everyone in their party. Participants must be at least five years old and weigh between 70 and 275 pounds. Zipline tours do run in the rain and snow but may be suspended on short notice if rain is heavy or if there's lightning or thunder. Advance reservations are highly recommended.

An outdoor pavilion for group events is planned for the near future, and Wahoo expects to be able to do zipline weddings then. They're also planning to offer combo packages with Scenic Helicopter Tours (see the Attractions chapter).

To get there from the Parkway, you have to go about 4 miles into the countryside, but it's not hard to find. From the courthouse, you'd take Chapman Highway (driving west) for about a half mile and turn left onto Hardin Lane. Follow this windy road about 2 miles, and then turn right onto Matthews Hollow Road. You'll find Wahoo up the road on the left. You can go any day— they're even open on Christmas.

Dollywood opened a zipline course in 2009 that is not as long as the course at Wahoo Ziplines but that's still a scream. Check out the Dollywood chapter for information on SkyZip and its five separate ziplines ranging in length from 100 to nearly 1,000 feet—as well as a 100-foot-long swinging bridge high above the amusement park.

ZORB SMOKY MOUNTAINS
203 Sugar Hollow Road, Pigeon Forge
(865) 428-2422
www.zorb.com/smoky

If you've ever wanted to climb into an 11-foot-diameter clear plastic sphere and roll down a 700-foot-long hill going up to 30 mph, you're in luck. Zorb Smoky Mountains made its debut in October 2007, and it's the only such site in the U.S. As a Zorbonaut (as those who participate in the Zorb experience are called), you need no safety gear. You need only climb through a tunnel-like opening into the center of a big hollow ball that rests inside an even bigger hollow ball, with a cushion of air in between the two that keeps your body from coming into contact with the ground.

Zorb gives you three options. For Zorbit, a dry ride, you are securely strapped inside the Zorb before rolling straight down the Zorb course, rotating head-over-heels with the ball. Zydro is a wet ride—you (alone or with up to two additional friends) sit on the bottom of the ball amid about 15 gallons of water sloshing about, freely slipping and sliding the whole way down. With Zydro, you can either go down a straight course (which is a bit faster) or take the zigzag course (which is more disorienting). Either way, you'll find it a cross between a roller coaster and a washing machine without the detergent—and you'll also want to thank the crazy people in New Zealand who came up with the whole Zorbing concept in the '90s.

Zydro costs $37 per person per ride for either the straight or zigzag course, and Zorbit is $44. If you're brave enough to do all three rides, it's $81. Zorbonauts must be at least eight years old and less than 285 pounds for Zydro or less than 220 pounds for Zorbit. For Zydro, you can wear either a bathing suit or shorts and a T-shirt, but remember to bring dry clothes to change into afterward (or you can buy a special sports bag with a Zorb-logo T-shirt, shorts, and towel for $22). Zorb provides changing facilities and lockers. You can also opt to buy a CD with photographs of you and your friends Zorbing.

BLUFF MOUNTAIN ADVENTURES ATV RIDES
2186 Parkway, Pigeon Forge
(865) 453-3717, (800) 462-2134
www.bluffmountainrentals.com/Adventures
.asp

Although the office for Bluff Mountain Adventures is in Pigeon Forge, the guided ATV trail rides actually take place on 6,000 acres of Bluff Mountain in Sevierville. After getting helmets and goggles and listening to a safety and orientation briefing, your group takes off with your guide, roaring and bumping along wooded trails, splashing across mountain streams as you go. (Yes, you'll probably get muddy if it's rained recently.) It's noisy, it's crazy, and it's totally exhilarating. For the best view (and the roughest ride), take the trail to the top of the bluff.

You can sign up for four different rides, ranging from the one-hour family introductory ride ($44.95 for anyone age 16 and up and $34.95 for children, who must be at least 12 to participate), to the two-hour "for the daring" custom ride ($94.95 per person; you must be at least 16 to participate). An additional charge of $2.75 per person is added to cover insurance. If you're staying at one of the Bluff Mountain accommodations, you'll get a 20 percent discount. Tours are weather permitting.

TUBING AND WHITE-WATER RAFTING

Tubing (floating down a river while sitting inside a huge, inflated inner tube) is one of the simple joys of life. There's hardly anything better to do on a hot summer day. If you want to try it, you basically have two options. But for either one,

you'll have to go to Townsend—the Blount County community at the other end of Wears Valley Road from Pigeon Forge. (See the Townsend section of the chapter on Getting Out of Town for more information.)

The first option is to buy an inflated inner tube from one of the places listed here (or from one of the gas stations or seasonal tubing shacks that line the main drag through Townsend) and go on your own. To do this, you'll need two cars (unless you want to walk a mile or so while carrying a large inner tube). Leave one car at a good parking spot off the side of the road somewhere downstream (wherever you want to climb out of the river—but take pains to heed "no trespassing" signs and avoid private property). Then take the tubes in the other car and drive upstream until you find a place where you want to start.

The most popular place for tubers to begin their float trips is inside the national park at a place along the Little River called the Townsend Wye (sometimes spelled Townsend Y, as in fork—not YMCA), located a few miles east of Townsend on TN 73. In fact, if you drive into Townsend from Gatlinburg (through the national park), you'll pass right by this longtime favorite tubing and swimming hole. There's a parking lot there, as well as portable toilets in the summer.

The second option is to rent a tube at one of the businesses in Townsend that provide shuttle service. That way, you need only one car, and you're not left with a huge hunk of rubber to try to figure out what do to with when your vacation (or even just the day) is over. For a modest fee, you can tube and ride the shuttle all day. Instead of truck-tire inner tubes, expect brightly colored super-thick vinyl tubes 4 feet in diameter and sporting handles. Some tubes even have "floors" so younger kids won't slip out. The tube shuttle companies will shuttle you to an area near the park border but won't cross it, due to various park regulations about commercial businesses using the national park. It hardly matters, though. You'll get a fabulous ride either way.

A few safety notes: Tubing looks simple and fun (and it is) but as with all water sports, it can be dangerous. The tubing outfitters supply life vests, and you will want to wear one. Avoid oversized clothing that may snag on branches or other obstructions, and wear something on your feet for protection. You might want to wear water shoes instead of flip-flops, which can easily get knocked off and float away forever, leaving you looking like a soggy Smoky Mountain Cinderella. If you do manage to fall out of your tube, try to float feet-first on your back until you can climb back in. And don't forget the sunscreen—the reflection from the water will cause you to burn more quickly than you think.

The following listings include two places in Gatlinburg where you can pick up tubes on your own, followed by the main tubing shuttle operation in Townsend (which provides tubes for rent). Rounding out the section is a white-water rafting operator.

SHIRLEY'S TEXACO SERVICE
1141 Parkway, Gatlinburg
(865) 436-4109
Located at traffic light #10, right at the park entrance, Shirley's maintains a large stock of truck tubes for sale only, at about $10 apiece.

MCKINNEY'S MARKET
831 East Parkway, Gatlinburg
(865) 430-5985
About a mile east of traffic light #3, McKinney's sells tubes for $15 each. Their tubes are extra thick and made especially for tubing, with rope handles.

SMOKY MOUNTAIN RIVER RAT
205 Wears Valley Road, Townsend
(865) 448-8888
www.smokymtnriverrat.com
This operation has been making certified (and certifiable) river rats out of patrons since 1995, when the business consisted of a 20-foot-by-20-foot building, an old 1976 Chevy van, and 50 tubes. Today, River Rat's modern facilities include changing stations, restrooms, a small store, and lovely picnic grounds right on the banks of the river. You'll find River Rat just 20 minutes from Pigeon Forge on Wears Valley Road (turn at traf-

fic light #3), a short distance before it dead-ends onto the main drag in Townsend.

You get two tubing options here. The Family Float (for ages two and up) is the gentlest option. For this one, you'll hop into your tube at River Raft's outpost and then float 1 1/2 miles downstream to a place where the shuttle bus will pick you up and bring you back. These trips generally take about an hour and a half. The second option is the Adventure Float (for ages five and up). For this one, you start out taking the shuttle bus for a 1-mile ride to the put-in. The float from here back to the tube shack is about an hour long. Another option is to rent kayaks that you can take on the same routes using the same shuttle.

River Rat operates from May through September. You'll also find a shop at the outpost that sells water shoes, towels, sunscreen, T-shirts, hats, and even underwater cameras—so if you forgot to bring something with you, you're covered. Tubing costs $13 per person, including tax, tube rental, life vest, and unlimited shuttle service for the entire day. Kayaking is $15 for the first trip and $5 for each additional trip, including tax, kayak rental, life vest, and shuttle. River Rat also operates a rafting company (USA Raft) as a sister business that can take you white-water rafting on the Pigeon River. Various combo tubing/rafting programs are available.

RAFTING IN THE SMOKIES
2470 East Parkway, Gatlinburg
(865) 436-5008, (800) 776-7238
www.raftinginthesmokies.com
One way to gain an appreciation for the awesome power of nature is to watch a National Geographic special on TV. But a much better (and wetter) way is to plunk yourself down right in the middle of it for some hair-raising, white-knuckle excitement in a fairly safe environment.

Here's how Rafting in the Smokies works: If you've made reservations in advance (highly recommended), you'll get your tickets in the mail, along with directions to the outpost in Hartford. The outpost is at exit 447 on Interstate 40, near the Tennessee/North Carolina border (about 45 minutes to an hour from downtown Gatlinburg).

🔍 Close-up

A Lovely Way to Spend a Day (or More)

Llamas aren't new to the Smokies. The staff at LeConte Lodge (see the chapter on the national park) counts on the lovable, furry beasts to ferry supplies up to the lodge (and to carry trash back down) once a week in season. If you want to get in on a little llama trekking action of your own, Sandy Sgrillo of Smoky Mountain Llama Treks is your llady.

Sandy offers several different trails to pick from (including some with mountain views and some leading to waterfalls) on mostly private property located between Sevier and Cocke Counties. (Sandy can't take you into the national park because commercial use of the park is prohibited, except for certain licensed operators who run specific park facilities.)

When you make your reservation, Sandy will give you excellent directions to the trailhead, where she and her beasts will be waiting. As Sandy will explain, llamas are as gentle and friendly as they look—if they're treated with respect. "They're a lot like house pets," Sandy says. "Big house pets. They're intelligent and respond to the treatment you give them. Since I love my guys and demonstrate it, they love me right back. And after they are introduced to other people, they're very easy to get along with." Each hiker will get his or her own llama as a personal companion for the hike—to lead, not to ride on.

Sandy's day treks range from two to six hours (and cost between $50 and $85, the latter including a full gourmet lunch). Overnight treks run $265, including meals and cushy sleeping arrangements (a tent with a queen-size air mattress and linen bedding). All trekkers must be at least six years old. For more information, contact Sandy at Smoky Mountain Llama Treks (865-428-6042; www.smokymountainllamatreks.com).

If you haven't made reservations, you can go either to the office on East Parkway, about 6 miles east of traffic light #3 in downtown Gatlinburg, or to the office at 3249 River Road in Pigeon Forge. (The Gatlinburg headquarters is actually in the mountain town of Pittman Center, a well-kept secret that would like to stay that way.) Then you'll drive to the outpost, following the directions you receive with your tickets.

Two trips are available on the Pigeon River. The hairier trip is the Big Pigeon adventure, which begins with a ride in a shuttle bus to the put-in, 5 miles upriver. This run offers both Class III and Class IV rapids and is rated as one of the most exciting white-water raft rides in Tennessee. Flanked by the national park on one side and Pisgah National Forest on the other, the Big Pigeon run drops sharply through 5 miles of almost continuous rapids in a fast-moving hour-and-a-half ride. Don't worry if you don't have experience— the expert guides (one is in every raft) will teach you everything you need to know. By the end of the trip, you'll end up back at the outpost.

Through the height of the rafting season (May through Labor Day), this trip runs on Tuesday, Wednesday, Thursday, and Saturday (the days water is released from the dam). In the shoulder seasons—in March and April and also from Labor Day through November—the schedule is different, so call for current information.

For a tamer trip, the Lower Pigeon float trip is just the ticket. Leaving from the outpost, your raft will follow the swift, gentle current for 6 miles through one of the most beautiful stretches of forest in North America. At some slow points, rafters can jump in the river and swim along with the raft. On this two-hour trip, you'll encounter Class I and II rapids and one Class III rapid at the end. The shuttle is waiting when you get out to return everybody to the outpost. Another option with this trip is to rent single or double inflatable kayaks called duckies that accompany the rafts.

The Big Pigeon white-water raft run costs $39 per person (children must be at least eight years old and weigh at least 70 pounds), and the float trip (either by raft or by duckie) is $35 a head (children must be at least three years old).

All rafting trips go as planned, regardless of weather conditions—if there's any question about what you're facing, pack a bathing suit, a complete change of clothes, and a towel. That'll do in warm weather. If it's cool or worse, wool socks and sweaters are recommended. And be sure of this: You are going to get wet, probably to your skin. Hot showers and changing rooms at the outpost will ensure you depart as warm and dry as when you arrived.

HORSEBACK RIDING

Sevierville

DOUGLAS LAKEVIEW STABLES
1650 Providence Road, Sevierville
(865) 428-3587
www.douglaslakestables.com
These riding stables are located among scenic rolling hills near Douglas Lake, just a few miles off TN 66. They've been providing guided horseback tours for more than a decade and offer approximately 40 different horses and 12 miles of trails for riders of all levels of experience.

Douglas Lakeview Stables offers packages that combine trail rides with a cowboy hat and color photos (your choice of an 8x10 group photo or a 4x6 individual photo). The cost is $29.95 for a one-hour ride package, $59.90 for a two-hour ride package, or $120 for a four-hour ride package. Prices include tax. Discounted rates are extended to groups of five or more, and kids three to six years old can ride in the saddle with an adult for about $10 each.

Typically, tours last from one to four hours. Trip options include lakeshore rides (ask about the old Indian burial ground), sunset rides, and moonlight rides for adults only. The property also features a free petting zoo for customers with goats, emus, and llamas. Owner Jim Chambers, a chaplain, also performs horseback wedding ceremonies and vow renewals at a variety of rustic sites. Weddings range from $259 to $1,199.

DEER FARM RIDING STABLES
478 Happy Hollow Lane, Sevierville
(865) 429-2276
www.deerfarmzoo.com
You'll find these stables in the scenic hills east of Sevierville off U.S. Highway 411. They're owned by the same family that operates the Smoky Mountain Deer Farm and Exotic Petting Zoo, which is located on the same property (see the Close-up in the Attractions chapter). The horses are gentle and the well-maintained trails are a comfortable 8 feet wide, shaded by trees for approximately 80 percent of the route. Deer Farm also provides riding instruction, mounting stands, padded equipment, and guides who will tow your younger riders if you wish. Pony rides are also available near the stables for $5 each.

Rides cost $15.95 for a half hour, $21.95 for a full hour, and $41.95 for two hours (by reservation only). Children small enough to share an adult's saddle cost $6.50 extra. The maximum weight for riders is 250 pounds. Stables are open weather permitting.

FIVE OAKS STABLES
1628 Parkway, Sevierville
(865) 453-8644
Although their address technically places them in Pigeon Forge, you'll actually find the entrance to the stables on the Parkway in Sevierville, just shy of the Pigeon Forge border. Their Parkway location makes Five Oaks one of the more conveniently located riding establishments in the area. The wrangler guides will help you mount your horse before leading you on a scenic trip through the 250-acre farm's rolling and wooded hills, with great views of the mountains and the city below.

Half-hour rides are $16.50, while one-hour rides are $22.00 (including tax). You must be at least six years old and less than 330 pounds to ride. The stables are open weather permitting, and no reservations are necessary. Five Oaks also has a gift shop and tack store.

Pigeon Forge

WALDEN CREEK RIDING STABLES

2709 Waldens Creek Road, Pigeon Forge
(865) 429-0411, (865) 429-0607
www.waldencreekstables.com

You'll find horseback riding and a whole lot more at these stables located just a few miles outside Pigeon Forge off Wears Valley Road. A scenic 500-acre ranch with about a hundred horses is the setting for guided day rides that last anywhere from 40 minutes to eight hours. Well-maintained trails take riders through valleys, over foothills, and across mountain streams. Undeveloped trails lead to nearby mountaintops.

Most folks take either the Valley Hill ride (which lasts 45 minutes to an hour and costs $25) or the Valley Mountain ride (which lasts an hour and a half to two hours and costs $40). The Mountain View ride for more experienced riders lasts two and a half hours and costs $50. Other options (including full-day rides, evening rides, and overnight excursions) are also available for more experienced riders. Walden Creek also performs wedding ceremonies on horseback.

On certain nights from May through October, you can join one of Walden Creek's Wild West shows, including both singing cowboys and rowdy "bandits." The cost is $25, but if you've gone horseback riding any day during the season (be sure to save your ticket), the dinner and show is half-price. You get a hayride to start, and then you'll enjoy a pulled-pork dinner and bonfire as well as a show featuring rope tricks, horse races, and trick riding.

While you're there, check out Walden Creek's extensive gift shop for all sorts of western wear, jewelry, T-shirts, and even saddles.

i Although most horseback-riding stables list specific closing times, it's important to note that the last ride of each day usually departs up to an hour before that closing time. In other words, you can't show up five minutes before closing and expect to ride.

BIG ROCK DUDE RANCH AT PONDEROSA RIDING STABLES

909 Little Cove Road, Pigeon Forge
(865) 428-9398
www.ponderosahorseriding.com

Big Rock Dude Ranch has some big horses (and easy-loading ramps), so there's no weight limit here. A one-hour ride on a multi-elevation trail is $26.95 (minus the $4 coupon you can get at the counter), or ride for two hours for $46.95. There's even a playground and a free petting zoo with chickens, goats, ducks, rabbits, and a pony. Big Rock also offers picnic tables, horseshoes, and a free heritage museum with Civil War artifacts and 400-year-old Bible pages. You can also fish in a stocked pond, with the pole and bait provided ($16.95 for all day). Or try panning for amethyst, pyrite, blue calae, peacock copper, tourmaline, jade, and other gemstones ($12.95 for a three-pound bag of mining ore). If you get the combo special for $29.95, you get a one-hour horseback ride, gem mining, a bag of corn for the petting zoo, and ice cream. Add $7 to that price and you can also fish all day.

Gatlinburg

SMOKY MOUNTAIN RIDING STABLES

1720 East Parkway, Gatlinburg
(865) 436-5634
www.smokymountainridingstables.com

Smoky Mountain Riding Stables is actually inside the boundaries of the national park, about 4 miles east of downtown Gatlinburg on US 321N. The stables are owned and operated by Kenny Kear, a Gatlinburg native with an impressive string of credentials as a trainer of champion show horses. Open from early March through November, Smoky Mountain Stables offers hour-long rides for $25 and two-hour rides for $50. You must be at least five years old (and under 225 pounds) to ride.

The same outfitter also operates Sugarlands Riding Stables (865-436-3535; www.sugarlands ridingstables.com), which is located just before the Sugarlands Visitor Center, not far from the Gatlinburg entrance to the national park. The rides at Sugarlands are a bit steeper than Smoky Mountain Riding Stables, but otherwise the prices and policies are the same.

SKIING AND SNOW TUBING

OBER GATLINBURG
1001 Parkway, Gatlinburg
(865) 436-5423 (ski line: 800-251-9202)
www.obergatlinburg.com

You don't hear the words *skiing* and *Tennessee* used in the same sentence very often, and there's a reason for that. In fact, there's only one ski resort in the state—Ober Gatlinburg. But the good news is that when you don't have lots of single-digit temperatures and great natural snow, you have to try harder. So what started in 1962 as a run down the mountain to a simple cinder-block building (when there was snow) has grown into a sprawling year-round ski resort/amusement park with some of the most advanced snowmaking equipment in the country.

Tucked into a five-acre niche in Mount Harrison (Ski Mountain to the locals), Ober Gatlinburg sits 1,400 feet above downtown, at an elevation of about 2,700 feet. Getting there entails a 2-mile ride from the tram terminal on the Parkway (highly recommended) or 7 miles of driving on a two-lane mountain road (not recommended at all, especially since the road is frequently closed to all but local traffic during the ski season). The aerial tramway (covered in the Attractions chapter) costs $10 for adults and $8.50 for children ages 7 to 11 for round-trip fare. And remember to hang on to your tram ticket. If you show it at the lift ticket window, you'll get a discount.

The frigid fun usually begins in early to mid-December (and generally runs until early March) with eight slopes, three lifts, a rental shop, and a ski school. A kaleidoscope of plans fits any budget, but a day of skiing costs about $80 per person (including tax) for the tram, ski rentals, ski clothing rentals, a one-hour group lesson (required for first timers), and a lift ticket. If you want to snowboard, tack on an additional $10. (By the way, children age six and under get free lift tickets with a paying adult.)

Among the eight slopes are Ober Chute (a 4,400-foot intermediate run with a vertical drop of 556 feet), Mogul Ridge (a 300-foot washboard with a near-vertical 235-foot drop), and the beginner run, Cub Way (a long, gentle slope). The two quad lifts and one double lift move a total of 6,000 people per hour, so there's seldom any waiting.

Lift tickets cover a dizzying array of scheduled sessions (including night skiing) that vary with the time of year. Call for the schedule that will be in use when you arrive, or check the Web site for details.

New for winter 2008 is a $1.5 million, snow-tubing park with ten 400-foot lanes (featuring a 50-foot vertical drop) and a Magic Carpet lift. You must be six years old and 42 inches tall to tube solo, but children ages three to five can ride with an adult. Tubing costs $20 per session, and each session lasts an hour and 45 minutes. The park is lit, so you can also tube at night.

DOLLYWOOD

One hundred and fifty acres of rides, attractions, music shows, and mountain crafts make Dollywood the cornerstone of many a Smoky Mountain vacation. Open since 1986, Dollywood is the namesake of Dolly Parton, renowned country music star, movie actress, philanthropist, and Sevier County's most notable native. She is also a part owner who remains very active in the continued development of the park.

Abundant greenery and beautiful flower gardens enhance the ambience of the park's numerous rustic wooden structures. Dollywood was built around a previously existing amusement park that had been in place for many years, operating most recently as Silver Dollar City theme park in the late '70s and early '80s. Since taking over, however, Dolly and company have continually added on to the complex—new features are introduced to the public every year. Since the closing of Opryland in Nashville, Dollywood is now the largest and most visited theme park in the state and hosts upwards of two million visitors each year. It has also been quite beneficial to the local economy, as evidenced by the fact that the various businesses that make up the Dollywood Company have become Sevier County's largest single seasonal employer.

OVERVIEW

Dollywood is open April through early January. The park is open daily throughout the summer and runs on a more limited schedule during the other months. Hours of operation vary, depending on the time of year. Generally, the park is open from 9 a.m. to 8 p.m. during summer and from 10 a.m. to 7 p.m. during spring and fall. The winter schedule generally runs Thursday through Sunday from 2 to 9 p.m., with extended hours on weekends. The park is closed Thanksgiving, Christmas Eve, and Christmas day.

The following prices are the most current available at press time, but please be aware that they are subject to change. One-day admission is $53.50 for ages 12 and older, $42.35 for ages 4 through 11, and free for children three and younger. Tickets are $50.20 for seniors (60 and older) or AARP members. All prices include tax.

Group rates and season passes are available, as well. In fact, if you purchase a one-day ticket and like what you see, you can apply the full value of your ticket toward a season pass that same day. And you're more than halfway there:

A season pass actually costs less than the price of two one-day tickets.

If you plan on attending both Dollywood and Dollywood's Splash Country (see the write-up at the end of this chapter), you can purchase Splash & Play tickets that allow three-day access to both parks for one discounted price. Or you can look into buying a Super Pass, a mega–season pass of sorts that gets you into both parks for the whole season. They are sold at varying price levels according to age and privilege options, but they usually include park admission as well as discounts on merchandise, and other regional attractions.

Another way to stretch your dollar at Dollywood is to arrive after 3 p.m. (or after 6 p.m. during the Smoky Mountain Christmas event), in which case your admission on the next operating day is free. This works especially well on hot summer days when you can take advantage of the cooler evening temperatures and the park's 8 p.m. closing time.

Admission prices include unlimited access to all regular shows, rides, attractions, craft showcases, and special events. As such, you can squeeze a lot of activity into one day (or two) without parting with too much more cash. But to park, eat, shop, and play games, you'll need to bring a good reserve of spending money.

Parking fees are $8 for cars ($11 for RVs and oversize vehicles), and trams will take you from your parking area to the main entrance (or you can take either of the Dollywood trolleys operated by the cities of Pigeon Forge and Gatlinburg; see the Getting Here, Getting Around chapter for details). Generally, expect to pay inflated prices at the theme park's restaurants and other food concessions—although honestly, the prices aren't any more inflated than they are at any other major theme park. Just be prepared!

Frankly, Dollywood's days and hours of operation change throughout the year (and the detailed pricing structure can be quite complex when you factor in all the different age groups, discounts, and passes). So call before you arrive for the most detailed and up-to-date information on schedules and prices.

Dollywood's address is 1020 Dollywood Lane, Pigeon Forge. For information on the park and its programs, call (865) 428-9488 or (800) 365-5996. Or you can check out the park online at www .dollywood.com.

GETTING THERE

There used to be two ways to get to Dollywood, but no longer. What locals used to call the back entrance (which was also the main entrance for Dollywood's Splash Country—Dollywood's water park) has now become the main entrance for both Dollywood and Splash Country, so if you're a return guest, you may be taking a new route. Turn off of the Parkway at traffic light #8 and follow Veterans Boulevard to the park's entrance, which is clearly marked by signs. An attendant is stationed to take your parking fee. When you find a parking space, be sure to note the lot number. You'll need to remember it when the tram takes you back to the parking areas later in the day.

NAVIGATING THE PARK

Dollywood is divided into several major sections that revolve around different themes and reflect various aspects of the Smokies and Americana. Within the boundaries of each, you'll find a variety of rides, attractions, shows, restaurants, and shops related to that zone's theme.

Wilderness Pass is the newest area, which now connects Timber Canyon and Craftsman's Valley and is home of the park's super soaker River Battle water ride. Timber Canyon features two thrill rides that are the only ones of their kind in the United States. Showstreet Palace is the site of DP's Celebrity Theatre and the Southern Gospel Music Hall of Fame. Adventures in Imagination features the Thunder Road movie ride and the Chasing Rainbows museum. Jukebox Junction takes you through a time warp back to the '50s, complete with a neato diner. Rivertown Junction features several shops as well as Smoky Mountain River Rampage, a white-water rafting ride.

You'll have trouble dragging your children away from the Country Fair area. With carnival midway rides, games, and 13 family rides all in one compact location, the young ones could linger in this section alone for hours. In the Village, you'll discover the depot for the Dollywood Express and an antique carousel. Dreamland Forest is where you'll find the Mountain Slidewinder ride in addition to many of the children's activities. In Craftsman's Valley, you can watch demonstrations of most of the old-time mountain arts as well as buy plenty of high-quality crafts to take home. You'll also find two roller coasters and a bald-eagle preserve here.

WHAT TO DO AT DOLLYWOOD

One of the best things about Dollywood is that it embodies in one (albeit expansive) location much of what people want out of a trip to the Great Smoky Mountains. Yes, it's a theme park with plenty of fun rides and attractions, but those thrills represent just one facet of your experience. In contrast to places like Six Flags, where rides are the staple, Dollywood also offers its visitors a broad canvas of options, including plenty of first-class musical shows and other entertainment. The setting represents an old mountain community of yesteryear. It serves a slice of Appalachian life, telling many a homespun tale via mountain music, crafts, and awesome wonders of nature. (You can even learn specifics about the history of the area by looking at the props and stories behind the rides.) Although this chapter can only scratch the surface, the highlights that follow will give you a good feel for what's in store.

Take Me for a Ride

Inside the park, you'll discover all sorts of rides (including relatively tame rides, thrill rides, water rides, and some rides designed just for the little ones). Amusement park mainstays like the Wonder Wheel (a classic Ferris wheel) and the Dollywood Express (an authentic steam-driven train) fall into the tame but classic category. The most-talked about thrill ride is the award-winning Mystery Mine—a one-of-a-kind indoor/outdoor roller coaster that includes a weightless inversion and a 95-degree, 85-foot vertical drop. Rounding out the thrill rides at the park are the Daredevil Falls log flume, the award-winning Thunderhead wooden roller coaster, and Timber Tower—the first of its kind in the country—which swings, spins, and drops you at 60-degree angles.

One of the newest rides, River Battle, is in the park's new area, Wilderness Pass. For this water ride, riders climb into eight-passenger rubber rafts, and everyone gets his or her own soaker gun. As the raft slips, spins, and bumps along its route, riders can shoot other rafters (or even those watching the ride from the sidelines) or take aim at any of the hundred or so special targets along the way. Some of the targets (including large-scale talking cartoon animals) shoot back when hit, while others dish out their own surprises. One fun twist is that spectators can also shoot the riders with soaker guns that line the walkways along the ride's path.

Wilderness Pass also has a brand-new ziplining course that takes visitors to new heights of adventure—quite literally! SkyZip, added in May 2009, consists of five separate ziplines ranging in length from 100 to nearly 1,000 feet. (The attraction also includes a 100-foot-long swinging bridge in the treetop canopy.) To ride, participants get into a seating apparatus that's attached to a pulley suspended from an elevated and inclined cable. Gravity carries riders from one end of the cable to the other as they literally zip along in midair above the trees, getting fabulous views of the Tennessee Tornado roller coaster, Eagle Mountain Sanctuary, and Craftsman's Valley in the process. Trained guides also share environmental and historical information about the undeveloped and unspoiled property surrounding Dollywood that the course zips through. SkyZip requires an additional fee that's over and above park admission ($40 plus tax, although Dollywood Gold Passholders get a 20 percent discount).

An Interactive Experience

Dollywood's attractions offer something for all ages. One of the highlights of Adventures in Imagination is Thunder Road—a movie-ride attraction that takes passengers on a rollicking journey with bootlegger Luke Doolin as he tries to evade the sheriff and the revenuers in a three-car chase that tells the incredible story one of the Smokies' most legendary moonshine runners. Children must be 42 inches tall to ride. (Note that Thunder Road doesn't operate during KidsFest or Smoky Mountain Christmas, when special seasonal movie rides replace it. See the descriptions of Dollywood's festivals below for more information.)

Another highlight here is Chasing Rainbows, an interactive museum/attraction that displays behind-the-scenes collections, stories, and memorabilia that relate to Dolly's life and career. See yourself on video as you share the stage with Dolly and Porter Wagoner or see what you look like in one of Dolly's wigs—if you dare!

One longtime favorite attraction is Eagle Mountain Sanctuary, the nation's largest preserve of non-releasable bald eagles. Presented in cooperation with the American Eagle Foundation, this 1.5-million-cubic-foot aviary recreates the natural habitat of our national symbol and is used for the purposes of education, rehabilitation, and breeding. This safe haven is also the site of the Wings of America Birds of Prey demonstration. Viewers can get up close and personal with some of nature's most interesting flying specimens, such as bald eagles that swoop down gracefully over the heads of the audience. (Of course, this is all done under the supervision of specially trained handlers!)

The Southern Gospel Music Hall of Fame and Museum, located next to Showstreet Palace Theatre, uses a variety of memorabilia and artifacts that pay tribute to the Southern gospel artists who have shaped and influenced their genre of music. The attraction also features a "living museum," which uses numerous exhibits to examine the past, present, and future of Southern gospel music.

Dreamland Forest is anchored by what Dollywood bills as "America's largest interactive tree house"—two large three-story structures that contain dozens of fun activities for kids ranging in age from toddlers to teens. Treetop games and gadgets include a birdhouse village, "grapevine gossip phones," and a magic looking glass. Further into the attraction, children will discover a three-level "beehive area" where they can shoot foam balls at targets (and each other) from air guns. Parents can get in on the fun helping gather balls on the lower level with their special collection devices. The Bullfrog Creek section of Dreamland Forest is where the younger ones can get wet with squirt guns, water blasters, fountains, and more.

i If you plan to spend more than one day at either Dollywood or Dollywood's Splash Country, buy a season pass. They cost less than two single-day admissions.

Music, Music, Music

Music is a given at Dollywood, and that's to be expected considering that music is Dolly's original claim to fame. You'll find is a definite emphasis placed on country and gospel music, although one of the shows (the award-winning *Dreamland Drive-In*) highlights songs and dances from the '60s and '70s. Much of what you'll see on the stages of Dollywood are straight-ahead, live music performances: In all, about a dozen occupy a variety of indoor and outdoor venues. One features longtime favorite James Rogers, while another showcases members of Dolly's family. Another popular show, *Heartsong*, takes viewers on a musically enhanced journey through the Great Smoky Mountains with a large-screen motion picture presentation that is enhanced with multisensory extras. (Warning: You might get a little misty—but not from crying!)

New this year is *Sha-Kon-O-Hey!*, a major stage production with eight new songs written by Dolly as a tribute to the spirit and heritage of the land that has become the national park. "Sha-kon-o-hey" is Cherokee for "Land of Blue Smoke," the local Native American's name for the Smokies. (Dolly has also released a new CD of the same name and is donating the first-year profits to the nonprofit organization Friends of the Smokies, in honor of the park's 75th anniversary.) The show will run in DP's Celebrity Theater through October 2009.

In addition to its regular daily musical fare, Dollywood presents lots of special musical options during its four annual festivals (some of the South's largest). See the section on festivals later in this chapter for details. Dolly herself occasionally performs in benefit concerts in support of the Dollywood Foundation, an organization devoted to improving education in Sevier County and beyond, with Dolly's Imagination Library.

Craftwork

One of the factors in the Dollywood equation that lends itself so well to the park's mountain home theme is the abundance of craftspeople who populate the complex. Craftwork has long been

Less Waiting in Lines with New Q_2Q

If you want to pack more into your time at Dollywood (or if you simply hate standing in line—and who doesn't?), Dollywood has a new program called Q_2Q that will electronically stand in line for you, saving you a place for select shows and rides while you're off enjoying other parts of the park. To use the new system, you have to rent a small portable device called a Q-bot from the Q_2Q Reservation Center in Adventures in Imagination.

You can then use your Q-bot anywhere in the park to electronically scroll through the possible rides and select which you want to reserve. The rides that are part of the Q_2Q program are Mystery Mine, Timber Tower, Thunderhead, Smoky Mountain River Rampage, Sky Rider, Dizzy Disk, River Battle, and Tennessee Tornado. To reserve a show once you have your Q-bot, you need to use special kiosks at the reservation center. Q_2Q reserves shows playing at DP's Celebrity Theater, Showstreet Palace Theater, and the Pines Theatre.

The Q-bot beeps and vibrates when it's time to make your way to the attraction. With rides, you simply go to the ride anytime after the time shown on your Q-bot, and you'll be admitted immediately. With shows, the Q-bot holds your place until five minutes before the designated show begins. At the end of the day, you simply return the Q-bot to the reservation center.

Renting a Q-bot costs $15 for the first person and $5 for each additional member of your party who is using the same Q-bot (tax is additional); up to six people can share the same device. The number rented each day is limited, and they're available on a first-come, first-served basis. You must be 18 years old (ID is required) to rent one, and you must leave a credit card or cash deposit of $225, which you will forfeit if you fail to return the device.

a staple of the mountain lifestyle in the Smokies, so it's only natural that those skills would be on display here. Masters of time-honored art forms like glassblowing, pottery throwing, candle making, and blacksmithing conduct impressive demonstrations of their skills on a regular basis. Be sure to ask them questions about their work. These friendly folks love to interact with visitors and share stories.

i To maximize your time and avoid heavy foot traffic, try getting to Dollywood when the gates open. Start your tour of the park in either Craftsman's Valley or Country Fair and work your way toward the front entrance.

ANNUAL FESTIVALS

Dollywood offers four themed festivals that run from opening day through the end of the season. For each, the park looks different, and the entertainment is often different to boot. In addition to the write-ups below, two of the following events are also covered in the Festivals and Annual Events chapter.

Dollywood Festival of Nations

Since 2001, Dollywood has gotten each season rolling with its Festival of Nations, a monthlong celebration that practically delivers the world to the heart of the Great Smoky Mountains. Some 200 performers from a dozen different countries share their acts throughout the park's many venues. In addition to the international guests, Dollywood's regular performers are scheduled as well, sharing the stage time at the park's various theaters. In previous years, DP's Celebrity Theatre has hosted the Moscow Circus, and at Showstreet Palace Theatre, the Russian Cossack Dance Troupe took the stage. Other acts have hailed from Trinidad, Kenya, Italy, and Ecuador.

Dollywood Festival of Nations isn't all music. Guests can get that Epcot feeling as they watch acrobatics and juggling on the streets of the park. At the international bazaar, street vendors have gifts and souvenirs for sale, and Dollywood's restaurants and food vendors serve the cuisine of many different countries. And remember, as with all festivals, Dollywood's regular attractions, rides, and shows are almost all up and running during this time.

i The annual April parade when Dolly rode down the Parkway in Pigeon Forge amid floats and marching bands for opening day has now been switched to May. The parade, complete with Dolly as grand marshal, now marks the start of Dolly's Homecoming and always takes place the Friday before Mother's Day.

KidsFest

KidsFest runs every year from mid-June through early August, when colorful roving characters (including Baxter Bear, Walker the bluetick hound, and Patches the scarecrow) wander throughout the park, interacting with visitors. While the festival's other elements change about every other year, they're all designed to delight children and inspire their imagination.

For 2009, the fun will include animal encounters in Dollywood's Valley Exhibition Hall, where handlers from the Knoxville Zoo will play show and tell with a variety of small animals, reptiles, and bugs. Sandscapes, the 12-time World Sand Sculpture Champions, will show off large-scale, three-dimensional sand sculptures made from 75 tons of sand in the Village area near the Train Depot. Also in 2009, the Kratt Brothers, stars of the popular PBS Zoboomafoo series, will put on a show in Showstreet Palace, sharing their menagerie of live critters.

During KidsFest, the Thunder Road motion movie ride in the Adventures in Imagination area will change to Journey to the Center of the Earth. This 4-D adventure stars Brendan Fraser as Professor Trevor Anderson in a quest to discover a lost world. Riders wear special 3-D glasses that make elements of the movie pop right out of the screen. This ride is billed as a 4-D experience, with the "fourth dimension" being a surprise scent. (Don't worry—it's a pleasant one!) Children must be 42 inches tall to ride.

National Gospel and Harvest Celebration

Plenty of craftspeople work in the Smokies year-round, but during the annual National Gospel and Harvest Celebration in October, skilled artisans from across the country converge on Dollywood. Typically, some two dozen guest crafters are on hand, in addition to the resident artisans featured in the Craftsman's Valley section of the park.

Dollywood is made over for fall with thousands of hay bales, pumpkins, cornstalks, and chrysanthemums. And the smells of traditional autumn foods like deep-fried turkey legs and homemade sorghum waft through the air, tempting guests as soon as they walk through the gates. The park also presents the joyful noises of dozens of Southern gospel acts performing more than 200 shows at different venues over the course of the festival; all of the shows are included in the price of regular park admission.

A Smoky Mountain Christmas

The arrival of winter doesn't necessarily put a chill on the fun at Dollywood. During its Smoky Mountain Christmas festival, which runs from early November until early January, the park takes on a whole new identity. It's really one of the single best seasonal celebrations in the county.

In terms of appearance alone, Dollywood is a spectacle, as more than four million holiday lights twinkle throughout the park. Look for Carol of the Trees, an attraction that incorporates synchronized music and special lighting effects. Meanwhile, the many music shows at Dollywood adopt holiday themes, such as Dollywood's *Babes in Toyland* (with impressive acrobatics and beautiful scenery). *Christmas in the Smokies*, the park's signature wintertime production, is a large-scale affair staged in the Showstreet Palace Theatre. The spirit of the season is best captured with the gospel music of the Kingdom Heirs and Dollywood's live, outdoor nativity pageant, O' Holy Night.

The Thunder Road motion movie ride in the Adventures in Imagination area will change to the Polar Express 4-D Experience, the story of a child who doubts the existence of Santa Clause and has a chance to change his mind on a unique train ride to the North Pole. Riders don special 3-D glasses that make the movie come to life, and they'll also experience special "fourth dimensional" effects, such as pine scent drifting through the air. (Children must be 42 inches tall to ride.).

Holiday foods and the lighted Christmas parade help round out the festival, and if that isn't enough for you, you can still ride the Tennessee Tornado in the middle of winter.

ℹ If you buy your ticket to Smoky Mountain Christmas after 6 p.m., you get the next day free.

DOLLYWOOD'S SPLASH COUNTRY WATER PARK

Dollywood's Splash Country, a $20-million 35-acre water park that made its debut in 2001, sits right next to Dollywood theme park. It features a wave pool, an 8,000-square-foot leisure pool (with geysers, slides, and waterfalls), a variety of single- and double-tube slides, and a family raft ride. The following descriptions hit the highlights, but know that there's plenty more in store.

Adventurous water lovers can try Fire Tower Falls, the tallest and fastest body flume slide in the state, with a 70-foot free fall and a 140-foot splash lane at the end. Big Bear Plunge takes you on a white-water rafting adventure through

winding, dark caverns with steep drops that ends with your raft exploding through a wall of water and sliding down a cliff face into a pool below. On SwiftWater Run, the current propels your tube through a corkscrew tunnel before plunging into a landing pool. (Note that all of the thrill rides have minimum height restrictions that vary from ride to ride, and some require younger riders to be accompanied by a chaperone who is 16 years or older.)

Younger kids might prefer Little Creek Falls, the children's play pool area with its own water slides and activity pool. Bear Mountain Fire Tower offers seven slides and a bucket that dumps a thousand gallons of water on whomever happens to be underneath it when the alarm sounds. All ages can kick back on the 1,500-foot "lazy river" that meanders the expanse of the water park or bob along in Mountain Waves, a 25,000-square-foot wave pool.

Waterfalls, mountain streams, and natural-looking terrain help create the overall look and echo the Smoky Mountain theme. Other amenities include shops for last-minute swimwear and sunscreen needs, a self-service restaurant, a snack shop, and lockers. By the way, you won't have to pay extra for the use of rafts or inner tubes. Those are free with park admission.

Dollywood's Splash Country is open Memorial Day weekend through Labor Day, and the gates open at 10 a.m. Admission prices are $43.50 for ages 12 and older, $41.25 for seniors, and $37.90 for kids 4 through 11. Season passes range from $77 to $110, depending on age. All prices include sales tax. As mentioned in the theme park section above, guests can purchase Splash & Play tickets or Super Passes that allow access to both Dollywood theme park and Splash Country water park for a discounted price. And just like at Dollywood, if you arrive after 3 p.m., you can splash the next day for free.

ℹ Season pass holders can get into Dollywood's Splash Country one hour earlier on Saturday.

FESTIVALS AND ANNUAL EVENTS

As if you didn't already have a million and one reasons to come to the Smoky Mountains, here are a few dozen more. You'll find commemorations of seasons and holidays as well as festivals for arts and crafts, nature, and mountain ways of life. Smoky Mountain communities celebrate automobiles, romance, and the performing arts. Along the way, look out for plenty of great music, delicious food, and festive decorations.

Although the events included here are by no means a complete representation of all the events that take place in the Smokies each year, these are the more popular ones as well as the ones with the most longevity. In some cases, you'll find that larger festivals are listed below, as well as many of the specific events that take place within them. For example, Winterfest is a countywide celebration that lasts from mid-November through February. Obviously, quite a few Winterfest-related happenings take place during this period, and you'll find the more notable ones included here.

What you won't see listed are events sponsored by retailers that are basically nothing more than gimmicks to enhance business, as well as most charity fund-raisers. Several of the events detailed in this chapter do raise money for specific organizations and causes, but only those that might be of practical interest to the out-of-towner—such as music concerts, craft fairs, food tastings—are included here. Activities like charity golf tournaments and walk/run events that rely almost exclusively on local or selective participation have been omitted.

If you're an admirer of customized cars, you might want to plan your Smokies visit to coincide with any of the area's many custom auto shows—better known locally as "rod runs." Held mainly during the summer and in Pigeon Forge, these events showcase everything from modified vintage classics to Volkswagen Beetles. They won't be described here because they usually generate more interest among show participants than with the typical tourist. But whether you like custom cars or not, you have no choice but to get an eyeful of them as you drive down the Parkway in Pigeon Forge!

The following events are listed in chronological, instead of geographical, order. Because most Smoky Mountain events take place on different dates each year, each listing gives the general time of month that the event occurs. Phone numbers that appear with listings sometimes correspond with the event sites, but in other cases the number will enable you to reach the event coordinators. The listings also give specific prices, but be aware that these are also subject to change from year to year.

JANUARY

Many of the events in January and February are part of Winterfest, which begins in November and runs through February. (Refer to the November section of this chapter for a general overview of the Winterfest celebration.) Also in January, the cities of Pigeon Forge and Gatlinburg are continuing the trolley tours of their respective city's Winterfest light displays. You'll find all the specifics about those trolley tours in the November section as well.

WILDERNESS WILDLIFE WEEK
Music Road Hotel and Convention Center
303 Henderson Chapel Road, Pigeon Forge
(865) 453-8574, (800) 251-9100

Although the events that take place throughout the week occur in different parts of the county, the Music Road Hotel in Pigeon Forge is headquarters for what has become one of the area's most popular annual events. Wilderness Wildlife Week is eight days of nature hikes and walks as well as seminars, displays, and workshops dealing with the study of Smoky Mountain flora and fauna. And you can't beat the fact that the whole thing costs absolutely nothing. More than a hundred scientists and other experts in the fields of wildlife, nature, and conservation lead the hikes and other programs. This all-volunteer staff converges from around the region to lend its expertise on subjects ranging from native black bears to wildflowers.

Although most Wildlife Week events don't require advanced reservations, some of the offerings limit the number of spots available. You can register for any of the week's approximately 50 hikes on a first-come, first-served basis the day before the hike at the Music Road Hotel. As for the hikes themselves, Pigeon Forge provides transportation to various points in the national park for the expeditions that range from short, casual nature strolls to overnight stays on top of mighty Mount LeConte. Most of the week's lecture-oriented programs take place at the Music Road Hotel.

AppalachiaFest is also part of the week's festivities (and is the only component that charges admission). This evening concert of traditional mountain music is held on Tuesday night in the Country Tonite Theatre. Performers vary but in 2009 included Grammy award-winner Tim O'Brien. Tickets are $15 for adults and $5 for those age 17 and under.

When Wilderness Wildlife Week was in its infancy, the turnout was pretty low, and the number of programs was limited. These days, 20,000 people from all over the country journey to the Smokies specifically for this event, which usually takes place during the second full week of the month.

More Information

Many of these inclusions are sponsored by the different cities in the county, so if you would like more information, contact:

Sevierville Visitor Center
(865) 932-4458, (888) 738-4378
www.visitsevierville.com

Pigeon Forge Department of Tourism
(865) 453-8574, (800) 251-9100
www.mypigeonforge.com

Gatlinburg Chamber of Commerce
(865) 436-4178, (800) 568-4748
www.eventsgatlinburg.com

SPECIAL OLYMPICS WINTER GAMES
Ober Gatlinburg Ski Resort
1339 Ski Mountain Road, Gatlinburg
(615) 329-1375, (865) 436-5423
www.specialolympicstn.org
www.obergatlinburg.com

Each year, scores of physically and mentally challenged youths go for the gold in the snow-covered mountains of Gatlinburg. Athletes as young as 11 compete in alpine skiing and ice-skating events during late January. The first day of the Olympics is usually reserved for coaching and training. During the next day, specific competitions take place between 8:30 a.m. and 4 p.m. Gold, silver, and bronze medals go to the top three finishers in each event, and all remaining participants receive ribbons. Closing ceremonies take place during the afternoon of the final day of competition.

Spectators don't have to pay admission, but if you opt to take the aerial tramway up to the resort, the round-trip fare will be $9.50, including tax, for anyone age 12 and up and $6.50 for ages 7 through 11. Children 6 and younger ride free with an accompanying adult. While you're at Ober Gatlinburg, which has hosted the Special

Olympics Winter Games since 1986, all the usual attractions and activities are available at their regular prices (see the Attractions chapter and the Active Outdoor Adventure chapter). (Note that while these Special Olympics used to take place in February, in recent years they've been moved up to January.)

ℹ️ You might want to check with area departments of tourism to see if any parades or road races (5K or 10K runs) are scheduled during your visit. If you know that sections of the Parkway and other side roads will be closed to cars during the event, you can adjust your travel plans for that day.

FEBRUARY

SADDLE UP!
Various venues, Pigeon Forge
(865) 453-8574, (800) 251-9100
This event, which debuted in 2001, has caught on right-quick-like and built up as much momentum as a cattle stampede. If you're a cowboy (or cowgirl) or have ever just fantasized about being one, Pigeon Forge is the place to be in February during this four-day immersion into all things western. Among the daily activities featured are chuck wagon cook-offs, a cowboy symphony, a western swing dance, and performances by cowboy poets and storytellers. Saddle Up! concerts feature musical acts steeped in the classic sounds of the American West. Most of the events are free except for the chuck wagon lunches ($5), the western swing dance ($5), and the Saddle Up! concerts (between $15 and $20).

MARCH

A MOUNTAIN QUILTFEST
Various venues, Pigeon Forge
(865) 453-8574, (800) 251-9100
www.mountainquiltfest.com
At this free show you'll find exhibits of another time-honored form of mountain arts and crafts. The centerpiece of the event is a juried show

with more than 300 quilts on display and for sale. Festivalgoers can also sign up for more than 80 classes and seminars (for which there is a fee) to help hone their skills. A Mountain Quiltfest takes place over a five-day period in mid-March.

APRIL

GREAT SMOKY ARTS & CRAFTS SHOW
Gatlinburg Convention Center
234 Historic Nature Trail, Gatlinburg
(865) 436-4178, (800) 568-4748
www.gatlinburgcrafts.com
Every Easter weekend approximately 10,000 visitors flock to the convention center to see artists from Gatlinburg's renowned Great Smoky Arts & Crafts Community (see the Shopping chapter) exhibit their talents and offer handcrafted treasures for sale. Craft products include baskets, candles, dolls, jewelry, pottery, quilts, toys, and much more. Representatives from nearly all of the community's studios, galleries, and shops are present for the four-day event (which takes place in March when Easter falls in that month).

Admission to this arts-and-crafts show is free. The doors open at 10 a.m. daily, and closing times vary, depending on the day of the week. This is just the first of several shows that the Arts and Crafts Community sponsors throughout the year; others take place during the Thanksgiving and Christmas holidays (see the November section of this chapter).

SPRING WILDFLOWER PILGRIMAGE
Gatlinburg Convention Center
234 Historic Nature Trail, Gatlinburg
(865) 436-7318
www.springwildflowerpilgrimage.org
Every April, near the end of the month, nature enthusiasts from near and far gather in Gatlinburg and the national park to experience the annual arrival of Mother Nature's blossoming beauty. Although most of the actual wildlife viewing takes place in Great Smoky Mountains National Park, the event is headquartered at W. L. Mills Auditorium in the Gatlinburg Convention Center.

For five days, more than 80 professional tour leaders selected from universities and colleges across the United States conduct some 90 different programs. Included in this staff are botanists, photographers, and hikers who are eager to share their expertise and experiences with their groups. Programs include half-day and daylong field trips, excursions that range from moderate scenic strolls to overnight trips to Mount LeConte. Meanwhile, at Mills Auditorium, visitors can view a collection of more than 200 flower and plant species native to the area.

The Wildflower Pilgrimage dates back more than 50 years, when the University of Tennessee Botany Department conducted annual field trips in the Smoky Mountains. In 1951, the pilgrimage was officially established in cooperation with the Gatlinburg Chamber of Commerce, the national park, and the Gatlinburg Garden Club. That first year, approximately 400 "posie pilgrims" took part in 11 tours over two days.

Today, registration fees are $30 for one day ($50 for two or more days) for adults and $10 for one or more days for high school and college students. Children ages 12 and younger are admitted free.

RIBFEST & WINGS
Ripley's Aquarium Plaza, Gatlinburg
(800) 568-4748

This festival on the outdoor plaza of Ripley's Aquarium of the Smokies has quickly become a local's favorite. In addition to live music and children's activities, including face painting, local restaurants cook up their best ribs and wings and compete for awards in six categories. The most coveted is the People's Choice Award (chosen, as you might assume, by popular vote). In order to do the careful research necessary in order to cast an informed ballot, you can sample all the ribs and wings you want for the price of an armband ($12). Otherwise, you can buy by the bite ($1 for one rib or for two wings).

SMOKY MOUNTAIN SPRING TROUT TOURNAMENT
Little Pigeon River in Gatlinburg, Pigeon Forge, and Sevierville
(865) 661-3474
www.rockytopoutfitter.com

After a long winter without restocking, more than 10,000 trout are released into the Little Pigeon River, running from the national park boundary in Gatlinburg all the way to Sevierville. Participants are allowed to keep what they catch, and more than $10,000 in prizes is up for grabs as well. Prizes include $500 cash awards for the largest (and smallest) trout, gift certificates, trophies, fishing gear, and more.

The two-day event takes place the first weekend of April. The competition is open to anglers of all ages, although entrants are separated into "tourist" and "local" divisions and then subdivided into "adult" and "children" groups. And tournament organizers say that no matter how they fare, all kids who enter walk away with a prize.

The $40 entry fee covers both days of the event (or pay $25 for either day), but a Tennessee fishing license and a trout permit in Gatlinburg are also required to participate (see the Parks and Recreation chapter for information on obtaining a license). In addition to the spring event, a fall tournament also takes place the last week of September.

i Every spring, Gatlinburg's parks department gets in step with the countywide Springfest celebration (which includes the annual Wildflower Pilgrimage, the Ribfest & Wings street fair, and other spring events). They adorn the streets and utility fixtures with thousands of blooms and bulbs, adding cheerful splashes of color to the downtown area to help usher in the warm weather.

MAY

DOLLY'S PARADE
Parkway, Pigeon Forge
(865) 453-8574, (800) 251-9100

Sevier County's most famous offspring marshals this annual parade in Pigeon Forge. The bands strike up and the floats start rolling down the Parkway as crowds line the streets, waiting to catch a glimpse of Dolly Parton. In past parades Ms. Parton has brought some of her friends along to help celebrate—stars like Burt Reynolds and Lily Tomlin. Around 6 p.m., the caravan starts on River Road, makes its way north along the Parkway, and winds up at the Wears Valley Road intersection. This parade used to be held in early April, but starting in 2009, it moved to the Friday before Mother's Day.

RAMP FESTIVAL
Kineauvista Hill, Route 321, Cosby
(423) 623-1009
www.cosbyrampfestival.org

This one may send you a few miles out of your way, but it's about as unique a festival as you'll ever see (or smell). First, you're probably wondering what a "ramp festival" is. No, it's not a day to celebrate motorcycle stunt paraphernalia or interstate access points. Ramps are a cross between onions and garlic, and believe it or not, thousands of people travel from all over the country to sample and celebrate this pungent plant. Taking place the first Sunday in May, the festival's activities include country, folk, and bluegrass music, as well as the always-popular Maid of Ramps pageant, a beauty competition for young ladies ages 16 through 21.

Naturally, with a gathering devoted to an edible plant, there's bound to be food involved. Indeed, in addition to barbecued chicken and pig, a variety of ramp dishes are served up. A couple of the more popular ones are ramps with scrambled eggs and ramps served with hoe cake, a type of skillet-fried corn bread. You might want to know that ramps are five times stronger than onions when uncooked. In fact, it's rumored that enough ramp consumption will cause an odor to be released through the pores of the body. Worry not. If you show up to the Ramp Festival, you will hear plenty of home remedies for getting rid of "ramp breath."

The history behind the festival dates back more than 50 years to when a visiting Knoxville News Sentinel columnist suggested to some of the Cosby locals that they start a festival in honor of the ramp. Several of the local men proceeded to form a club for just such a purpose, and the rest is history. Today, the event is sponsored by the Cosby Ruritan Club, whose members dig up 50 to 60 bushels of ramps in preparation for the festival. Admission is $7 for adults and $5 for children ages 6 to 12. Children age 5 and younger get in free. Parking is free, too.

> **i** Traffic slows to a snail's pace on the Parkway during most of the custom car shows or "rod runs." In traffic, the custom-car drivers like to move very slowly; when parked, the cars themselves draw lots of stares from rubbernecking motorists. If you get stuck, take one of the local shortcuts listed in the Getting Here, Getting Around chapter.

GATLINBURG SCOTTISH FESTIVAL & GAMES
Downtown and Mills Park, Gatlinburg
(865) 436-4178
www.gsfg.org

When the Smoky Mountains were settled about 200 years ago, many of the newcomers who settled were Scottish. Today, quite a few descendants of those pioneers still reside in these mountains (Gatlinburg's high school sports teams are even nicknamed the Highlanders). Since the early 1980s, Scots from all across the country (and even Scot wannabes) have gathered in Gatlinburg to celebrate that country's heritage. During the third weekend of each May, members of more than 60 clans drink deep from the well of their culture.

Things get kicked off on Friday with a parade through downtown Gatlinburg featuring kilted men and bagpipe bands. On Saturday and Sunday, the events move to Mills Park off US 321. The festivities include bagpipe competitions, Highland dancing, and border collie demonstrations. The different clans set up tents where visitors can learn about each clan's history and colors. Authentic Scottish cuisine is available for the tasting—including hot dishes such as meat pies and baked goods such as scones.

The Scottish athletic events are always popular with the spectators. Women especially enjoy the men showing their legs in the bonniest knees competition, and the caber throw (where contestants toss a telephone-pole-like log) is a test of raw strength and skill. Then there's the haggis hurl! Haggis, for those who don't know, is a traditional Scottish dish prepared by taking the organs of a sheep or calf, mincing them with a few more palatable ingredients, and boiling them in the animal's stomach. It's not hard to imagine why people want to hurl them!

Admission to the Scottish Festival & Games is $18 for Saturday and $13 for Sunday, or $25 for both days. One-day tickets for children ages 5 to 14 are $5.

BLOOMIN' BARBEQUE & BLUEGRASS FESTIVAL
Downtown Sevierville
(888) 889-7415
www.BloominBBQ.com
One of the highlights of this festival, the largest in Sevierville, is the state championship barbeque cook-off, with barbeque teams from around the country competing for $15,000 in cash prizes. Each team serves up 20 pounds of pulled pork, 24 pounds of brisket, 5 pounds of chicken, and 10 pounds of ribs!

The festival also includes bluegrass concerts, kids' games (including climbing walls and bounce houses), food, and authentic mountain crafts. At the Bluegrass Music Tent, you can even learn to play a banjo, guitar, mandolin, or a fiddle.

Another highlight is the Annual Mountain Soul Vocal Competition Finals, in which male and female contestants from around the country sing any of the 3,000 songs penned by Sevier County native Dolly Parton. The goal isn't to imitate Dolly or to do an impression of her, but to perform the song in the singer's own style (be that rock, rap,

swing, soul, bluegrass, or—of course—country). The winner not only gets cash, but also a recording session in Nashville and an autographed guitar by Dolly herself.

Admission to the entire festival is free, even for the concerts.

JUNE

SMOKY MOUNTAINS STORYTELLING FESTIVAL
Various venues, Pigeon Forge
(865) 453-8574, (800) 251-9100
The mountain art of storytelling gets into high gear with a weekend of fun taking place in early June at several different Pigeon Forge music theaters. Specific venues for this event, sponsored in part by the National Storytelling Network, change from year to year. Regardless of which events or sites you choose, get ready to be mesmerized by noted local storytellers from the Smoky Mountains and the rest of the nation. The event includes storytelling concerts and workshop, the National youth Storytelling Showcase (for storytellers ages 17 and younger), and an evening of family-friendly ghost stories called Haunts 'n' Haints.

Day passes to most of the festival events are $10 (free for ages 17 and younger), while weekend passes are $25. Haunts 'n' Haints Tales is an additional $5 per person. (This festival formerly took place in February but has recently been moved to June.)

SMOKY MOUNTAIN TUNES & TALES
Downtown Gatlinburg
(800) 568-4748
Each evening around 5 p.m. from early June through early August, a horse-drawn wagon totes at least a dozen colorfully costumed folks through the streets of downtown Gatlinburg and drops them off in various places to perform for whomever gathers to watch. Offerings include clogging (a type of mountain dancing), dulcimer music (from a string instrument originating in the mountains), and storytelling, in addition to information about local wildlife and plants.

JULY

4TH OF JULY MIDNIGHT PARADE
Parkway, Gatlinburg
(865) 436-4178
This event has the distinction of being the nation's first Independence Day parade each year. Just after the stroke of midnight on the 4th, the long procession of floats and marching bands winds its way down the Parkway. Naturally, there's no charge for watching.

PATRIOT FESTIVAL
Patriot Park, Old Mill Avenue Pigeon Forge
(865) 453-8574, (800) 251-9100
Join nearly 30,000 revelers to observe Independence Day. Things get under way at 1 p.m. with an arts-and-crafts exhibition. Children's games and live entertainment begin at 3 p.m. and continue until 7:30 p.m., when the headline music act takes the stage. Headliners in recent years have included stars as well known as the Charlie Daniels Band. At 9:30 p.m., get ready for a spectacle of fireworks. The event is free, but due to the limited amount of on-site parking, spectators are asked to park elsewhere and take a trolley to Patriot Park (see Getting Here, Getting Around). Be sure to bring blankets and chairs to sit on for the fireworks.

GATLINBURG CRAFTSMEN'S FAIR
Gatlinburg Convention Center
234 Historic Nature Trail, Gatlinburg
(865) 436-7479
www.craftsmenfair.com
This 10-day event in late July is the first of two Gatlinburg Craftsmen's Fairs held between July and October. Visitors can see time-honored mountain crafts and other traditional art forms created before their eyes. More than 150 artisans from across the country are on hand, demonstrating their skills in areas such as folk art, wood turning, and ceramic making. Finished products include works in all kinds of media, from leather to oil painting to sculpture.

The event has grown into one of the most notable crafts happenings, not just in the Smok-

ies but in the entire southeastern United States. The show's quality is maintained through a jury system, which is used to evaluate potential entries. Although new exhibitors participate each year, roughly 80 percent are regulars. Some have been displaying their skills and wares since the fair originated. In addition to arts and crafts, live bluegrass and country music performances keep things hopping.

Admission is $6 for adults and free for children age 12 and younger. See the October listings for the particulars of the second fair.

AUGUST

STRINGTIME IN THE SMOKIES
Old Mill Square and Patriot Park, Pigeon Forge
(865) 453-8574, (800) 251-9100
Bluegrass performers strum their stuff at the Old Mill in Pigeon Forge at 11 a.m. and 1 p.m. Bring your own instruments and join in at Jammin' at the Old Mill from 2 to 9 p.m. Bring chairs and blankets to sit on for the evening concerts on both Friday and Saturday nights from 6 to 10 p.m. All events are free.

WORLD PREMIERE GOSPEL CONCERT
Grand Resort Convention Center
3171 Parkway, Pigeon Forge
(865) 453-1000
www.grandresorthotel.com
This three-day event, which takes place in late August, features some 60 different gospel groups representing more than 400 individual artists. The 3,000-seat convention center hosts two shows daily, from 1 to 5 p.m. and from 7 to 11 p.m. The concerts are sponsored by Gospel Music Television Network, which is based in Pigeon Forge and is North America's only all-gospel channel, broadcasting inspirational acts 24 hours a day, seven days a week. GMTN broadcasts the World Premiere concerts worldwide via satellite and cable, reaching an audience of millions in the United States and Canada.

Other activities related to the concert include morning devotional services and a lecture series.

Vendors of religiously themed merchandise are on hand throughout the event, and the performers themselves set up product tables where fans can buy CDs and T-shirts and even get handshakes and autographs from their favorite acts. At the cafeteria, attendees can meet, greet, and eat with the stars. One-day tickets for the event start at $29.95 plus tax; multiday packages that include lodgings, meals, and show tickets are available.

SEPTEMBER

OLD-FASHIONED WAGON RIDES
Downtown Gatlinburg
(865) 436-3897
From September 1 through the end of October, the city offers wagon rides through the streets of Gatlinburg. The departure point is traffic light #6 at Mountain Mall. The rides run Sunday through Thursday (excluding Thanksgiving and Christmas), and the cost is $4 per ride.

BOOMSDAY
Downtown Knoxville
www.boomsday-knoxville.com
Boomsday, which takes place the Sunday night of Labor Day weekend, is the largest fireworks display in the Southeast—it was even filmed for a National Geographic special. All kinds of carnival-style events and live entertainment are offered throughout the day, but the best part is the fabulous fireworks display. In about 20 minutes, four tons of pyrotechnics explode over the Tennessee River in downtown Knoxville in a show that takes almost 48 hours to set up. This is not a truckload of fireworks; it's a trainload. For the statistically inclined, more than 60 miles of wire are used to connect the computers that time more than 12,000 explosions. Local radio station 104.5 FM provides musical accompaniment.

If you're staying anywhere in Sevier County, plan to be on Chapman Highway (U.S. Highway 441N) no later than 7:30 p.m. Follow Chapman into Knoxville until you are required to turn away from the Henley Street Bridge, where the fireworks are set up. Turn in either direction, go anywhere from a few blocks to a mile to get a good view of the bridge, and find a place to park. Get as close to the river as you can (you won't be alone) in time for the explosive fun to begin at 9:30 p.m..

SEVIER COUNTY FAIR
Sevier County Fairgrounds
754 Old Knoxville Highway, Sevierville
(865) 453-0770
www.myseviercountyfair.com
There's nothing like a good old-fashioned county fair. This week of food, rides, games, and exhibits gets started each Labor Day and continues through Saturday night. The fairgrounds, which flank the Little Pigeon River in Sevierville, are the site for the festivities, which include midway rides and games, home-baked pies and preserves, and exhibits of prize-winning livestock, fruits, and vegetables. Several events are annual favorites, like the tractor pull and the watermelon seed–spitting contest. Another highlight of the week is the beauty competition, in which young ladies from across the county vie for the title of Fairest of the Fair. Admission is $3 for adults, and children ages 12 and younger get in free. Once on the grounds, you can buy individual ride tickets or pay $18 for an armband that gets you unlimited ride access.

SMOKY MOUNTAIN HARVEST FESTIVAL
Sevierville, Gatlinburg, and Pigeon Forge
Smoky Mountain Harvest Festival begins in mid-September and runs to the end of October. During this period, you'll see a number of craft fairs and music festivals throughout the county. The centerpiece is the countywide decorating contest in which area businesses, governments, and civic organizations adorn their buildings and grounds with traditional harvest decorations like hay, pumpkins, cornstalks, and gourds. Awards are given to winners in a number of different categories.

With the exception of the Trout Tournament, all of the events included in this chapter for the remainder of September and October are considered to be official Harvest Festival Events by their respective host cities.

Major special events in Gatlinburg, such as the 4th of July Midnight Parade and the Christmas Parade, can have equally major effects on traffic. It's not unusual to see traffic into the north end of the city backed up for miles on US 441 (The Spur). Entering Gatlinburg via US 321 may be a quicker alternative during these celebrations.

SMOKY MOUNTAIN FALL TROUT TOURNAMENT
Little Pigeon River in Gatlinburg, Pigeon Forge, and Sevierville
(865) 661-3474
www.rockytopoutfitter.com
This is the fall edition of a popular trout-fishing event that brings anglers of all ages to the shores of the Little Pigeon River. The September tourney takes place the last weekend of the month. See the write-up in the April section of this chapter for a more comprehensive overview.

A TASTE OF AUTUMN
Gatlinburg Convention Center
234 Historic Nature Trail, Gatlinburg
(865) 436-4178
Late in the month, you can get your fill of great food prepared by local eateries. At this one-day event, you can sample items from the menus of participating restaurants beginning at 5:30 p.m. for a cost of $25. You can purchase tickets in advance from Gatlinburg City Hall or either Gatlinburg welcome center. Along with the food tasting, the event features live entertainment, a cash bar, and a charity auction benefiting United Way of Sevier County.

OCTOBER

ROTARY CLUB CRAFTS FAIR
Patriot Park, Pigeon Forge
(865) 453-8574, (800) 251-9100
This arts-and-crafts event features dozens of local crafters as well as those from the Midwest and Southeast, displaying such skills as glassblowing, wood carving, and basket making. The festival takes place under a 200-foot tent at Patriot Park and runs for most of the month. Admission is free, but donations made during the festival benefit the many community projects sponsored by the Pigeon Forge Rotary Club throughout the year.

DOLLYWOOD'S NATIONAL GOSPEL & HARVEST CELEBRATION
Dollywood
1020 Dollywood Lane, Pigeon Forge
(865) 428-9488, (800) 365-5996
www.dollywood.com
Colorful autumn decorations abound throughout the park during Dollywood's National Gospel & Harvest Celebration, combining music, crafts, fall food, and fun throughout the month of October. Featured is the Smokies' only outdoor crafts festival with scores of visiting craftspeople from across the nation, showcasing and demonstrating their talents. Also, witness the country's largest Southern gospel music event. One-day tickets to Dollywood range from $42.35 for ages 4 through 11 to $53.50 for ages 12 and older (including tax). Note that Dollywood is closed on Tuesdays and Thursdays in October. See the Dollywood chapter for a complete profile, including more detailed admission and schedule information.

GATLINBURG CRAFTSMEN'S FAIR
Gatlinburg Convention Center
234 Historic Nature Trail, Gatlinburg
(865) 436-7479
www.craftsmenfair.com
For nearly three full weeks beginning in early October, the Gatlinburg Convention Center hosts tens of thousands of people who come to see live craft demonstrations by artisans from all over the country. See the listing for the summer fair in late July for information on what can be found at both Gatlinburg Craftsmen's Fairs. Admission is $6 for adults and free for children ages 12 and younger.

NOVEMBER

WINTERFEST
Sevierville, Pigeon Forge, and Gatlinburg
www.smokymountainwinterfest.com
Originally developed as a means of drawing more tourists to the Smokies during the winter, this nearly four-month-long festival has now become the big kahuna of annual area festivals. Beginning in early November, the county's three main cities each host their own respective kickoff celebrations on different nights to launch an entire season of music, parades, decorations, shopping bargains, and millions of holiday lights.

In Sevierville, you can enjoy live music performances, a lighting festival, kid's games, fireworks, and decorations at the Community Center on Gary Wade Boulevard. (Special 3-D glasses are available free from the Sevierville Visitor Center until they run out; the glasses make each point of light look like a snowflake.) Pigeon Forge's kickoff ceremonies take place at Patriot Park and include the turning on of the city's light displays, fireworks, live entertainment, food vendors, and free trolley tours of the holiday lights. In Gatlinburg, the kickoff is at Ripley's Aquarium of the Smokies, where you can sample entries in the chili cook-off and watch city officials flip the switch on millions of spectacular lights. Live bands are also on hand.

Most of the events listed for the months of November and December are part of the official Winterfest celebration. For more information, refer back to the January and February sections of this chapter.

WINTERFEST TROLLEY TOURS OF LIGHT
Pigeon Forge
(865) 453-6444, (865) 453-8574
Starting on the Friday after Winterfest gets under way, you can see the lights of Pigeon Forge without the hassle of driving. Tours run through January and are offered to all who want to enjoy the city's five million lights. Heated buses and informed hosts will guide you through the history of the displays. The cost of each trolley ride is $5 per person. The tours run Monday through Friday

evenings until New Year's Day and then Monday and Friday only through January. Tours depart the trolley office beginning at 6:30 p.m. Tickets may be purchased beginning at noon on the day of your tour, and reservations are encouraged. (For more specifics about the Pigeon Forge trolley system, see the Getting Here, Getting Around chapter.)

WINTERFEST TROLLEY RIDES OF LIGHT
Gatlinburg
(865) 436-3897
From early November until the end of January, these sightseeing trolleys offer spectacular views of Gatlinburg's Winterfest light displays. Tours depart from the Trolley Center at traffic light #5 (near Ripley's Aquarium of the Smokies) at 6:30, 7:30, and 8:30 p.m. and cost $5 per person. In November and December, they run every night; in January, they run Saturday only. However, since tours don't run on Thanksgiving, Christmas, and a few other selected days, it's best to verify specific times and dates. (For more information about Gatlinburg trolleys, see the Getting Here, Getting Around chapter.)

DOLLYWOOD'S SMOKY MOUNTAIN CHRISTMAS
Dollywood
1020 Dollywood Lane, Pigeon Forge
(865) 428-9488, (800) 365-5996
www.dollywood.com
Dolly's theme park is once again the setting for a large-scale seasonal celebration, beginning just after the Winterfest kickoff and running through the day after New Year's. During this time, Dollywood takes on a whole new character. The first thing you notice is all the lights—four million to be more precise— arranged on buildings, trees, shrubberies, and attractions.

As during the rest of its season, music is a staple of Dollywood's Christmasfest. A number of holiday-oriented shows are presented, such as *Dollywood's Babes in Toyland*, *Christmas with the Kingdom Heirs* (a gospel group), *Christmas in the Smokies,* and *O' Holy Night.*

Although Dollywood's water rides are closed for winter, the other rides here are up and running most of the time. Do take note, however, that the roller coasters close down when the weather hits 32 degrees—so if you want thrills and chills, get them before the sun goes down. Additional special attractions appear only for the holiday season. Kids will love Santa's Workshop, home to Santa Claus and his merry elves. Don't miss Carol of the Trees, an impressive synchronized lighting and music display. On top of all the lights, shows, and attractions, Smoky Mountain Christmas still offers plenty of shopping opportunities and holiday foods as well.

Dollywood is generally open Thursday through Sunday only from mid-November through the first Saturday in January (except for Thanksgiving Day, Christmas Eve, Christmas Day, and New Year's Eve). Call first to verify specific operating hours. Admission for one day ranges from $42.35 for ages 4 through 11 to $53.50 for ages 12 and older (including tax). Children 3 and younger get in free. See the Dollywood chapter for more detailed information on Dollywood, including admission and schedules.

i How many individual lights shine in Sevier County during Winterfest? More than 12 million lights in city-operated displays alone! Area departments of tourism estimate the following totals by city: Sevierville—120,000; Pigeon Forge—5 million; Dollywood—4 million; Gatlinburg—3 million. And these figures don't even take into account lights that are displayed by businesses and residents.

GREAT SMOKY ARTS & CRAFTS SHOW
Gatlinburg Convention Center
234 Historic Nature Trail, Gatlinburg
(865) 436-4178
www.artsandcraftscommunity.com
For more than a week surrounding Thanksgiving, this crafts event features the work of artisans from Gatlinburg's Great Smoky Arts & Crafts Community. It's a great way to get a start on holiday shopping. Admission is free. See the write-up in the April section of this chapter for more details

on what you'll find at the Arts and Crafts Community's annual shows.

THE NUTCRACKER "SWEET" AND FESTIVAL OF TREES
Gatlinburg Convention Center
234 Historic Nature Trail, Gatlinburg
(865) 680-7369, (865) 436-4178
See dozens and dozens of ornately decorated Christmas trees guaranteed to lift your holiday spirits just in time for Thanksgiving weekend (as will the free admission). Then, at 7 p.m., watch local kids as young as five perform this classic ballet put on by the nonprofit Smoky Mountain Dance Theatre. (Every child who auditions gets a part.) If you reserve one of the "sweet" seats (in the first ten rows of the middle section) for $25, you'll also get a $3 program and candy with your seat. Otherwise, tickets are $15 in advance or $18 at the door. Students can get in for $10, and those ages four and younger are admitted free.

DECEMBER

GATLINBURG'S FANTASY OF LIGHTS CHRISTMAS PARADE
Downtown Gatlinburg
(865) 436-4178
Lighted floats, marching bands, giant helium balloons, and, of course, Santa Claus trek along the Parkway, basking in the glow of the city's numerous Smoky Mountain Lights displays. The mile-and-a-half-long parade, which takes place the first Friday of the month, starts rolling at 7:30 p.m.

CHRISTMAS PARADE
Downtown Sevierville
(865) 453-6411
This Christmas parade makes its way along the Parkway and surrounding streets located in and around downtown Sevierville. You'll see marching bands, twirlers, decorative floats, and, of course, ol' Saint Nick himself. Parade spectators are invited to bring new, unwrapped toys that are taken up by Santa and his helpers as they make their way along the parade route. Donations go to Toys for Tots.

NEW YEAR'S EVE FIREWORKS AND BALL DROP

Space Needle
115 Historic Nature Trail, Gatlinburg
(865) 436-4178

It may not be Times Square in the Big Apple, but standing shoulder to shoulder with 25,000 other New Year's Eve revelers under the Space Needle isn't too bad for downtown Gatlinburg. The festivities start around 11:30 p.m., leading up to the lowering of a lighted ball from the top of the Needle (near traffic light #8). When midnight strikes, the attraction suddenly sparkles from top to bottom in a seven-minute display of pyrotechnics—about $10,000 worth, to be specific.

SHOPPING AND MOUNTAIN CRAFTS

While the national park draws millions of visitors to the Smokies every year, quite a large contingent of Smoky Mountain visitors come not to exhaust themselves on rugged mountain trails but instead to shop 'til they drop. Their prime plastic-melting territory includes the ever-expanding major outlet malls in Pigeon Forge (and now also in Sevierville), as well as countless specialty shops in all three Smokies Corridor towns and the numerous craft shops sprinkled throughout Gatlinburg's celebrated Great Smoky Arts & Crafts Community. After all, there's bargains in them thar hills!

For each Smokies Corridor community, this chapter will first give a sampling of specialty stores in that town (as always, traveling from the northern end of the corridor by exit 407 of Interstate 40 to the southern end, toward the entrance to the national park) before moving on to list the town's shopping centers and/or outlet malls (in the same north-to-south order). At the end of the chapter is a special section on shopping for mountain crafts, which is concentrated in Gatlinburg.

OVERVIEW

The stores listed here are by no means a comprehensive list. These pages focus on the more distinctive and unusual shops that visitors aren't likely to find at home. The Smokies Corridor does have a Walmart (it's on the parkway in Sevierville, not far from the Pigeon Forge border), but you won't generally find national discount chain stores like that listed in this chapter. (By the way, you might also want to look through the chapter on Festivals and Annual Events, because a number of them offer good Smokies shopping opportunities, as well.)

All of the shops, malls, and galleries listed in this chapter are interspersed with the attractions, restaurants, and motels throughout the Smokies Corridor and operate primarily on the same schedule. From Easter through Thanksgiving weekend, the vast majority of businesses will be open every day from about 9 a.m. to at least 9 p.m. Because the term *off-season* is rapidly becoming an anachronism in the Smokies, you can expect enough shops to be open year-round that you can shop anytime you're here, although a lot of businesses are closed after 6 p.m. from

January through March. The only day when most stores are closed is Christmas. Call the individual merchants for exact hours if you want to be sure because hours do vary widely with the season and sometime with the whim of the owners.

A few notes about outlet shopping: If this is your primary interest, you'll want to spend most of your time in Pigeon Forge and Sevierville, where most of the outlet shopping is located. Gatlinburg just doesn't have the space necessary for the large-scale construction that such malls require (although it does have smaller-scale shopping malls, listed below, with eclectic collections of individual stores).

The majority of outlet mall stores have honest-to-goodness bargains available in every product line you can think of. It's a good idea to do a little homework before venturing onto the outlet scene so you'll have a good sense of what truly is a bargain price. The good news is that the worst you'll do is pay retail for some things in stores that call themselves "outlets" but are not actually franchised by a company.

Outlet mall hours are often more predictable than those at individual shops elsewhere in town. In general, the most common hours in high season are at 9 a.m. to 9 p.m. (except for Sundays, when stores might not open until 10 or 11 a.m. and typically close between 6 and 7 p.m.). During the off-season, the outlet malls open between 10 or 11 a.m. and close between 5 and 6 p.m. (or 9 p.m. on Friday and Saturday nights).

SEVIERVILLE

Although Sevierville has always had an interesting selection of individual shops (and antique markets), it has not traditionally been known for its glorious shopping opportunities. All that has changed recently and continues to change at a dizzying speed. Although it's true that Sevierville doesn't have as many outlet malls as Pigeon Forge, for example, its Tanger Five Oaks Outlet Center is the largest outlet mall in the entire Smokies region—hardly something to sneeze at!

When the huge Bass Pro Shop went up in 2005 in what's now known as the Sevierville 407 district (at exit 407 on I-40, at the northern end of the Smokies Corridor), there was a corresponding boom in area hotels, restaurants, and retail shops. Watch for this area to be red-hot shopping spot in the future, especially with the 190-acre Dumplin Creek shopping complex on the drawing boards. Dumplin Creek, to be developed by the same builder responsible for the upscale 300-acre Turkey Creek complex west of Knoxville, will include not only shops, but also movie theaters and restaurants, and eventually hotels.

Here's a sampling of what's in store for Sevierville-bound shoppers.

BEEF JERKY OUTLET
3609 Outdoor Sportsman's Place, Kodak
(865) 932-4333, (866) 876-3626
www.tennesseejerky.com
Ever have a hankering for ostrich jerky? How about alligator or even arctic ox jerky? If so, you're in luck because this outlet near the Bass Pro Shop in Kodak carries more than 200 varieties of jerky, sold by the bag, by the jar, and in bulk. The exotic jerkies (kangaroo, caribou, and salmon among them) are made elsewhere, but the Smoky Mountain beef jerky is made locally. This outlet

also carries flavored peanut butters, deep-fried peanuts (eaten shell and all), and locally made jellies and jams. A second shop operates in Pigeon Forge (in Walden's Landing; 865-774-3441), and the newest location is in Gatlinburg (903 Parkway; 865-277-9019).

GREAT SMOKY MOUNTAINS ASSOCIATION GIFT SHOP
Sevierville Chamber of Commerce Visitor Center
3099 Winfield Dunn Parkway
(865) 436-7318
www.thegreatsmokymountains.org
If you want to help the national park, make it a point to patronize the well-appointed shops run by the nonprofit Great Smoky Mountains Association, of which this is the first you come to when traveling down the Smokies Corridor from I-40. Located within the new light and bright Sevierville Chamber of Commerce Visitor Center, this shop stocks a wide variety of Smokies-related apparel, stuffed animals and other toys, local specialty foods, CDs, posters, postcards, calendars, mugs, trail maps, and all manner of excellent books on the Smokies. Books for sale include various park guides, picture books, histories of the area, tomes about the park's flora and/or fauna, and plenty of great nature-oriented books for children. All purchases made at GSMA shops benefit the national park.

If you really want to help the park and save money, become a GSMA member. Memberships start at $30 per year, with benefits including a 15 percent discount in all GSMA shops (and with all online orders) as well as a variety of discounts at all sorts of local shops, galleries, accommodations, restaurants, and other businesses. You'll also get *Smokies Life* magazine and the association's newsletter, *Bearpaw*, twice a year, as well as the quarterly *Smokies Guide* newspaper—not to mention a snazzy lapel pin, a coupon for 20 percent off a one-time purchase, and other assorted goodies. Oh, and a great feeling that you're helping to support one of America's greatest national treasures.

In addition to this particular location, you'll find similar GSMA shops inside both of the

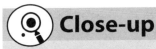

Close-up

Bass Pro Shops

Saying the Bass Pro Shop in Kodak is a retail store is like saying trees grow in the Smokies. It's true, but so much else happens there. This two-level, 130,000-square-foot complex at exit 407 on I-40 (the exit for Highway 66 to the Smokies) also houses a restaurant, a coffee shop, a waterfall, a trout stream, archery and rifle ranges, and countless wildlife displays. And that just scratches the surface.

The fun begins when you approach the huge log and rock entrance and find all sorts of animal tracks in the cement sidewalk. Once inside, you'll see a stone and stucco fireplace reminiscent of an old lodge, with wildlife displays, local memorabilia, and old-fashioned photos adding to the atmosphere throughout the store. Murals of local scenes adorn the walls (the 90-foot-long masterpiece in the camping department depicts the Appalachian Trail). Museum-quality wildlife exhibits are everywhere and include state-record fish mounts, turkeys, native waterfowl, bear, elk, and full-body whitetail deer and bear mounts. One remarkable example is a group of five elk overlooking the showroom as though it were a Smoky Mountain meadow.

Water is a key element in the outdoorsy decor here. Examples (all indoors) include a 15-foot waterfall, an 18,000-gallon aquarium (with more than 200 fish native to the area), and a 7,000-gallon trout stream that flows through one section of the store and is stocked with live brook, brown, and rainbow trout. (Anglers, please note: Hands off your hooks here!)

If you get hungry hiking about the displays, grab a latte and a snack at Starbucks (by the aforementioned trout stream) or stop at Islamorada Fish Company, an upscale seafood restaurant with its own saltwater aquarium. (See the Restaurants chapter for more information on this eatery.)

Want to practice your aim? The archery department in the mezzanine includes a bow setup shop and a 25-yard live archery range. You'll also find a rifle arcade that boasts 50 animated targets. Fishermen won't be encouraged to cast indoors, but fly-fishing enthusiasts can watch experts tying one on in the fly-fishing department (generously bedecked with antique and collectible fly-fishing memorabilia).

Oh, yeah, you'll also find merchandise for sale at Bass. In addition to a host of fishing and hunting equipment, Bass sells gear for camping, hiking, bird-watching, and water sports (in the marine and boat center, which offers everything from big boats to kayaks). To bring the great outdoors inside your own home, check out the outdoor-themed artwork and home decor items, including lamps, bird feeders, furniture, kitchen equipment, and more. Bass Pro Shop also offers a variety of outdoor skills workshops for adults and children.

Bass is part of the newly named Sevierville 407 community of businesses clustered around exit 407 on I-40. (Technically, this area is known as Kodak, although it's officially part of Sevierville). Guys will find this a particularly interesting part of town because it's home not only to the Bass Pro shop, but also to a professional baseball stadium (see the Attractions chapter for information about the Smokies Stadium) and even the Beef Jerky Outlet described elsewhere in this chapter.

For more information, call (865) 932-5600 (or 800-BASS-PRO) or visit the store's Web site at www.basspro.com.

Gatlinburg Welcome Centers (on The Spur, US 441 South, between Pigeon Forge and downtown Gatlinburg and also at traffic light #3 on the Parkway downtown) and in each of the three visitor centers inside the national park (at Sug- arlands, near the Gatlinburg entrance; at Cades Cove, halfway around the 11-mile loop drive near Townsend, TN; and at Oconaluftee, near the Cherokee, NC, entrance).

COUNTRY CHRISTMAS & COLLECTIBLES
3044 Winfield Dunn Parkway, Kodak
(865) 933-9115, (888) 314-0173
www.countrychristmasonline.com

This 23,000-square-foot store carries an enormous array of Christmas decorations at a discount, but what makes it even more notable is that their in-house designer can create custom wreaths, swags, and centerpieces to your exact specifications. This is also the store that custom-makes many of the county's outdoor lighting displays for Winterfest (including the one directly across the street at the Sevierville Chamber of Commerce Visitor Center). In fact, you can flip through their book of examples to get ideas for ordering your own, just in case you'd like to have some Winterfest magic in your front yard back home.

i Blazing-hot summer sun notwithstanding, Tennessee law requires that shirts and shoes be worn in all places where the public congregates.

SMOKY MOUNTAIN KNIFE WORKS
2320 Winfield Dunn Parkway, Sevierville
(865) 453-5871, (800) 251-9306
www.smkw.com

This place bills itself as "The World's Largest Knife Showplace." Once you've strolled through its three levels and 55,000 square feet of sales and display floor space, you probably won't dispute the claim. On the main level, you'll find display case after display case filled with just about anything that cuts—pocketknives, hunting and fishing knives, and hatchets. Look for brand names like Case, Buck, Gerber, and Remington. Another area is devoted to out-of-the-ordinary weaponry like machetes, swords, Ninja gear, blowguns, and even paintball equipment.

On the lower level you'll find sections containing kitchen cutlery, jewelry, toys, T-shirts, gift items, and a knife-sharpening service. There are also several displays that will make your visit even more visually interesting. Look for the life-size dioramas depicting an African watering hole, an American Indian with his canoe, and a Civil War soldier with cannon. The kids will be entertained by the Bubba Bear Band, a singing animatronic attraction.

The centerpiece of the lower level is the working gristmill apparatus. Complete with original gears and pulleys, this water-powered wheel works just like it did in the olden days.

The upper level is practically a museum, with many display cases filled with collections of rare and antique knives and related memorabilia. Many of the collections are arranged thematically, including those devoted to film and TV westerns, weapons of Native American tribes, and Civil War weaponry (similar displays are on the main level near the front entrance as well). Although most of these collections are for display purposes only, Smoky Mountain Knife Works does have other cases filled with antique and collectible knives that are for sale.

While you're upstairs, check out Trophy Mountain, a display that the store claims is the Smokies' largest indoor mountain and waterfall. Like other parts of the store, Trophy Mountain is home to a veritable zoo made up of stuffed game and mounted game trophies. Before you leave Smoky Mountain Knife Works, be sure to visit the gift and collectibles area and the sweetshop. The business also publishes several catalogs annually through which you can place orders over the phone by calling the toll-free number.

CHEROKEE TRADING POST
1590 Winfield Dun Parkway, Sevierville
(865) 453-1247, (877) 723-2608

The Cherokee Trading Post is a fun and funky little shop that carries just about any Native American crafts you can imagine, including pottery, jewelry, blankets, leather goods, animal skins, and even arrowheads. They have a large selection of leather moccasins (as you might infer from the huge white letters proclaiming "Deerskin Moccasins" on the roof as you drive by) and leather gloves, as well as plenty of T-shirts, and even a case filled with unusual knives.

MUSIC OUTLET
1050 Winfield Dunn Parkway, Sevierville
(865) 453-1031
www.musicoutlet.net
This outlet store in a pretty stacked stone building with a white second-floor balcony has a huge selection of discounted musical instruments (including guitars, banjos, fiddles, dulcimers, keyboards, and electric pianos). They also sell professional audio gear and music accessories, and they give music lessons, too.

EVERYTHING NATURAL
209 Forks of the River Parkway, Sevierville
(865) 453-6112
www.everythingnaturaltn.com
Although you can find quite a few health-food stores in Sevier County, this Sevierville store has been around longer than most, since 1985, and has an experienced, knowledgeable staff. Naturally (pun fully intended), they carry several lines of vitamin, mineral, and herbal supplements. In the back room, they also have a selection of ground herbs that you can buy loose for use in preparing foods or drinks. You'll also find sections devoted to homeopathy, aromatherapy, and healthy pet food products. Everything natural also has a good selection of healthy snacks and hiking foods, as well as natural cosmetic items like shampoos and soaps, and relevant books and magazines.

S & G COMICS & COLLECTIBLES
464 Forks of the River Parkway, Sevierville
(865) 908-8346
www.sgcomics.com
Kids and adults alike will have no trouble losing themselves in any number of fantasy worlds after stepping inside this place. Comic books, both new and used, are the staple product, but sports card collectors will find a fair amount of merchandise as well. Many of S & G's display cases are filled with baseball, football, and basketball cards ranging from the common to the rare and valuable. Sports collectors will also take interest in the poseable action figures and other athletic memorabilia for sale, some of which is autographed.

Sci-fi collectors can check out all the different *Star Trek* and *Star Wars* collectibles, including trading cards, figures, and models. Many of the shop's collectible figures are current hot items from the worlds of film, television, and music. Naturally, trading cards like Pokemon and Dragonball Z are quite popular as well.

Are you thinking that's all? Wrong, laser breath! S & G Comics & Collectibles has books, figurines, dice, cards, and other supplies for all kinds of role-playing games like Dungeons and Dragons. It's time to beam down!

i Antique hounds take note: The eight-mile stretch of Winfield Dunn Parkway (Highway 66) between I-40 and downtown Sevierville is antiques and flea-market heaven. You could spend a full day poking about the seemingly endless rows of booths and stalls at the various businesses here. Merchandise ranges from legitimate antiquities to junk, but the browsing is priceless.

YOUR SCRAPBOOK SUPERSTORE
250 Collier Drive, Sevierville
(865) 428-9980
This huge store in the Governor's Crossing shopping center has the largest inventory of scrapbooking merchandise in the country, including an extensive Disney section. Their sister business, the Scrapbook Clearance Center (865-908-7747), is just a few doors down and sells discontinued and closeout items for unbeatable prices.

Shopping Centers and Outlet Malls
GOVERNOR'S CROSSING
212 Collier Drive, Sevierville
Governor's Crossing is a planned development encompassing accommodations (like the Resort at Governor's Crossing), a number of restaurants, attractions (such as Rainforest Adventures), and entertainment theaters (like the Smoky Mountain Palace, home to the Cirque De Chine show) that are all covered in their own chapters. In addition,

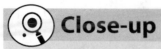

Close-up

Apples to the Core

If you're a lover of apples, you will truly be in your element at this working apple farm, with more than 4,000 apple trees providing 14 different varieties of apples. But even if you're not much of an apple fan, you'll probably enjoy yourself anyway. The complex, which is open year-round, is nestled along the banks of the Little Pigeon River. The hillside apple orchards and whitewashed buildings are the giveaway that you've reached your destination—about a half-mile off the Parkway at the Sevierville–Pigeon Forge border on Apple Valley Road.

While this community of businesses may be most known for its two restaurants, the Applewood Farmhouse Restaurant and the newer Applewood Farmhouse Grill (both described more fully in the Restaurants chapter), there's much more to the place than eateries.

The Apple Barn General Store (800-421-4606; www.applebarncidermill.com) was one of the first commercial ventures to appear on the property, created in 1981 as a place to market the apples from the orchard. It was constructed inside the old barn dating from 1910 that had stood on the property when the current owners purchased the farm in the early '70s. The General Store still carries bushel baskets full of fresh apples, as well as cheeses, smoked hams, bacon, dried fruits, apple butter, apple jelly, and a variety of popcorn. In addition to food, you'll find gift items and an upstairs craft-and-basket loft.

Around the same time the General Store opened, the owners also cranked up the Cider Mill so that customers could see the apples being processed into apple cider. Nowadays, you can still see the mill at work, and in the Cider Bar, visitors can purchase fresh apple cider along with fried pies, apple dumplings, and old-fashioned apple stack cake made in the Apple Pie Kitchen.

Since the early 1980s, the Applewood Farms complex has been fruitful and multiplied. At the Candy Apple and Chocolate Factory, you can watch workers make candied and caramel apples as well as homemade fudge, taffy, stick candy, and lots more. Experienced candy makers use all-natural ingredients in their old-fashioned recipes. Next door is the Creamery, an old-time ice-cream parlor complete with antique soda fountain. Here, you can order homemade ice-cream sundaes, sodas, and shakes and you can even buy fresh-baked apple breads.

Wine connoisseurs will definitely want to stop by the Apple Barn Winery (865-428-6850; 866-428-6850). Since the winery opened in 1995, many of the winery's labels have won numerous awards at national and international wine competitions. At the tasting bar, you can sample from their menu of 12 different wines, most of which are made from apples. Their most popular vintage is the Apple-Raspberry, a medium-sweet apple wine blended with raspberry juice.

The final business in the complex is the Christmas & Candles shop (865-774-9502), which as you might imagine, is a year-round Christmas shop that sells custom-made wreaths, tree ornaments, gift items, and figurines—not to mention candles. About half the candles they carry are actually made in the shop, and not surprisingly, they do indeed sell apple-scented merchandise (in six different scents).

the complex includes about 20 shops, such as Vanity Fair Outlet, Shoe Carnival, BonWorth, Country Clutter, Books-a-Million, and the Scrapbook Superstore (described earlier in this chapter). By the way, Collier Drive, which goes through Governor's Crossing, is the connecting road between the Parkway and Veterans Boulevard.

TANGER FIVE OAKS OUTLET CENTER
1645 Parkway, Sevierville
(865) 453-1053, (800) 408-8377
www.tangeroutlet.com

The entrance to this outlet mall (commonly called Five Oaks) is on the Parkway about a half-mile south of Governor's Crossing. With more than a hundred shops, Five Oaks is the largest outlet mall in the area—big enough to have its own free trolley shuttling passengers around the acreage during high season, from April through Thanksgiving.

Stores here include The Gap, Old Navy, Liz Claiborne, Coach, American Eagle, Calvin Klein, J.Crew, Tommy Hilfiger, Perry Ellis, 9 West, Chicos, Coldwater Creek, Children's Place, Carter's, Lennox, Jones New York, Bath & Body Works, Zales, Harry & David, Aeropostale, Bass, Eddie Bauer, Gymboree, Naturalizer, Nike Factory Store, Polo Ralph Lauren, and Rockport—and a ton more.

PIGEON FORGE

Pigeon Forge was where the outlet craze began in the Smokies Corridor in 1983 when the first outlet mall went up—a strip mall with about ten shops that was then known as the Factory Merchants Mall (now the very much expanded Pigeon Forge Factory Outlet Mall). The "if you build it, they will come" philosophy certainly held true here, and shoppers have been streaming to this small town in the foothills of the mountains ever since for the chance to melt a little plastic in pursuit of the hottest of bargains. In addition to the plethora of superstores and outlets touting national-name recognition, you'll find many smaller, locally owned stores and shops in the region, both dotting the parkway as well as clustered around the historic Old Mill downtown. They offer plenty of personality and charm in place of rock-bottom prices, not to mention fabulous regional finds you won't see in the bigger malls.

The following is a sampling of what you'll encounter on your Pigeon Forge shopping expedition.

THE INCREDIBLE CHRISTMAS PLACE
2470 Parkway, Pigeon Forge
(865) 453-0414, (800) 445-3396
www.christmasplace.com
Since Hurshel and Marian Biggs opened their store in 1986, the 43,000-square-foot Bavarian-style complex containing many "shops" under one roof has grown into one of the top 10 Christmas and collectible destinations in the United States. You'll find it just north of the Wears Valley Road intersection, right across the street from the Inn at Christmas Place (see the Hotels and Motels chapter).

The Bavarian village setting is quite attractive. The buildings themselves reflect old-world architecture and are surrounded by cobbled brick walkways, wildflowers, and greenery. In the center of the courtyard, a large model train setup features cars winding their way through a village scene and running waterfall.

When you walk through the doors, you enter a year-round Christmas fantasyland filled with thousands of Yuletide decorations. Although an all-Christmas store could easily be presented in a tacky or junky fashion, Christmas Place is first-class all the way. Dozens of lighted and decorated tree displays fill the main showroom, along with plenty of figurines, decorations, and gift items.

In the North Pole Village area, you'll find a wide selection of artificial trees, ornaments, and lights. Look for collectible names like Department 56, Lee Middleton, Fontanini, and Christopher Radko. There's a personalizing gallery, a large department of miniature village scenes, and an in-house floral department. At the east end of the store, keep an eye out for the large stained-glass window that looks down on a peaceful nativity scene. If you've got kids, check out the displays of model train kits in addition to the toys and games. Every so often, some of the collectibles artists come to meet customers and sign their own creations.

The Incredible Christmas Place also has a Singing Santa who strums his guitar and visits with children from Easter weekend to December 23rd each year. You can even have a portrait made, if you want to beat the rush at your mall back home. The store also has a guest rewards program; for every $250 you spend in a two-year period at either at the store (in person or online) or at the hotel across the street, you'll receive a $10 coupon.

Two other shops that are part of the complex but have separate entrances are Mrs. Claus's

Candy Kitchen, which sells hot and cold sandwiches and a selection of delectable fudges and cookies, and the Vera Bradley boutique, which carries a full line of Vera Bradley designer handbags and other gift items.

i Pick up copies of Smoky Mountain tourist-oriented magazines to find discount coupons on merchandise at many of the county's most popular shopping destinations. Some of the publications include the *What-To-Do Magazine, Tennessee Smokies Visitors Guide, Best Read Guide,* and the *Sevier County Shopping Guide.*

CHINA AND GIFT MART
2680 Parkway, Pigeon Forge
(865) 453-5679, (888) 314-0174
www.chinagiftmart.com
More than 300 different patterns of china are discounted up to 70 percent at this shop that's been in business since the mid-'80s. They stock more than a dozen name brands, including Noritake, Royal Worcester, Wedgewood, Nikko, Lenox, Royal Doulton, and Muirfield. The selection is all first-quality and includes complete place settings and accessories.

In addition to china, China and Gift Mart carries flatware by Oneida, Retroneu, and Towle Silversmith as well as collectibles by Precious Moments, Cherished Teddies, and Emmett Kelly Jr. The Christmas and Collectibles department offers 15,000 square feet of gorgeous Christmas decorations, fine collectibles, dolls, and more.

CIRCLE E FACTORY BOOT OUTLET
2746 Parkway, Pigeon Forge
(865) 453-1749, (800) 611-0012
www.circleewestern.com
When Circle E opened its doors in the '60s, it was about the only building at the south end of Pigeon Forge. Now it's surrounded by motels and restaurants. Circle E is also reputed to be the first business in Pigeon Forge that used the word *outlet* in its title. Circle E features an impressive selection of boots from utility (Dan Post and Dingo) to

full-dress (Tony Lama and Justin) at competitive prices, along with work shoes, Stetson hats, and one of the most complete lines of square-dance apparel in the Southeast. How can you resist a place that sells boots called Peanut Brittle Iguana Lizard?

STAGES WEST
2765 Parkway, Pigeon Forge
(865) 453-8086, (877) 717-8243
www.stageswest.com
Saddle on up, pardners, and head to Stages West, the Smokies' largest western store, with more than 100,000 items at discount prices. There are more than 5,000 pairs of boots in stock by manufacturers like Durango, Tony Lama, and Acme-Dingo. For kids, they have more than a thousand pairs of boots from which to choose. Their leather goods also include handcrafted purses, wallets, belts, and moccasins. If you like to do-si-do, you'll definitely want to visit Stages West, which specializes in western wear and square-dance apparel.

i Several of the merchants' associations in the Smokies publish coupon books that provide discounts and premiums. Check the local welcome centers, lodging places, and brochure racks everywhere (including your hotel lobby) for some hidden bonuses.

SMOKY MOUNTAIN CANDY MAKERS
2880 Parkway, Pigeon Forge
(865) 453-9213
www.smokymountaincandymakers.com
Since 1973, this family-owned confectioner has been turning out delectable treats like taffy, fudge, candy apples, suckers, and hand-dipped chocolate and nut clusters. About 90 percent of the goodies in stock are made on the premises. In fact, if you visit at the right time, you'll be able to see the staff of candy makers turning out their products before your eyes. If you're lucky, you might even get to see the old-fashioned taffy-wrapping

machines pull, roll, and wrap! They carry the usual assortment of flavors, including chocolate, bubble-gum, licorice, watermelon, cotton candy, banana, peppermint, rum, and chocolate-covered peanut butter. But you'll also see some unusual varieties thrown in the mix, such as clove, sassafras, and teaberry. There's even a line of sugar-free taffy.

DIXIE DARLIN
3355 Butler Street, Pigeon Forge
(865) 453-3104
www.dixiedarlin.com
This 3,500-square-foot shop is one of the biggest and oldest needle art shops in the country. It features an extensive collection of supplies for counted cross-stitch, counted canvas needle-point, punch needle, stitchery, and embroidery. Owner Cindy Smelcer also offers her exclusive Dixie Darlin Designs, featuring local subjects, folk art, and primitive designs. The shop also carries framing supplies, including hard-to-find sizes of frames and mats. To get there, turn onto Old Mill Avenue at traffic light #7, cross the bridge, and you'll soon find Butler Street on the left.

PIGEON RIVER STRING INSTRUMENTS
165 Old Mill Avenue, Pigeon Forge
(865) 453-3789
www.pigeon-river.com
This shop features a wide collection of string instruments, including banjos, fiddles, harps, and Appalachian hammer dulcimers—everything you could ever need to make sweet mountain music. At least some of the stock here is made locally, and you'll also find all sorts of music-related items, from lamps to neckties.

THE BARN OWL
3629 Parkway, Pigeon Forge
(865) 428-0846, (800) 874-3147
A collector's must-see, the Barn Owl carries Hall-mark and Precious Moments items (some that go back a few years) as well as high-class figurines and sculptures. They also carry an excellent selec-tion of expert-level jigsaw puzzles from Milton Bradley, Springbok, and Ravensberger.

Shopping Centers and Outlet Malls

WALDEN'S LANDING
2530 Parkway Pigeon Forge
www.waldenslanding.com
This is one of Pigeon Forge's newer shopping centers, and it's built to resemble a small town from yesteryear. The complex has about 20 shops (including a Harley-Davidson shop, John Deere Country, and a nostalgia and pop culture shop called Red Rocket) and five restaurants (including the Smoky Mountain Brewery—see the chapter on music and entertainment theaters and night-life). They're all clustered around an adorable miniature golf course called Firehouse Golf (see the Attractions chapter) in the center. You'll find Walden's Landing at traffic light #2B.

THE SHOPS OF PIGEON FORGE
161 East Wears Valley Road, Pigeon Forge
(865) 428-7002
www.shopsofpigeonforge.com
Formerly called Tanger Outlet Center (not to be confused with the huge Tanger Five Oaks mall in Pigeon Forge), The Shops of Pigeon Forge is a medium-size strip mall, kitty-corner from Belz Outlets, that offers 24 shops in a compact two-level setting with convenient parking. A sampling of the stores here include Oshkosh B'Gosh, Ree-bok Outlet Store, Tommy Hilfiger, Liz Claiborne, Kitchen Collection, and an Easy Spirit Outlet.

To get to The Shops of Pigeon Forge and the other outlets on Teaster Lane (including the huge Belz Outlets, profiled next) turn left at traffic light #2 (Teaster Lane) or #3 (East Wears Valley Road). If you're coming from the south, turn right at traf-fic light #5 (Jake Thomas Drive), and then left at Teaster Lane.

BELZ OUTLETS
2655 Teaster Lane, Pigeon Forge
(865) 453-7316
www.belzoutlets.com
Boasting the biggest parking lot of the bunch, the Belz mall consists of two large malls with a freestanding anchor outlet on the north side of Teaster Lane (building #1 is the only truly

enclosed mall in the area) and a strip annex with its own parking lot on the south side. The number of shops in both total more than 65 in more than 450,000 square feet. The main mall building offers Burlington Brands, Dickies, Black and Decker, Jewelry Outlet, and Camp Coleman, while the annexes include stores such as Old Time Pottery, Tuesday Morning, and Nike.

The quickest access to Belz from the Parkway is to turn at East Wears Valley Road (traffic light #3, directly across from Wears Valley Road) and go up to the traffic light at Teaster Lane. If you're coming from Sevierville, turn left on Teaster Lane (traffic light #2) and follow it around.

RIVERVIEW OUTLET MALL
2600 Teaster Lane, Pigeon Forge

RIVER VISTA OUTLET MALL
2700 Teaster Lane, Pigeon Forge

These twin strip malls, built side by side just one year after the Belz outlets, seem to be merely an extension of the Belz annex on Teaster Lane because Belz has them surrounded on two sides. They're actually not part of the Belz conglomerate, although both Riverview and River Vista are themselves owned and operated by the same parent company.

You won't find more than a handful of shops between the two, including Clothing World; Handbags, Etc.; Workshop Tools; Candle Carvers; Smoky Mountain Babies & Tots; and The Arbor. This is also the home of the Great Smoky Mountain Murder Mystery Dinner Show (see the Music and Entertainment Theaters and Nightlife chapter). By the way, these malls are appropriately named. They offer a lovely view of the Little Pigeon River from their rear balconies.

PIGEON FORGE FACTORY OUTLET MALL
2850 Parkway, Pigeon Forge
(865) 428-2828
www.pigeonforgefactoryoutlet.com

This is the area's original outlet mall, located on the west side of the Parkway, identified by its distinctive sloping red metal roofs (which gave it its nickname: Red Roof Mall). It includes about 50 shops on two levels, with offerings such as New York New York, Carter's Childrenswear, Black and Decker, Oneida Factory Store, a L'Eggs/Hanes/Bali/Playtex outlet shop, Rack Room Shoes, a Corningware/Corelle/Revere shop, and some lesser-known favorites such as the Handbag Superstore and Wilsons Leather/Wallet Works.

The best way to get into the Pigeon Forge Factory Outlet Mall (as well as the Z Buda Mall, described next) is to turn right at the driveway at traffic light #4 and follow it to the upper level. Most parking is here, with access and egress available on Florence Street at the back. If parking is available to your right at the top, take it—it's your best chance to see both malls without getting too far from your vehicle.

Z BUDA MALL
2828 Parkway, Pigeon Forge

Z Buda sits both behind and beside Pigeon Forge Factory Outlet Mall, and for all the world it appears to be part of the same complex. (It was built shortly after its larger neighbor and they even share the upper-level parking lot.) But you won't find big names among Z Buda's dozen or so shops and eateries. Instead, you'll find shops like Discount Souvenirs, Just Stop Smokies (gifts and toys), Shirt World, Bumbershoot Books, and Atrium Flowers. This mall is a fun place to prowl because unexpected bargains pop up in the least likely places. Its unusual name came from its original owner, the late Mr. Zee Buda. The mall is now owned by his son, Zandy. One can only wonder if Zachary will be next.

i Most of the Pigeon Forge outlet malls are served by the Pigeon Forge trolley system. This is a convenient way to see the outlets but could be a problem if you have to ride the trolley back to your lodging place with a good-size load of packages.

OLD MILL SQUARE
Old Mill Avenue and Veterans Boulevard, Pigeon Forge
(865) 428-0771, (888) 453-6455
www.old-mill.com

One block off the parkway from traffic light #7, Old Mill Square is a shopping district that's sprung up around the historic Old Mill, an active gristmill built in 1830 on the banks of the Little Pigeon River (see the Attractions chapter).

The square is home to two main eateries—the Old Mill Restaurant and the Old Mill Pottery House Café & Grille (see the Restaurants chapter), as well as the Old Mill Creamery. A host of shops also come under the official Old Mill umbrella.

The Old Mill General Store sells yellow and white cornmeal and a variety of flours ground at the Old Mill itself, as well pancake and specialty mixes, homemade jams, fudge, crafts, and various Smoky Mountain memorabilia. The Old Mill Pigeon River Pottery is located in what used to be the studio of legendary local potter Douglas Ferguson, founder of Pigeon Forge Pottery. (The serving pieces in both Old Mill restaurants come from here.) In addition to plates, bowls, and other ceramic kitchenware, this shop also sells adorable ceramic bears.

The Old Mill Candy Kitchen cooks their confections in copper kettles, hand-dips many of their chocolates, and relies on machines that have been pulling and cutting taffy for more than 75 years. Be sure to try one of their famous Bear Paws, a combination of milk chocolate, homemade caramel, and fresh pecans. If you like something you ate at either of the Old Mill's restaurants, you may be able to find it for sale as a dehydrated mix at the Old Mill Farmhouse Kitchen. The corn chowder is a big seller here, as are the signature bread mixes and salad dressings. The Old Mill Toy Bin and the Old Mill Pigeon River Potting Shed round out the options here.

You'll find plenty of individually owned shops that are not officially part of the Old Mill Square complex, but that are all clustered around it (and known informally by the locals as Old Mill Village). These lovely shops include the Twisted Vessel Gallery, Candles by Donna, Kitchen Kupboard, Something Special by Sue, Angel's Among Us, Diane's Resale Shop, Smoky Mountain Dog House, Smoky Mountain Cat House, and Gourmet Coffee Shop, to name just a very few.

Most of the shops in this area offer free parking, and there's plenty of free parking at nearby Patriot Park. Or you can take the trolley to the Pigeon Forge Fun Time Trolley office, which is smack in the middle of the village. From there, you can find most of what's available within a block or 2.

THE SHOPS AT PATRIOT MILL
3475 Parkway, Pigeon Forge
This small shopping center (formerly the Log Cabin Shops) has recently been considerably spiffed up and now sports a brand-new look and a brand-new name. It includes about 10 shops, such as Great Smoky Fashion & Collectibles, Rocky Top Leather, 101 Gifts, and Yash Jewelers—not to mention Ole Country Store, which has been at this location for more than 25 years.

GATLINBURG

Gatlinburg may not have outlet malls, but it's still a super shopping spot. The city has crammed more than a dozen shopping malls and more than a hundred freestanding retail shops of dizzying variety into less than a half mile, and that only tells about half the story. You can walk the full length of the Parkway from traffic light #3 to traffic light #10 in about 15 minutes—if you're wearing blinders. The experienced shopper (appropriately shod in comfortable shoes) will take anywhere from three to six hours to do justice to a single side of the Parkway. In fact, the best way to make your shopping assault is to do just that—hit one side of the street, cross, and return on the other side.

What follows is an overview of the more established and/or more unusual shops in town, as well as a listing of the malls and shopping villages on the Parkway.

GAZEBO
377 Parkway, Gatlinburg
(865) 436-4064
www.gazebogatlinburg.com
Predating the 1975 tourism boomlet, the Gazebo is one of the longest-running art galleries in town. This gift shop, owned and operated by Kay Mor-

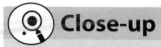 **Close-up**

Business as Usual in Gatlinburg

If you spend enough time in Gatlinburg, you'll learn that a lot of the downtown property is owned by two families, the Ogles and the Reagans. They share a pretty hard-nosed attitude about selling land: Don't. The Ogle family is large, robust, and given to long lives. They're also one of the oldest English-speaking families on the planet, with an unbroken line of succession that goes back 30 generations to 11th-century England. Until her death at 104 in 2002, the matriarch of the local Ogle clan was the estimable Hattie Maples Ogle McGiffin, born in 1898. Hattie started a handicrafts store in Gatlinburg in 1932 and later built two motels and an RV court before eventually established herself as one of the finest business minds anywhere in the United States.

Hattie's first husband Charlie Ogle (1893–1945) was one of the most beloved people in Gatlinburg's history. He inherited the family grocery store started by his grandfather Noah (on the present site of the Mountain Mall). Hattie and Charles had four children, and their line now includes more than 40 direct descendants (and counting) in just three generations. Many of the Ogles continue to own and manage the family empire, which now includes three shopping malls, several motels, a couple of office/retail buildings, two downtown markets, and long-term land leases on the sites of several large motels.

The Reagan story has the same result with a completely different approach. Brownlee Reagan was born in Gatlinburg in 1926. His great-great-grandfather, Daniel Wesley Reagan (1802–1892), was a native of Sevier County before the establishment of White Oak Flats. The Reagans are an industrious lot, known for their hard work and community service. Brownlee Reagan appeared to be headed down the family's established path as a police officer and eventually police chief, but he combined his public service with an unusual perception of Gatlinburg's future. He began accumulating land before the tourist boom of the '70s by buying whatever land he could afford that came on the market, and building motels.

His current holdings include five downtown motels (plus another motel out of state), a couple of shopping malls, and a lot of undeveloped land. Not blessed with a large family, Brownlee Reagan has pretty much handled it all by himself, with some of the load being picked up by sons Lee and John.

The Ogle and Reagan families have controlled their holdings and their destinies by maintaining active interests in the community: Hattie Ogle McGiffin lent her name and considerable talents to a variety of civic and charitable causes. Both families are deeply involved in local politics—Charles Earl Ogle Jr. (Hattie's grandson) and Brownlee Reagan have both served the city as commissioners, mayors, chamber of commerce presidents, and civic philanthropists.

In the cosmic scheme of things, Gatlinburg is still a young and growing city. Just two centuries old, it has considerable growth potential in the undeveloped land to the east. When that potential is tapped, the local feeling that Gatlinburg is an Ogle/Reagan empire will probably dissipate. Who knows how that will change the course of Smokies Corridor commerce?

ton, is now located in a log building that was at one time the first icehouse in Gatlinburg. The Gazebo sells specialty bottles and a gorgeous array of handblown art glass. Their collection of ANRI wood carvings (Hummel-like carved wood figures) is one of the largest in the eastern United States. Your children are welcome, but hang on to them.

MORTON'S ANTIQUES
409 Parkway, Gatlinburg
(865) 436-5504
Doing business at the same location since 1949, Morton's is noted for its art glass and porcelain antiques and for its spectacular line of Italian inlaid wood furniture. Morton's also sells a

small selection of very rare (and very pricey) old coins and baseball cards, which has in the past included vintage Babe Ruth, Willie Mays, and Mickey Mantle trading cards.

THE HEMP STORE
411 Parkway, Gatlinburg
(865) 436-8300
Here's a kicky little shop featuring clothing and accessories from natural fibers. Tie-dyed clothing and New Age jewelry items are also available, along with a selection of in-your-face environmental bumper stickers, pins, and posters. And if you have any need for hemp rope, this is one of the few places where you'll find it sold in bulk. The Hemp Store is about to undergo an expansion, so additional merchandise will ultimately be added.

BENEATH THE SMOKE
467 Parkway, Gatlinburg
(865) 436-3460
www.kenjenkins.com
This shop, the gallery of local photographer Ken Jenkins, is dedicated to Mother Nature in all her splendor. In addition to stunning photography prints, Beneath the Smoke carries sculpture, camping products, and an impressive selection of handbooks and guidebooks to the flora and fauna of the Southeast. The variety of bird guides is simply the best in the area.

GREAT SMOKY MOUNTAINS ASSOCIATION GIFT SHOP
Gatlinburg Welcome Center
(865) 436-7318
www.thegreatsmokymountains.org
This is another of the wonderful little shops run by the nonprofit Great Smoky Mountains Association, which stocks a wide variety of Smokies-related goods including apparel, toys, local specialty foods, gifts, and books. All purchases made at GSMA shops benefit the national park. If you become a member, you'll get a 15 percent discount on all GSMA shop purchases, as well as discounts at many local businesses.

This is one of two locations for GSMA shops in Gatlinburg. The other is inside the Gatlinburg Welcome Center on the Spur, US 441 South, a few miles before the start of downtown. You'll also find GSMA shops in Sevierville as well as in each of the three visitor centers in the national park. For a more detailed description of what the shops carry, where they are, and what the membership benefits include, see the write-up in the Sevierville section of this chapter.

SMOKY MOUNTAIN ANGLER
466 Brookside Village Way, Gatlinburg
(865) 436-8746
www.smokymountainangler.com
Smoky Mountain Angler is the oldest fly-fishing shop in Gatlinburg. They sell tackle, locally hand-tied flies, clothing, and accessories, but they also rent fishing equipment, sell fishing licenses, and provide professional guide services for a half-day or full-day of fishing (including loaned gear if you need it). The shop is located above Papa John's Pizza in Winery Square, half a mile from traffic light #3 on East Parkway.

O2 BEAD EXPERIENCE/BEAD XP
511 Parkway, Gatlinburg
(865) 430-9115
www.beadxp.com
Owners Glen and Susie Gothard, artisans themselves, offer a wide variety of beads, including those fashioned from sterling silver, semiprecious gemstones, Czech glass, shell, bone, wood, copper, Swarovski crystals, and freshwater pearls. They also carry all the beading tools you'd need to create something special with whatever beads you choose.

But the shop (located in the Riverbend Mall) goes one further. They also offer three beginners' classes to help you discover what you can do with all those amazing beads in the first place. Classes include a two-day fusing class (where you make two dichroic glass cabochons), a four-hour glassblowing class (where you make a basic pendant with clear and colored borosilicate glass rods), and a two-day lamp-work bead class (where you learn to create glass lamp-work beads). All supplies, tools, and equipment are provided for the classes.

CLOCK PEDDLER OF GATLINBURG
608 Parkway, Gatlinburg
(865) 436-5605
It's all about time at the Clock Peddler. If it tells time, they've got it or can get it. From bedside and kitchen novelty clocks to grandfather models with everything short of a symphony orchestra, and movements from windup and pull chain to the latest quartz model, the Clock Peddler has it all. And don't worry about getting your grandparent clock home in the family sedan— the Clock Peddler will arrange shipping for any large purchase.

RANGER BOB'S TRADING POST
624 Parkway, Gatlinburg
(865) 436-7835
Ranger Bob has apparently led an interesting life. His trading post runs the gamut from animal pelts you can wear to black-light lamps and posters. A wide array of puzzles (jigsaw and brain-bender) could keep a puzzle nut of any stripe occupied for days, especially if they're worked under a black-light lamp. The kids' backpacks in the form of woodland creatures are interesting enough to make Bob's worth a look.

i It only shows if you're really looking for it, but the Parkway in Gatlinburg runs steadily uphill toward the national park entrance. Consider that when planning your assault on the downtown shopping district.

THE KARMELKORN SHOP
647 Parkway, Gatlinburg
(865) 436-4373
www.karmelkorngatlinburg.com
Rick Berrier is as established a Parkway fixture as the weekend traffic. He's been up to his elbows in the wonderful things he does with popcorn since 1961, and he still looks like a kid. Get to the Karmelkorn Shop early in your stay—Rick's deals on refillable boxes will keep your fingers sticky for your whole trip at a remarkably low cost.

Both this shop a second location at 651 Parkway offer a veritable korn-ucopia of flavors, including traditional karmelkorn, cheesekorn, white cheddarkorn, butter-rum korn, toffee korn, and kettlekorn (not to mention just regular old buttered popcorn).

OLD TYME PORTRAITS BY TREADWAY
702 Parkway, Gatlinburg
(865) 436-0458
Gatlinburg's oldest "dress-up" photo shop has more interesting and amusing getups that allow you to express your personality in graphic new ways than any other photo shop in Gatlinburg. The Treadway brothers have been in the novelty photo business for more than 40 years (that's longer than anyone else in town), and it shows in the imaginative way they approach their craft. For one, the sets you're photographed in are real—they're not mere pull-down backdrops. While this location has the most sets to choose from (including a bar, a parlor, a gangster car, and a '57 Harley Davidson), the Treadways also operate more than half of the dozen or so other old-fashioned photo shops in town, as well as one in the Pigeon Forge Factory Outlet (or "Red Roof") mall.

i Gatlinburg has an ordinance that bans the wearing of masks or face coverings in the downtown shopping area. The city makes an exception for Halloween, but only for kids.

AUNT MAHALIA'S CANDIES
708 Parkway & Mountain Mall, Gatlinburg
(865) 436-7992, (800) 438-7992
www.auntmahalias.com
The first candy shop in town to open multiple locations, Aunt Mahalia's has been threatening the dental health of three generations of visitors to the Smokies. It's hard to imagine the Parkway without the distinctive red-and-white-striped Aunt Mahalia's stores. The handmade candy they sell includes fudge, pecan logs, taffy, peanut brittle, stick candy, and more. For those who want to indulge with less guilt, there's also a sugar-free line.

WOOD SIGNS OF GATLINBURG
715 Parkway, Gatlinburg
(865) 436-9640, (866) 436-9640
www.woodsignsofgatlinburg.com
This is Gatlinburg's oldest sign-carving shop, family-owned and family-operated in the same location since 1971. The Jones family's signs are made of mahogany, cedar, or redwood. Some are machine-engraved, while others are hand-carved. Their huge variety of designs includes specialty signs in the shape of bears, fish, horse heads, porpoises, dogs, ducks, pigs, campers, saws, arrowheads, cowboy hats, anchors, and even fire trucks. Admit it, you've always wanted your family name carved on the side of a bass, haven't you?

GLASSBLOWERS OF GATLINBURG
729 Parkway, Gatlinburg
(865) 436-9114
Bob Myrick and his family started out in the early '70s with a small storefront operation on the present site of their three-story shop. The Myricks, one of Gatlinburg's leading merchant and philanthropic families, carry an impressive array of high-class glass and ceramic sculpture and a huge selection of souvenir jewelry. They'll even personalize glass items while you wait.

JONATHAN'S
733 Parkway, Gatlinburg
(865) 436-7148
www.jonathansgatlinburg.com
A downtown mainstay since the late '70s, Jonathan's features an extensive line of upscale name-brand sportswear and accessories, collectibles (like Willow Tree figurines and Big Sky Carvers lovable bears and moose figures) and a broad line of camping supplies and literature.

MAGNET-O-WORLD
738 Parkway, Gatlinburg
(865) 430-9022
If it sticks to metal, it's here. More than 100,000 magnets line the walls of this fun house that passes for a retail store. There's enough variety of amusing, amazing, and appealing magnetic note holders in this place to make you go home and buy a bigger refrigerator.

OLE SMOKY CANDY KITCHEN
744 Parkway, Gatlinburg
(865) 436-4886
Back when Gatlinburg was a lot smaller, the Candy Kitchen provided some of the town's most popular entertainment. Tourists came by the score to sit on the benches out front and watch the candy makers work their magic in the big picture window. Then they went inside and bought everything they saw being made, and usually more. The news is all good: Despite the fact that new forms of entertainment have thinned the crowd a bit, the benches are still there, and so are the candy makers in the window. Shops like this one are the reason Gatlinburg still enchants a large number of visitors looking for a simpler, gentler way of life.

THE ROCK SHOP
1007 Parkway, Gatlinburg
(865) 436-4106
Established in the '60s, the Rock Shop carries anything that started out as a piece of some kind of stone. You'll find arrowheads, custom jewelry, sculpture, and geodes for sale here. It's the sort of place people love to poke around in just to see what they can discover, and kids are guaranteed to find a treasure or two.

Shopping Malls and Villages
CAROUSEL MALL
458 Parkway, Gatlinburg
Standing at the intersection of the Parkway and East Parkway at traffic light #3, Carousel Mall is built into a hillside so steep that ground level on the East Parkway is three stories above ground level on the Parkway less than 100 feet away. Either way you enter, short stairways and a central elevator take you through several levels of shops.

At press time, only a handful of places (none of them true shops) were doing business here, thanks to a fire in December 2007 that destroyed much of the structure, including one of Jim Gray's galleries. Rebuilding has commenced, so look for an unveiling soon.

RIVERBEND MALL
511 Parkway, Gatlinburg
At traffic light #3 on the Parkway, Riverbend Mall offers two levels of gift shops, a restaurant, and a few other businesses. This is the home of Things Unique, Gatlinburg Cutlery, and O2 Bead Experience/Bead XP (see the description of this shop earlier in this chapter).

MOUNTAIN MALL
611 Parkway, Gatlinburg
www.gatlinburg-mountainmall.com
The largest retail concentration in town, Mountain Mall is a six-level structure containing about 40 shops at traffic light #6. The split-level design makes stair climbing more negotiable, and the elevator stops at all levels. There's also an interesting little escalator that only goes up. A three-story wooden fountain at the west end sends water plummeting through a fascinating series of weight-activated ducts.

Among the original tenants when the mall opened in 1978 are the Rhythm Section, the city's first record business; the Gatlinburlier, the only shop in town that's dedicated entirely to the smoker; and Aunt Mahalia's Candy (described earlier in this chapter). Additional shops include Pepper Palace, where you can choose your poison if inner heat is your thing, and the Black Bear Tea Company, which sells a grand selection of teas, tea ware, and tea accessories—and even coffee.

BASKINS SQUARE MALL
631 Parkway, Gatlinburg
Running away from the Parkway toward River Road, not far after traffic light #6, Baskins Square Mall has shoehorned more than a dozen shops and restaurants into a deceptively small area with an inviting brick courtyard. They include the Little Sparrow Gallery (which specializes in Native American products), Mountain Woodcarvers, Scents of Gatlinburg, and one of the Old Tyme Portraits by Treadway locations (described

earlier in this chapter). Sometimes, the folks at Scott Compton Magic Shop go out in the courtyard and show off some of their tricks—and if you end up buying the trick in their upper-level store, they'll coach you in how best to perform it. If you get hungry, stop at the Funnel Cake Company or the New Orleans Sandwich Company.

One weekend a year, you can forget about sales tax in Tennessee. The Sales Tax Holiday begins the first Friday in August and ends the following Sunday. Tax-free items include clothing as well as school supplies and school art supplies that cost $100 or less. Computers selling for $1,500 or less are also tax-free that weekend.

THE VILLAGE
634 Parkway, Gatlinburg
www.thevillageshops.com
Right across the road from Baskins Square Mall, after traffic light #6, this group of 27 shops and eateries appears in a charming Old World setting, with pedestrian entrances on the Parkway and Baskins Creek Road. Its idyllic backdrop includes rock gardens, wildflowers, water fountains, and interesting relics like a British phone booth. Local wildlife are no strangers to the Village—squirrels, hummingbirds, and even the occasional bear have been known to pay visits to the courtyards.

The shops themselves generally convey an old-world look through an eclectic mix of architectural styles and designs, with moss and vine thriving on their facades. A great many of the furnishings and fixtures that go into the makeup of each shop are either unusual, antique, rare, or some combination of the three. For example, the front porch of one particular shop was obtained from the old parsonage of Knoxville's Second Baptist Church.

Other shops use pieces like beveled glass, wormy chestnut wood, and antique staircases to flesh out the old-world effect. Even the archway that forms the main entrance to the Village is historically significant. The bricks are believed to have been made by area slaves around 1843. Supposedly, they were used to construct the first brick building in Sevier County around that same time.

A sampling of tenants includes the Day Hiker, the Honey Pot (glassware, pottery, and clay gift items), Verbenas (body, bath, and home delicacies), the Taylor Girls (two ladies' boutique shops), the Silver Tree, Life According to Jake (colorful "Life is Good" shirts and other gear), Smoky Mountain Babies (clothing and toys), Candle Cottage, Hofbrauhaus Restaurant & Cheese Cupboard, Thomas Kinkade at the Village (the art of Thomas Kinkade), Crystalix (which puts your 3-D photo in a crystal cube) and Celtic Heritage (Scots-Irish merchandise).

THE MARKETPLACE MALL
651 Parkway, Gatlinburg
Just down the street from Baskins Square Mall, close to traffic light #6, the Marketplace Mall recently underwent an extensive refurbishment and now looks exactly like the sort of adorable European cottages that are the highlight of the most charming of all ceramic Christmas villages. This mall consists of one aisle of shops running back toward the park from the street, just five on each side. The two businesses flanking the entrance are Lids (which sells all sorts of hats) and For Bare Feet (which carries all manner of socks). The Discovery Store stocks interesting electronic toys for kids and adults alike. You'll also find a few eateries, including the Greenbrier Coffee & Tea Company and the colorful Henbender Grill (named for the largest salamander species in the Smokies).

REAGAN TERRACE MALL
716 Parkway, Gatlinburg
Halfway between traffic lights #6 and #8 (remember, there is no light #7), and built around a courtyard on the Parkway, is Reagan Terrace. The dozen or so shops here (including the Candle Shoppe, Medieval Blades, Southern Outfitters, Relaxation Station, and the Fragrance Connection) are flanked by Hauntings and World of Illusions (see the Attractions chapter for descriptions of both). Eateries in Reagan Terrace include Famous Fries and the Fudge Shoppe.

DOWNTOWN TRADERS MALL
805 Parkway, Gatlinburg
This one is different in that it's entirely below the sidewalk, underneath Midtown Lodge, right before traffic light #8. A pretty little brick walk leads to a courtyard with a rock garden waterfall that provides a nice photo opportunity. Stores here include the Buckboard, which carries a collection of Tom Clark gnomes, local crafts, and western-themed goods. Mountain Leather Company has offered locally handcrafted leather items since 1980, and Smoky Mountain Collectibles has a broad line of NASCAR merchandise.

ELKS PLAZA
968 Parkway, Gatlinburg
As you might guess from the name, this is the home of Gatlinburg's Elks Lodge #1925, which takes up the second story. Included in the street-level mall below (right before traffic light #9) are the Best Italian Cafe and Pizzeria (see the Restaurants chapter), the Hillbilly Gift Shop, One Happy Place (selling '70s smiley-face merchandise), and Southern Pride Décor and More.

TRAMWAY MALL
1001 Parkway, Gatlinburg
(865) 436-5423
www.obergatlinburg.com/tramshop.htm
The jumping-off point for the aerial tramway to Ober Gatlinburg (see the Attractions chapter), the Tramway Mall at traffic light #9 has goodies at the Kandy Kitchen and the Tramway Snack Bar, gifts at the Silver Galleon and Country Corner, and the chance to pose in old-fashioned togs at Miss Sadie's Old Time Photos.

CALHOUN'S VILLAGE
1004 Parkway, Gatlinburg
The last mall before the entrance to the national park, Calhoun's Village sits between traffic lights #9 and #10. It's anchored by Calhoun's Restaurant (as you might imagine) as well as Cherokee Grill and Smoky Mountain Brewery and Restaurant, Gatlinburg's only minibrewery (see the Music and Entertainment Theaters and Nightlife chapter). This small group of shops includes the funky

Earth to Old City gift shop, Bampton-Greene Native American Tribal Arts Gallery, and the fantastically frenetic Toy Crazy.

MOUNTAIN CRAFTS

Before the outlet malls, waterslides, amusement parks, and myriad other attractions brought tourists to this valley, even before Great Smoky Mountains National Park was anything more than a gleam in the eye of a group of conservationists around the region, Gatlinburg was nationally known for its crafts. The variety and enduring quality of the handcrafted merchandise being produced in practically every home and marketed nationally by the Pi Beta Phi women's fraternity was legendary. Gatlinburg was the center of the industry, which flourished in the mountainous areas where farming wasn't practical, as increasing numbers of craftspeople from Pigeon Forge and the eastern areas of the county brought their crafts into Gatlinburg to sell.

This section of the chapter is dedicated to the small number of native and immigrant craftspeople who are trying to keep the heritage of handcraft alive in the Smokies. It will also expose one of the area's best-kept secrets—one that has been known to extend some trips to the Smokies for a few days. To keep things on a fairly level plane here, a few ground rules have been established: First, the term *handcraft* is narrowly defined. To qualify, goods must be produced either by guiding material through a stationary tool (like cutting on a band saw or weaving on a loom) or by guiding the hands or a handheld tool over moving or stationary material (like throwing on a potter's wheel or whittling a piece of wood). Additionally, the artisan must begin working with unfinished raw material, like wooden or composition boards, bolt cloth, hides, or tubes of paint.

The development of the handcraft industry was the result of a great deal of bush-beating by the Pi Beta Phi teachers when they arrived in 1912. They provided a market for the local artisans without requiring the locals to do anything more than they'd been doing all along, and everybody was happy with the arrangement. The

trailblazers who subsequently opened businesses to increase their merchandising possibilities gave the large cottage industry a more localized group of outlets without significantly reducing Pi Beta Phi's slice of the pie. The local businesses gave the home-based craftspeople a chance to produce more merchandise without really straining themselves and encouraged the idea of crafts as a family trade. The craftspeople who migrated to the area brought new crafts with them, which had no adverse effect on the existing home-based producers.

Although the number of craft businesses has increased steadily, Gatlinburg still has a lot of people who work at home. These are the "invisible craftspeople," and this chapter is not going to expose them beyond noting the fact that they're still out there. These artisans are content to work in privacy and to sell their production to area shops, which then sell them to the public. The number of cottage businesses is probably larger than ever before, for a couple of reasons: First, there are more sales outlets available to the artisans; second, the life cycle of craftspeople usually finds them retiring from the public view into the cottage end. The financial rewards are smaller because they're selling at wholesale prices instead of retail, but the general feeling is that the freedom to work at their own pace is adequate compensation.

Today's invisible craftsperson is most likely a woodworker, a basket maker, a weaver, or a quilter. In addition to being native crafts, the time required for most of them to be done properly almost dictates that the work be done without distraction. The number of cottage woodworkers is very large (it's well over half the total of active craftspeople) because woodworking, as one of the oldest and more popular crafts, is in more demand than the public artisans can hope to supply. The common bond of the invisible craftspeople seems to be the desire to work in solitude. Whatever their reasons, these craftspeople have chosen the reclusive lifestyle of many country artisans, and their counterpart shops respect that choice. As it was in the beginning, the cottage craft industry of the Smokies remains an integral part of the heritage and attractiveness of the mountains, perpetuating the deep-seated conviction of the Appalachian people that they alone will choose the terms that define their lives.

With that in mind, what follows is a listing of some of the more notable places to buy mountain crafts in the area, starting with a few Sevierville and Pigeon Forge institutions and then moving down the road to Gatlinburg, where Pi Beta Phi's large footprint is still clearly visible. Special pains will be taken to point out the shops where you can expect to watch craftspeople actually plying their trades.

One final disclaimer: These businesses are for the most part small, family-operated enterprises, with no more than a few employees. Expect hours of operation to be limited to daylight hours, with at least one day a week off, usually Sunday. (A lot of the craftspeople don't even post their hours because they live basically from day to day.) Your best bet would be to call ahead on the day you want to visit to make sure the shop you want to see is open.

By the way, pricing, like most everything else the craftspeople and artists do, is a very personal matter, and it leads to some interesting variations. As a rule (to the extent that rules apply to craftspeople), you can expect to find prices that are surprisingly low when you consider what you're getting. The best way to put it into perspective is to think what you pay for a skilled tradesman like a plumber, an electrician, or an auto mechanic for an hour's work, and compare it to the price of a broom that took a few hours to make or a fine carving that may have taken several days. The best way to approach craft shopping is to consider that, in most cases, your purchase is worth what you pay for it. And the current craze in collectibles notwithstanding, handmade craft items have great potential for being upgraded to heirlooms in the histories of most families.

Sevierville

Pickings in Sevierville are pretty slim because the city has always been the center of government and local commerce. The ongoing entry into the tourism market has brought Sevierville into the overall tourism picture in a big way, but handcrafts and art were never a big part of that. The artisan listed here, however, is one of the most important artists in the area.

THE ROBERT A. TINO GALLERY
812 Old Douglas Dam Road, Sevierville
(865) 453-6315
www.robertatinogallery.com
The Robert Tino Gallery is located in a family-owned farmhouse clearly visible and accessible from Winfield Dunn Parkway (Tennessee Highway 66), about a mile north of Dolly Parton Parkway. Robert Tino, one of the younger artists in the area, has built an admirable reputation within the local artists' community. His sensitivity to the natural beauty of the world around him is translated to canvas in whatever medium Tino chooses. A Sevier County native, Tino has benefited from the tutelage of several artists in the area, and has returned the favor by assisting several promising young artists in starting their own careers. Tino's work, and that of his protégés, is displayed in a century-old farmhouse that's listed on the National Register of Historic Places.

Pigeon Forge

Pigeon Forge's move toward a family-centered commercial base took a toll on that city's craftspeople by covering them up with a lot of noise and neon lights. A few stubborn souls have survived the onslaught, and they've pretty much concentrated themselves in the Old Mill area, the heart of the oldest continuing craft business in the city. To get there, turn east off the Parkway at traffic light #7 (Old Mill Avenue), cross the river, and look for a place to park. Every shop listed here, and many of the others that are described in the previous sections of this chapter, is within walking distance.

JIM GRAY GALLERY
3331 South River Road, Pigeon Forge
(865) 428-2202
www.jimgraygallery.com
Jim Gray is one of the better known of the Smokies' large group of superb artists. In addition to his flair with paint and canvas, Gray is a sculptor of considerable talent. His most visible local work is the Dolly Parton statue on the courthouse lawn in Sevierville (see the Attractions chapter). This Pigeon Forge gallery, set on the west bank of the Little Pigeon River, displays a sampling of Gray's talents in various artists' media. Established in the area since the early '70s, Gray is a prime benefactor of Great Smoky Mountains National Park; he's created several original paintings for the park's benefit. He was also an early resident of the Great Smoky Arts & Crafts Community and has another gallery in a converted church there.

OLD MILL PIGEON RIVER POTTERY
175 Old Mill Avenue, Pigeon Forge
(865) 453-1104, (888) 453-5455
www.oldmillsquare.com/pottery.htm
Located in the heart of the Old Mill area, Pigeon River Pottery is just about what you'd expect from local craftspeople. An impressive collection of useful and decorative pottery items in blue and earth tones is complemented by a whimsical collection of black bears created by artist-in-residence Thomas Bullen, a third-generation native artisan. Some of the potters in Pigeon River's on-site workshop have been in the business in Pigeon Forge since the '50s and '60s. All of the pottery produced at Pigeon River is protected with lead-free glazes and is microwave and dishwasher safe. The idea here is that you're buying pottery for its intended use before mass-

The visiting artisans who come here for the many craft shows are pretty good or they wouldn't be here, but they leave when the tourists do. If you have a problem with an item you bought at a craft show, it's sometimes hard to find the craftsperson. You won't have that problem if you buy from a local establishment.

produced dinnerware came along. This shop is part of the larger Old Mill Square complex, described fully earlier in this chapter.

RANDALL OGLE GALLERY
169 Old Mill Avenue, Pigeon Forge
(865) 428-2839
www.randalloglegallery.com
A self-taught native artist and great-grandson of early mountain pioneers, Randall Ogle is well known for his portrayals of Cades Cove historic buildings and pastoral scenes. In fact, his gallery offers the largest collection of Cades Cove artwork in the Smokies. Ogle's nostalgic collection of Sevier County farm scenes and community landmarks, as well as his wonderfully detailed reproductions of vintage cars, is generating new interest in old times.

Gatlinburg
Still the area leader, Gatlinburg's craft heritage is going through the same growing pains as the rest of the city. It's not easy to find actual craftspeople downtown, but locally made handcrafts and art are available if you know where to look. These listings start with the downtown area and then move out East Parkway to highlight some real treasures on the way to the biggest concentration of independent artisans in North America—the Great Smoky Arts & Crafts Community.

Downtown
ARROWCRAFT
576 Parkway, Gatlinburg
(865) 436-4604
www.arrowcraft.org
Built in 1926 by Pi Beta Phi (the nation's oldest college women's fraternity) as a local outlet for Gatlinburg's artisans, Arrowcraft is the oldest gift shop in Gatlinburg. The shop was purchased in 1993 by the Southern Highlands Craft Guild. As a regional outlet for one of the nation's largest craft associations, Arrowcraft is an outstanding gallery of traditional Appalachian crafts of all kinds, produced by the best of several hundred regional artisans. The nicest part of visiting Arrowcraft is the knowledge that everything displayed in the

museum-like setting is a handmade item you can take home with you. Arrowcraft is located adjacent to the campus of the Arrowmont School of Arts and Crafts, which has a national reputation. Also on the grounds of the shop is the reconstructed cabin originally built from the logs William Ogle cut for the home he never saw, but which housed his widow, Martha Jane, and members of her family who were the first white settlers of the area that became Gatlinburg. (See the Attractions chapter for more information about the cabin.)

East Parkway

Heading out of downtown Gatlinburg on East Parkway (U.S. Highway 321N) toward the Great Smoky Arts & Crafts Community, you will find a few notable shops that are worthwhile stops.

A TOUCH OF TIFFANY
1003 East Parkway, Gatlinburg
(865) 436-9456
What Dorothy and Herb Jones do with stained and beveled glass is a sight to behold. From simple (and simply beautiful) night-lights and suncatchers to stained-glass lamps and windows, the Joneses' artistry with glass is impressive indeed.

THE GREAT SMOKY ARTS & CRAFTS COMMUNITY

The Great Smoky Arts & Crafts Community, (www .artsandcraftscommunity.com) lies 3 miles east of downtown Gatlinburg's traffic light #3 on East Parkway (US 321). The community begins at the intersection with Glades Road at traffic light #3A.

Technically, the Great Smoky Arts & Crafts Community is both a geographic area (bounded by the loop formed by Glades Road, Buckhorn/ Bird's Creek Road, and East Parkway—almost entirely within the city limits of Gatlinburg) as well as the organization of artists and craftspeople who own and operate businesses within the loop. The organization prints and distributes the excellent brochure and map that describes the area, lists the approximately 120 member businesses, and is the best guide through the neigh-

> **i** Don't be afraid to ask pointed questions in craft shops. A working craftsperson has very few secrets as far as what he or she does and how.

borhood. If you don't already have one, you can pick one up at just about any shop in the loop.

Here's a quick geography lesson: Traffic light #3A (Glades Road) is the starting point in this tour, if you come east from downtown Gatlinburg. There are two other ways you can approach the community:

1. If you're coming in from Sevierville or Pigeon Forge on Bird's Creek Road, you'll see a sign that says, Now Entering The Great Smoky Arts & Crafts Community on your right about 4 miles from Caton's Chapel school.

2. If you're coming from the east on US 321, turn right at Buckhorn Road a mile after you cross the Little Pigeon River on the Conley Huskey bridge—look for the sign on the left as you approach Buckhorn.

The Great Smoky Arts & Crafts Community got started in 1937 when Carl Huskey opened the Village Craft Shop in Whippoorwill Hollow. Carl's son Charles Ray keeps the family business alive as a cottage industry provider to several shops in the area. The area was pretty sedentary until it zoomed from a dozen or so shops in 1970 to 25 in 1975. The organization was formally chartered in 1978 with 28 member businesses, of which almost half are still operated by their founders or a succeeding generation. By the end of the '80s the secret was out among artisans, and the area has bloomed into a major commercial district (albeit a sprawling one, covering an 8-mile loop) with more than a hundred businesses of various types.

The community is laid out along the corridor described earlier, with a few side trips to shops a little more remote, but all the roads are hard-surfaced. The area is laced with signage that keeps you from getting terribly lost, and every shop offers ample parking. You'll even find several places to grab a bite to eat (see the Restaurants chapter for descriptions of some of them.)

Once you're safely into the bosom of the community, you're in a mostly rural area populated by the shops and galleries of the local artisans. These people are preserving Gatlinburg's original industry by keeping alive the local heritage of handwork and fine art. Some of the shops are operated by second and third generations of local families who've been engaged in their crafts for about a century. Others are professional artisans who came here to practice their crafts because the area is one of the few in this country where craftspeople can still make a living on their own terms. The combination of native and immigrant craftspeople and artists makes this the largest concentration of independent artisans in North America, and no other area even comes close. The operative word here is *independent:* For the most part these people depend on their own talents for their income, without subsidies.

Because of its size, it's difficult to see the entire Great Smoky Arts & Crafts Community in a single day. Either decide which shops are most appealing and limit your visit to those, or slice the trip into a couple of days and see it all. One other suggestion: The city operates a trolley through the community that's designed for tourism. From April through December, you can board the yellow-route trolley at the Gatlinburg city hall parking lot on East Parkway (parking is free). For $1, you can ride the trolley through the Great Smoky Arts & Crafts Community, get on and off as often as you like, and see most of the community. The trolley stops at most of the shop complexes along the way and takes about 30 minutes to make a complete loop. Consider using the trolley to scope out your route: Ride around first without getting off, making mental notes about where you want to go, and then once you get back to your car, drive through at your leisure with a more informed perspective.

The listings that follow include shops that are known to produce a significant percentage of the merchandise they sell and where you may expect to see craftspeople working. This route begins at the Buie's Landing complex just before the intersection of East Parkway and Glades Road (at traffic light #3A) and travels clockwise through the community, following the route of the community's brochure.

BUIE POTTERY
1360 East Parkway, Gatlinburg
(865) 436-3504
www.buiepottery.com
A fine arts graduate of the University of Tennessee, Buie Hancock creates a colorful variety of useful and decorative pottery from start to finish. From bathroom items to oil lamps, every product at Buie Pottery is one of a kind.

LICKLOG HOLLOW BASKETS
1360 East Parkway, Gatlinburg
(865) 436-3823
Billie Canfield and her daughter Lisa Canfield augment their own excellent basket-making talents with those of several area wicker workers. An interesting array of ironwork and folk art complement the basketry.

VILLAGE CANDLES
1400 East Parkway, Gatlinburg
(865) 436-4299
This is Gatlinburg's original candle maker. Stephanie Lang casts more than a thousand different designs from her own molds and finishes them in a fashion so attractive that you wonder if anyone would actually dare to burn them.

LUCITE BY LOUISE
1400 East Parkway, Gatlinburg
(865) 436-8849
http://lucitebylouisereversecarving.samsbiz .com
Harry Maloney uses new technology to create his handcrafted masterpieces. Using tools designed primarily for woodworking, Harry cuts intricate designs into clear Plexiglas. Key chains, desk accessories, and one-of-a-kind lamps and plaques can be personalized while you wait. And get Harry to talk to you while you're there; you'll figure out quickly that he's not from around here.

THE LEATHER WORKS
1400 East Parkway, Gatlinburg
(865) 436-4014
Founded by Al Shirley in the early '80s, the Leather Works produces a variety of custom articles and represents the works of several area craftspeople. Their selection of leather handbags may well be the biggest in Gatlinburg, and thanks to their recent expansion, they now also carry a large selection of leather jewelry, hats, and key chains. If you buy a belt here, they can even put your name on it. If you're interested in doing some of your own leatherworking, Leather Works will even sell you a full hide.

SCRIMSHAW, KNIVES, SILVERSMITHING
1402 East Parkway, Gatlinburg
(865) 430-3496
The influence of the southwestern Indians is clearly visible in the silver work of Paul Stewart. Sterling silver and semiprecious gemstones dominate Stewart's handiwork in this shop, which also features knives and scrimshaw by Newman and Peggy Smith. Jewelry repairs are available.

GLADES HOMEMADE CANDIES
1402 East Parkway, Gatlinburg
(865) 436-3238
Here's another Gatlinburg tradition practiced by another native family. Connie and Ronnie Bohanan whip up daily batches of fudge, brittle, taffy, and hand-dipped chocolates to satisfy the most demanding sweet tooth. Helped when necessary by Connie's parents, Billy Ray and Helen Moore, Glades also produces a full line of sugar-free candies.

LORELEI CANDLES
331 Glades Road, Gatlinburg
(865) 436-9214, (800) 432-7077
www.loreleicandlesonline.com
When Lori Tierney was a college student in 1979 (she still looks like one), her father's candle factory in Sevierville was destroyed by a fire. Lori dropped out of school, bought a building on Glades Road, and sifted the ashes of her father's business until she had reclaimed enough molds

to start her own factory. Some of those resurrected molds are probably still in use among the several thousand novelty candles produced daily at Lorelei, along with a line of original art candles that's constantly being updated and expanded.

GEMSTONE CUSTOM JEWELRY
337 Glades Road, Gatlinburg
(865) 436-4448
www.jewelrybygemstone.com
Malcolm (Mac) and Susie MacDonell stopped off in Gatlinburg in 1976 on their way to their planned retirement home in Costa Rica. The visit was extended when Mac rented a shop to store his jewelry-making equipment and set it up to give himself something to do. Gemstone Custom Jewelry was an instant hit with the locals, who know a good thing when they see it, and became a landmark business in the Great Smoky Arts & Crafts Community because of the excellent work and outgoing personalities of its owners. Costa Rica will have to wait: Gemstone Custom Jewelry, a charter member of the Great Smoky Arts & Crafts Community, will probably go on producing fine jewelry from precious metals and stones for a long, long time.

LEATHER—THE REAL MCCOY
513 Glades Road, Gatlinburg
(865) 621-0679
www.leathertherealmccoy.com
You'll know Gary McCoy is in his shop if you see his motorcycle parked outside. "Free spirit" is an appropriate description of this longtime resident, but the quality and beauty of his belts and leather accessories are solid testimony to his ability. It's no wonder he's also known as "The Real McCoy." For over 40 years.

GATLIN COUNTY LEATHER
517 Glades Road, Gatlinburg
(865) 430-5840
Custom-made leather clothing is the main draw at this shop, where Marsha Fountain fashions Native American–inspired war shirts, dresses, and more contemporary coats and vests from deer and elk hide. In addition, she also carries

hats, belts, moccasins, drums, flutes, hand-carved pipes, bows, and quivers as well as lots of Native American jewelry, music, and books. Many folks also stop in to visit with Shadow, Marsha's young and quite friendly wolf dog.

An interesting aside: Marsha, who is of Cherokee and Creek Indian descent, is also related to Radford Gatlin—the man for whom Gatlinburg was named (see the History chapter).

MORNING MIST GALLERIES
601 Glades Road, Gatlinburg

Morning Mist is a large shopping mall—in excess of 20 shops with a high turnover. Among the regulars are a couple of food service facilities, several gift shops that come and go on a regular basis, and the following four shops where craftspeople produce and sell their wares.

HENRY PARKER'S LIGHTHOUSE GALLERY
601 Glades Road, #1, Gatlinburg
(865) 430-9449

Nobody can quite figure out why an artist with a national reputation for painting lighthouses and other maritime subjects lives in the mountains, but then Henry's not the easiest guy in the world to get a handle on. Henry delights his visitors with an off-the-wall sense of humor that makes his artwork make perfect sense. A visit to Henry Parker's gallery is worth the trip just to meet an artisan with a completely unique point of view.

BEECH BRANCH CRAFTS & SIGNS
601 Glades Road, #3, Gatlinburg
(865) 436-9065

Gatlinburg natives Teddy and Sandy Osborne personalize their own slate signs, brick buildings, and fireplace screens. They're also one of the last places in the Arts & Crafts Community where you can get a totally personalized routed redwood sign.

SMOKY MOUNTAIN GOLD 2
(SMOKY MOUNTAIN ROSE LADY)
601 Glades Road, #8, Gatlinburg
(865) 436-6805

Proprietor Carolyn Mikles is truly an alchemist. For the past quarter century, she's been taking all sorts of natural items (acorns, flowers, leaves, and even pinecones) and turning them into fabulous gold-plated jewelry. In addition, she also creates beads from dried rose petals and other flowers and makes jewelry out of them. (You can even send her the petals from your wedding bouquet or any other sentimental occasion and she'll create a special piece just for you—although her waiting list is 12 months long.)

> **i** The local craftspeople take a lot of pride in what they do, and it's usually their principal source of income. It bugs them when tourists treat them like flea market exhibitors. Bargain with them if you want, but don't be surprised if their normally cheerful attitude chills quickly.

CANDLES BY DICK AND MARIE
601 Glades Road, #15, Gatlinburg
(865) 430-9148

Dick and Marie Pinner have taken an entirely new slant to the ancient craft of candle making. Using a modern casting material instead of paraffin, the Pinners create crystal-clear candles that would be gorgeous if they were just left alone. But that's just the beginning; the clarity of the material lets this talented couple then create artworks by adding natural and artificial materials, making every candle a work of art. And if that's not enough, they're also scented. Sacrificing nothing for the sake of art, the Pinners' candles will burn as long or longer than wax candles, and they smell good, too.

FIRST IMPRESSIONS POTTERY
612 Glades Road, Gatlinburg
(865) 436-3642

The first impression you get in this shop is that a lot of really talented people are contributing some really nice handcrafts to it. The reality is that it's all being done by Jim Coffelt, a multitalented Sevier County native who can work magic with whatever tool he picks up. Coffelt started out as a wood carver in high school, worked as a potter's apprentice for a while, and dabbled in art and serious woodworking during a few winters. Now he spends his winter as a guest instructor in woodworking at the Arrowmont School of Crafts (see the History chapter).

ALEWINE POTTERY
623 Glades Road, Gatlinburg
(865) 430-7828
www.alewinepottery.net
Function and form come together in Robert Alewine's beautiful and useful pottery items. From kitchen utensils to bathroom accessories to oil lamps, Alewine's attention to detail and special painting and glazing techniques set his work apart from any other. Alewine is the only potter in the area who is known to "foot" every piece he produces to ensure that all his pieces sit evenly without rocking.

SPINNING WHEEL CRAFTS
711 Valley Road, Gatlinburg
(865) 436-4493
Bea Bakley is a third-generation native weaver who's been doing her rag rugs, place mats, and table runners forever. Husband Elmer keeps just enough space cleared on his workbench to produce a complete line of traditional folk toys and intricate wind-driven whirligigs that will dress up any yard or patio needing a truly unusual decoration.

CLIFF DWELLERS GALLERY
668 Glades Road, Gatlinburg
(865) 436-6921
www.cliffdwellersgallery.com
This historic building was built in downtown Gatlinburg in the 1930s as the home, gallery, and studio of artist Louis E. Jones. In 1995, Jim Gray (whose gallery is next door) and his son Chris moved the building to the Arts & Crafts Community and restored it. Now a fine art and craft gallery featuring the works of several contemporary and traditional artisans, one or more of whom demonstrate their craft on-site regularly.

JIM GRAY GALLERY
670 Glades Road, Gatlinburg
(865) 436-8988
www.jimgraygallery.com

Jim Gray's gallery is in a restored church building that's more than a hundred years old (the new church is a few blocks up the road). A complete collection of Gray prints and sculpture is available, along with the works of several regional artisans. A special feature is the amazing stone sculpture of noted Canadian Mohawk artist Thomas Maracle. Jim Gray also has a second gallery in Pigeon Forge, which is described earlier in this chapter.

THE SMITHS
680 Glades Road, Gatlinburg
(865) 436-3322
www.thesmithsshop.com
Scrimshaw by Cherokee artisan Peggy Smith and custom knives and silver work by her husband, Newman, stand out in this shop featuring local and regional Native American artifacts and handcrafts. Newman Smith's custom knives are nationally known for their originality and durability.

A TROLL IN THE PARK
680 Glades Road, Gatlinburg
(865) 436-0091
www.trolls.com
Smoky Mountain Trolls have been part of the area's folklore for more than 30 years. The Arensbak family produces the trolls and their individual histories, along with an unusual line of accessory items.

COSBY HILLPEOPLE CRAFTS
680 Glades Road, Gatlinburg
(865) 430-4675
From useful to whimsical to just nice to look at, the products of Carl and Libby Fogliani remind us of the way the hill people used to live. Simple hand toys of wood and cloth, bird feeders, pinecone wreaths, and quilts and quilting supplies (including hard-to-find quilt frames) all flow from the hands of these versatile craftspeople.

OGLE'S BROOM SHOP
680 Glades Road, Gatlinburg
(865) 430-4402
http://oglebrooms.tripod.com
Ogle's Broom Shop is a name that's been around

almost a century. David Ogle, the current proprietor with his wife, Tammie, is a fourth-generation broom-making Ogle; his father, Wayne, was a nephew of Lee M. "Pop" Ogle, credited by many as the father of the broom industry in Gatlinburg. David and Tammie employ the same techniques that the Ogles have used since the beginning—advances in technology are helpful to the cosmetic appearance, but a broom tied by Tammie Ogle today is in no way different from one tied by Lee Ogle in 1925.

OWNBY'S WOODCRAFTS
704 Glades Road, Gatlinburg
(865) 436-5254
One of the area's oldest working craftspeople, James "Lum" Ownby and wife, Jan, produce a broad line of wood products from native materials, assisted by their daughter Jody and son-in-law David Penny. Lum Ownby is one of the few craftsmen still active who started out whittling at a card table in downtown Gatlinburg.

SMOKY MOUNTAIN POTTERY
744 Powdermill Road, Gatlinburg
(865) 436-4575
www.smokymountainpottery.com
A true production pottery, Smoky Mountain Pottery is a constant beehive of activity. Dennis and Gay Ann McEvoy seem to be everywhere at once, throwing pottery on their own wheels or supervising the pouring of clay into molds for the hundreds of wall plaques and other accents and ornaments they sell.

WHALEY HANDCRAFTS
804 Glades Road, Gatlinburg
(865) 436-9708
Opened in 1954 by Frank and Augusta Whaley as a weaving business, the shop is now operated by son Randy, a wood carver of the highest order. Randy Whaley has earned a reputation as a master carver with his large renditions of animals, birds, and fish. Lathe turnings and carvings by other members of the large Whaley family find their way into the shop, and Frank shows up now

and then with some of his exquisite woven place mats. Whaley Handcrafts is a charter member of the Great Smoky Arts & Crafts Community.

THE CHAIR SHOP
830 Cantrell Circle, Gatlinburg
(865) 436-7413
Randy Ogle is the fourth generation of his family who believes the only way to produce quality furniture is to use solid American hardwoods and methods that have passed every test time can devise. It's not really a cash-and-carry operation; your custom order will probably take the Chair Shop a while to build and deliver, but you and your great-grandchildren will have the rest of your lives to enjoy it.

GATLINBURG CERAMICS
805 Glades Road, Gatlinburg
(865) 436-4315
The ceramicists' profession is proud to have Judy Bailey as a member since 1973. A nationally recognized producer and teacher, Judy does the job from start to finish. She pours her own molds (several of which she makes herself) and hand-paints and fires a dazzling selection of useful pitchers, bowls, and decorative holiday items. Reproductions of antique oil and electric lamps are also a favorite here. Judy is a charter member of the Great Smoky Arts & Crafts Community and has been a board member and president of the organization almost continuously since the organization was formed in 1978.

BAXTER'S STAINED GLASS
1069 Ogle Hills Road, Gatlinburg
(865) 436-5998
Visitors are always welcome at Baxter's, and they'll find themselves right in the middle of whatever John and Donna have going on— there's really no point where the workshop ends and the showroom begins. The Baxters have been making their sun-catchers, candleholders, nightlights, and windows since 1984 in the shop that adjoins their home, a short drive back into the woods off Glades Road.

JOHN COWDEN WOODCARVERS
4242 Bird's Creek Road, Gatlinburg
John Cowden is a third-generation whittler who learned cabinetmaking from Shirl Compton after World War II. Following in his father's and grandfather's footsteps, John carved animals on the front porch of Hattie Ogle's Bearskin Shop in the '40s until he opened his own shop in the Glades in 1954. A charter member and original director of the Great Smoky Arts & Crafts Community, John is arguably the oldest remaining active wood carver in the Smokies today.

G. WEBB GALLERY
795 Buckhorn Road, Gatlinburg
(865) 436-3639
www.gwebbgallery.com
Located in a 1910 homestead at the corner of Glades and Buckhorn Roads, the G. Webb Gallery has a garden so rich in wildflowers and other natural wonders that the artist needs only to walk out the front door for a lot of his inspiration. Custom matting and framing are available while you wait.

SMOKIES' EDGE
540 Buckhorn Road, Gatlinburg
(865) 436-3988
Don Getty was one of the first tenants of the Mountain Arts complex when it was built in 1985. His distinctive style in original leather handbags, wallets, and decorative accessories has been expanded to include a line of beautiful lathe turnings he started producing after attending winter classes at the Arrowmont School a few years back. Maybe it's something about leather, but Don's another free-spirited type who uses a motorcycle as basic transportation. It's not unusual for him to load up his equipment and head west in the dead of winter to indulge his passion for skiing in the mountains of Colorado.

OTTO PRESKE—ARTIST IN WOOD
535 Buckhorn Road, Gatlinburg
(865) 436-5339
When Otto Preske built his two-story log cabin home and showroom in 1976, it was the only shop on his side of the road for 2 miles. He's now in the middle of several buildings. Otto's skill as a wood sculptor is unmatched in the area, and his large commissioned sculptures of sacred objects are in churches throughout the midwestern and southern United States. How good is Otto Preske? Give him your picture and enough time to do the job, and Otto will carve your likeness.

VERN HIPPENSTEAL GALLERY
480 Buckhorn Road, Gatlinburg
(865) 436-4372, (800) 537-8110
www.vernhippensteal.com
Possibly Gatlinburg's most successful native artist, Vern Hippensteal came to prominence when he built this imposing gallery in 1982. His reputation has grown steadily since as his watercolor depictions of the mountains he's always called home have increased in popularity. His work is also available at Hippensteal's Mountain View Inn (see the Bed-and-Breakfasts and Country Inns chapter).

TERRI WATERS GALLERY
438 Bebb Road, Gatlinburg
(865) 436-5647
www.terriwatersgallery.com
Terri Waters is a Gatlinburg native and one of a family of distinguished artists—she'll tell you which family. Her stunning triptych *Mt. LeConte Dawn* would be a crowning achievement for any artist, but Terri is best known for her Smokies Wildflowers watercolor series. Terri's gallery recently moved from its downtown location in the Baskins Square shopping mall to the house where she grew up in the Arts & Crafts Community. In addition to her stunning art, her gallery also sells locally made pottery and jewelry.

TURTLE HOLLOW GALLERY
248 Buckhorn Road, Gatlinburg
(865) 436-6188
Wood turnings and original basketry are the hallmarks of this gallery, which features the work of several regional artisans. Proprietor Ross Markley is also a guest lecturer and instructor at the Arrowmont School of Arts and Crafts.

GREAT SMOKY MOUNTAINS NATIONAL PARK

Why do nearly nine million people visit Great Smoky Mountains National Park each year (making it the nation's most visited)? To begin with, it's easy for most folks to get to. Straddling the state line between Tennessee and North Carolina, the Smokies is within 550 miles (equivalent to a day's drive) of one-third of the U.S. population. The folks who flock here find 800 miles of nature walks and hiking trails, 550 miles of horse trails (and four commercial stables), 700 miles of fishable streams, 11 developed picnic areas, 10 front-country camp-grounds, and nearly 400 miles of roads for auto touring. And that's just for starters.

The Smokies is also filled with wildlife—including some life-forms that exist only in these hills and hollers. The 800 square miles that make up the park are home to at least 10,000 identi-fied species of plants and animals (including more species of salamanders than anywhere else in the world). Yet biologists currently keeping count of the critters expect the final tally to be closer to 100,000! Without a doubt, the Smokies is the most biologically diverse national park in the continental United States. No wonder it's been designated as a United Nations Interna-tional Biosphere Reserve.

Unlike other national parks, the Smokies' human history is a huge highlight. The park houses the best and most complete collection of historic log buildings in the eastern U.S. More than one hundred modest homes, gristmills, one-room schoolhouses, barns, outbuildings, and churches (all open for people to explore) remain to tell the story of the European settlers who began to arrive here in the late 1700s, as well as their descendants who lived and worked here until the national park was established in 1934. Thanks to this painstaking preservation of the area's rich and colorful Appala-chian history, the United Nations also declared the park to be a World Heritage Site.

Finally, it's also free: The Smokies is one of the few national parks that won't ever charge an entrance fee—thanks to agreements made when it was established. Great Smoky Mountains National Park is unique among federally operated American facilities because the government didn't originally own it. The land was in private hands in the early part of the 20th century, largely owned by various lumber companies, and 80 percent of it was cut. The area along the Tennessee–North Carolina border was purchased through an orga-nized effort by people in both states and donated to the government to be preserved as a national park. Most of the work of actually creating the park (building roads, bridges, and so on) was done by the Civilian Conservation Corps (CCC), one of the myriad federal programs designed to help end the Great Depression of the '30s.

It is commonly held among the locals that any visit to the Smokies isn't complete without spending some time in Great Smoky Mountains National Park. Even if your only real purpose in coming here is to shop the outlets, you should at least get a look at the beauty of the park. You wouldn't go to Myrtle Beach and not look at the ocean, would you? Of course not.

Two nonprofit organizations provide major assistance to the park through fund-raising and cooperative efforts. The Great Smoky Mountains Association, established in 1953, produces most of the printed material offered in the park and funds projects that don't fit into the normal

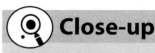 **Close-up**

Happy Birthday, Ole Smoky

The Great Smoky Mountain National park celebrated its 75th birthday in 2009 with special programs and events spread throughout the year. One of the main events occurring on the very day of the anniversary was the groundbreaking for a much-anticipated new visitor center at Oconaluftee on the North Carolina side (2 miles north of the town of Cherokee). The new $2.5 million, 7,000-square-foot building is scheduled to open at the end of 2010 and will replace the current 1,100-square-foot visitor center, a much smaller building that was never meant to be a visitor center to begin with. Built in 1940 by the Civilian Conservation Corps (the CCC), the old structure was originally planned as a ranger station and a magistrate's courtroom.

The new visitor center will include a cultural history museum with changing exhibits highlighting the park's Southern Appalachian culture. Some of the exhibits will focus on industries that were common in the area before the park's establishment, including logging and milling. Still other exhibits will focus on the Cherokees who made this area their home before the national park existed.

The park system has designed the building to be LEED (Leadership in Energy and Environmental Design) certified for environmental efficiency. (For more about LEED-certified building in the Smokies, see the Close-up in the chapter on hotels.) For example, the park service enlisted the help of the Oak Ridge National Laboratory to take solar measurements ensuring that the new visitor center's windows will be oriented and sized to allow for the exact right amount of light to stream through them, offsetting the need for heat in the winter.

When the new building opens, the older one will then be used as a classroom for educational programs and as a meeting space for community outreach events. Architectural details, such as its large stone fireplace, lovely grey quartzite stone floors, and chestnut trim salvaged from trees victimized by the chestnut blight, make it well worth saving. In addition, the adjacent Mountain Farm Museum (a group of historic log homes and other buildings illustrating mountain life that are connected by a self-guided nature trail) will remain unchanged.

For updated information on anniversary programs, visit the park's special anniversary Web site, www.greatsmokies75th.org.

---

budget process, such as wildlife management programs and educational exhibits. (For information on becoming a member, see the organization's Web site at www.thegreatsmokymountains .org or stop by any of the organization's stores listed in the Shopping chapter.)

Friends of Great Smoky Mountains National Park, organized in 1993, helps provide funding for larger-scale projects and services by raising money and public awareness. For information on how to donate, visit www.friendsofthesmokies .org, or just drop a donation in one of the colorful collection boxes you'll see throughout the park.

These two organizations have put their considerable influence and talents behind the most ambitious project ever undertaken by the National

Park Service or any other research organization on the planet: a complete inventory of plant and animal life in the park that's under way as you read this page. The All Taxa Biodiversity Inventory (ATBI) is the biggest long-term scientific program ever undertaken in the history of the world and is expected to take a team of several hundred (perhaps thousands) knowledgeable scientists and support staff 10 to 15 years to complete. That's what those people you might see with clipboards, laptop computers, and calculators are doing. They're even using global positioning satellite technology to document the exact location of everything they find. Discover Life in America, a national nonprofit research organization, is coordinating the project.

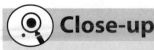

Close-up

Don't Feed the Wildlife

Your first close-up encounter with some of the resident wildlife in the national park could very well occur at Sugarlands, where deer and a variety of smaller furry creatures graze on the lawn and occasionally try to mooch a treat from the visitors roaming the grounds. But whether you're hiking in the backwoods or standing in front of the visitor center, don't approach any wild animal—anytime!

The animals may well appear to be friendly, which will probably cost them their lives someday, but they're really just hungry, which could cost you (or someone close to you) a body part that you probably had other plans for. First, none of the forest animals know where the food ends and your fingers, hands, or even your arm begins. Further, the preservation of the wildlife in the park depends on their being required to find their own food. If they depend on humans to feed them, either they will starve to death when there aren't any humans around, or they'll be put to death because they become dangerous and aggressive beggars. Not to mention the fact that Twinkies and potato chips are probably not the healthiest of snacks for wild critters.

You're going to hear this a lot in the park, and everybody here knows it's tough to resist the temptation to feed an animal that will come to you for a handout, but you must resist. If it's a truly hungry animal, it may take your hand as part of its handout.

When the ATBI is completed sometime in the second decade of the 21st century, it's anticipated that the number of known species within the park will increase tenfold. For example, when a small group of scientists came into the park for a three-day weekend to study algae and diatoms (this is deep scientific stuff—diatoms are single-cell algae), 85 percent of what they found was previously undiscovered.

Although the great majority of new discoveries will probably remain obscure or unnoticed outside of the scientific community, new species of butterflies and fish could attract public attention. During the planning stages of the inventory alone, while the whole idea was still being considered, scientists discovered two new flies and one turtle never before seen on the planet. And two new salamanders and a toad that had never been seen before popped up in Cades Cove! Because the researchers will study areas most people bypass, this inventory may also be the greatest thing going on in the park that you never see.

Great Smoky Mountains National Park is situated in one of the world's few mountain ranges that runs predominantly north and south.

During the most recent ice age (about 10,000 years ago—you probably missed it), the Smokies became home to many northern species of plants and animals that migrated south ahead of glaciers moving down North America from Canada. These species then moved up to the mountain peaks as the glaciers retreated. As a result, the Smokies now contain more native tree species (100 and counting) than all of northern Europe and more flowering plants, ferns, fungi, mosses, and lichens than any other spot on earth. All told, there are more than 5,600 different vegetative plant species (not including trees) in the park's 800 square miles.

The park is one of the best-preserved temperate deciduous (leaf-bearing) woodlands in the world, and the 100,000 acres of virgin timber within its boundaries make up the largest pristine forestland east of the Mississippi. A three-hour hike from 1,500 feet to the range crest above 6,500 feet contains as much diverse forest growth as you could see in a three-day drive-and-hike marathon from Georgia to Maine. The wildflowers here are nothing short of legendary. In fact, you can see enough different flowering plants bloom to make you wonder if the Smokies have a perpetual spring season. Some flowers in the park bloom as early as February, and the show doesn't stop until the last ones bloom in November.

The story on animal diversity is equally impressive: Great Smoky Mountains National Park is home to at least 66 mammal, 240 bird, 50 fish, 39 reptile, and 43 amphibian species. The latter group includes 31 species of salamander alone, the largest collection in the United States. The red-cheeked salamander is a local phenomenon found nowhere else on the planet.

What follows is a description of what you can expect in a visit to the park. For information about current programs and road conditions, call (865) 436-1200.

i Not only is the Smokies the most visited national park in the country, but it has more than twice the number of visitors as the second-most-popular park. Grand Canyon National Park has the number two position, with 4.4 million visitors a year compared to the Smokies' 9 million.

INTO THE WOODS!

Sugarland Visitor Center, a few minutes into the park from the Gatlinburg entrance, is an excellent place to begin any park adventure. From anywhere in Gatlinburg, just head for traffic light #10 and don't turn; from Pigeon Forge, come down the Parkway Spur about 4 miles to the park bypass on the right (just past the Gatlinburg welcome center) and take it around Gatlinburg. You'll find great photo opportunities at the two scenic overlooks along the bypass. Either route will bring you straight into the park, where you'll soon see Sugarland Visitor Center and its ample parking lot on the right, at the intersection of U.S. Highway 441 and Little River Road.

Sugarlands is an attraction all by itself, with museum-type exhibits of flora and fauna, an outstanding 20-minute film about the park shown in a comfortable theater, an excellent bookstore run by the nonprofit Great Smoky Mountains Association (see the Shopping chapter), and a staff of rangers who can tell you anything you want to know about the park. Check the posted schedules for the times and locations of the "Ranger Walks and Talks" and other free ranger programs, and if you have kids, ask about the Junior Ranger program. By fulfilling a list of qualifications in a fun activity booklet, kids can earn a badge of their own (and even have their name announced in the visitor center when they get it).

Ranger programs include classic Smokies activities, such as guided walks on some of the shorter trails, evening campground talks, hayrides in Cades Cove, and streamside salamander expeditions. Some of the craft-oriented programs include the chance to make old-fashioned toys, weave bookmarks on a loom like the early settlers, create Cherokee-inspired clay pots, play Appalachian instruments like the dulcimer, and even create a dinner bell the way a 19th-century blacksmith would have. A few ranger programs have even gone high-tech, including one that focuses on using GPS (global positioning system) technology.

Sugarlands is also the place on the Tennessee side of the park to pick up reams of literature on every developed attraction within the park. You can also become acquainted with the rules of conduct in the park. The rules may seem a bit restrictive, but think about what your backyard would look like if 9 million people came into it over the course of a year, and each one of them picked one blade of grass and left one plastic soft drink bottle. A visit to the Sugarland Visitor Center is a great way to temporarily restore your faith in government; it's an uplifting demonstration of your tax dollars at work.

i There are 23 species of snakes in the park, of which only two are poisonous: the timber rattler and the copperhead. Snakes like warm spots and sunlight, so be careful when climbing on rocks.

When you leave the Sugarlands Visitor Center, you'll come out on Little River Road, and it's time to make your first big choice: Turn right if you're headed for Elkmont, Metcalf Bottoms, the Sinks, Tremont, or Cades Cove (each described below in the order you'll encounter them).

If your goal is the Chimneys, Alum Cave, Morton Overlook, Newfound Gap, or anything in North Carolina, turn left on Little River Road, go back to US 441 (about 100 yards), and hang a right.

If You Turned Right Leaving the Visitor Center

You're on Little River Road, and it'll be more than 18 miles before you see another building. Little River Road is flat and serpentine and was almost totally destroyed by the devastating flood of 1994. Rebuilding took two years to complete, so you're on one of the better roads in the park. Along with some spectacular scenery, Little River Road has much to offer.

About 4 miles from Sugarlands, the Laurel Falls trail goes off to the right. It's paved, and for the 1-mile stroll (one way) back through the pine-oak forest to Laurel Falls, it's as level as you're going to find in the park. The falls themselves are quite lovely, and the trail passes directly across them.

Another mile up the road, the Elkmont campground road goes off to the left. Elkmont campground is a favorite jumping-off place for some of the more challenging hiking trails in the western sector of the park. The campground is near the site of the original Wonderland Hotel and 70 cabins that once belonged to a group of influential citizens who were able to lease land from the park, some as late as the early 1990s. The buildings were then deserted and fell into disrepair while the park service and local preservation groups decided their fate. Recently, the park service announced plans to restore 19 of the buildings for future public use (although they won't be used for overnight accommodation). The rest of the buildings will eventually be removed; as long as any are left, entry is prohibited for safety reasons.

Continuing west another 5 miles, you'll next come across Metcalf Bottoms picnic area, which stretches for about a half mile along the Little River, with plenty of tables and charcoal grills. The river is shallow (and very cold), excellent for wading, and one of the most popular places in the

park to begin a tubing adventure (see the Active Outdoor Adventures chapter).

A short drive across the river, the entrance road goes onto an unpaved trail. Turn right on the trail, and a short distance up is the parking area for the Little Greenbrier School, an original one-room schoolhouse. Warning: If you miss the trail, or turn right instead of left coming back out, you're headed for Wears Valley, which is outside the park. If you wind up at Wears Valley Road, turn right; you'll soon be in Pigeon Forge.

Little River runs right alongside the road from Metcalf Bottoms for a couple of miles to the Sinks, so tubers can be escorted without losing sight of them. Tubers: Get out of the river before you get to the Sinks, which is extremely dangerous for tubing. There's room along the river as soon as the bridge comes into view.

One of the truly awesome works of nature in the park, the Sinks is a sinkhole of undetermined depth that causes the Little River to roar and swirl madly in a maelstrom that's every kid's dream and every mother's nightmare. Although you may see people diving into the river from the tops of the cliffs here, this is against park regulations and is very dangerous. A couple of young people die here every year trying to do something stupid. Enjoy it from your car, or stand a respectful distance back along the edge.

A mile or so farther, Meigs Creek joins Little River. If you look up the creek to the left, you'll see Meigs Falls, one of the prettiest waterfalls in the park. Meigs Creek is one of the places where river otters were reintroduced to the park several years ago in a highly successful program. There is no more delightful creature anywhere than the otter at play, which is how it spends most of its life. If you really get lucky, you may see one here.

The next several miles of Little River Road follow the river on the right with sheer metamorphic sandstone crags coming down the left side. At the intersection of Tennessee Highway 73, you can go off to the right for gas, food, snacks, or a meal in Townsend, if you're so inclined. If you keep going, Little River Road turns into Laurel Creek Road, and the entrance road to the Great Smoky Mountains Institute at Tremont is about 0.1 mile up on the left (see below for more on Tremont). Continuing past Tremont, you'll be in Cades Cove in about 7 more miles. If you go into the cove, buy a copy of the self-guiding brochure—a great little guide with a useful map of the cove.

To do the trip justice, figure on an absolute minimum of two hours in Cades Cove—an hour or so of driving around the full 11-mile loop (one-way traffic only) and at least an hour's combined time spent at the several home sites and churches you'll pass along the way. Be prepared: Gridlock happens. Animal sightings along the road usually bring traffic to a stop, and traffic can get tied up for hours. If you brought a picnic with you, you're welcome to pull over and enjoy it anywhere along the loop road where there's space to pull completely off the road.

Cades Cove is your best chance to see wild turkeys, groundhogs, whitetail deer—and even coyotes. Various mammals—raccoons, rabbits, and relatively harmless skunks—hang around the parking lot at Cable Mill and the Oliver homestead. The Cades Cove campground (see the Campgrounds and RV Parks chapter) and picnic area are near the beginning of the loop road, as is a commercial horseback riding stable. A snack bar and refreshments are available at the campground store after you exit the loop.

i **Hunting is absolutely forbidden in the park. Fishing is permitted (see the Parks and Recreation chapter for details), but only with a single hook and artificial flies or lures. While the native brook trout were off limits for decades, successful restoration efforts now allow the taking of brookies from all but three well-marked park streams.**

Tremont—
Connecting People and Nature
GREAT SMOKY MOUNTAINS INSTITUTE AT TREMONT
9275 Tremont Road, Townsend
(865) 448-6709
www.gsmit.org

About 18 miles west of the Sugarlands Visitor Center, Great Smoky Mountains Institute at Tremont conducts a series of educational programs designed to provide hands-on training to nature lovers of all ages. Using the national park as a classroom, the institute's educational programs are internationally renowned for their leadership in the field of residential environmental education.

A wide variety of 3- to 10-day residential programs year-round emphasize the cultural and natural history of the Smokies for kids, families, teachers, and seniors. Participants stay in a dormitory that holds up to 125 people and eat family-style in a dining hall. Classes meet in several indoor classrooms and one huge outdoor facility. Prices are relatively affordable but vary with the specific program, so for up-to-date adult scheduling and fees, contact the institute or visit the Web site.

Some of the most popular of Tremont's programs are the age-sensitive adventure camps lasting for either 5 or 10 nights. Campers hike, swim, and sing around the campfire, and choose their own schedules from a fascinating menu, all under the watchful care of environmental educators. Many of Tremont's programs are specifically for adults as well, including hiking adventures, wilderness first-aid courses, photography workshops, and Elderhostel programs.

Whatever your destination when you left Sugarlands and turned right on Little River Road, bear in mind that on your return you're going back over the same road you traveled. If it's late afternoon, the traffic is going to increase a bunch when you get to US 441. Be prepared to move slowly toward Gatlinburg, and consider taking the bypass toward Pigeon Forge. Even if you're heading for Gatlinburg, taking the bypass and doubling back on the Parkway is an option.

If You Went Back to US 441 (Newfound Gap Road) and Turned Right

If you went the other way when you left Sugarlands Visitor Center, you'll be on a road that goes south and uphill for the next 16 miles, after which it goes downhill for another 17. Newfound Gap Road has lots of curves that some might call dangerous, so be careful. It's a good road; it's just not straight or level. As a matter of information, this the highest thoroughfare in the eastern United States. It's also usually self-governing because the volume of traffic makes it hard to drive too fast.

You'll find pull-offs for several short nature trails called quiet walkways on Newfound Gap Road. They're usually no more than a quarter mile into the woods, and they're a nice opportunity to stretch your legs.

The first landmark on the right is the Chimneys picnic area about 5 miles from the Sugarlands Visitor Center. Situated along a particularly noisy and rocky stretch of the West Prong of the Little Pigeon River about 2 miles below its source, Chimneys is a big local favorite, and daylong parties are commonplace at this picnic area. If you happen to see a bear here, don't reward the bear for aggressive behavior. Scream, yell, wave your arms, and run it off. The bear will leave if you're very clear that it's not welcome.

Continuing up (literally) Newfound Gap Road, the over-and-under loop is a creative approach to road building in an area not designed for such things. To avoid tunneling through the mountain, the CCC road builders constructed a 360-degree loop where the road travels up the mountainside in a constant spiral and passes over itself, all in less than half a mile.

A few miles farther on, the popular Alum Cave trailhead is on the left (along with its large parking lot). The Alum Cave trail runs about 5 miles to LeConte Lodge, where it meets the Boulevard Trail, which leads to the Appalachian Trail (a wonderful way to travel from Maine to Georgia if you really enjoy hiking). Many dedicated hikers walk the Appalachian Trail in several stages over a period of time, and hundreds will take it on as a summerlong project.

Alum Cave is one of the more popular trails in the park in its own right and leads to rock overhangs where the Confederate army supposedly mined alum to make gunpowder during the Civil War. The hike has a 1,400-foot elevation gain and is moderately strenuous, but if you start early and take it slow, it's not that bad. If you're headed for LeConte Lodge (see the Close-up in this section), you can leave your vehicle at the Alum Cave lot, but be sure not to leave any valuables. Be sure you're wearing good, strong hiking-style shoes and that you bring along appropriate survival equipment (water, a first-aid kit, food, rain gear—check with the rangers for details).

Driving a few more miles on Newfound Gap Road will bring you to Morton Overlook on the right. This is one of the more popular scenic stops, providing a panoramic view of totally unspoiled wilderness. It's worth a few minutes. Panhandling bears frequent this area in the late afternoon.

i **In cold-weather seasons, be particularly careful to avoid hypothermia, the potentially fatal lowering of the body's core temperature. Hypothermia happens even in the summer, especially when you don't have dry clothing to change into if you get wet in a cold stream or a sudden rainstorm.**

Newfound Gap (elevation is 5,048 feet) is the next stop, after a couple of miles of extreme turns on a fairly steep grade. Here, a tablet marks the spot where President Franklin Roosevelt dedicated the park to the American people in 1940. The parking area has been enlarged and improved in the time since FDR was there, but the view you're seeing is exactly what he saw in 1940.

Proceeding south, the Tennessee–North Carolina border and Clingmans Dome Road come up almost simultaneously. Clingmans Dome Road goes off to the right and leads to the Clingmans Dome observation tower 7 miles away. The tower, about a half mile up a strenuous trail from the parking lot, is reputed to be, at 6,643 feet, the highest point in Tennessee. Some people will present a persuasive argument (like any accurate map) that Clingmans Dome is in North Carolina, but the park service and the two states say otherwise.

Clingmans Dome Road is "trailhead central," with five locations along the road and at the

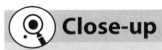 **Close-up**

LeConte Lodge

LeConte Lodge is a mountain retreat perched atop the third-highest peak in the entire Smokies range. At 6,500 feet above sea level and 1 vertical mile above Gatlinburg, it's is an overnight haven for the ambitious hiker in search of a satisfying meal, rustic accommodations, good company, and unparalleled views.

For those wary of long, strenuous hikes, this journey may not be your cup of tea. There's only one means of getting to the top of Mount LeConte, and that's by foot. Five hiking trails lead to the lodge from different starting points in the national park. They range in length from the Alum Cave Trail (4.9 miles each way) starting on Newfound Gap Road to the Trillium Gap Trail (17.8 miles each way), accessible from Cherokee Orchard Road/Roaring Fork Motor Nature Trail near downtown Gatlinburg.

LeConte Lodge, the highest-elevation guest lodge in the eastern United States, was built in 1924 and today serves up to 60 guests nightly between late March and late-November. Advance reservations are required and should be made about a year prior to visiting (call 865-429-5704 or visit www.lecontelodge.com for information).

Don't expect luxury. The cabins have no electricity, telephone service, or running water. Light is provided by kerosene lamp, and heat by stove. The lodge has flush toilets, but they're in a separate building, and you won't find any showers. Because there is no road to the top of the mountain, supplies are airlifted up to the retreat each spring. During the rest of the season, llamas bring up fresh supplies, including food and clean linens, three times a week. The native South American beasts ferry dirty linens and garbage on their trips down.

The outpost is laid out like a compact little village, a collective of primitive cabins anchored by an office, a dining hall, and common bathrooms. There are seven one-room cabins with bunk beds that sleep four to five people each, as well as three group cabins with either two or three bedrooms and a shared living room. Scattered about the grounds are picnic tables and old-fashioned water pumps for drinking, hand washing, or tooth brushing.

Guests get dinner and breakfast (and lunch in between if they're staying more than one night). Dinner is usually a traditional "meat and potatoes" affair with soup, roast beef, mashed potatoes, green beans, corn bread, canned peaches, baked apples, and chocolate chip cookies. Wine is served with dinner for an additional fee. Breakfast consists of eggs, Canadian bacon, hotcakes, grits, biscuits, hot chocolate, and coffee.

Between meals, overnighters are on their own as far as keeping themselves entertained. In colder weather many huddle in the warmth of their cabins, passing the time by reading, making music, playing games, or engaging in pleasant conversation with new friends. On temperate days you're more likely to find guests outside enjoying the views of surrounding mountain peaks or Gatlinburg in the valley far below.

The lodge itself doesn't really provide the best views from LeConte. For that, you can either hike a half mile to Myrtle Point, an excellent spot to view sunrises, or you can climb two-tenths of a mile to Cliff Top, which has a 180-degree western exposure for remarkable sunsets.

overlook parking lot. The trails along this road are rated from medium to strenuous, and all are long and mostly downhill from the road, which means you'll be coming uphill to get back. The Spruce-Fir Nature Trail, about midway between Newfound Gap and the Dome, is a short, nearly level walk through a high-elevation forest. It's the only one of the five on this stretch that's recommended for nonserious hikers.

Back to Newfound Gap: The road you've followed up out of Gatlinburg for what seems to be a lot longer than 16 miles is now over the top, and if you continue to follow it, you're going to descend steadily for about 17 miles to the Ocon-aluftee Visitor Center at the south end of the park. Along the way you'll have several opportunities to pull over and enjoy the scenery, which is little different than north of the gap. The Smokemont Campground on the left as you descend is a few miles short of Oconaluftee, and Mingus Mill is just ahead on the right. At the end of a short walking trail, Mingus Mill is a working gristmill, grinding corn into meal with an enclosed water turbine.

One more mile takes you into the Mountain Farm Museum (a collection of historic structures moved here from elsewhere in the park) at the Oconaluftee Visitor Center. This is a real-life exhibit of how the settlers of Appalachia lived in times past, and it's worth your time to check it out. Dead ahead is Cherokee, North Carolina. It's covered in detail in the Getting Out of Town chapter.

It probably would be a good idea to head back toward Gatlinburg in time to be off New-found Gap Road in daylight. In the summer this would mean leaving Cherokee by 6 p.m. and leaving Newfound Gap no later than 7 p.m. If those curves just short of Newfound Gap impressed you coming up, they're even more impressive going down in daylight. Going down after dark? Make up your own adjectives.

This section has covered the two most popular excursions in Great Smoky Mountains National Park, and each of them will pretty well use up a day because of the distances they cover. Also, because you know where they are, you might choose to devote some more time to picnicking at Metcalf Bottoms or Chimneys, or to a tubing

i To help you plan your day a little better, here's a mileage chart of distances from the Sugarlands Visitor Center to some of the more popular destinations: Chimneys picnic area: 5 miles; Newfound Gap: 16 miles; Clingmans Dome: 23 miles; Cherokee, North Carolina: 34 miles; Elk-mont picnic area: 7 miles; Metcalf Bottoms picnic area: 12 miles; Cades Cove: 27 miles.

excursion with an extended visit to contemplate the wonder of the dreaded Sinks.

The next section covers a couple of lesser-known but wonderfully satisfying side trips that afford a deep-in-the-woods experience without ever getting more than a few miles from civilization.

The Cherokee Orchard–Roaring Fork Motor Nature Trail

The trip described here is tailor-made for those who feel obligated to see the park because they're here anyway, and it just happens to be one of the most beautiful ways you'll ever spend a couple of carefree hours. The Chero-kee Orchard–Roaring Fork Motor Nature Trail is another locals' favorite. This is a one-way drive on the northern slope of Mount LeConte, and you leave downtown Gatlinburg to start it. The Motor Nature Trail (local parlance) is about 10 miles long from start to finish, and you can make it in an hour or you can choose to spend a day. Most non-hikers spend up to three to four hours on the Motor Nature Trail, including a stop somewhere along the way for a picnic lunch, if you're so inclined (and prepared).

For starters, you want to be on Historic Nature Trail heading out of downtown Gatlinburg. You can get there by going through town to traffic light #8. Just stay on Historic Nature Trail past Mynatt Park (another nice picnic site with charcoal grills—see the Parks and Recreation chapter) and into the woods. About a mile up is the Noah Ogle Homestead, the first of several homesites the park service has preserved along the trail. Take a few minutes and tour this farm and mill settled by the son of Martha Jane Huskey Ogle, Gatlinburg's first white settler. A pamphlet you can pick up at the start of the nature trail explains what you'll see.

Continuing away from town, you'll see a turnout or two if you're interested (they're trail-heads for the Rainbow Falls and Bull Head trails—serious stuff) and maybe some wildlife. You might notice that the trees on the left are in more orderly rows than usual; that's the remnant of Cherokee Orchard, one of the last settled areas of the park.

Approaching the Roaring Fork Motor Nature Trail, you'll see that the road you're on continues. It loops around the orchard and returns to Gatlinburg. You want to turn right onto the Motor Nature Trail (it's clearly marked), and it's highly recommended that you buy the self-guiding brochure at the entrance. If you're not already sold on the value of these little pamphlets, this one should do the trick. It's $1 on the honor system. Let the pamphlet be your guide around the Motor Nature Trail, along with a small amount of advice to follow.

Pine Tops, an early landmark, offers an interesting view of Gatlinburg and a nice picnic site. It's also known as a hangout for hungry bears, so be vigilant. If a bear joins your picnic, excuse yourself, take your food, and go sit in your car until the bear leaves. You're on its turf, and the bear is neither a gracious host nor a grateful guest. Because they're so used to having people around, bears in the Smokies don't always fear people the way they should. Don't, under any circumstances, try to pet or feed a bear.

Regardless of how cute you find them, these are wild animals that should be treated with respect and given a wide berth whenever you encounter them. Be especially cautious if you see a mother bear and a cub; the mothers are terribly protective and won't think twice about attacking if they feel their youngsters are threatened.

Heavy traffic could slow you down at the Trillium Gap Trail parking lot. Unless you want to hike to Grotto Falls on the Trillium Gap Trail (moderate to difficult, 2.8 miles), get through this area as quickly as possible. This is the point where you stop going up and start going down.

You'll find a couple of neat things at the turn-off by the old cemetery, a short distance from the Trillium Gap Trail parking lot. First, across the road is a good-size confluence of three streams. A short scramble down the bank (stay on the path for better traction) will give you a view of some real busy water at a decibel level you won't believe.

Back across the road, if you take the path past the cemetery (very short), take your camera; there's a meadow where the sight of young animals playing is fairly common. This isn't well known or publicized—if you're treated to a Bambi moment, enjoy it and kind of keep it to yourself. And you're welcome. Shortly after the cemetery, the Baskins Creek Bridle Trail crosses the road. Be alert for riders on horseback—they have the right-of-way.

The Ephraim Bales place is very popular among picnickers. It's the largest open space on the trail and has a great stream with large rocks you can relax on. The Bales place is also a fascinating look at how the original settlers lived. The living quarters will make you wonder how the high birthrate in the mountains was possible. You should stop here for a few minutes to let your brakes cool.

Now you're really going downhill. You're also going to encounter a few fairly sharp turns and a narrow bridge or two. Stay alert. As you near the end of the trail, the Reagan tub mill and farmhouse is an interesting departure from the rest of the architecture in the park—the house was ordered precut from a Sears catalog. The last stop on the trail is the Place of a Thousand Drips, and it's worth a look (unless there's been a particularly long dry spell); it's not often you see a waterfall coming right down on the road.

When you exit the Motor Nature Trail, you'll be on Roaring Fork Road. A short drive through a residential/condo neighborhood will bring you to traffic light #1A at East Parkway (U.S. Highway 321). Turn left to go back to downtown Gatlinburg. The Parkway and traffic light #3 is less than a mile away.

i **To help alleviate the air pollution that threatens its very existence, Great Smoky Mountains National Park has begun using Green Power, a TVA electrical-use plan that generates electricity without the use of fossil fuels, and has acquired an electric-powered pickup truck for use inside the park.**

Greenbrier

There's one more picnic/wildlife area that's nice to visit because of its isolation, and that's the Greenbrier picnic area about 5 miles east of Gatlinburg on East Parkway (US 321). The road goes off US 321 to the right and runs along the Little Pigeon River, another usually busy stretch of water. After you've passed Buckhorn Road at the bottom of the long, steep grade on US 321, look for the Greenbrier sign about a mile farther on. If you miss it, you'll cross the river immediately. Just turn around and go back.

The Greenbrier road is about 5 miles long, quite narrow, and mostly unpaved. Since it runs alongside the river, the number of parked cars can make it practically a one-way road at some points. As a matter of local custom, the cars coming out have the right of way. Be alert for pedestrians and bicyclists.

At several points along the road, small parking areas have been carved out of the woods for people to get out and walk down to the river.

The Middle Prong is moderately deep and fairly wide with a strong current, and it's a favorite swimming site because of the large rocks that serve as jumping and sunbathing platforms (although the park service discourages jumping and diving). Tubing is also popular here. The river turns away from the road about 5 miles in from the highway, providing a beautiful picnic area with tables, charcoal pits, and restrooms. Another great local favorite because of its accessibility and privacy, the Greenbrier picnic ground is also popular with deer, who will roam through without paying much attention to the human population, as long as said population returns the favor.

About a mile past the picnic grounds, a bridge across the river leads to the Ramsey Cascades Trail (not for novices). The remnants of several residence fence lines are visible in the area around the parking lot. Greenbrier Cove was once a bustling community, populated mostly by Whaleys, and a few of them are still around.

Beyond the bridge, there's a picnic pavilion with tables and a concrete floor—a really nice spot for family or small-group gatherings. The road ends in a loop at the trailhead for the Porter's Creek Trail, an easy 2-mile walk beside a stream with a lot of pretty cascades. There's an original cantilever barn at the end of the trail. The cantilever barn is an architectural style that's disappearing quickly. This barn, and one in Cades Cove that the park service built in the 1960s, may soon be the only ones left in the area.

Greenbrier is there because the Greenbrier Cove settlers created the road before the park was established, and it made sense to keep it open without a lot of preservation or construction necessary. Although overuse has the potential to easily destroy the natural beauty here, it hasn't done so yet and probably won't as long as the public continues to obey the park maxim, "Take nothing but pictures; leave nothing but footprints."

> **i** In case of unsafe driving conditions (usually due to snow and ice or occasionally other events such as a rock or mud slide), the rangers close certain roads. Call (865) 436-1200 for an automated road condition report and a very detailed weather forecast (including sunrise and sunset times) that's updated daily by rangers.

A-CAMPING WE WILL GO

According to figures developed by the park's public affairs office, less than 10 percent of the nine million people who visit Great Smoky Mountains National Park every year ever get off the pavement. That means that more than 795 square miles of backcountry are seldom seen and never felt. This is good news to the park service folks, who are trying to keep the wilderness serene, and it's even better news to those visitors who come here seeking solitude and oneness with nature.

If you want to enjoy nature up close and personal, you can choose two ways to "rough it" in Great Smoky Mountains National Park. You can stay in a developed campground in your RV, trailer, or tent, like civilized campers. Or you can go out into the wild and live like Tarzan. Both choices are easy on the pocketbook, especially the Tarzan route—it's free. And both are described below, starting with the developed campgrounds.

The Campgrounds and RV Parks chapter describes four developed park campgrounds that are close enough to the Smokies Corridor to be considered part of it. Listed here are the remaining six, four of which are in North Carolina. The two Tennessee sites are listed first, followed by the North Carolina campgrounds listed from east to west. But be warned: Even the closest of these six is more than 50 miles from Gatlinburg. None of the campgrounds listed in this section take reservations. They're all available on a first-come-first-served basis. For more information and a complete list of national park campgrounds, visit the park's Web site at www.nps.gov/grsm and follow the links for camping.

Tennessee
LOOK ROCK CAMPGROUND
Foothills Parkway
The Foothills Parkway runs outside of the western border of Great Smoky Mountains National Park; the section where Look Rock Campground is located is accessible only off TN 73, about 10 miles west of Townsend. At an elevation of 2,600 feet, the Look Rock Campground is the highest in the Tennessee side of the park. Look Rock is open mid-May to October 31 and has 68 sites. Site rental is $14, and RV length is not limited.

ABRAMS CREEK CAMPGROUND
Happy Valley Road, somewhere in east Tennessee
Remember the old line, "You can't get there from here?" Well, here it is. Abrams Creek Campground is on the extreme western edge of Great Smoky Mountains National Park, convenient to nowhere and accessible only by taking Happy Valley Road off U.S. Highway 129, some 30 miles south of Maryville, which is about 15 miles west of Townsend. The campground is open from mid-March to October 31 and has 16 campsites. Site rental is $14 per night, and RV length is restricted to 12 feet.

North Carolina
BIG CREEK CAMPGROUND
Waterville
The Big Creek area is about 6 miles south of exit 451 on Interstate 40, right at the Tennessee–North Carolina border. The campground is in a valley surrounded by woods. No RVs are allowed in this 12-site enclave, which is open from mid-March to October 31. Campsite rental is $14 a night.

CATALOOCHEE CAMPGROUND
Way deep in the woods and way up in the mountains, Cataloochee Campground really requires a map to find. The Great Smoky Mountains Trail Map ($1 at any visitor center) will show the unnamed roads that lead to the campground at location D-11. Cataloochee is 2,610 feet up in the mountains, with 27 available campsites. Open from mid-March to October 31, campsites at Cataloochee are $17. RV length is restricted to 31 feet.

BALSAM MOUNTAIN CAMPGROUND
If you like the idea of going to Cataloochee, you'll love Balsam Mountain. This campground, at 5,310 feet in elevation, is the highest campground accessible to vehicles in the park. The 46 campsites are open from mid-May to mid-October, and RV length is restricted to 30 feet. Campsite rental is $14 a night. To get there, take the Blue Ridge Parkway north from Newfound Gap Road (US 441) about 12 miles to Heintooga Ridge Road on the left. Don't worry about missing Heintooga Ridge Road—it's the first road you'll come to. Turn left and follow the road into Balsam Mountain, about 8 miles.

DEEP CREEK CAMPGROUND
This one's also pretty remote from the Tennessee side, but it's convenient to the Fontana resort area. The best way to get there is off U.S. Highway 19, about 3 miles east of Bryson City or 20 miles west of Cherokee. Deep Creek has 92 campsites, many of which are for tent camping only. The campground is open from early April until Octo-

ber 31 and has a 26-foot trailer length limit. All campsites are $17 a night.

ℹ️ Because of highly destructive insects that are threatening much of the woodland in the Smokies, the U.S. Department of Agriculture has quarantined firewood from the states of Michigan, Illinois, Indiana, Maryland, Missouri, Ohio, Pennsylvania, Virginia, West Virginia, Wisconsin, New Jersey, and New York. If you're driving to the Smokies from these states, leave your logs at home!

Camping au Naturel

It would be nice to say you're welcome to just go lose yourself in the forest for whatever time you'd like, but you can't. The park service is a branch of government after all, and although they have no problem with your wandering in the wilderness for an indefinite period, they want to know you're out there. They'd also like to know approximately where you are during your stay, so they're quite insistent that you register for a backcountry permit at any ranger station, campground, or visitor center. They're free—the only cost is the time it takes you to fill out the simple form.

All camping in the park requires planning. All shelters and the more accessible campsites are rationed due to space limitations. To stay at these sites, you will have to make reservations by calling the Backcountry Reservation Office at (865) 436-1231. On the other hand, you'll have to hike a greater distance to reach the 70-plus non-rationed sites. To start your planning, spend a buck for the Great Smoky Mountains Trail Map, which will identify all 88 of the backcountry campsites and all 16 of the trail shelters in the park. The map and any park personnel will answer all of your questions, but a few of the more important points are listed here just to give you an idea of what you're getting into.

1. It's strongly recommended that you stay on the trails at all times. There are 800 miles of these; that should be plenty.
2. Maximum party size is eight.
3. You can spend no more than three consecutive nights at a campsite and no more than one night in the same trail shelter.
4. You must stay each night in a designated site and follow your identified itinerary.
5. Horses are permitted in the park on marked trails, and horse parties may only stay at campsites designated for horse use on the map—50 such campsites are so designated, of which 9 are rationed.
6. All food for horses must be packed in—grazing is prohibited.
7. Horses are not permitted within 100 feet of trail shelters or in cooking areas of campsites.
8. When not being consumed or transported, all food and trash must be suspended at least 10 feet off the ground and at least 4 feet from any tree branch to keep it out of the reach of bears (all campsites have cable-and-pulley systems to facilitate pack suspension).
9. All plants, wildlife, and historic features are protected by law. Do not cut, carve, or deface any trees or shrubs.
10. Polluting park waters is prohibited—do not wash dishes or bathe with soap in any stream.
11. Firearms and hunting are prohibited.
12. Open fires are prohibited except at designated sites. Use only wood that is dead and on the ground, and build fires only in established fire rings.
13. Toilet use must be at least 100 feet from a campsite or water source and out of sight of the trail. Human feces must be buried in a six-inch-deep hole.
14. All trash must be carried out.
15. Pets, motorized vehicles, and bicycles are not permitted in the backcountry.

Anyone arrested by park rangers for violation of any rule is subject to trial in a federal court. The maximum fine for the conviction of any misdemeanor is $5,000 and/or six months in jail for each violation.

i Leave as small a footprint as you can. This area will remain virginal as long as everybody makes an effort to remove all traces of human presence in Great Smoky Mountains National Park.

TAKE A HIKE!

Several of the more convenient hiking trails in the park have been described at the points where they begin, with brief descriptions concerning length and degree of difficulty. Stick to these trails and the quiet walkways that the park service has provided. Most of the 800 miles that cross the park like a giant spiderweb are intended to connect primitive campgrounds and trail shelters so any hiker can see the park without having to strike into uncharted forest.

It's difficult to argue with the folks who believe the park should be a deeply tactile experience and can only be truly appreciated if you go out and get semi-lost in it, but the fact is that the park is there for what you want it to be. If that involves walking around in it, wonderful. If not, that's okay, too. But if you do plan to hike anywhere in the park beyond a short stroll, talk to the park service people at the Sugarlands, Cades Cove, or Oconaluftee Visitor Centers, and get whatever literature you can to make your hiking experience safe and memorable. In addition to the invaluable Great Smoky Mountains Trail Map, you can also choose from a huge selection of books on the subject by park service and civilian experts.

PARKS AND RECREATION

Whether you live here or just visit, you'll surely find that the area's trademark backdrop of mountains, woodlands, and waters make the Smokies a natural when it comes to outdoor recreation. This chapter covers what outdoor and indoor recreational opportunities various city governments have provided as well. The chapter starts out with a profile of Douglas Dam Park in northern Sevier County. Following that are sections on the facilities and recreational programs offered by each of Sevier County's three primary cities—including information on fishing.

Of course, the biggest park in town—Great Smoky Mountains National Park—is such an exhaustive subject in its own right that it has its own chapter. Outfitters who take you horseback riding, white-water rafting, tubing, and llama trekking are covered in the Active Outdoor Adventures chapter. And golf is, appropriately enough, in the Golf chapter.

DOUGLAS DAM PARK
Tennessee Highway 338 or
Tennessee Highway 139

In 1942 the Tennessee Valley Authority (TVA) constructed Douglas Dam on the French Broad River, primarily to help provide the surrounding area with much-needed electricity. The man-made reservoir that resulted was appropriately named Douglas Lake, a great spot for outdoor recreation, as is the developed area surrounding the dam itself. Visitors can access both the waters above and below the dam at little to no cost, enjoying gorgeous summertime views and a variety of warm-weather activities like fishing, boating, swimming, and camping.

From Tennessee Highway 66 (Winfield Dunn Parkway) you can access the area via TN 139, although the more logical and direct approach is to go east on TN 338 (both routes are known as Douglas Dam Road—see the Getting Here, Getting Around chapter for clarification). No matter which route you choose, you'll encounter small markets along the way that sell food as well as fishing and camping supplies. If you haven't already stocked up before leaving on your outing, these convenience stores might be your last best chance for provisions. Once you get into the TVA area, the pickings are slim (more on that below).

On arriving at the park, you'll see signs that will give you a choice of heading toward the "headwaters" or the "tailwaters." Headwaters are the lake waters above the dam, and tailwaters refer to the continuing French Broad River below the dam. The descriptions here will begin with the headwaters. (Please note: As you near this area, you'll find Mountain Cove Marina and RV Park, a commercial operation that is not at all affiliated with TVA. Mountain Cove offers gasoline and permanent boat docking and is described fully in the Campgrounds and RV Parks chapter.)

The TVA headwater facilities include a free boat-launch ramp, restrooms, picnic areas, and a designated swimming area, complete with sand. The best time to swim there is during the peak summer months, when lake levels are at their highest. Regardless of the time of year, however, you swim at your own risk—there are no lifeguards on duty.

Most of the headwaters area is devoted to camping spots, some of which include RV hookups. Primitive camping is allowed as well. Most sites include a parking spot, picnic table, and a barbecue grill. Nightly rates are $24 with full hookups, $20 with just water and electric, or $16 with no hookups. Payments are deposited on the premises on the honor system. For more information on amenities and payment procedures at Douglas Dam Park, see the Campgrounds and RV Parks chapter.

Once you get out onto the lake itself, you've got 30,600 acres of water before you, not to mention 550 miles of shoreline. The waters are ideal for boating, waterskiing, or using various personal watercraft. For the safety of yourself and your fellow boaters, please be sure to observe all TVA water regulations, which are posted at the boat launch.

If you choose to go to the tailwaters area on the other side of the dam, you'll be faced with a few more forks in the road and more well-signed destination choices as you approach. Just above the tailwaters you'll find two overlook areas, both of which provide stunning views of Douglas Dam itself (in case you're curious, it's 705 feet long and 202 feet high). The upper overlook has restrooms, free picnic sites, and a covered picnic pavilion, which can be reserved for $50 a day by calling (866) 494-7186.

A campground and a boat launch are located farther below, right on the French Broad River. As with the headwaters area, use of the ramp is free, and the same rules and regulations apply to the campground (see the Campgrounds and RV Parks chapter). As you near the ramp and the camping area, you'll see Douglas Canteen (865-453-9683), a small store where you can purchase a fishing license, bait, and snacks. The store's selection is fairly narrow, but it will do in a pinch. For more details on requirements for purchasing a Tennessee fishing license, refer to the Gatlinburg section of this chapter.

i **Douglas Lake makes for great fishing. The best time to drop lines in either the headwaters or tailwaters is in spring. Depending on your bait, you're likely to do better in the river than in the lake. The main thing you'll need to watch out for is the surge in waters that occurs when the dam's generators are running.**

SEVIERVILLE

One of the best things about living in or even visiting Sevierville is the number of programs offered through the city's department of parks and recreation. What's even better is that much of what's available is either free or very reasonably priced, and it's accessible to anyone, even vacationers. Most of these activities have two centralized locations, the Sevierville Community Center, which opened in 1982, and Sevierville City Park, established in 1974. To reach either by phone, call (865) 453-5441.

SEVIERVILLE COMMUNITY CENTER
200 Gary R. Wade Boulevard, Sevierville

Conveniently located near downtown, just 1 block off Dolly Parton Parkway, the community center provides many diverse forms of recreation, mostly in a climate-controlled, indoor environment (outside, there are walking/ jogging trails and a playground for the kids).

The center is open seven days a week year-round except for the months of June, July, and August, when it's closed on Sunday. Normal hours of operation are 6 a.m. to 9 p.m. Monday through Friday, 9 a.m. to 4 p.m. on Saturday, and 1 to 6 p.m. on Sunday (September through May). While it wouldn't be practical to completely cover all of the center's specific schedules and fees here, the description below provides you with a good starting point.

One of the center's more popular offerings is the 25-meter, six-lane swimming pool. Open year-round, the pool's daily schedule is generally divided between lap swimming, exercise classes, and open swimming (just for fun). A certified lifeguard is always on duty. Several instructional programs are available, including swimming lessons and water exercise classes. They'll even teach you how to be a water safety instructor or a lifeguard.

The base fees for pool access are $2.50 for adults, $2.00 for children, and $1.25 for spectators. Booklets of 25 tickets as well as four-month and yearly passes are available at discounted prices. Group rates are available for birthday parties and other private groups, but reservations must be made in advance. At all times, children 10 and younger must be accompanied by someone age 18 or older, and normal pool schedules are subject to change due to swim meets.

The gymnasium can be used as a full-size basketball court or divided into two volleyball courts. If you want to just show up and shoot hoops with whoever else happens to be there, the charge is $3, but the cost to rent part or all of the space for either basketball or volleyball costs $25 per hour or more. The two racquetball/wallyball courts on the premises cost $3 per person per hour before 4 p.m. After 4 p.m. and on weekends, the rates are $4.50. With all of the above sports, you can bring your own stuff or rent balls and other equipment from the office.

Adult leagues include three-on-three basketball, volleyball, wallyball, and racquetball. Most of these leagues play in fall and winter, and registration fees can range from $42 per person to $125 per team.

The gymnasium is also a great place to get an aerobic workout. Instructors use step aerobics, interval aerobics, cardio kick-boxing, and body design programs (using hand weights) to work with anyone from beginner to advanced at both low- and high-impact levels. Classes are offered Monday through Thursday, generally in the early morning and/or late afternoon. Daily fees are $3.25 for adults and $3.00 for seniors. Twelve-class passes are available at a discounted price.

The fitness center includes multi-station weight machines, free weights, rowing machines, stair climbers, and stationary bikes to help you in your strength and/or cardiovascular training. If you're interested in combining both types of exercise, the center offers aerobic weight-training classes Monday through Thursday in the early morning.

Fees for regular use of the fitness center are $2.25 daily for adults and $1.75 daily for seniors. Discounted rates are offered for four-month and yearly passes. Aerobic weight-training classes cost $3.50 per individual class session or $46.00 for a three-month session.

The building's bowling center offers 10 air-conditioned lanes with state-of-the-art pin replacement and scorekeeping equipment. Operating hours are Monday through Saturday from 11:30 a.m. to 10 p.m., and Sunday from 1 to 6 p.m. (closed Sunday, June through August). Fees range from as low as $2.35 per game for kids' and seniors' open bowling before 5 p.m. to as high as $2.95 per game for open adult bowling after 5 p.m. The shoe rental fee is $2. On Friday and Saturday, the center offers Cosmic Bowling; when the lights go down, the music cranks up, and the pins glow in the dark! Cosmic bowling costs $9.95, and shoe rental is included in the fee. In addition to open play, the center hosts several monthly tournaments and bowling leagues; the latter generally run September through May.

If you have children, you'll appreciate the community center's many kid-oriented recreational programs. These programs are fun-filled, educational, and affordable and allow the kids to participate in activities like swimming, arts and crafts, games, and bowling. There is an ongoing after-school program as well as Christmas, spring break, and summer camps. Annual events include a kids' dog show.

SEVIERVILLE CITY PARK
1005 Park Road, Sevierville
Especially during the summer months, Sevierville City Park becomes a beehive of community activity. Softball teams go head-to-head out on the diamond, families hold reunions in the covered pavilions, and friends enjoying strolls around the walking trail.

The favorite park hangout from late May through Labor Day weekend is the outdoor pool and food concession area. Pool hours are Monday through Friday from 11 a.m. to 6 p.m., Saturday from 10 a.m. to 6 p.m., and Sunday from 1 to 6 p.m. The main pool is quite large, with shallow and deep waters as well as a diving area. Smaller wading pools accommodate younger children, and two certified lifeguards are on duty at all times. The main building houses showers and restrooms. Fees for swimming at the park are slightly higher than those for the community center pool. You can use the pool for private functions, but these events must be held after regular pool hours and by reservation only.

Outdoor playing surfaces include a four-goal basketball court, a regulation soccer field, two junior-size soccer fields, and eight tennis courts, four of which are lighted for night play. Four lighted baseball/softball fields are used for Little League programs as well as adult league play. Men's and women's softball leagues play during spring and summer, and a coed league goes into action in the fall. Entry fees are $375 and $235 per team, respectively.

One section of the park is located along the banks of the West Prong of the Little Pigeon River. This area is dominated by large shade trees and features a number of picnic tables and barbecue grills. Several covered picnic pavilions are on-site as well. The cost is $7.00 per hour for the first three hours and $3.50 per additional hour. Because demand for them is high (especially in summer), it's best to make reservations in advance through the parks department.

Circling the majority of the City Park complex is a half-mile-long walking/jogging trail. Near the west side of the park, you'll find an entrance to another trail, the Memorial River Trail Greenway. This 8-foot-wide path runs for 2 miles, starting at City Park and running alongside the West Prong of the Little Pigeon River. The trail, which crosses the Parkway and continues north to Main Street, is well landscaped and has plenty of lighting and park benches. There's also a gazebo looking out over the river.

i In addition to its main park, Sevierville operates several smaller neighborhood parks throughout the city, including the McMahan Addition and J. B. Waters–Love Addition parks and Northview Optimist Park in northern Sevier County.

PIGEON FORGE

PIGEON FORGE COMMUNITY CENTER
170 Community Center Drive Pigeon Forge
(865) 429-7373

When it comes to civic recreational facilities, Pigeon Forge now finds itself on more-than-equal footing with its fellow Sevier County cities. This 86,000-square-foot, $13-million complex opened in 2000, giving both locals and visitors access to year-round opportunities for fun and conditioning. The center is open weekdays from 6 a.m. to 9 p.m., Saturday from 8 a.m. to 6 p.m., and Sunday from 1 to 6 p.m.

The daily usage fee for the center is $5 per person plus tax ($6 if you are not a resident of Sevier County). Weekly passes ($20 plus tax) and monthly passes ($50 plus tax) are available. Annual memberships offer even more value and cost $50 plus tax for Pigeon Forge residents, $75 plus tax for those who work in Pigeon Forge but live outside the city, $100 plus tax for residents of Sevier County who don't live or work in Pigeon Forge, and $120 plus tax for nonresidents. Student, senior citizen, and family memberships offer even better savings and are set up under the same resident/worker/nonresident structure. These fees and memberships allow access to and use of most of the center's facilities, with two exceptions noted below.

On the first floor of the community center is a 10-lane bowling center, featuring state-of-the-art pin placement and scoring equipment. Just off the entrance to the bowling center are vending areas and a video arcade. New bowlers can take lessons, and everyone can get involved in league play. The center also hosts Cosmic Bowling nights on Friday and Saturday, featuring special music, lights, and late-night hours.

The bowling center operates on its own schedule, so call for particulars. The cost of bowling is not covered by standard usage or membership fees. Day rates range from $1.90 per game for members to $2.45 per game for nonmembers. Evening rates are 35 cents higher, and renting shoes will set you back $1.50 a pair. Cosmic Bowling costs $8.25 per two-hour session. The bowling center also has a pro shop.

The gymnasium occupies 22,000 square feet of the two-acre community center building. Curtains can be drawn to separate the three full basketball/volleyball courts or to subdivide one of the courts into two half-courts. Just off the main floor are two racquetball/handball courts.

The third major component of the ground floor is a six-lane, 25-yard indoor pool. The pool's schedule is divided throughout the week, with times slotted for lap swimming, open swimming, exercise classes, swim lessons, and swim meets. Although the indoor pool is open year-round, it's primarily used as an instructional facility during summer.

The outdoor pool, open generally from Memorial Day through mid-August when school starts, is identical to the indoor pool, except that it has a waterslide and diving board. Outside swimmers will also find a concession stand and shower facilities. This pool is not covered by community center fees.

Rounding out the first level are a dividable, multipurpose conference room that can accommodate 300, a food preparation area that serves the conference area, and a child-care center that takes potty-trained kids ages two through eight. If you are a member, child care is free. Otherwise, child-care rates are $2 per child per visit with a maximum of two hours per day.

The highlight of the community center's upper level is the Fort Sanders Fitness Center, filled with more than $100,000 worth of cardio and weight-training equipment. The center's staff is able to offer health and conditioning assessments, equipment orientation, personal training, and weight-loss programs. Fitness classes are taught in aerobics, indoor group cycling, kickboxing, yoga, senior exercise, circuit training, and group weight training. Classes cost $3 each or $32 for 16 classes.

The fitness center opens directly onto a walking/running track that circles the perimeter of the gymnasium at second-floor level. Nine circuits equal 1 mile. Administrative offices are also located on this floor.

i If you want to use any of the local fitness facilities, remember to bring along a picture ID. You'll need it to sign in as a guest and get a locker key.

The community center hosts a variety of general-interest classes for both adults and children. Adults can take art, crafts, and CPR/first aid. Kids can take cheerleading, tumbling, and dance. Most classes cost around $30 to $50 per month. Karate classes are also offered for both kids and adults, with a separate fee structure.

The center also has after-school sports camps for ages 6 to 11 as well as summer camp programs.

Currently, two city parks serve the folks of Pigeon Forge well with free, easily accessible facilities. For more information on both parks as well as any of the city's recreation and athletic programs, you can contact Pigeon Forge's Department of Parks and Recreation at (865) 429-7373.

PIGEON FORGE CITY PARK
2446 McGill Street, Pigeon Forge
This park is handily located just off Wears Valley Road, only a couple of blocks from the Parkway. The site features five lighted baseball/softball fields, two outdoor basketball courts, six lighted tennis courts, a lighted volleyball court, a horseshoe pit, and a playground. A 1.25-mile walking/jogging trail surrounds most of the area, and you'll also find two covered picnic pavilions here. Although there is no cost to use the pavilion, city officials do recommend making reservations since it is frequently in use.

PATRIOT PARK
Old Mill Avenue, Pigeon Forge
Patriot Park is located just 1 block off the Parkway in the heart of Pigeon Forge's Old Mill Community. And as the site of the city's main trolley office (see the Getting Here, Getting Around chapter) as well as many of its special events (see the Festivals and Annual Events chapter), the park is frequented by locals and vacationers alike.

At the southwest corner of the park, a charming gazebo has even been used for private wedding ceremonies. At the northwest corner is a covered picnic pavilion, which, like the one at the city park, can be used at no cost (again, reservations are encouraged). Surrounding the open field is a half-mile walking/jogging trail.

Before the city educational/recreational complex on Wears Valley Road was completed, this was Pigeon Forge's only public park, and it didn't have an official name. When the new city park opened in 1990, during the Persian Gulf War, Patriot Park was christened. On display in a glass enclosure near the park entrance is a Patriot missile (don't worry, it's unarmed) that's identical to the ones used by U.S. forces during the Persian Gulf War. The missile battery was donated by the Raytheon Corporation, the manufacturer of Patriot missiles. This is one of only four on display in the United States. Also on the premises, at the far east end of the grounds, is a 32-foot-high, 28-foot-wide replica of the Liberty Bell, constructed out of an aluminum frame with a shell made of woven metal lace. Both displays help play up the park's patriotic theme.

Patriot Park is the site of a number of city-sponsored special events held each year in Pigeon Forge. Among them are traditional holiday events like the annual Patriot Festival on the 4th of July and the city's official Winterfest Kickoff celebrations (as described in the Festivals and Annual Events chapter).

GATLINBURG

Long a leader in entertaining visitors, Gatlinburg takes excellent care of her own as well, with a wide variety of recreation programs designed to provide cradle-to-grave diversion for whatever interests may develop. Although these programs are designed primarily for local use, visitors can also get involved in most local activities.

One of the more interesting activities is the trout-fishing program, which allows game fishing right in the middle of town. You need three items to fish in Gatlinburg: a federal stamp, a state license, and a municipal permit. A special federal stamp is required for trout fishing in Tennessee. It costs $18 a year and can be purchased with a Tennessee fishing license.

The state fishing license availability chart looks like a train schedule, but the essence is

this: Any child under 13 can fish in Tennessee without a license. Adult licenses are based on resident and nonresident status—an annual fishing license costs $28 for a resident and includes hunting privileges, while a nonresident annual fishing license (no hunting allowed) is $81 ($41 without a trout license). A one-day fishing license is available to residents only for $5.50. Nonresidents may purchase a three-day fishing license for $33.50 (or $16.50 without trout privileges) or a 10-day license for $50.50 ($25.50 without a trout license). Tennessee or North Carolina fishing licenses are required to fish in Great Smoky Mountains National Park, and each is honored at all locations inside the park, regardless of which state you might be in at the time. Other licenses (handicapped, veterans, junior and seniors) can be purchased at Tennessee Wildlife Resources Agency field offices—call the East Tennessee Regional Office at (423) 587-7037 or (800) 332-0900 for details.

Finally, to fish inside city limits, you also need a special municipal permit, which can be purchased for $2.50 per day.

You can also buy a fishing license over the phone (with a credit card) by calling (888) 814-8972 or online by visiting www.tnwildlife.org.

The Gatlinburg Recreation Department raises trout from fingerling to adult size in feeding pens at Herbert Holt Park and releases them into the city's streams on a weekly schedule through the tourist season. The local trout program has a creel limit of five fish per day during the April through November catch-and-keep season, and possession of more than five fish at any one time is prohibited. From December through March, all fish caught must be released unharmed, and possession of trout during that season is prohibited. Fishing is permitted daily except Thursday (the day the streams are stocked) from a half hour before sunrise until 30 minutes after sunset.

A single rod and single hook are required year-round. There are no bait restrictions or minimum length requirements during the catch-

and-keep season, but artificial lures are required during the catch-and-release season. Two areas are designated as "children's streams," where only children 12 and under can fish, with a daily creel limit of two fish. The designated children's streams are Dudley Creek and the Little Pigeon River at Herbert Holt Park, and LeConte Creek in the Mynatt Park area. Local police are authorized to act as game wardens within the city limits.

This is a great way to teach a kid how to fish without ever leaving civilization, and the stocking program almost guarantees a good-size trophy sometime during the season. The two most popular adult fishing spots in the city are both on the West Prong of the Little Pigeon River, right in the middle of town. The area along River Road between near the national park's entrance and the bridge at Greystone Heights Road is easily accessible from the Riverwalk (see the Attractions chapter) and is usually well stocked. The stretch that runs parallel to the Parkway heading north from behind Applebee's restaurant to the bridge at traffic light #2 is a little more private, with motels and a few businesses hiding the river from the street traffic. Details of the program are available at city hall, the Gatlinburg welcome centers, or either Ace Hardware or Smoky Mountain Angler, both on East Parkway (U.S. Highway 321N) between downtown and city hall.

Gatlinburg operates three beautiful municipal parks, each with its own special attraction. All three have covered pavilions with picnic tables and cooking facilities, which are available for group use. If you're a Gatlinburg resident, there's no charge for your group; if your group is from out of town, you'll have to pay a nominal fee. Either way, make reservations by calling the Gatlinburg Recreation Department at (865) 436-4990.

HERBERT HOLT PARK
Pigeon River Road, Gatlinburg
This award-winning facility is on the site of the old sewer plant at the north end of the city and is only visible from The Spur. The road into the park is north of traffic light #1 (turn right coming toward town, left going out). Herbert Holt Park's

picnic pavilion has a huge barbecue grill for sheltered cooking. Picnic tables with individual cooking grills along the stream are convenient to the playground and horseshoe pits. You'll also find a short hiking trail above the restrooms.

The city's trout-rearing facility lies beside the pavilion at Herbert Holt Park in what used to be the sewage plant settling beds. Trout of various sizes are visible to the public, along with special provisions made to foil the flock of blue herons that moved into the park the day after the first trout fingerlings were brought in. This park is one of the two "children's only" fishing zones, and it recently also became one of the first places (if not the only place) in the state to have a fast-water handicap fishing pier. A concrete ramp gradually winds down the slope of the riverbank from the parking area to the pier, built right next to the river, enabling handicapped people to fish streamside.

MYNATT PARK
Asbury Lane, Gatlinburg
The biggest, oldest, and most complete municipal recreational site in the city, Mynatt Park is about 6 blocks from traffic light #8. An absolute jewel, Mynatt Park pretty much has it all, including picnic tables and charcoal grills in a shaded section alongside a busy stream, a large pavilion for group use (call 865-436-4990 for reservations), a lighted basketball court, six tennis courts, horseshoe pits, playground equipment at two sites, a baseball diamond, and plenty of open land. There's even a gazebo convenient to the pavilion that's become a popular spot for alfresco weddings. (This is also one of the two places in town with "children's only" fishing areas.) Mynatt Park is a great favorite with local residents, who turn out in force to walk their pets and watch Little League baseball. A word to the wise: The Mynatt Park pavilion is the most-requested facility in the city. If you're planning anything that includes this particular site, call as far in advance as possible.

MILLS PARK
Mills Park Road, Gatlinburg
Adjacent to the community center and Gatlinburg-Pittman High School, Mills Park is primarily an

athletic venue. Lighted softball and football fields are in almost constant use by high school and youth organizations, and the high school uses the quarter-mile track as its home oval. The only concession stand in the municipal park system is convenient to the football and softball fields and sits right in front of the new skateboard park. A new nine-hole disc golf course also runs throughout the park.

At the other end of the park, a pavilion with picnic tables is close to the playground and jogging trail. Mills Park Road runs off East Parkway (US 321N) about 5 miles from downtown. Two parking lots are convenient to whatever type of activity you've planned, and the high school and community center parking lots handle the overflow for large events like the Scottish Games each spring (see the Festivals and Annual Events chapter).

GATLINBURG COMMUNITY CENTER
Mills Park Road, Gatlinburg
(865) 436-4990
www.ci.gatlinburg.tn.us/parksrec/parks.htm
The Gatlinburg Community Center is a 50,000-plus-square-foot indoor facility that's jam-packed with things to do. To get there, take East Parkway (US 321N) about 5 miles from traffic light #3 in Gatlinburg to Mills Park Road. Turn left and go about a half mile until you see the big sign, and turn left again. The parking lot is at the top of the hill. Usage fees are moderate to dirt cheap, and the center is open seven days a week.

The community center's 25-yard swimming pool is available for open swimming any time there's not a swim meet or a group activity (adult lap swimming is allowed during afternoon and evening water exercise classes). Pool admission is $2.00 a session for those age 13 to 65 and $1.50 for both children 12 and younger and for seniors 65 and over. Frequent swimmers can buy extended-use passes to the pool—a pass good for 25 visits is $30.00 for adults and $22.50 for children and seniors. For the truly addicted aquaphile, an unlimited-use six-month pass is available at $72 and $54, respectively. Water exercise classes are conducted Monday, Wednesday, and

Friday from 11 a.m. to noon, and Tuesday and Thursday evenings from 6:30 to 8 p.m. The cost is 25 cents plus the pool admission fee. Certified lifeguards are on duty at all times that the pool is open. (All prices include tax.)

On the community center's second floor, a patio area with tables and chairs provides a bird's-eye view of the pool. Snacks and soft drinks are available at vending machines nearby. The multipurpose room next to the upstairs patio is big enough to accommodate a meeting of 300 people or can be divided for two smaller events. The hourly rental rate includes use of the fully equipped kitchen. The multipurpose room is the meeting place for the Gatlinburg Garden Club, the Gatlinburg Retired Citizens Club, and the Gatlinburg Community Chorale. It's also used for specialty classes that occur through the year in subjects as varied as line dancing and CPR/first aid.

The central hallway that runs the length of the building looks down into the racquetball courts. The double gymnasium has several basketball goals, including junior-height models. Equipment is free during open play, but some form of collateral is required (car keys and driver's licenses are the usual adult fare; kids can leave textbooks, wallets, etc.). During fall and winter, the gym is booked pretty solid on weekday evenings for adult basketball and volleyball leagues. Aerobex classes are conducted in the gym on Monday, Wednesday, and Friday mornings from 9 to 10 a.m. Daily admission to Aerobex is $3, a 12-ticket booklet is available for $25, and a yearly membership is $270.

The Tone Zone, an exercise area with weight machines, provides a complete fitness center with qualified supervision available for counseling. An orientation session is required on your first visit. Pick your price: Admission to the Tone Zone costs $4 a day, $10 a month, $50 for six months, or $100 for a whole a year. Seniors pay $3 a day or $7 per month.

Back downstairs, the four racquetball courts that line the central hallway are very popular with the locals and have spawned several champions at the local and regional level. Racquetball courts are rented on an hourly basis. An hour's use is $2.75 per person Monday through Friday before 5 p.m., and on evenings and weekends the rate is $3.75 per player. Racquets are available for rental at $1.25 per hour, and racquetballs are sold for $3.50 a can. A 15-hour racquetball card costs $34 and can be used in either prime or non-prime time. Wallyball, a singular twist on volleyball, is a popular game for groups. Rental of a racquetball court for wallyball is $8 an hour, including the net and ball.

Large locker and shower rooms have direct entry to the swimming pool. If you want a locker for storage while using the facilities, that'll set you back anywhere from 25 to 75 cents per day, depending on locker size. Long-term locker rental rates are also available.

The bowling center and game room are on the first floor, with separate entrances that also open to the rest of the building. The bowling center has eight synthetic lanes. Local leagues take up most of the lanes through the week from October through March, but open bowling is available every day and most weekend nights. Open bowling before 6 p.m. is $1.75 per game.

After 6, the price jumps to $2 for adults 19 to 65, while junior and senior citizen rates don't change. Shoe rental costs $1.25 a pair. Channel bumpers for kids that prevent gutter balls can be installed in the lanes for 50 cents extra per game. Open bowling discount cards provide 25 games at a 40 percent savings: The adult card is $30.00, and juniors and seniors can buy a discount card for $26.25. Specialty tournaments (moonlight bowling, no-tap, Scotch doubles, etc.) are conducted most Saturday nights during the bowling season. Cosmic bowling is offered on Friday nights from September through May from 8 to 10 p.m. at a cost of $4.50 per hour, including shoe rentals, for as many games as you care to play.

Adjacent to the bowling center and its refreshment area is the game room, containing two professional billiard tables, two world-class ping-pong tables, and an air hockey table. Thirty minutes of billiards costs $1. Ping-pong is free, but you need your own ball. They're available at the bowling counter for 25 cents if you don't have one with you. Air hockey costs 50 cents a game—first player to seven goals, or the leader after seven minutes of play, wins.

GOLF

Compared to other vacation spots in the South, like Myrtle Beach, South Carolina, or the Pinehurst area of North Carolina, the Smokies aren't huge as a golf destination. The landscape doesn't lend itself to multiple course layouts, and the mountain lifestyle that's been in place here since, well, forever, isn't one that leads to a lot of golf.

That doesn't mean, however, that you should leave your clubs at home. Four beautiful golf courses are spread about Sevier County, and all but one is within 5 miles of the Smokies Corridor. Two are municipally owned, and topflight course architects designed all four. Greens fees vary slightly from course to course, and most have in-season and off-season rate schedules—all rates quoted here are in-season. Because the local temperatures remain moderate through December, it's not unusual to see golfers out on most of the area courses year-round, but the idea of coming to the Smokies to play golf in January and February isn't really a good one.

Reserved tee times are recommended from spring through fall, and some form of golf/lodging packages are available at most courses. They're described here from north to south, starting with the newest.

EAGLES LANDING GOLF CLUB
1556 Old Knoxville Highway, Sevierville
(865) 429-4223
www.seviervilletn.org/DepartmentPages/Golf.htm

Laid out along Tennessee Highway 66 between Interstate 40 and Dolly Parton Parkway, Eagle's Landing opened in 1994. The course is owned by the City of Sevierville. *Golf Digest* gave this course three and a half stars—the only rated course in the county. From downtown Sevierville, go west on Dolly Parton Parkway (U.S. Highway 411/441) less than a mile from the TN 66 intersection to the next traffic light at Old Knoxville Highway. Turn right and go about 2 1/2 miles. You'll see the course on the right before you see the driveway. If you're somewhere on TN 66, go west on Boyd's Creek Road (Tennessee Highway 338—there's a traffic light) about 1.2 miles to Old Knoxville Highway and turn left. The course entrance is a little more than a mile on the left.

The course is essentially flat, wide open for now (that'll change as the trees planted along the fairways mature), and very forgiving. The par-72 layout runs from 6,900 yards at the championship tees to an almost pitch-and-putt 4,600 from the ladies' tees. Rough that isn't a real hazard borders wide Bermuda grass fairways. The Little Pigeon River wanders through the course, providing more scenery than anything else, but it can jump up and bite you if you're not paying attention.

Information on course layout approaches the overload stage, with five tee levels to shoot from. Pin placements are changed daily according to a zone diagram, and all pins are placed in the same zone every day. The scorecard shows the zoning for each green, and they'll tell you before you tee off which zones to shoot for.

Eagles Landing breaks the day into three parts, with fees sliding to match the time of day. Regular fees (opening until 2 p.m.) are $41 weekdays and $51 weekends. From 2 to 4 p.m., fees are $36 and $46, respectively, and the twilight rate of $26 kicks in at 4 p.m. every day. Carts are required, and all fees include carts.

Eagles Landing is a member course of the National Audubon Cooperative Sanctuary Program, a national organization dedicated to preserving wildlife on golf courses. Nonplay areas of the course are maintained as wildlife refuges, and sightings of deer, otters, beavers, several duck species, Canada geese, and even wild turkeys lend a grace note to playing the course. American bald eagles have been seen over the course as well. Eagles Landing has golf package tie-ins with several area lodging facilities; detailed information is available on the Internet. Advance tee times are recommended during the summer to avoid long waits once you arrive.

At press time, Eagles Landing was planning to add 18 more holes, making for 36 holes in all. Construction is expected to begin in the fall of 2009, and the new course should be ready for play in spring of 2010.

i **The Smokies is one of the few mountain communities in the United States where you can play golf year-round. It has been known to get a bit cold in the winter, but the courses remain open and the fairways are pretty uncrowded.**

RIVER ISLANDS GOLF CLUB
9610 Kodak Road, Kodak
(865) 933-0100
www.riverislandsgolf.com
River Islands is a spectacular golf course. Laid out alongside and in the middle of the French Broad River, this course is visually as pleasing as any course you'll play anywhere. Getting there requires a little more attention to the road than the other three area courses, but it's worth it.

Coming out of Sevierville on Winfield Dunn Parkway (TN 66), turn left at the traffic light at Tennessee Highway 139 (Kodak Road). It's the first traffic light after you cross the river on TN 66. Look for the blue and white signs. About 3 miles in on TN 139, look for the Northview fire hall on the right, and take the next left (it's a four-way stop). Less than a mile later, turn right at Kodak Road, and follow it about 3 miles to the course entrance on the left. You'll see most of the course before you get to the driveway.

River Islands is an Arthur Hill design. It's a classic links-style layout, with five holes distributed among three natural islands in the French

Broad River. Being laid out entirely along a river bottom, it's pretty level; it's also heavily forested. This course also has the interesting distinction of being located in two counties; from the tee at the par-3 third hole in Knox County, your drive crosses the river and the county line, (hopefully) coming down 175 yards later on the green in Sevier County. Tee layouts make River Islands whatever you want it to be: The forward tees neutralize the ever-present river, and the back tees will test your club selection skills. The fairways are a particularly lush Zoysia grass that feels almost spongy but sets a ball up nicely. Of the four courses, this is the one that can bring you to your knees the quickest and for the longest time. Played from the championship tees, River Islands is a test of every shot-making skill in the game. From the two intermediate tees, it's a constant challenge, and from the ladies' tees it's not really a pussycat but it's a lot drier.

Greens fees are $56, including cart and tax, from Monday through Thursday until 1 p.m. After then, it's $46. On Friday, Saturday and Sunday, greens fees are $60 until 1 p.m., when the cost goes up to $50. This is an arduous course despite its relative flatness, and carts and spikeless shoes are required. Due to its extreme popularity, River Islands requires reserved tee times during the tourist season.

GATLINBURG GOLF COURSE
520 Dollywood Lane, Pigeon Forge
(865) 453-3912, (800) 231-4128
www.golf.gatlinburg-tn.com
ci.gatlinburg.tn.us
The Gatlinburg Golf Course is the oldest and most mountainous of the bunch. It was established in 1955 in Pigeon Forge—because that's where the land was available. This course recently underwent a much-anticipated $2 million renovation, including both the clubhouse and the course itself, which was designed by noted golf course architect William Langford.

To get there, turn off the Parkway at traffic light #8 (the Dollywood light) in Pigeon Forge. You'll see the course on the right long before you get to the clubhouse driveway.

Gatlinburg is the only course of the four in the area that's landlocked, and the only water at all is two artificial lakes that play with your head on the 18th hole. The layout is about 6,300 yards and par 71 from the longest tees, and 4,710 yards and par 72 from the ladies' tees. It's like playing two completely different courses. The front nine is reasonably level and sandy, with three long par 5s. Fairways are broad, and most of them run downhill to the greens. Indian guides are no longer required on the back nine, but you may feel the urge to yodel from time to time. The 12th hole, aptly named "Sky Hi," is internationally known for its 200-foot drop from tee to green, making the 195-yard length look like a green-side chip shot. Play it long—there's nothing between the tee and the green but deep wilderness and the occasional cloud. There are very few sidehill lies on the back nine; most of the fairways look like canyons.

Gatlinburg is a lot of fun to play if you really enjoy variety. Just over 50 years old, the course lets its natural growth provide most of the challenge and scenery. Carts are required on this course, and you'll appreciate that fact after a round. From June through October, greens fees for 18 holes are $60 before noon, $50 from noon to 4 p.m., and $40 after 4 p.m. The rest of the year, fees range from $45 to $55. If you want to golf for just nine holes, the fee is $30 any time of the year. All prices include cart and tax, and you can now reserve your tee-time online. A hundred memberships are available at $1,200 a year for a family.

BENT CREEK GOLF VILLAGE
3919 East Parkway, Gatlinburg
(865) 436-3947, (800) 251-9336
www.bentcreekgolfcourse.com
The farthest course from the Smokies Corridor,

Bent Creek lies along the foot of Webb's Mountain about 10 miles east of Gatlinburg on U.S. Highway 321. A word of warning: Bent Creek is situated on a large resort property named Sunterra Resort. Don't be confused by the presence of signs bearing both names as you approach the course.

The course is a Gary Player design, running from a fairly flat front nine to a couple of mountain goat specials on the back. At 6,200 yards from the championship tees to 5,100 for the ladies', the course is medium length par 73, with generous fairways and forgiving rough. Most of the greens are moderately sloped with practically no bunkers in front. There's a lot of water on the course, but it only comes into serious play on a couple of holes. This is a very playable course for the intermediate golfer.

Regular greens fees are $49.50 from Sunday through Thursday and $57.50 on Friday and Saturday. Twilight fees, starting at 3 p.m., are $29.50 and $34.50, respectively. Tax and carts are included in all rates. The resort also offers several combination golf/lodging packages. Bent Creek's easy accessibility and long-term reputation make it a local favorite, and tee times are at a premium during the season.

The national move to spikeless or soft-spike golf shoes has finally made its way to the Smokies. Most of the courses in the area "strongly recommend" spikeless shoes—Gatlinburg Country Club and River Islands Golf Club require them. Don't be surprised if you're turned away for spiked shoes, especially when the greens have been dried by the summer sun.

WEDDINGS

How serious is the wedding business in the Smokies? More than 17,000 couples tie the knot here each year—more than any other destination in the United States except Las Vegas. As a possible spin-off of the area's reputation as a premier honeymoon and romantic getaway destination, the Smokies have become a favorite spot for both weddings and marriage renewals.

Not too many years ago, you could count the number of wedding chapels in the county on one hand; these days you need both hands—about four times. As the scenic backdrop of the Great Smoky Mountains became a natural honeymoon destination, the wedding chapel industry slowly took root. Some say that the chapels were meeting an already existing need. Others contend that the Smokies became the "Wedding Capital of the South" because of the proliferation of chapels. In actuality, there's probably a little bit of truth to both schools of thought.

Chapels range from rustic log structures to more elegant southern colonial or Victorian chapels, and most of them can provide you with everything you need (including ministers, music, flowers, videos, photos, limos, and even honeymoon suites)—everything, that is, but a mate. You're on your own for that!

THE PRELIMINARIES

Tennessee's fairly liberal marriage laws probably have a lot to do with the wedding boom. No blood test or waiting period is required, and a duly empowered official is as near as the telephone. First, you don't even have to be a Tennessee resident to get a license here, and if you're a Tennessean from outside Sevier County, chapels will honor a license you purchased in your home county, provided your ceremony takes place within 30 days of its issue.

If you can provide proof of age with a valid ID, you can get a marriage license at age 18 without parental consent, or at 16 with on-site parental consent. (That means all parents involved—if there's a single parent, the other parent's absence must be documented by a death certificate, custody agreement, or other proof and be presented with the license application.) In extreme circumstances, a court order can be requested for people as young as 14, with the same parental stipulations (for Sevier County residents only).

As for marriage license fees, that's where Tennessee has made it a little harder to say "I do"

these days. In an effort to lower the state's high divorce rate, the laws were changed to encourage couples to take advantage of premarital counseling.

The upshot is if you are both Tennessee residents, you'll pay $38.50 for a license in Sevier County, provided you and yours receive four hours of premarital counseling from an approved institution (church, family therapist, and so on). Otherwise, you'll pay $98.50 for the privilege of rushing blindly into matrimony. So far, the majority of couples seem to be skipping the advice and paying more money for the sake of convenience. If you're from out of state, however, none of this applies—you'll simply pay the $38.50.

You can get your **marriage license** from the Sevier County Court Clerk. The main office is at the courthouse in Sevierville (865-453-5502). Office hours are Monday through Thursday from 7:30 a.m. to 5:30 p.m. and Friday from 7:30 a.m. to 5 p.m. There are two branch offices as well. In Gatlinburg, go to the Shilling Center office building, about 2 blocks off the Parkway on Reagan Drive. The phone number is (865) 430-3404, and office hours are Monday and Friday from 8 a.m.

🔍 Close-up

Making a Career Out of "I Do"

One of the best-known ministers in the Smokies, Gatlinburg's Rev. Ed Taylor, retired in 2009 at 77 years old. The ordained Baptist minister affectionately known in these parts as "Reverend Ed" estimates that he's performed about 85,000 weddings during his long career, which spanned more than three decades. He's even married the likes of country singers Billy Ray Cyrus and Patty Loveless (although not to each other). He got to meet country star Tanya Tucker, too, who sang at a wedding he performed for one of Tucker's band members.

Rev. Ed was the first minister to make weddings here a big business. People from out of town already had the idea that the Smokies was a great place to get married (naturally), but when they got here, most of them had to say their "I dos" before a justice of the peace who held his ceremonies in a local farm supply store. Figuring that couples might prefer a wedding that didn't involve climbing over feed sacks, Rev. Ed began providing them with something a little more special—and the rest is history. At the time of his retirement, he owned four wedding chapels.

At last count, some 17,000 weddings were held annually in Sevier County (although that figure has gone as high as 21,136 in the year 2000), thanks in large part to the reverend's visionary abilities. Rev. Ed's famous Valentine's Day "marrythons" have hitched as many as 60 couples in 24 hours. He charged $120 and up for his 20-minute ceremonies, which were definitely not the "drive through" variety. Rev. Ed reminded couples of the sanctity of marriage during the ceremony and always presented his newlyweds with a copy of the New Testament at the close of their nuptials.

to 5 p.m., Wednesday from 8:00 a.m. to noon, and Saturday from 9 a.m. to 1 p.m. In Pigeon Forge, visit city hall on Pine Mountain Road (865-908-6613); this branch is open Saturday only from 9 a.m. to 5 p.m.

ℹ️ Sevier County is now the only county in the country where you can complete your paperwork for a marriage license online, and most people get their marriage licenses that way. To apply, go to www.marrymeintennessee.com and click first on the link for east Tennessee and then on the link for Sevier County on the bottom of the page.

GOIN' TO THE CHAPEL

The option of a chapel wedding can be attractive to prospective married couples for a number of reasons. For one, they are often less expensive than large church weddings, and they offer

unique alternatives to traditional nuptials, including multidenominational services and out-of-the-ordinary locations. They're also easier to plan in a short period of time—all of the elements of the event can be coordinated in a cooperative effort between the couple and the chapel's staff.

Admittedly, when one hears the term *wedding chapel*, images of the cheesy glitz of Las Vegas may come to mind. But the chapels listed here aren't the quickie-marriage type of operation where you'll be hitched in less than 10 minutes by an Elvis clone who hands out casino chips as a gift. Yes, you can get married in a relatively short period of time, but the chapels in this chapter are established, reputable businesses with tasteful, attractive facilities that use ordained ministers to perform legal ceremonies. (Just to be on the safe side, however, always ask about your minister's credentials, no matter where you choose to wed.) Although all the chapels listed here offer nondenominational, Protestant-based ceremonies, some are also willing to provide marriage rites in other religious faiths.

WHAT TO EXPECT FROM A CHAPEL

The listings here will present you with a fairly wide range in terms of price and available services. Just about every chapel offers its own preset wedding packages, and you'll also find those that are willing to work with you to put together whatever kinds of services and amenities that you'd like.

What you get boils down to how much you're willing to spend. You can get a basic, straightforward ceremony for as little as $60 in some places. On the other hand, you can still spend thousands of dollars, just like you would in a larger church wedding. In between the extremes is where you have to decide what you want out of your wedding—a simple exchange of vows in a chapel or a more elaborate ceremony in a unique setting like a gazebo, waterfall, or scenic garden. Some chapels can even arrange for you to be married on horseback or in a helicopter!

The chapels profiled here provide most of the traditional tokens that are associated with wedding ceremonies themselves. Depending on the specific package, your wedding can include music (live or recorded), flowers, a garter, a cake, candles, mints and nuts, a wedding album, and more. All of the wedding providers here can either directly supply or make arrangements with other businesses for related services like photography, videography, limo transportation, and honeymoon lodgings, as well as receptions and catering. In some instances, a chapel might offer wedding packages that include honeymoon vacation activities like horseback riding, snow skiing, whitewater rafting, or music-theater shows.

For payment, you'll find that most major credit cards and cash are accepted. If you are

i If you're planning a chapel wedding in the Smokies, consider making your wedding arrangements before making your honeymoon lodging reservations. You may get a better accommodations deal as part of your wedding package than if it had been purchased separately.

reserving a chapel for a specific date, you will likely have to post a deposit of some sort; the deposit may vary depending on the total price of the wedding and the length of time between reservation and wedding. In most cases, deposits can be paid with either credit card or cash.

Most chapels will take walk-ins, but whether they can take you on demand depends on whether the chapel has already been booked and whether a minister is available. If you drop by on a Saturday from May through October or in February, you're not likely to have much success. You'll probably have better luck with a walk-in wedding on a weekday morning in the off-season.

Finally, bear in mind that the addresses below are primarily for the companies' business offices. In some cases, the chapel itself is not located at that address, and you'll need to start your inquiry by either calling or stopping by the business office first. For this chapter, the listings are divided by city, and within each city, the listings are alphabetical.

SEVIERVILLE

SMOKY MOUNTAIN WEDDING CHAPEL
158 Court Avenue, Sevierville
(865) 428-4741, (800) 922-2052
www.smokymountainweddingchapels.com
Couples have been saying "I do" at this downtown Sevierville chapel for more than a decade. Because it's located across from the Sevier County Courthouse, you won't have much ground to cover between getting your marriage license and walking across the street to the chapel. The interior features an altar surrounded by white lattice, colorful flowers, and greenery. The facility accommodates up to 25 people.

Smoky Mountain Wedding Chapel can make arrangements for weddings in other locations. Previous ceremonies have taken place at sites like Cades Cove in the national park and the Old Mill in Pigeon Forge. In addition to the Sevierville chapel, this outfit also has wedding chapels in Pigeon Forge that operate under the same business name.

PIGEON FORGE

IN THE SMOKIES WEDDINGS
2036 Ridge Road, Pigeon Forge
(865) 429-1440, (800) 893-7274
www.smokyweddings.com
In the Smokies' Mountain Mist Chapel is located in a secluded country setting and features a heart-shaped candelabra with more than 70 candles. The chapel can handle up to 80 people. In the Smokies has been conducting weddings since the early 1990s. They have access to five church-ordained ministers and employ a staff of four wedding coordinators. They provide a number of different wedding packages, some of which include gazebo weddings, off-site receptions, and honeymoon accommodations.

ℹ Throwing rice is illegal in Tennessee. And birdseed (although it won't land you in jail) is often frowned upon for the same reason—because it can make surfaces slippery. Many wedding chapels forbid it. While transgressors are not likely to end up behind bars, they may well be charged an extra cleanup fee by the chapel—so think twice before tossing rice!

MOUNTAIN VALLEY WEDDING CHAPEL
2256 Parkway, Pigeon Forge
(865) 453-6343, (800) 729-4365
www.marryonamountain.com
A rustic cedar and glass exterior and classically decorated interior make for a charming juxtaposition of styles at this chapel. The hilltop location (they call it a mountaintop, but that's a bit of a stretch) offers some pretty decent views and creates a general feeling of seclusion; ceremonial settings include a gazebo and a waterfall. Inside, the tastefully decorated, candlelit chapel can handle up to 100 guests.

Mountain Valley's office is right on the Parkway in Pigeon Forge, but the chapel itself is just off Wears Valley Road—only a couple of miles off the Parkway. The chapel offers custom-tailored ceremonies, dependent on the couple's specific needs. Receptions, photography, and in-house videography are among the services provided.

GATLINBURG

CHALET MOUNTAIN WEDDING CHAPEL
890 Holly Branch Drive, Gatlinburg
(865) 430-5568, (888) 686-5683
www.chaletmountain.com
High on Mount Harrison, near Chalet Village, sits this sparkling white Victorian-style chapel. You'll find a predominance of white on the inside as well, along with wooden pews (seating 25 to 30), burgundy carpeting, and a 6-foot-tall stained-glass angel. Other settings include a gazebo and a 25-foot waterfall.

The chapel offers a full slate of wedding package amenities, including fully catered wedding receptions in the on-site banquet facility. The company also has a rental and realty office that offers approximately 60 chalets for honeymoon lodging.

CHAPEL AT THE PARK
1844 East Parkway, Gatlinburg
(865) 430-3372, (800) 693-6479
www.chapelatthepark.com
The chapel partially borders the national park on U.S. Highway 321. It's in a quiet, wooded setting, surrounded by native dogwoods and seasonal flowers. The building exudes elegance with a mountain theme.

Outside, the traditional Appalachian-style exterior features white wood, a green tin roof, bell tower, and lots of windows. Inside, 50 guests can be seated in a plush room that boasts a large chandelier and candlelit pews. Outdoor weddings in front of the gazebo or waterfall can accommodate up to 70 people. Other amenities include separate dressing rooms for the bride and the groom and a state-of-the-art, three-camera videotaping and editing system.

The business office is in a separate location. Owner and minister Lee Bennett prefers that physical separation between the main office and the chapel because it affords more privacy for the ceremonies themselves.No more than one wedding per hour is scheduled.

CHAPEL IN THE GLEN
412 Glades Road, Gatlinburg
(865) 436-5356, (800) 537-1505
www.chapelwedding.com
A beautiful hilltop in the Great Smoky Arts & Crafts Community is the setting for the Chapel in the Glen. The white pine chapel (complete with bell tower) and award-winning landscaping welcome couples into an interior decor replete with "woodsiness." A stacked-stone wall and candelabra highlight the altar, and the chapel seats 40 comfortably.

Outdoor ceremonial settings here include a gazebo, a reflecting pond, and a waterfall. Chapel in the Glen provides a full-time staff of six to help couples with wedding preparations. They do perform walk-in ceremonies. They will not, however, join couples who have just met and are looking for a speedy wedding.

ℹ One question to ask when you are looking for a wedding chapel is the size of its dressing room—if that's important to you. Some wedding chapel facilities offer more spacious changing facilities than others.

CUPID'S CHAPEL OF LOVE
706 East Parkway, Gatlinburg
(865) 430-3851, (800) 642-8743
www.cupidschapeloflove.com
Owner Rose Fisher opened her chapel in 1995, and in the years since she has built up her business to the point that she sometimes has bookings as far as two years ahead. That doesn't mean she's booked solid for the next two years, but it does mean that her available spots for walk-ins are few and far between.

The quaint chapel is built of whitewashed, hand-hewn logs. Inside, the pew cushions and carpeting are shades of burgundy, and the walls are lined with colorful stained-glass windows. Seating is available for up to 65 guests. Near the altar is a trellis with a climbing vine and magnolias. Outdoor settings include a bridge over a stone waterfall and a gazebo.

Cupid's Chapel offers several wedding packages, including the '50s Nostalgia package complete with oldies music. Some packages include lodging at Cupid's Love Nest, the chapel's own honeymoon accommodations. In addition to traditional, nondenominational ceremonies, Cupid's can also make arrangements to perform weddings of other religious faiths. They are open every day except Sunday.

GATLINBURG'S LITTLE LOG WEDDING CHAPEL
1350 East Parkway, Gatlinburg
(865) 436-8979, (800) 554-1451
www.logchapel.com
This new chapel that opened in April 2009 is located on Glades Road in the Great Smoky Arts & Crafts Community off East Parkway/US 321. As the name states, the building itself is of log construction and offers a combined decor of rustic log and refined elements like stained-glass windows, flowers, and candelabra. It accommodates 80 people. Little Log Wedding Chapel has been in business since 1992, although the company's original log chapel was 3 miles away near the entrance to the Arts & Crafts Community.

VICTORIAN GARDENS WEDDING CHAPEL
571 East Parkway, Gatlinburg
(865) 430-5683, (800) 597-1371
www.victorianweddingchapel.com
As you're driving away from downtown Gatlinburg on East Parkway/US 321, you can't help but notice this grand, Victorian-style chapel—with a seating capacity of 80, it's one of the largest ones in the area. The interior's colors are white with burgundy and mauve accents. Two-story stained-glass windows and large chandeliers add to the elegance.

Victorian Gardens has been in business since 1997. They offer a broad range of options in their wedding packages and can also feature on-site receptions in their adjacent solarium. Victorian Gardens maintains a staff of 8 to 10 people to assist spouses-to-be.

GETTING OUT OF TOWN
(CHEROKEE, NC, & TOWNSEND, TN)

Although the Smokies Corridor is so filled with things to see and do that it's hard to imagine anyone wanting more, a few outlying areas are special enough to deserve some attention here. Cherokee, NC, is steeped in the culture of the Native Americans who lived on this land long before the white settlers moved in and started building their homes and businesses. And tiny Townsend, TN, the town at the entrance to Great Smoky Mountains National Park that is closest to popular Cades Cove, offers a laid-back atmosphere that provides a totally different way to experience the Smokies.

CHEROKEE, NORTH CAROLINA

Like the Tennessee cities of the Smokies Corridor, Cherokee is a growing tourist center that serves as a gateway to Great Smoky Mountains National Park, offering its fair share of shopping, attractions, and entertainment opportunities. But most everything in this town is very much flavored by the character and the culture of the Native American people who inhabit the region. You'll find a lot to do here—in fact, there's more than you could possibly take on in one day.

The 100-square-mile Cherokee Indian Reservation, known by Cherokees as the Qualla Boundary, borders Great Smoky Mountains National Park on the south and also includes the southern terminus of the Blue Ridge Parkway. At one time the Cherokee culture was prevalent throughout the Carolinas. Its influence can still be seen today in the names of many towns and other geographic features in this area (such as the Nantahala National Forest and the Tuckasegee River) as well as in the foods that are staples in western North Carolina. The 11,000 members of the Eastern Band of the Cherokee (as opposed to the Western Band, relegated to Oklahoma) have done their part to keep the culture alive. For more about the history of the Cherokee, see the History chapter; for even more detailed information than this book can provide, pick up a copy of the *Insiders' Guide to North Carolina's Mountains*.

Like that of Sevierville, Pigeon Forge, and Gatlinburg, Cherokee's tourism season generally runs from May through October. From November through April, some businesses here are closed, although lately many are finding it easier to stay open all year as larger numbers of tourists discover everything Cherokee has to offer. If you plan a visit to Cherokee during the off-season, check ahead of time to make sure that what you want to do will be open when you're there.

If you want to stay overnight, you'll find a lot of accommodations to choose from. Cherokee offers some 50 motels, nearly 200 rental cabins, and approximately 25 campgrounds, many of which are easily accessible from the center of town. Other locations offer scenic riverside and mountainside settings. Most of the hotels and motels are independent mom-and-pop establishments, but several nationally known franchises are also a part of the mix.

Understandably, craft and gift shops abound here, dealing in everything from tourist souvenirs to art, jewelry, and clothing. If you're interested in narrowing your search for shopping finds to authentic products made by Native American craftspeople, you might want to start with this list of shops and galleries (a few of which are described further below): Bearmeat's Indian Den, Carol's Handmade Crafts, Cherokee Heritage Museum & Gallery, FBI Trader, Great Smokies

Fine Arts Gallery, Joel Queen Gallery, LIFT Culture House, Medicine Man Crafts, Museum of the Cherokee Indian, Native American Craft Shop, Qualla Arts and Crafts, Talking Leaves Bookstore, and Trail of Tears Gallery.

Getting There and Getting Around

The simplest way (although not always the quickest) to get to Cherokee from Sevier County is to take U.S. Highway 441 from Gatlinburg into the national park and simply follow it all the way into Cherokee. As the crow flies, it's about 35 miles from Gatlinburg, but the road is curvy and often steep. Especially during peak-season periods, traffic consists of large numbers of sightseers, so you'll be lucky to ever do more than 40 mph. Count on a good one-hour drive from Gatlinburg. During the winter, US 441 is sometimes closed because of snow, ice, or landslides. Always be sure to contact the national park's information line if you're in doubt about road conditions.

The drive along US 441 is worth it, however. You'll see vast, towering mountainsides and deep valleys that stretch toward the horizon. In October, when the leaves are changing, the foliage becomes a patchwork quilt of fiery color blanketing the landscape. Along the way, there are a good number of pull-offs and parking areas where you can stop and relax while you take in the views or put your camera to work. See the chapter on Great Smoky Mountains National Park or call the park headquarters at (865) 436-1200 for more information about what you'll encounter along the way.

Once you get to Cherokee, you'll find that things are laid out pretty simply. US 441 merges with U.S. Highway 19 (which runs perpendicular to US 441), forming a T. Most of what you'll be interested in lies on or just off these two roads within a radius of only a few miles. The area has a lot of signs, and with the aid of a map, you shouldn't have much trouble finding what you're looking for.

Native-American-Themed Attractions

An exploration of the Cherokee Indian Reservation reveals a wealth of Native American cultural activities that are both educational and entertaining. What follows are the highlights. For additional information, contact the Cherokee Welcome Center at (800) 438-1601, or visit their Web site at www.cherokee-nc.com.

OCONALUFTEE INDIAN VILLAGE
Drama Road, off US 441 Cherokee, NC
(828) 497-2111, (866) 554-4557
www.cherokee-nc.com
The Oconaluftee Indian Village is a re-creation of a Cherokee village from around the mid- to late 1700s that gives visitors an authentic glimpse into traditional Cherokee ways of life. Cherokee guides lead visitors on tours depicting history through replicas of tool workshops, various types of early homes, a seven-sided Council House, and a sweat house (different from a sweat lodge) as well as by demonstrating beadwork, basket making, pottery making, as well as the making of canoes, blowguns, and more. The tour ends up at the sacred Square Grounds, where you will hear about the spiritual practice of the ancient Cherokees and possibly see some examples of dancing. While you're at the village, check out the indigenous plant life in the adjacent Cherokee Botanical Garden.

The Oconaluftee Indian Village is open from May through late October. Prices are $15 for adults and $6 for ages 6 through 12 (tax included). Admission to the gardens is free.

THE MUSEUM OF THE CHEROKEE INDIAN
US 441 at Drama Road Cherokee, NC
(828) 497-3481
www.cherokeemuseum.org
Thanks to a $3.5-million renovation that the Museum of the Cherokee Indian underwent several years ago, the museum now uses state-of-the-art technology to tell the story of the tribe's history. The interactive exhibits teach visitors about the Cherokee's past as they walk through "time zones" representing specific periods and events, from prehistory through modern times—including the infamous Trail of Tears.

Along the way, computer-generated images, lasers, lights, and sound effects (designed in part by Disney Imagineers) enhance the rituals and history that have long been kept alive by Cherokee "myth keepers." For example, watch for the medicine man to appear by the crackling fire, sharing a Cherokee myth. The gift shop is also first-rate. Admission is $9 for adults and $6 for children ages 6 through 13 (including tax). The museum gives AAA and AARP discounts.

UNTO THESE HILLS . . . A RETELLING OUTDOOR DRAMA
Drama Road and US 441 Cherokee, NC
(828) 497-2111, (866) 554-4557
www.cherokee-nc.com
You can absorb even more Cherokee history at this acclaimed outdoor drama, up the street from the Museum of the Cherokee Indian and near the Oconaluftee Indian Village. The show, which has gone through a major overhaul recently and now features Native Americans in the majority of the cast, is the longest-running outdoor drama in the U.S. Since the original version made its debut in 1950, more than six million people have come to see the performance. The story tells the history of the Cherokee, starting with their creation myth, moving through the Trail of Tears, and ending with the present day. Unto These Hills is performed nightly (except Sunday) between mid-June and late August in the Mountainside Theatre, a 2,800-seat outdoor amphitheater. Reserved tickets are $22 for adults and $10 for children ages 6 to 12. General admission is $18 for adults and $8 for anyone 12 or younger. All prices include tax.

CHEROKEE HERITAGE MUSEUM AND GALLERY
Saunooke Village, US 441 Cherokee, NC
(828) 497-3211
www.cherokeeheritagemuseum-gallery.org
This fabulous museum-plus-gallery houses the largest collection of contemporary Cherokee arts and crafts in the world. More than one thousand pieces of art are on display here, although the museum's total collection contains at least 10 times that many pieces. The displays include paintings, dolls, baskets, masks, beadwork, pot-

tery, sculptures, weaponry, tools, and gourd art made with a variety of mediums, including clay, bone, leather, wood, stone, and feathers. The most prized piece on display is a cherrywood sculpture of an eagle dancer by John Julius Wilnoty.

Curators and codirectors R. Michael Abram, PhD., and Susan M. Abram add new pieces to the existing exhibits as the artists produce them, so the collection keeps growing. The Abrams started collecting Cherokee art in 1973 and opened their museum-gallery in 1984.

The displays offer much more than merely pretty things to look at. In keeping with Cherokee's oral tradition, visitors listen to audio-guided tours as they explore the museum, and the effect is much like having a personal guide. Instead of merely cataloging or describing each artist's work, the museum offers an interpretation of the art that shows how it fits within the context of both the traditional Cherokee culture and the modern one.

This museum's extensive gallery gift shop is also a great place to shop for authentic Cherokee arts and crafts, as well as works of art from other tribes. It also sells educational books, videos, and CDs. The museum is open from mid-March through November. Admission is $6 for ages 11 and older, $4 for children ages 6 to 10, and free for anyone under age 6. Prices include tax.

i Ask before you take any pictures or videos of Native Americans. Not everyone will give you permission, but you're much more likely to get cooperation if you show some respect.

QUALLA ARTS & CRAFTS MUTUAL
645 Tsali Boulevard, Cherokee, NC
(828) 497-3103
www.cherokee-nc.com
This craft cooperative across the street from the Museum of the Cherokee Indian displays and sells the works of some 250 Cherokee artisans, in addition to offering art from other American Indian craftspeople across the country. Founded in 1946, this is the oldest and most revered Native

American cooperative in the U.S. The Members Gallery displays the cooperative's permanent collection of historical-quality pieces mostly by deceased artists. Historical baskets, beadwork, pottery, masks, finger weaving, wood carving, stone sculpture, jewelry, and even blowguns are examples of what you can buy here. The cooperative is open year-round, except for two weeks in January when they close for inventory. Admission is free.

i **If you see some funky-looking bears on the streets of downtown Cherokee, don't worry. You're not hallucinating. The colorfully painted beasts were painted by several Cherokee as part of a program that started in 2005. The idea was to instill community pride while at the same time raise awareness of the talent of the many tribal artists.**

OCONALUFTEE RIVER TRAIL
US 441 at the national park entrance
Cherokee, NC
Oconaluftee River Trail is a 1.5-mile trail (one-way) that runs from the Great Smoky Mountains National Park entrance sign on US 441 on the edge of town to the Oconaluftee Visitor Center inside the park. The trail is flat and well maintained and takes visitors on a peaceful trek through a wooded setting accented by the sounds of the Oconaluftee River. Five interpretive exhibit panels along the way retell traditional Cherokee stories, in both Cherokee and English.

Other Attractions
HARRAH'S CHEROKEE CASINO AND HOTEL
777 Casino Drive, Cherokee, NC
(828) 497-7777, (800) HARRAHS
www.harrahscherokee.com
This legal gambling establishment, operated by the Eastern Band of Cherokee Indians, did for Cherokee what Dollywood did for Tennessee's Smokies—that is, helped it start the transition from a seasonal destination to a year-round one.

Since 1997, Harrah's has provided gaming action and live entertainment 24 hours a day, seven days a week. It's very much like what you'd find in Las Vegas or Atlantic City, with a few notable exceptions.

If you arrive at Harrah's in your car, you can either park free in one of the many parking areas or pull up to the main building and have your car valet-parked for an extra fee. If you park in the lots, you can either walk to the casino or take Harrah's free shuttle to the front doors. The casino also has on-site accommodations for its guests in the form of a 576-room luxury hotel. The 15-story facility features two restaurants, a conference center, gift shop, indoor swimming pool, fitness room, and much more. Native American crafts and artwork adorn each floor.

You must be 21 or older to set foot inside the casino, and although alcohol is not permitted on the premises, smoking is. Videotaping is not allowed, but flash photography is welcome. The casino offers more than 3,400 video gaming machines spread out over nearly 88,000 square feet of floor space. Some 8,000 square feet of that is smoke-free.

Harrah's is in the middle of a $650-million expansion that will double everything when it's completed in 2013. The expansion will bring the total number of gaming devices to 5,200 and will double the gaming floor. A 3,000-seat event center (double the current size) will be added to the hotel, as well as a 22-story, 500-room tower (bringing the hotel's tower count to three), 28 low-rise suites, a new restaurant, and a 16,000-square-foot spa.

All of the gambling at this Harrah's is done on video machines, although you will find live dealers assisting on the video blackjack games. And you'll still find video versions of all the typical casino games like poker, keno, and Lock 'n' Roll, Harrah's own version of the basic slot machine. The games have minimum costs ranging from 1 cent to $25. The maximum house payout on many of the games is unlimited thanks to changes in state law. In addition to quarters, machines also take small- and large-denomination bills. Harrah's has also recently added a video poker room.

Near the main entrance is the Games Master area, where staff members will help you learn how to play the different games. Although the games are all played on machines, they're very user-friendly once you figure out what you're doing. There are no buttons to push or levers to pull. All actions are conducted by simply touching a finger to the appropriate spot on the video screen. When you're ready to start pumping quarters, you'll find three cashier areas along the perimeter of the main floor. After that, you're on your own. If you need assistance with a particular game, you can call for an attendant by pushing a button on your machine. You'll also find plenty of servers on the floor distributing free nonalcoholic beverages.

There is more to Harrah's than just gaming, however. Harrah's hosts concert performances and show revues. Performers such as B. B. King, Bill Cosby, Willie Nelson, and Wayne Newton have appeared in the past. Tickets to these shows range anywhere from $35 to $100, depending on the performer, and you can purchase them at the box office in the casino. There's an average of one show a month.

Harrah's Cherokee Casino has five eating establishments on the main premises and two more in the hotel. In the casino itself, you'll find the Fresh Market Square, serving lunch and dinner in an all-you-care-to-eat buffet format. For one price, you can choose from a wide selection of international and traditional dishes. The Fresh Market Express offers 24-hour counter service if you're looking for something quick and light—sandwiches, pastries, ice creams, and coffees. For full sit-down dining service, step into Sycamores On the Creek, a restaurant featuring steaks, seafood, pasta, desserts, and more.

In the hotel are the Selu Garden cafe (which serves a well-rounded menu for breakfast, lunch, and dinner) and Club Cappuccino (a great place to go for all kinds of coffee drinks, not to mention pastries, desserts, and fresh fruits). Other amenities at Harrah's include a kids' arcade, a passenger lounge area for those awaiting bus transportation, and two gift shops.

i You can't take anyone under 21 into Harrah's Cherokee Casino, even if you're just going to a restaurant. If you want to gamble, you can leave any child 13 or older unattended at Harrah's video arcade, located in the hotel, which is separate from the casino.

TRIBAL BINGO
U.S. Highway 19, Cherokee, NC
(828) 497-4320, (800) 410-1254
At Tribal Bingo, which is also operated by the Eastern Band of Cherokee Indians, you can play one of the South's favorite games of chance for $5,000 as well as progressive jackpots. All prizes are awarded in cash. The facility accommodates up to 1,000 players and is open Wednesday through Sunday year-round.

i If you're traveling to Cherokee to visit Harrah's Casino, consider taking a shuttle. Rocky Top Tours (865-429-8687; www.rockytoptours.com), runs buses departing from Pigeon Forge and Gatlinburg on Tuesdays and Thursdays. The 90-minute ride costs $30, but you get $20 worth of tokens from the casino on arrival if you bring a photo ID (you must be 21).

SANTA'S LAND THEME PARK & ZOO
571 Wolfetown Road/US 19, Cherokee, NC
(828) 497-9191
www.santaslandnc.com
It's always Christmas (or at least it is from early May through the end of October) at Santa's Land Theme Park and Zoo. Ride the Rudi-Coaster or the Ferris wheel, take a train ride, cruise on the paddleboats, or visit with Santa and his elves. At Santa's Land Zoo, you can pet and feed a variety of domestic and exotic animals. Santa's Land also offers live shows (including a baby bear feeding show), an arcade, restaurants, and plenty of shops. Admission is $18.46, plus tax, for everyone except children under two—they get in free.

OCONALUFTEE ISLANDS PARK
US 441N, Cherokee, NC

Oconaluftee Islands Park is located on a patch of ground in the middle of the Oconaluftee River adjacent to the downtown area. Wheelchair accessible by footbridge, this thoroughly delightful park has picnic tables, grills, a covered pavilion, a beach volleyball court, and a walking trail. Along the trail, you'll encounter nine different audio stations that are part of the park's Talking Trees project. At the stations, visitors learn about the use of the different trees present in the park as well as their value to the Cherokee culture. There is no charge for use of park facilities.

If you'd like to take a more active role in Cherokee's great outdoors, many other activities are available, including mountain biking, tubing, white-water rafting, trout fishing, and horseback riding. Contact the Cherokee Welcome Center for more information (800-438-1601; www .cherokee-nc.com).

TOWNSEND, TENNESEE

For years this small burg—located about 20 miles west of Gatlinburg in Blount County—has made a name for itself as "the peaceful side of the Smokies." That billing is based on the fact that although Townsend and its surrounding environs are every bit as scenically fetching as what you'll find in neighboring Sevier County, the city has managed to escape many of the pitfalls that go hand in hand with high-traffic tourism.

In other words, Townsend offers much of what Smokies purists desire from a trip to the mountains without all the inconveniences and hassles. Visitors get quick, handy access to the national park, exposure to mountain crafts and culture, and views and scenery galore—but they are spared going shoulder to shoulder with teeming throngs of fellow visitors and miles and miles of bumper-to-bumper traffic. (In fact, the traffic lights aren't numbered in Townsend the way they are in the other Smokies Corridor towns, and there's a good reason for that. Townsend has only one traffic signal!)

Compared to much of Sevier County, Townsend aptly embodies its "peaceful side"

moniker. Even so, you will see a few telltale signs of tourist-targeted influence. US 321 is now a spacious four-lane highway running through town. New cabins and rental homes are springing up like mushrooms. And yes, you'll even find tacky souvenir shops. But overall, a day in Townsend is a day well spent.

Getting There and Getting Around

If you're leaving from Gatlinburg, go to the national park's Sugarland Visitor Center and head west on Little River Road as if you were going to Cades Cove. When you get to the Townsend Wye, turn right and follow the road straight into Townsend, which will be about 20 miles from your starting point. (If by some chance you see the turnoff to Tremont on the left, you went too far. Turn around and take your first left onto the road out of the park that goes to Townsend.)

From Pigeon Forge, take U.S. Highway 321 (Wears Valley Road) and follow it for a little more than 15 miles until you hit a stoplight. Bingo, you're in Townsend. (And you've also just come to the only traffic light in town.) Both routes are generally curvy and scenic, and traffic runs slowly on them in peak season, so don't get in a hurry.

Townsend is laid out in a long, narrow strip that stretches for several miles along one major road, although it has a few names, which can be confusing. The best way to explain it is to say that if you came from Pigeon Forge and you're sitting at the traffic light at the T intersection at the end of Wears Valley Road, the road you are facing is Townsend's main drag, which is called East Lamar Alexander Parkway. If you turn left, you're turning onto TN 73, which eventually heads into the national park. If you turn right, you're turning onto a continuation of US 321, which stretches to the western edge of town.

That's about the only complicated thing there is to Townsend, and it really isn't all that complicated at all, once you're there. Sticking to this main drag gives you access to the majority of what Townsend offers. Some businesses, such as cabin rental offices, are often located within a few miles on smaller county roads.

What to Do in Townsend

For outdoor recreation, you can take advantage of horseback riding, hiking, or—perhaps Townsend's favorite summertime activity—inner tubing on the Little River. (See the chapter on Active Outdoor Adventures).

If fishing is your sport, the Little River is good for that, too. Stop by Little River Outfitters (865-448-9459; www.littleriveroutfitters.com) to stock up on fly-fishing gear essentials as well as to get a little advice about where to fish and with what bait.

Golfers might want to tee it up at Laurel Valley Golf Course (865-448-6690).

Although no real attractions exist in Townsend, at least not in the sense that they do elsewhere in the Smokies Corridor, one site is definitely worth a stop. The Great Smoky Mountain Heritage Center (865-448-0044; www.gsmheritagecenter.org) is a fabulous place for learning all about the history and culture of both the Native Americans in this area as well as the early European settlers. The main exhibit hall houses a huge collection of Native American artifacts as well as exhibits on pioneer and mountain culture with interactive displays that make the history come alive. The outdoor gallery offers a collection of historic buildings, including an 1892 log cabin, a smokehouse, two cantilever barns, a gristmill, a granary, a wheelwright shop, and even an outhouse (complete with Sears catalog)!

For shoppers, Townsend has its share of antiques and craft shops, where you'll find everything from handmade wood carvings and stringed musical instruments to baskets and patchwork quilts. Look for establishments like Smoky Mountain Woodcarver (865-448-2259; www.woodcarvers.com), Wood-N-Strings (865-448-6647; www.clemmerdulcimer.com), and CAM Cabin Crafts (865-448-5940; www.appalachianministry.org).

For fun dining, be sure to stop by Deadbeat Pete's (865-448-0900), serving hearty Tex-Mex lunches and dinners throughout the week (except in winter, when dinner is served daily but lunch is served only on weekends). You'll love the laid-back atmosphere, particularly the graffiti-covered one-dollar bills stapled to nearly every square inch of wall space. Other restaurants to keep in mind are the Back Porch (865-448-6333), Trailhead Steakhouse (865-448-0166), Carriage House Restaurant (865-448-2263), Riverstone Family Restaurant (865-448-8816), Wild Mountain Rose Bakery/Pizzas (865-448-6895), and Miss Lily's Cafe (865-448-1924). All offer home-cooking with a small-town touch.

Townsend hosts a number of special events each year, most notably the fall and spring editions of its Heritage Festival. That's when locals and visitors alike gather to celebrate the area's history and culture. The event showcases crafts, barbecue, storytelling, and live country and bluegrass music. The festival is also a good opportunity to meet descendants of the families who once lived in the areas now occupied by the national park. Many of those displaced families make their homes in Townsend today.

For more information about Townsend, contact the Townsend Visitor Center at (865) 448-6134 or (800) 525-6834 or visit their Web site at www.smokymountains.org.

RELOCATION

If you're lucky enough to be relocating to the Smokies, welcome to town. You've picked a place to live where the people are friendly, the cost of living is relatively low, and the scenery is simply outstanding. This chapter is meant to help make your transition a little smoother. It will begin with a discussion of real estate in the various neighborhoods throughout the Smokies Corridor, giving you an idea of where you might want to live and how much it will cost. Next, the chapter offers listings of various schools, health-care facilities, and places of worship. (Community centers and municipal recreation opportunities are covered in the Parks and Recreation chapter.)

REAL ESTATE

If you browse through Smoky Mountain area real estate listings, you'll frequently come across the headline "Views, Views, Views!" It's no wonder. Though abundant, views of the majestic Great Smoky Mountains are a treasured commodity around here. You could argue that views are what it's all about when it comes to the local real estate market. Those mountains are what brought tourism here in the first place, and time has proven that many who find the Smokies "a nice place to visit" do, indeed, want to settle among them as well. Then, consider all the people who have migrated to Sevier County to work in the businesses and industries that service the vacationer. The result has been long-term growth in the sheer numbers of properties being developed, bought, and sold.

That said, the current market volatility is shifting the real estate landscape from month to month. Interest rates are generally low right now, but mortgages are very hard to get. Although that may seem like a downer, the fact is that there's no better time to purchase property if you've got deep pockets (meaning you won't have a problem qualifying for a mortgage). It's also an excellent time to upgrade to a house with more square feet, because even if you lose money on the property you sell, the discount

you'll be getting right now on your new bigger house will put you much further ahead in the long run. Here's some more good news: Thanks to the large amount of revenue generated by tourism in Sevier County, the property tax rates are among the lowest in Tennessee.

Not only have things shifted economically, but new roads are also changing things. Collier Drive in Sevierville and Veterans Boulevard in Pigeon Forge are not 100 percent developed at the moment, but as more and more subdivisions and businesses go in, properties around the former major entryways to town that have traditionally been more valuable may not appreciate as much.

Another thing to consider is that Sevier County generally has a high regard for personal property rights. In other words, there's a relative lack of zoning and other restrictions here compared to other parts of the country. Here's what that means for you as a new homebuyer: If you buy or build a fairly nice home in an area with no restrictions, your neighbor could drag a beat-up mobile home onto his property, or even start a used-car lot next door. If you want to be sure something like that doesn't happen, your best bet is to buy in a subdivision that has restrictions already in place.

If your idea of a "dream house" is a historically significant structure on a quaint, tree-lined street, you're going to find slim pickings. With certain exceptions, the communities of the county are characterized by neighborhoods and subdivisions that have generally been around fewer than 40 years, much of that being developed just within the last 10 to 15 years. In the more isolated, rural areas outside the main communities, you'll find mixes of both newer and older homes; it's not uncommon to find an old, fixer-upper farmhouse situated within a mile of a new, sprawling, cedar and stone home perched on multiple grassy acres.

i **You can sometimes get a good deal purchasing a property meant for rentals as a permanent residence. But be sure it meets your needs. Although it may appear to be a bargain, the kitchen and storage spaces, especially the closets, are typically much smaller than they are in homes designed for permanent residence. You might even lack a washer-dryer hookup.**

You'll also find that Sevier County is an architectural patchwork quilt in which the styles and types of homes vary from community to community, depending on the prevalence of tourist activity in that area. Part of one town might have a generous supply of ranch-style homes. Another section of another town might be saturated with chalets built into steep hillsides. Yet another area might provide a steady landscape of newly constructed log cabins. Condos are becoming increasingly popular countywide, and in both the cities and the rural areas, there are numerous sites to place mobile homes. In the northern half of the county, variations on the standard ranch-style house are typical, while southern Sevier County has more cottages, cabins, condos, and chalets. What you ultimately choose depends on your aesthetic preferences, your price range, and, to some degree, your motives for moving here in the first place.

Please note that although the selling prices listed here were accurate at press time, relatively few properties have actually sold at those prices (or any others) from the fall of 2008 through the

i **If you're buying a home in a planned community with shared facilities, ask your real estate agent about the home owners' dues. While some have none at all, others have fees as high as $600 per month. Some condo complexes also tack on additional fees (like a pool usage fee, for example). When added up, these fees can sometimes double your home owners association (HOA) fee.**

spring of 2009. So be sure to ask your real estate agent for up-to-date figures when you start looking.

Sevierville

One of the more rapidly expanding areas in Sevier County, both commercially and residentially, is the Tennessee Highway 66 corridor that runs for about 8 miles from Interstate 40 to Sevierville, also encompassing the small, unincorporated community of Kodak. This whole area, residentially speaking, is an especially popular location among couples for whom one partner might work in Sevier County and the other may commute to a neighboring market like Knoxville or Jefferson City. Kodak's proximity to a number of surrounding job markets and its relatively light traffic make it a favorite site to put down roots. In 2008 the average selling price for a home in Kodak was $164,153.

Anyone who's home shopping in this territory can use some advance information about the utility services available. First, note that the City of Sevierville has annexed the narrow strip of land bordering both sides of TN 66, from I-40 all the way in to the main part of the city. The homes and businesses that are so annexed receive all city utilities, including sewer service, all the way to I-40 and a little beyond (into what's now being called the Sevierville 407 area). Most of the residential locations along TN 66, however, lie outside the annexation boundaries. Some of those still receive city services but at higher rates. In the other cases, utilities are either provided by companies that service surrounding areas, or ℹ️ **Many areas in Sevier County have well water with a high sulfur and mineral content. Taste the water before you buy a home with a well, and check for mineral deposits in the lower rack of the dishwasher and in the toilet tanks. It may be wise to do a well test for any property you're serious about buying.**

septic and well-water systems are used. When looking at a home that borders TN 66, be sure to ask your real estate agent about its sources of electricity, water, and sewer.

The Kodak/TN 66 area has a number of subdivisions, some of which are worthy of mention here. Bentwood, which started development in 1990, had several of its speculative homes featured in the local Parade of Homes showcase during its first year of existence. Houses in Bentwood start around $250,000. Another subdivision in this region is Grandview. It was first developed as an exclusively upscale neighborhood, but after years of subsequent phases, many of its initial restrictions have been relaxed. As a result, less expensive homes are more prevalent farther back into Grandview's newer additions. You'll find homes here ranging from around $145,000 up to $449,000.

The Royal Heights neighborhood lies within Sevierville city boundaries. It consists of more upscale homes, and prices generally start at about $180,000 and peak in the $330,000 range, with little change over time. Union Hill, located off Allensville Road, is a newer development popular with first-time home buyers. New homes here can be purchased in the $79,000 to $117,000 range.

Taking a slight detour and briefly leaving Sevierville altogether, you'll find the Seymour/Boyds Creek area, which is similar to Kodak in that it offers a convenient location for the couple who have careers split between Sevier and Knox Counties. Seymour, a small community about 12 miles from Sevierville, lies in the extreme northwest end of the county, right along the Knox County border. Although it is regarded as a "hot"

area in terms of commercial development, Seymour is primarily a residential suburb of Knoxville with handy access to the rest of Sevier County via Chapman Highway. Boyds Creek Highway connects Seymour to TN 66 with a 12-mile stretch of road. On this scenic drive, you'll find a mixture of older, historical homes and newer construction of subdivisions like Valley View Farms. This area serves its residents well with distant but sometimes unobstructed views of the Great Smoky Mountains.

Newer homes in the Seymour area run from $119,000 to $400,000. Although buyers can usually get more bang for their real estate buck here compared to other communities in the market, the downside is that these properties don't appreciate as quickly as in places like Pigeon Forge or Gatlinburg. For that reason, Seymour is a better buy for someone who plans on staying put for a while. If you're buying in this area, consider staying within the Sevier County border due to the lower taxes and higher appreciation. Initial prices will be a little bit higher, but it will pay off in the long run. Again, many new residents are choosing to buy in newer subdivisions. Some of the popular developments are Van Gilder, Van Haven, Sharps Vista, and Clydesdale.

Back in Sevierville, you'll find several major pockets of residential concentration that offer homes with a more diverse range of prices and ages. The average selling price of homes in Sevierville was $187,415 in 2008. If you're driving in to Sevierville on Chapman Highway from Seymour, you'll come across the Hardin Lane neighborhood just as you near downtown. As you turn off onto Hardin Lane, you'll encounter several apartment complexes, but farther back, you'll enter a nice, established neighborhood where the homes date back to the 1970s. The streets are quiet and the yards are green and wooded—this could explain, in part, why these homes appear on the market infrequently. Prices here hover in the $174,900 to $265,900 range, although several homes in the neighborhood are more upscale and more expensive. In the past several years, there has also been a lot of new construction activity in nearby developments like Paine Lake,

Steeplechase, and Saddleback Ridge. There, you'll find homes in an assortment of scenic settings, including the banks of the Little Pigeon River and a nearby hillside. Prices are in the $189,900 to $600,000 range.

Downtown Sevierville is home to many of the older two-story homes with wooden exteriors. Some of these date back to the early 1900s and have historical value. This section of town is noteworthy for its proximity to retail businesses and schools as well as county and city government offices. However, the same families have occupied a lot of these homes for years, and they don't appear very frequently on the market.

The area east of Sevierville along Dolly Parton Parkway has recently become an established commercial and residential area with many offices, retail space, and restaurants. Much of this came in response to the rapid residential growth in that part of town. The area in general has thrived because of a migration of local residents away from the more central, tourist-trafficked areas of Sevierville. As for housing, quite a few neighborhoods, both new and old, border key streets and roads like Dolly Parton Parkway, Earnest McMahan Road, and Pullen Road. Broadly speaking, this area features rolling countryside with awesome Smoky Mountain views.

Among the more well-established areas are upscale neighborhoods like Birchwood and Blalock Woods. These both date back to the 1970s and are marked by large, handsome homes that are fairly well separated from one another and sit on wooded tracts. Birchwood homes start around $156,000. In Blalock Woods, values are higher, with homes starting around $235,000.

Rivergate is a popular area that offers housing in the $144,900 to $200,000 range with the benefit of city utilities. Since lots were first auctioned off there in 1996, homes have sprung up like dandelions. Somerset Downs falls somewhere in between the old and new classifications. It also has large, attractive homes in a more sprawling setting but uses water wells and septic tanks. Prices there start around $169,900.

Near Somerset Downs are the newer Sunrise Estates and Snappwood, where nice, modern homes started going up in the early 1990s. They start as low as $174,500 and go as high as $299,000.

Other names to look for include Shaconage, which is located off Pittman Center Road, and Victoria Landing, a hilltop condominium development with units starting at around $162,000. One of the best-known subdivisions in this neck of the woods is Belle Meadows. The homes there are large and attractive, but because it does receive city utilities, the lots are somewhat small and the houses are situated pretty close to one another. Nevertheless, it's a very popular neighborhood for families with children. Prices start around $234,000.

If you travel even farther east on Dolly Parton Parkway (U.S. Highway 411, which eventually becomes Newport Highway) and turn south onto Long Springs Road, you'll be on your way to two towns that are favorites among those who desire scenic, remote settings. New Center and Jones Cove, both of which are unincorporated, are 10- and 20-minute drives from downtown Sevierville, respectively. Although these communities offer little commercially, each has its own elementary school. In addition to the more idyllic atmospheres found there, the property values of these two hamlets can sometimes be more competitive compared to their neighboring markets. The average selling price of a home in New Center was $167,666 in 2008; for Jones Cove the corresponding figure was only $91,728. These figures are in line with a general assumption to be made about real estate prices in Sevier County: You'll usually find better prices on houses and land located in the more rural undeveloped areas.

Another section of Sevierville that offers nice homes in varying price ranges is the residential area that lies just west of the Parkway and runs from Forks of the River Parkway south to Lynn Road near the Governor's Crossing development. A conglomeration of different subdivisions, this area is sometimes generally referred to as Marshall Woods, which is actually the name of just one of its more popular neighborhoods. Within its streets, you'll find a little bit of everything, from large, split-level homes on quiet, shaded streets to houses that are more of the cookie-cutter variety but still make for good values in this popular family setting. This area hasn't seen a lot of recent construction. Most of the building activity there took place from the 1960s through the 1980s.

i Property taxes in Sevier County are among the lowest in the state of Tennessee. In 2008 the rate was $1.54 per $100 of assessed value. City rates are 31 cents in Sevierville, 12.42 cents in Pigeon Forge, 14.93 cents in Gatlinburg, and 77 cents in Pittman Center.

Pigeon Forge

Pigeon Forge accounts for the second-smallest population among Sevier County's three main towns. Upon seeing nothing but tourist-oriented businesses along the Parkway, vacationers to Pigeon Forge have often asked, "Where do people around here live?" One only needs to travel a block or two in either direction off the Parkway to answer that question. Although the main strip consists of one commercial venture after another, bands of residential areas run parallel to the Parkway on both sides, from one end to the other. When you drive into these neighborhoods, it's like entering a whole new world. The often-chaotic atmosphere of amusement rides, attractions, and traffic is immediately supplanted by tranquil environs consisting of ranch-style homes and cabins on quiet streets. At the same time, however, you're never far away from all the shopping and recreation. When home shopping in this area, be sure to ask your real estate agent about whether there's back-road access to the neighborhood you're interested in—that may be an important factor during the height of tourist season (and therefore, the height of traffic jam season).

There are also residential areas along the arteries that feed into Pigeon Forge's city limits from the county. Side roads like Henderson Chapel Road, Wears Valley Road, Mill Creek Road, Dollywood Lane, and Veterans Boulevard/Middle Creek Road all contain quite a mix of homes in terms of age, style, and price. Speaking in general terms, the residential construction in Pigeon Forge has gradually evolved over the decades. The real estate picture is one of old frame farmhouses, brick ranchers, and cabins often mixed together in a random fashion, with few clearly defined "neighborhoods." In 2008 the average home in Pigeon Forge sold for $215,807.

Much of Pigeon Forge's more recent construction is geared to the vacation and overnight rental markets and usually consists of cabins, cottages, and condos (see the Vacation Rentals chapter). These types of properties can be found on or near the secondary roads mentioned above.

A heavy concentration of cabins and log homes can also be found in the community of Wears Valley, which also has its own back entrance to Great Smoky Mountains National Park via Lyon Springs Road. About 8 miles southwest of Pigeon Forge, this unincorporated town has become a heavy contender in its own right in the second-home market. A popular location with retired people as well as vacation/investment home buyers, Wears Valley is very much of the same nature as Gatlinburg when it comes to real estate. For one, property values are a little higher than those in other parts of the county. Undeveloped house lots can go for as much as $124,900, and the average sale price of a home in 2008 was $303,206. What makes this area so popular is its setting. Nestled in a peaceful valley at the foot of Cove Mountain, Wears Valley provides its residents with tremendous views in a laid-back country setting.

Another community that's easily accessible from Pigeon Forge is Caton's Chapel. Traveling approximately 10 miles out Dollywood Lane will take you to this unincorporated town, the location of which makes for handy back-road access to Pigeon Forge, Sevierville, and Gatlinburg. In addition to convenience, Caton's Chapel also retains a tranquil country setting. Outside of a few small stores and an elementary school, there's not a lot of activity. The growth that has taken place out there has been primarily in vacation/second-home/rental properties.

Gatlinburg

Like Pigeon Forge, its neighbor to the north, Gatlinburg gets more than 10 million visitors a year, although only about 5,400 people call Gatlinburg "home" on a year-round basis. Because the city is surrounded by the national park on three sides, it is somewhat limited when it comes to finding new areas into which this permanent population base can expand. Gatlinburg is also topographically confined by its location, tucked in the narrow valleys among the Smoky Mountain foothills. A lot of businesses and homes are packed and wedged into the compact dimensions of central Gatlinburg. The surrounding hills and mountainsides are also liberally dotted with chalets, cabins, and condos. Because of its location next to the national park, the only release valve that has been able to allow for physical expansion has been the area surrounding U.S. Highway 321 (East Parkway), heading north and east away from downtown Gatlinburg.

Also, as with Pigeon Forge, the makeup of Gatlinburg's residential communities is a jigsaw puzzle of development that has evolved over the years. Locals live in a hodgepodge of commingled house styles, including cabins, chalets, cottages, condominium developments, and even some traditional ranch-style homes. Many of these homes are found along the numerous side roads that feed into US 321. Near that highway, you'll find Quail Run, where homes go for $124,900 to $695,000.

One of the more recent subdivisions on the scene is Brent Hills, also located off US 321 in the neighborhood of Mills Park and Gatlinburg-Pittman High School. Several established residential pockets can also be found fairly close to central Gatlinburg. These include the Roaring Fork area, the Baskins Creek neighborhood, the McClain addition off River Road, and the neighborhood near Gatlinburg's Mynatt Park. Outside Gatlinburg city limits, there seems to be an endless network of intertwining country back roads, along which you'll find random scatterings of homes that can include cabins and older farmhouses.

Because of its proximity to the national park, Gatlinburg real estate prices tend to be higher than those in other markets in the county. Although the selling prices of homes there averaged $215,611 in 2008, there are more-affordable permanent homes to be had. You can find prices in the $79,900 ballpark, and of course, the diligent home shopper should always keep his or her eyes open for the "steals" that pop up constantly due to today's economic environment.

Another section of Gatlinburg deserves to be treated as an entirely different animal when it comes to real estate—the area generally referred to as "Ski Mountain." This unique section of town, which began developing in 1968, is spread along the east face of Mount Harrison and occupies more than a thousand gorgeous, wooded acres. Driving just a couple of miles up Ski Mountain Road from downtown Gatlinburg, you'll reach Chalet Village, a realm where the chalet indeed reigns supreme. Quite a few condominium developments are farther up the mountain as you near the top. (By the way, the ski resort/ amusement park of Ober Gatlinburg is located at the summit of this mountain; see both the Attractions chapter and the chapter on Active Outdoor Adventures for more on this.)

Overall, rental chalets and condos account for the vast majority of the homes in this region; there's only a sprinkling of permanent residences. Although condos are covered in more detail in the Vacation Rentals chapter, several names are worth mentioning here, including the Summit, Edelweiss, High Alpine, and High Chalet.

Those fortunate enough to live in the Ski Mountain area never grow tired of viewing the nearby mountains that dominate the view from their picture windows. The terrain here is hilly and sometimes downright steep, but the setting is unsurpassed with its abundant woodland growth, rugged complexion, and the always-present native black bear.

The trade-off is that this is some of the most expensive property in the entire county. In 2008, the average selling price of a chalet was close to $205,955. Properties in the $200,000 and $300,000 range are common. Condominiums can be found in a wide range of prices, starting as low as $49,900 for a one-bedroom unit to as high as $232,500 for a three-bedroom unit. Prices often depend on the condo's location as well as its amenities.

Another part of the county that's attracted both permanent residents and investment is the corridor of land along US 321 between Gatlinburg and the community of Cosby in neighboring Cocke County. Along this stretch of real estate, you'll find resort communities such as Cobbly Nob, Arcadia, and Deer Ridge, where you can buy houses and condos for both permanent or vacation residence. All of the properties mentioned offer outstanding mountain views in a remote country setting as well as numerous amenities and convenient access to Bent Creek Golf Course. Homes and condos in this area range from about $47,900 to $600,000, with a few even higher.

Finding Real Estate Listings

Any search for property within the Smoky Mountain region should start off with a visit to the Web site of the Great Smoky Mountains Association of Realtors at www.gsmar.com. This is the same multiple listing service (MLS) that the Realtors use, and you'll be able to find properties listed by every real estate agent in the county here. This Web site gives the most comprehensive and up-to-date information available about the properties for sale in the county. There's also a list of Realtors to choose from. Since the economic turndown, the number of Realtors has significantly decreased. You will have no problem finding a full-time, quality agent who is on top of his or her game, returns your calls, and keeps you informed.

Another resource for the Smoky Mountains property-seeker is *Homes and Land* of the Smokies. The Smoky Mountains edition of Homes and Land is generally regarded as the area's primary printed source for real estate listings, second only to the MLS. *Homes and Land* of the Smokies turns out 12 slick, full-color issues per year distributed in typical high-traffic areas throughout Sevier County. The magazine's list of properties is also accessible via the Internet at www.home sandland.com. This Web site does not have as much or as up-to-date information as the MLS, but when used in conjunction with the MLS, it can give you valuable added information. In 1998, this site was recognized by the *Wall Street Journal* as being one of the best real estate Web pages in the nation. Those wishing to subscribe to *Homes and Land* by mail can do so at a cost of $60 for 12 issues or $30 for six issues. If you call (865) 675-1622, they will send you a free copy of the publication.

Another resource for listings is the *Mountain Press*, the county's daily newspaper. Properties for sale and lease are listed in the paper's classified section each day. It will also include properties for sale by the owner (designated "FSBO"), which would not show up in the MLS nor in *Homes and Land*.

i Even if you're buying a brand-new home from the builder, be sure to shop around first to compare prices. Buyers who just pay what the builder is asking often shell out anywhere from $10,000 to $30,000 too much for a property. When you eventually sell, you may not get your investment back, even if the property is in good shape.

EDUCATION

Sevier County children and adults alike have access to a full slate of progressive educational programs on all levels, both public and private. To be sure, some school systems in the region, especially those in more rural areas, aren't so fortunate. But Sevier Countians have built an educational infrastructure that emphasizes quality teachers and up-to-date facilities..

Construction of new schools and additional classrooms has just barely managed to keep up with swelling enrollment, and local schools have also benefited from broad-minded approaches to curriculum and solid accreditation standards. Regardless of whether a child attends public or private school, the state of Tennessee requires that he or she attend kindergarten. To register, the child must be five years old on or before September 30 of the year he or she plans to attend. The registration procedure requires parents to provide a certified copy of the child's birth certificate along with an up-to-date immunization record and medical examination forms signed by the child's physician or the Sevier County Department of Health. Such health records are considered valid if they are dated any time between the start of school and the previous January 1. The public school system has a prekindergarten screening process as well, while most private schools, of course, have their own individual application and interview processes.

This section begins with an overview of the Sevier County public school system, followed by a look at area private schools. You'll also find profiles on the many adult education programs found in the county, including the local community college annex.

Public Schools

SEVIER COUNTY SCHOOL DISTRICT
226 Cedar Street, Sevierville
(865) 453-4671
www.sevier.org

Unlike many districts, Sevier County allows parents to send their children to any school within the system, regardless of residence. A family in Sevierville may enroll their teenager at Gatlinburg–Pittman High School, for example, or a younger child who lives in Seymour might attend Sevierville Primary.

As mentioned previously, one of the primary challenges the local school board has faced is how to accommodate the growing number of children who enter the school system each year. That number is currently over the 14,200 mark and rising.

The county's incorporated and unincorporated communities include 13 elementary or primary schools, 4 intermediate and middle schools, and 4 high schools. Also included in the public system are a vocational center (at Sevier County High School) as well as institutions that serve adults and special-needs children.

Teacher-student ratios are favorable: By 2001, Tennessee was required to have maximum ratios

of 1 to 20 for kindergarten through third grade, 1 to 25 for fourth through sixth grades, and 1 to 30 for seventh and eighth grades. Since 1991, every school in the system has been accredited by the Southern Association of Colleges and Schools. Its requirements for educational standards and student-teacher ratios are tougher than the minimums set forth by the state. Incidentally, the county does not operate on a "track system" that separates classrooms according to student ability. Rather, classes contain children with a mix of ability levels, although a full slate of advanced and honors classes is available.

i Since 2000, the transition for incoming freshmen at Sevier County High School and Seymour High School has been made a lot easier thanks to the schools' Freshmen Academy program. Highly rated teachers, a team approach to education, and age-segregated classrooms have all helped to slash the schools' dropout rate among sophomores.

In the area of special education, the Sevier County school system is well equipped to serve the educational needs of learning-disabled and handicapped students ages 3 to 22. Every school in the district has some sort of special education program. In some cases, special-needs children are integrated into regular classrooms; there are also self-contained classes for students with significant disabilities who can't be served in regular classrooms. Students who are more severely impaired can be enrolled in Parkway Academy, a facility that uses specially trained instructors and individualized curricula. The school system also offers outlets for exceptionally gifted students with its Children with Special Abilities program.

i Sevier County boasts more than 170 National Merit Scholars in the history of the school district. This number is fairly high compared to the numbers in other districts in the state.

Private Schools

The small number of private schools in Sevier County might be evaluated from different perspectives. An argument could be made for the fact that the broad base of laborers in the tourist industry (who make between $5 and $7 per hour) simply can't afford private schools. Although there is some validity to that, it's also true that many residents are simply happy with the public school system.

On the flip side of the coin, some parents enroll their children in private schools because of dissatisfaction with the public system. One of the primary complaints received about public schools is that they lack the Christian emphasis that a growing number of parents desire for their children (the same rationale applies to homeschoolers). One of the two private schools included here is a church-affiliated institution.

COVENANT CHRISTIAN ACADEMY
1625 Old Newport Highway, Sevierville
(865) 429-4324
www.covenantchristianacademytn.org
This private school started out with only six students in 1989. Almost two decades later, the school boasts an overall enrollment of more than 400 (including homeschoolers). The student body ranges from three-year-olds to 12th-graders and is split into two different facilities. The original Sevierville site serves 124 kids in first grade through 12th grade. The preschool is in a separate facility on Longsprings Road in Sevierville (call 865-429-1282 for information) and has about 75 children.

The curriculum is a nondenominational Christian-based one, with all subjects taught from a Christian perspective. Although the school is on land owned by Christ Covenant Reformed Episcopal Church, the school is not owned or run by the church. Daily activities include a chapel service and prayer. Covenant Christian is a day school that runs on typical school day hours. Pickup for enrolled students can be as late as 5:30 or 6 p.m. for the preschool.

Covenant Christian School also serves as a satellite facility for its homeschool program. Of the school's total enrollment of 420, nearly 220 are educated at home by their parents. Parents who wish to participate in the program must submit an application (and fee) and on approval pay an annual tuition as well as the cost of the curriculum. The curriculum can be purchased through the school, but if it is obtained elsewhere, it must be approved by the school.

i **Reflective of the demographic makeup of the county's general population, the students in Sevier County schools are overwhelmingly white. Minorities make up just about 6 percent of the student population; 1.3 percent is African-American, 1 percent is Asian, and 3.8 percent is Hispanic.**

KING'S ACADEMY
202 Smothers Road, Seymour
(865) 573-8321
www.thekingsacademy.net
Founded in 1880, King's Academy is the oldest continuously run school in Sevier County. It provides a high-quality college preparatory education, not only for local children but also for those from across the nation and beyond. Over the years, students have come from a total of about 50 different countries.

Originally known as Harrison Chilhowee Baptist Academy, the school is run by a president and board of trustees appointed and approved by the Tennessee Baptist Convention. Accordingly, students study a well-rounded curriculum presented with a Christian-centered worldview.

The school, for prekindergarten through 12th-graders, operates as both a day and boarding facility; the boarding program is available only to 7th through 12th grades. To be accepted, children cannot have been expelled from another school, nor can they have had severe behavioral problems, and administrators look for previous exemplary behavior in the application process.

The school's recent enrollment was 380 students, the highest number since the community

(Q) Close-up

The Dollywood Foundation

In 1988 hometown girl Dolly Parton and the Dollywood Corporation jointly established the Dollywood Foundation to develop and support educational programs in Sevier County. In its two decades of existence, the foundation has raised millions of dollars; funds have come from individual and corporate donors as well as through celebrity benefit concerts staged by Ms. Parton herself.

One of the foundation's hallmark achievements has been the Imagination Library, which began in 1995. The Imagination Library is designed to foster an interest in reading among preschool children and to help kindle their imaginations. Any child four or younger may register to receive a free, hardcover book in the mail once a month until he or she turns five years old. Children born at Fort Sanders Sevier Medical Center in Sevierville automatically receive their first book and registration form at birth. Children who begin collecting the library at birth will amass a total of 60 books by the time they graduate from the program at five.

This program began with the distribution of about 2,000 books a month to Sevier County kids. Since then the program has expanded, and the Dollywood Foundation now gives out more than 500,000 books each month in almost every state in the United States (including Alaska and Hawaii) as well as in Canada and the United Kingdom. Plans are to expand the program even farther afield. The foundation also sponsors a scholarship program in Sevier County. Based on an essay students submit, one high school senior from each of the four high schools is awarded $15,000 over four years for college tuition.

of Seymour built its own public high school in 1961. Contributing to that growth has been the school's elementary program, implemented in 1995. Of the students who graduate from King's Academy, approximately 95 percent go on to college, the highest such percentage among area secondary schools.

The school boasts a state-of-the-art computer lab and offers special programs such as the Experiential Curriculum for the Outdoors classroom (ECO). A required course in the upper-level grades, ECO takes students into the Smoky Mountains twice a year. The intent is to teach them skills like hiking, camping, rappelling, and canoeing while at the same time developing an appreciation of God's glory through the wonders of nature.

Extracurricular activities are well supported at King's Academy. The school maintains a full sports program, fielding secondary-level teams in sports like football, basketball, soccer, tennis, golf, and track. The campus also has a pool and gymnasium. Overall, the school is spread out over

a 67-acre campus and exudes the feel of a small college. During the summer months its retreat and conference center hosts activities such as band clinics, athletic camps, and church retreats.

Adult Education

Who says you can't teach an old dog new tricks? In Sevier County, educational opportunities for adults include classes within the public school system as well as on the private level. Whether you're going for your high school equivalency, interested in taking a computer class, or starting on a college degree, several options await you here in the Smokies.

ADULT EDUCATION PROGRAM
226 Cedar Street, Sevierville
(865) 429-5243
www.sevier.org

Partly funded and administered through the county's public school system, the Adult Education Program offers free classes on a variety of levels, serving hundreds of adults each year. Basic skills classes help adults improve in the areas of reading, writing, and math. English as a Second Language courses are also taught. Those pursuing a high school diploma can choose from two routes. They can attend classes at White's Adult High School in Sevierville, or they can take any of the GED equivalency classes offered at various times and different locations throughout the county.

TENNESSEE TECHNOLOGY CENTER
109 Industry Drive, Sevierville
(865) 453-5644

This vocational school operates through 26 sites statewide, including the one in Sevierville. Accredited by the Council of Occupational Education, the Sevierville branch teaches courses in industrial electricity and computer electronics. Each course is worth 27 college credit hours, and upon completion students may then seek certification in their field if they wish. Graduates are qualified to work in such occupational fields as residential and industrial wiring as well as repair of heating and air-conditioning systems, refrigeration systems, and various electronics.

The center maintains an average of 19 full-time students who attend class five days a week for six hours per day. There are usually about 28 part-time students attending two nights per week. All students must have a high school or GED diploma to enroll.

WALTERS STATE COMMUNITY COLLEGE
1720 Old Newport Highway, Sevierville
(865) 774-5800
www.ws.edu

Calling itself "The Great Smoky Mountains Community College," Walters State is a two-year, nonresidential college serving more than 6,000 students among its different campuses. Sevierville's annex is one of three branches of the main campus, which is based in Morristown, Tennessee (about a one-hour drive from Sevierville). Individual courses are taught in various facilities in more than 10 east Tennessee counties. The Sevierville site has an enrollment of around 1,300 students per semester. About 60 percent of

day students are recent high school graduates, while 60 percent of those who attend evening classes are older students seeking continuing education.

Accredited by the Southern Association of Colleges and Schools, Walters State offers associate of arts, associate of science, and associate of applied science degrees. The first two degrees are university parallel programs easily transferable to most four-year colleges; the majority of Walters State students pursue one of these degrees. The associate of applied science degree is a nontransferable, technical education path. For many years the Sevierville campus had not been equipped to teach science classes, so those requirements had been met at the Morristown campus in order to complete a degree. However, a $6.5 million, 68-acre campus opened a few years ago in Sevierville, offering science courses and allowing for full satisfaction of most areas of study.

Dozens of courses are offered in Sevierville, including computer science, math, English, and history. Two of this campus's flagship programs are studies in culinary arts and hospitality management.

The first gives students real-world experience in food preparation by cooking and serving lunches and dinners that are available to the public (see the Restaurants chapter). Hospitality Management prepares students for careers in hotel and motel management, an appropriate field for such a tourist-oriented area. In December 2007, a new building opened that is devoted entirely to culinary arts and professional entertainment (called CAPE).

Another unique program, Professional Entertainment, provides education and training for all aspects of show business, from acting, singing, and dancing to set design, television/record production, and management. The school even provides training for auditions at entertainment companies like Dollywood and Busch Gardens.

To enroll, new students must provide proof of two doses of measles, mumps, and rubella immunization since their first birthday. They must also submit an application and corresponding fee, provide a high school transcript, have ACT or

SAT scores sent to the admissions office, and, of course, follow the appropriate class-registration and fee-payment procedures.

In addition to degree-related studies, Walters State offers a number of other programs designed to reach out to all segments of the population. Each semester, the school teaches about 25 noncredit, "community-oriented" classes in subjects ranging from art to business education; the majority are in the field of computer studies. For prospective college students, college credit courses are available to high school juniors and seniors with a B average. Students who have difficulty attending classes at the main campus might want to take advantage of the college's distance-learning opportunities such as Interactive Television courses (which use closed-circuit TVs) and Internet courses, through which some or all of a course's work can be completed online.

i What's better than free college? Not much, especially if you plan on attending the local campus of Walters State Community College. Sevier County government pays full tuition for any student who graduates from a county high school with a minimum 2.7 GPA, scores at least 19 on the ACT test, and meets minimum residency requirements.

HEALTH CARE AND WELLNESS

In what is probably a rare turn of events, the medical-care field has actually stayed ahead of the curve during the explosion of tourism and population in Sevier County over the past decade. Rescue services and medical care have stayed abreast of the increasing demand by training practically every city and county employee in first aid and cardiopulmonary resuscitation (CPR), and the combination of a constantly growing population and the still-rural charm of the area continues to attract medical professionals to the mountains.

The county's only hospital has also committed itself to medical excellence by attracting generous donations for building and service expansions. By joining a large regional medical system, Fort Sanders Sevier Medical Center has made available to its patients facilities and services far beyond the reach of a "rural" hospital. Mental health has also become a significant concern as the nation's attention has shifted from restorative to preventive care, and several

Local Emergency Numbers

Any emergency—911

Tennessee Highway Patrol—(865) 594-5793

Sevier County Ambulance Authority—(865) 453-3248

Sevier County Sheriff's Department—(865) 453-4668

Sevierville Police Department—(865) 453-5507

Sevierville/Sevier County Fire Department—(865) 453-9276

Pigeon Forge Police Department—(865) 453-9063

Pigeon Forge Fire Department—(865) 453-4044

Gatlinburg Police Department—(865) 436-5181

Gatlinburg Fire Department—(865) 430-1330

Pittman Center Fire Department—(865) 436-9684

Pittman Center Police Department—(865) 436-5499

area churches conduct ongoing family-centered "wellness" programs. The single public mental-care facility and the oldest retreat center in the city are also listed here.

The list of medical services and facilities that follows covers a wide geographic area. All of the facilities listed accept most insurance programs and national credit cards. If payment is a problem, they'll work something out. The clinics usually operate Monday through Friday from 8 or 9 a.m. to 4:30 or 5 p.m., but calls at all hours are answered.

Hospitals and Convalescent Care Centers

Sevierville

FORT SANDERS SEVIER MEDICAL CENTER
709 Middle Creek Road, Sevierville
(865) 429-6100
www.fssevier.com

What was a small, well-run, but very limited rural hospital as recently as 1990 has grown into one of Tennessee's recognized leaders in overall health care. Fort Sanders Sevier Medical Center, still locally referred to as "Sevier County Hospital," has expanded in every direction (including straight up and down) until the original building is no longer visible. The current emergency room alone is larger and has a bigger staff than the original hospital had, and the addition of special-care facilities like the state-of-the-art intensive-care unit and the six-bed Dolly Parton Birthing Center has raised its level of available service to that of most metropolitan hospitals.

The current configuration includes an acute-care facility with 79 beds in private rooms, and an on-site 54-bed nursing home providing intermediate and skilled long-term care. Complete in- and outpatient surgical services are provided in more than a dozen specialties. Therapeutic services are available in long- and short-term programs, and support group contacts are usually on hand. As the hospital has continued to grow in a largely unsettled area of the county, it has had the added benefit of becoming the geographic center for the construction of several professional

centers offering medical service in every conceivable fashion, with most of the specialists having hospital certification.

A new $115 million hospital to be called LeConte Medical Center will open in 2010 right across the street from the current facility. This new hospital will have expanded services in the same areas of expertise Fort Sanders now offers, as well as several new features, as well. Planned for the new hospital are a sleep center, an expanded emergency department, all private patient rooms (with beautiful mountain views, no less), an ICU step-down unit, the Dolly Parton Center for Women's Services, the Dr. Robert F. Thomas Professional Building, and a Sevier County location of Thompson Cancer Survival Center.

FORT SANDERS SEVIER NURSING HOME
709 Middle Creek Road, Sevierville
(865) 429-6694
www.fssevier.com

Adjacent to and operated as a satellite service of the Fort Sanders Sevier Medical Center, the Fort Sanders Sevier Nursing Home provides 24-hour nursing care and service to residents at ICF Level I and skilled Level II. Various activities such as exercise classes, craft classes, and special holiday programs are available for all residents.

SEVIER COUNTY HEALTH CARE CENTER
415 Catlett Road, Sevierville
(865) 453-4747

Dedicated to more serious care of the aging and terminally ill, the Sevier County Health Care Center has 149 beds and is certified in all phases of treatment, rehabilitation, and hospice services.

Pigeon Forge

PIGEON FORGE CARE & REHABILITATION CENTER
415 Cole Drive, Pigeon Forge
(865) 428-5454

Pigeon Forge Care & Rehab is a recently renovated nursing home that also specializes in rehabilitation services intended to return injured and incapacitated patients to mainstream living through individually designed inpatient and out-patient programs. Physician involvement is one of this 120-bed facility's keys to developing and implementing programs to suit the needs of the individual patient.

Walk-In Clinics
Sevierville
ROCKY TOP MEDICAL CLINIC
1105 Oak Cluster Drive, Sevierville
(865) 908-3636
Rocky Top is staffed by a medical doctor and an osteopathic medical physician, with a sizable administrative staff. Rocky Top provides a full range of services, including diagnostic and urgent care, with the latest technology available. The clinic is open Monday through Thursday from 8:30 a.m. to 5 p.m., and Friday from 9:30 a.m. to noon. Walk-ins are accepted until about two hours before closing. Most insurance plans are accommodated, and the clinic accepts major credit cards.

Pigeon Forge
PIGEON FORGE MEDICAL CLINIC
3342 Parkway, Pigeon Forge
(865) 453-1924
This clinic sits right in the center of Pigeon Forge, at traffic light #7. One medical doctor and a physician's assistant are assisted by a nurse practitioner. The clinic provides full X-ray and diagnostic services. Treatment is available for up to simple fractures, and the drugstore next door can fill prescriptions. The Medical Clinic is an independent clinic, open Monday through Thursday from 8:30 a.m. to 4 p.m., on Friday from 8:30 a.m. to 3 p.m., and on Saturday from 9 a.m. to 1 p.m. Most insurance programs are accepted, as are major credit cards.

Gatlinburg
FIRST MED FAMILY MEDICAL CLINIC
1015 East Parkway, Gatlinburg
(865) 436-7267
First Med is operated by a medical doctor during the week and a physician's assistant on Saturday and Sunday. This independent clinic is equipped for urgent care and diagnostic services but doesn't apply casts. First Med is open weekdays from 8 a.m. to 2:30 p.m., (except Wednesday, when they close at 11:30 a.m.), on Saturday from 9 a.m. to 1 p.m., and on Sunday from 9 a.m. to 1 p.m. Some insurance plans are accepted, along with major credit cards.

While this was Gatlinburg's original walk-in clinic, First Med is technically a family clinic now. Walk-ins are taken, however, on Saturdays and Sundays. While you will need to call for an appointment if you want to come in during the week, same-day appointments are often available.

Chiropractic Clinics
Sevierville
RATCLIFF CHIROPRACTIC CLINIC
826 Middle Creek Road, Sevierville
(865) 453-1390
www.ratcliffchiro.com
The Doctors Ratcliff (there are two of them) apply the techniques of spinal manipulation to promote healing and better general health through nonsurgical means. Specializing in personal and sports injuries, the Ratcliff Clinic is one of the area's oldest practices in continuous operation. The clinic is open Monday and Wednesday from 8 a.m. to 6 p.m., Tuesday and Thursday from 8 a.m. to 4 p.m., and Friday from 8 a.m. to 5 p.m. They close for lunch every day from noon to 2 p.m. Most insurance programs that cover chiropractic care are accommodated, and major credit cards are also accepted.

Mental Health Care
Sevierville
PENINSULA HEALTH CARE
124 North Henderson Avenue, Sevierville
(865) 970-9800
www.penninsulabehavioralhealth.org
Peninsula provides crisis intervention services and long- and short-term counseling. For emergency services, call the mobile crisis line at (865) 539-2409. Peninsula takes most commercial insurance plans and accepts major credit cards.

WORSHIP

East Tennessee is smack in the center of that portion of middle America that's referred to as the "Bible Belt." Overwhelmingly Christian in orientation, most Sevier County natives continue to practice the old-time religion of their forebears. Meanwhile, nonnative residents who couldn't bring themselves to accept the deep fundamental religious attitudes they found here have brought their own more liberal brands of faith with them. When you think about it, you can understand the depth of religion in a place like the Smokies—it's difficult to look at the grandeur of these surroundings and question the existence and the awesome power of a supreme being.

Because the original settlers took their religion seriously, the church was the major center of social life. Church services were the only social activity that operated on a dependable schedule, and the mountain people of the southern end of the county moved quickly to establish chapels instead of hiking 15 or 20 miles to Sevierville or Wear's Fort, usually carrying their shoes. (This was an interesting conceit found among mountain people: They carried their shoes to church and to school so they wouldn't get scuffed and worn out on the dusty, rocky roads, and so they'd look their best during services and classes. It's kind of ironic that one of the few vanities actually practiced by these people was to surrender the protection of their feet so the covering would look good.)

Mostly Presbyterian on arrival, the settlers took to the Baptist faith early on when they found that seminary-trained ministers of other faiths were not exactly standing in line to move to the mountains and work for livestock instead of a salary. In contrast, any member of a Baptist congregation who "felt the calling" could preach if he was approved by the local church board. The Baptist system of homegrown preachers ministering to their own flocks is still in widespread use in east Tennessee, and its effectiveness is proved by the fact that Sevier County alone has a separate Baptist church for about every 75 residents.

The Baptists had another advantage in the early days. They were more tolerant than their Presbyterian and Methodist brethren of some of the mystical practices that bordered on voodoo in the deeper recesses of the mountains, particularly those involving the occasional sacrifice of poultry. The Baptists reasoned that most of these practices were harmless, and nearly all of them were used for medicinal purposes.

As the population of the area grew more by emigration than reproduction, other Protestant faiths took hold. The county today is still more Baptist than anything else, but just about every Protestant denomination currently in practice has a home in the Smokies. Roman Catholicism, unlike the pioneer trends of its missionaries elsewhere in the world, was a latecomer to the scene. The first established Catholic church opened in 1950 in Gatlinburg as a chapel extension of a Maryville church, and St. Mary's Catholic Church was consecrated there in 1953. Forty years later, a second Catholic church named Holy Cross was built in Pigeon Forge, and it reaches out to the migrant worker population by celebrating the Mass in Spanish at a special service every Sunday evening.

i **Smoky Mountain religious services are offered in some pretty unconventional places. Several motels have services in their meeting facilities, and some of the music theaters offer nondenominational services on Sunday morning. Services are also available at Ober Gatlinburg, Dollywood, and even in the national park. Ask your desk clerk for details.**

There are 145 churches of various Christian denominations within 3 miles of the Smokies Corridor, many of them on or in sight of the Parkway. Sevierville's two biggest churches (Baptist and United Methodist) are on the Parkway just south of Dolly Parton Parkway.

The same is true of Pigeon Forge, where the biggest Baptist church is on the Parkway just north of traffic light #7, and the Methodist church is on River Road just south of the same light.

Gatlinburg has six churches of varying denominations (including Catholic and Church of Christ) in a 4-block area of Historic Nature Trail (formerly Airport Road) and Reagan Drive near the center of town. In keeping with the character of the area, the churches all welcome visitors.

For detailed information on church schedules and programs (including revivals), visit the Web site www.discoverachurchinthesmokies .com. This Web site covers churches in Cosby, Sevierville/Kodak, Pigeon Forge, and Gatlinburg. The site also gives phone numbers, addresses, and photos of each church.

The local telephone directory's yellow pages contain a complete list of churches by denomination, and the Saturday edition of the *Mountain Press* has a full page listing the locations and worship services of every church that provides the information.

Several non-Christian faiths are accommodated in Knoxville, about 30 miles west of Sevierville. These include:

1. **Baha'i Faith,** (865) 673-8744
2. **Knoxville Jewish Alliance,** (865) 693-5837
3. **Muslim Community of Knoxville,** (865) 637-8172

In addition, several interdenominational churches are located in the area. The Center for Peace, a holistic spiritual center in Seymour, offers nondenominational programs based on ancient-wisdom traditions, including sweat lodges, visionary dances, and other activities. Contact the Center for Peace for a current schedule of events by calling (865) 428-3070 or visiting their Web site at www.centerforpeace.us.

INDEX